Approaches to Teaching the Works of Miguel de Unamuno

Approaches to Teaching the Works of Miguel de Unamuno

Edited by

Luis Álvarez-Castro

The Modern Language Association of America
New York 2020

Library of Congress Cataloging-in-Publication Data

Names: Álvarez-Castro, Luis, editor.
Title: Approaches to teaching the works of Miguel de Unamuno / edited by Luis Álvarez-Castro.
Description: New York : The Modern Language Association of America, 2020. | Series: Approaches to teaching world literature, 1059-1133 ; 164 | Includes bibliographical references.
Summary: "Offers pedagogical techniques for teaching the fiction, poetry, plays, and philosophical works of Miguel de Unamuno in college Spanish and comparative literature classrooms, including considerations of Romanticism, modernity, Catholicism, existentialism, autofiction, and metafiction. Includes information on reference works and online resources. Gives syllabus suggestions for undergraduate and graduate courses"—Provided by publisher.
Identifiers: LCCN 2019049223 | ISBN 9781603294713 (hardcover) | ISBN 9781603294423 (paperback) | ISBN 9781603294430 (EPUB) | ISBN 9781603294447 (Kindle)
Subjects: LCSH: Unamuno, Miguel de, 1864–1936—Study and teaching. | Unamuno, Miguel de, 1864–1936—Criticism and interpretation. | Unamuno, Miguel de, 1864–1936—Outlines, syllabi, etc. | Spanish literature—Study and teaching (Higher)
Classification: LCC PQ6639.N3 Z5466 2020 | DDC 868/.6209—dc23
LC record available at https://lccn.loc.gov/2019049223

Approaches to Teaching World Literature 164
ISSN 1059-1133

Cover illustration of the print and electronic editions:
Darío de Regoyos, *Vendredi Saint en Castille (Viernes Santo en Castilla)*, 1904.
© Bilboko Arte Ederren Museoa / Museo de Bellas Artes de Bilbao.

Published by The Modern Language Association of America
85 Broad Street, suite 500, New York, New York 10004-2434
www.mla.org

CONTENTS

PREFACE

In 1963, one year before the first comprehensive biography of Miguel de Unamuno was published in Spain, the American Hispanist Margaret T. Rudd wrote in the preface of her groundbreaking book, *The Lone Heretic: A Biography of Miguel de Unamuno y Jugo*: "as essayist, dramatist, novelist, poet, and philosophical thinker, he is Spain's most outstanding literary figure of the twentieth century; and as a disturbing, contradictory, controversial man whose influence has spread beyond the boundaries of the Iberian Peninsula into the infinite realm of the human spirit, he is one of the most fascinating individuals of modern times" (vii). Indeed, Unamuno has long been a canonical figure in Spanish culture. Even during the Francoist dictatorship, a time when some of Unamuno's religious and political propositions were either condemned or silenced, his works began to inspire a critical bibliography whose size has continued to grow to this day. On this side of the Atlantic, Unamuno was chosen as the special topic of *Revista hispánica moderna*'s first issue, in 1934, thus playing a leading role in the nascence of American hispanism.

While Unamuno's critical relevance in Spanish studies is secure and indisputable, the author's standing is less prominent in other academic fields and in Spanish literature syllabi at the undergraduate level. With regard to the former point, Unamuno is greatly underrepresented in the broader context of comparative studies, such as general education courses on world literature. Similarly, his name is rarely brought up in courses taught by departments of philosophy, religion, French, and English, on subjects such as existentialism, the faith-reason dichotomy, modernist literature, intertextuality, and Romantic thought.[1] Yet Unamuno would prove a valuable addition to those courses, for his works represent a point of convergence for many different traditions at a time when modernity underwent a fundamental crisis that ultimately resulted in the shift to postmodernity. A professor of Greek who experimented with modernist fiction and anticipated concepts in literary theory such as reader response and the death of the author, Unamuno assimilated a wide range of international influences—to name only a few, Arthur Schopenhauer, Søren Kierkegaard, William James, Thomas Carlyle, Samuel Taylor Coleridge, Gustave Flaubert, Walt Whitman, and Henrik Ibsen—into his own writing.

While a wide selection of Unamuno's works are consistently included on reading lists and in seminars at the graduate level, Spanish undergraduate courses tend to focus on just one of his novels: *San Manuel Bueno, mártir* ("Saint Manuel Bueno, Martyr"). Customarily reprinted in anthologies of Spanish literature aimed at college students in the United States, this work has virtually obscured the rest of Unamuno's production for many instructors and, consequently, for their students; the pedagogical potential of his essays, poetry, drama, and complete fiction has thus been neglected. These circumstances provided the impetus for this volume, which seeks to promote Unamuno as a key figure in contemporary Western culture in fields outside hispanism and to offer an expanded range of titles, methodologies, and perspectives to instructors of Spanish already teaching Unamuno.

NOTE

[1] Two publications are broadly suggestive of Unamuno's status outside hispanism. He is the only Spanish prose fiction writer to merit a brief biographical entry in the classic Penguin manual *Modernism: A Guide to European Literature, 1890–1930* (Bradbury and McFarlane 37–38), but he is not the subject of any of the volume's chapters. In Sarah Bakewell's study on European existentialism, *At the Existentialist Café*, named one of the ten best books of 2016 by *The New York Times* ("Ten Best Books"), the only reference to Unamuno is a passing mention in an endnote (393n286).

Part One

MATERIALS

Overview

The following pages provide a comprehensive overview of pedagogical resources available to instructors wishing to teach Unamuno's works in their courses, be they in literature, philosophy, religion, or related fields. First, brief descriptions are given of the most relevant editions of Unamuno's works in the original Spanish, followed by descriptions of the English translations and bilingual editions. Next, "The Instructor's Library" introduces the most significant book-length studies on Unamuno's life, literature, and thought, as well as monographs providing background on his literary and intellectual contexts. (Readers will additionally find information regarding journal articles on Unamuno in the essays in part 2.) While a good deal of this critical bibliography is written in Spanish, instructors will also find ample references to the rather extensive Unamuno scholarship published in English. The fourth section presents the growing catalog of online editions of Unamuno's works, both in Spanish and English, along with audiovisual resources for the teaching of his literature and thought, including film adaptations of some of his fictional works.

Given the lack of an authoritative edition of Unamuno's complete works, contributors to this volume use different editions according to their respective teaching practices. In cases where English translations are not available, they have provided their own. A note at the end of each essay will inform the reader of the specific texts employed, and full bibliographical information for those texts may be found in the works-cited list.

Editions

Despite Unamuno's undisputable relevance both in Spanish culture and the field of hispanism, there is no canonical edition of his complete works. Owing to the monumental size of Unamuno's epistolary and journalistic essay production, there is not even a truly comprehensive edition of his writings. There exist, however, three incomplete collections of Unamuno's works—nevertheless called *obras completas* 'complete works.' The first was initially published by Afrodisio Aguado between 1950 and 1958 and reprinted by Vergara between 1958 and 1964, ultimately containing sixteen volumes. Its initial editor, Manuel Sanmiguel, unapologetically explained in the opening volume that censorship had been applied to any "frase hiriente" 'offensive statement' (Sanmiguel 15). The second collection, edited by Manuel García Blanco—who had prepared several volumes of the Afrodisio Aguado / Vergara series—and published by Escelicer in nine volumes between 1966 and 1971, was similarly affected by the ideological constraints of the Francoist dictatorship, resulting in redactions of

Unamuno's political writings.[1] This edition is the most widely quoted in Unamuno scholarship and, arguably, the most readily available in college libraries in the United States. It covers the following topics and genres: travel literature and essays (vol. 1), novels (2), new essays (3), race and language (4), drama (5), poetry (6), spiritual essays (7), autobiographical writings (8), and speeches and press articles (9). A third compilation of Unamuno's works was edited by Ricardo Senabre and published by Turner in ten volumes between 1995 and 2009. It shares with its precursors the omission of most of Unamuno's journalistic writings as well as the author's complete correspondence. From a scholarly standpoint, the introductions by Senabre to each volume are notably less informative than those prepared by García Blanco for the Escelicer series. The contents of the ten volumes are as follows: novels (vol. 1), novellas and short fiction (2), drama (3), poetry (4–5), travel literature and autobiographical writing (6–7), and essays (8–10).

In addition to these collections, there are genre-based anthologies such as *Novelas completas* ("Complete Novels"), a 1,340-page volume edited by Juan Antonio Garrido Ardila and featuring a 150-page introduction; the two-volume *Ensayos* ("Essays"), published by Aguilar, with prologues by Fernando G. Candamo; *Teatro completo* ("Complete Theater"), edited by García Blanco; and the four-volume *Poesía completa* ("Complete Poetry"), published by Alianza Editorial, with prologues by Ana Suárez Miramón. Those interested in Unamuno's short fiction can make use of the two-volume *Cuentos* ("Short Stories"), prepared by Eleanor K. Paucker, or the more recent *Cuentos completos* ("Complete Short Stories"), edited by J. Óscar Carrascosa Tinoco. The first volume of Unamuno's correspondence, *Epistolario* ("Correspondence"), edited by Colette and Jean-Claude Rabaté and published by Ediciones Universidad de Salamanca, covers the years 1880–99 in more than a thousand pages, including a seventy-page introduction and a hundred pages of useful indexes; a total of eight volumes are planned. Lastly, instructors seeking a one-volume anthology of Unamuno's most popular titles can use *Antología: Poesía, narrativa, ensayo* ("Anthology: Poetry, Fiction, Essay"), prepared by José Luis López Aranguren, or *Obras selectas* ("Selected Works"), published by Espasa-Calpe in 1998 (coinciding with the centennial of the Generation of 1898), which includes *Del sentimiento trágico de la vida* ("On the Tragic Sense of Life"), *Niebla* ("Mist"), *Abel Sánchez*, *La tía Tula* ("Aunt Tula"), *San Manuel Bueno, mártir* ("Saint Manuel Bueno, Martyr"), and a selection of Unamuno's poetry.

While editions of complete works are certainly lacking, the variety of editions of individual titles, annotated or otherwise, can be overwhelming. (The number of editions has rapidly increased since Unamuno's oeuvre became public domain.) Editions of individual titles vary in the depth of their introductions and explanatory notes. Among the most popular publishers, Espasa-Calpe's Colección Austral and Alianza Editorial offer editions of many of Unamuno's major titles for the general public. On the opposite end of the critical spectrum, Ediciones Cátedra—a favorite of many survey participants and contributors to this

Dionisio Ridruejo; *Cartas del destierro: Entre el odio y el amor, 1924–1930* ("Letters from Exile: Between Hate and Love, 1924–1930"), edited by Colette Rabaté and Jean-Claude Rabaté; and Laureano Robles's editions of *Epistolario americano, 1890–1936* ("American Correspondence, 1890–1936"); of *Epistolario completo Ortega-Unamuno* ("Complete Correspondence Ortega-Unamuno"); of *Azorín-Unamuno: Cartas y escritos complementarios* ("Azorín-Unamuno: Letters and Supplementary Writings"); and of *Epistolario inédito* ("Uncollected Correspondence") offer valuable insights into Unamuno's personal and political struggles as well as into his relations with leading writers and intellectuals of his time.

Lastly, instructors wishing to go beyond Unamuno's classic titles can turn to modern editions of some of the works that were unpublished in his lifetime. These include the novel *Nuevo mundo* ("New World"), a modernist bildungsroman available in an edition by Laureano Robles; the facsimile edition prepared by Etelvino González López of *Diario íntimo* ("Intimate Diary"), which chronicles Unamuno's existential crisis of 1897; and *Filosofía lógica* ("Logical Philosophy"), a sketch of sorts for the magnum opus *Del sentimiento trágico de la vida* that has been edited by Ignacio García Peña and Pablo García Castillo.

Translations and Bilingual Editions

Considering that there is yet no truly complete edition of Unamuno's collected works in Spanish, it is hardly surprising that not all of his writings are available in translation. Nevertheless, instructors wishing to teach Unamuno in settings other than the Spanish classroom have at their disposal a number of English translations of his major titles. The first ones to appear were J. E. Crawford Flitch's versions of *The Tragic Sense of Life in Men and in Peoples* and *Essays and Soliloquies*, quickly followed by *Life of Don Quixote and Sancho* (by Homer P. Earle), *The Agony of Christianity* (by Pierre Loving), *Mist* (by Warner Fite), and *Three Exemplary Novels* (by Ángel Flores). After a hiatus during the Spanish Civil War and World War II, the catalog of translations increased with the addition of *Perplexities and Paradoxes* (a rendition of *"Mi religión" y otros ensayos* ["'My Religion' and Other Essays"] by Stuart Gross); *The Christ of Velazquez* (by Eleanor L. Turnbull); Abel Sánchez *and Other Stories*, which includes *The Madness of Doctor Montarco* and *Saint Emmanuel the Good, Martyr* (by Anthony Kerrigan; reprinted in 1996 with an introduction by Mario J. Valdés); and a new version of *The Agony of Christianity*, by Kurt F. Reinhardt.

In the late 1960s, shortly after the centennial of Unamuno's birth, Princeton University Press began releasing the seven volumes of *Selected Works of Miguel de Unamuno*, featuring translations by Anthony Kerrigan (along with those by Allen Lacy and Martin Nozick in the first two volumes) plus introductions and notes by various authors. This series entailed a pioneering—and still unparalleled—attempt to offer scholarly editions of Unamuno's major works to an English readership, and the volumes are present in many college libraries across the United States. Some of the titles included in this collection have not been subsequently translated into English. A weakness of the collection is that Unamuno's theater is represented only by *El otro*, while his poetry is utterly absent. The contents of the seven volumes are as follows: *Peace in War* (vol. 1); a translation of *Diario íntimo* plus a selection of his correspondence (2); *The Life of Don Quixote and Sancho* with related essays (3); *The Tragic Sense of Life* (4); *The Agony of Christianity* with essays on faith (5); *Mist*, *Abel Sánchez*, and *How to Make a Novel* (6); four short novels and a play: *La tía Tula*; *Saint Manuel Bueno, Martyr*; *The Novel of Don Sandalio, Chessplayer*; *The Madness of Doctor Montarco*; and *The Other* (7). More recent translations of Unamuno's fiction include Michael Vande Berg's version of *Love and Pedagogy* and two versions, by Juan Cruz (*A Translation of* Niebla) and by Elena Barcia, of *Fog* (a conspicuous departure from the conventional rendition of *Niebla* as "Mist"). As for poetry, *The Christ of Velázquez* is available in editions by Jaime R. Vidal and by William Thomas Little (the latter is titled *The Velázquez Christ* and features a 150-plus-page introduction). Lastly, Unamuno's unpublished *Tratado del amor de Dios*, an early version of his celebrated essay *Del sentimiento trágico de la vida*, has been translated as *Treatise on Love of God* in an annotated edition by Nelson R. Orringer.

Selections of Unamuno's poems are available in side-by-side bilingual editions by Eleanor L. Turnbull (*Poems*) and more recently by C. A. Longhurst (*Miguel de Unamuno: An Anthology of His Poetry*), the latter a fifty-poem anthology featuring an introduction that explores Unamuno's main poetic themes plus short commentaries on each composition. Unamuno's fiction, however, is the best represented genre in this format: besides Francisco de Segovia and Jean Pérez's bilingual edition of *San Manuel Bueno, mártir*, instructors have access to a Spanish-English annotated edition of *La tía Tula / Aunt Tula* by Stanley Appelbaum as well as the four titles published to date in the Aris and Phillips Hispanic Classic series: *Saint Manuel Bueno, Martyr* (edited by Paul Burns and Salvador Ortiz-Carboneres), *Aunt Tula* (edited by Julia Biggane), *Abel Sánchez*, and *Mist* (the last two edited by John Macklin).

As a supplement to translations and bilingual editions, classroom-oriented editions intended for nonnative learners, featuring a combination of introductions, glossaries, explanatory notes, and comprehension questions, can prove useful to instructors of Spanish. While some of these volumes are certainly dated, such as Ángel del Río and Amelia del Río's edition of *Abel Sánchez*; James R. Stamm and Herbert E. Isar's edition of *Dos novelas cortas* ("Two Novellas"), including *San Manuel Bueno, mártir* and *Nada menos que todo un hombre* ("Every Inch a Man"); and the anthology *Relatos de Unamuno* ("Short Stories by Unamuno"), prepared by Eleanor Krane Paucker, more recent examples include the annotated edition of *San Manuel Bueno, mártir* by Paola Bianco and Antonio Sobejano-Morán and that of *Abel Sánchez* by Susan G. Polansky.

The Instructor's Library

Background Studies

Regrettably, Unamuno tends to be absent—or, at best, mentioned in passing—in handbooks on existentialist philosophy or modernist literature produced outside the field of hispanism. Paul Ilie approaches existentialism in *Unamuno: An Existential View of Self and Society*, while C. A. Longhurst's *Modernismo, noventayochismo y novela: España y Europa* ("Modernism, 1898, and the Novel: Spain and Europe") offers a useful introduction to Unamuno and modernist literature. For a primer on Unamuno's significance within the Spanish literary canon, the following histories are a good starting point: volume 9 of *Manual de literatura española* ("Handbook on Spanish Literature"), titled *Generación de fin de siglo: Prosistas* ("Turn-of-the-Century Generation: Prose Writers"), by Felipe B. Pedraza Jiménez and Milagros Rodríguez Cáceres; *A New History of Spanish Literature*, by Richard E. Chandler and Kessel Schwartz; and *The Cambridge History of Spanish Literature*, edited by David T. Gies. Luis Fernández Cifuentes's *Teoría y mercado de la novela en España: Del 98 a la República* ("Theory and Market of the Novel in Spain: From 1898 to the Republic") provides an excellent account, from a sociological and aesthetic perspective, of the literary context in which Unamuno's works appeared. Studies on Spanish metafictional literature with references to Unamuno include Carlos Javier García's *Metanovela: Luis Goytisolo, Azorín y Unamuno* ("Metafiction: Luis Goytisolo, Azorín, and Unamuno") and Ana M. Dotras's *La novela española de metaficción* ("The Spanish Metafictional Novel").

Instructors seeking an overview of the intellectual climate of Unamuno's era can peruse the classic study *La edad de plata, 1902–1939* ("The Silver Age, 1902–1939"), by José-Carlos Mainer; Pedro Cerezo Galán's in-depth analysis in *El mal del siglo: El conflicto entre Ilustración y Romanticismo en la crisis finisecular del siglo XIX* ("The Century's Malady: The Conflict between Enlightenment and Romanticism in the Crisis of the Late Nineteenth Century"); and volume 39 of *Historia de España* ("History of Spain"), *La edad de plata de la cultura española, 1898–1936* ("The Silver Age of Spanish Culture, 1898–1936"), edited by Pedro Laín Entralgo. The catalog of the exhibition *El tiempo de Miguel de Unamuno y Salamanca* ("Miguel de Unamuno's Time and Salamanca") includes essays on Unamuno's literary production and its historical context, while Roger Patrick Newcomb's *Iberianism and Crisis: Spain and Portugal at the Turn of the Twentieth Century*, which devotes a chapter to Unamuno, offers an Iberian perspective on the literary-historical context. Lastly, those interested in the critical concept of the Generation of 1898 can consult Luis Granjel's richly documented handbook, *Panorama de la Generación del 98* ("Introduction to the Generation of 1898"); the now dated, critically speaking, *Modernismo frente a noventa y ocho* ("Modernism Versus 1898"), by Guillermo Díaz-Plaja; the more balanced approaches of *The 1898 Movement in Spain*, by H. Ramsden, and of *The Generation of 1898 in Spain*, by Donald Shaw (also available in Spanish); as well as the historical perspectives of Joan Mari Torrealdai's *La censura de Franco y los escritores vascos del 98* ("Franco's Censorship and the Basque Writers of 1898") and the rather comprehensive collection *Los significados del 98* ("The Meanings of 1898"), edited by Octavio Ruiz-Manjón and Alicia Langa. For a revisionist approach that doubles as an informative introduction to this critical controversy, three recommended readings are José Luis Calvo Carilla's *La cara oculta del 98* ("The Dark Side of 1898"), Antonio Ramos Gascón's article "Spanish Literature as a Historiographic Invention: The Case of the Generation of 1898," and the collective volume *Spain's 1898 Crisis: Regenerationism, Modernism, Post-colonialism*, edited by Joseph Harrison and Alan Hoyle.

Studies on Unamuno

As of this writing, the *MLA International Bibliography* listed more than 1,600 entries in a search of "Unamuno" in the title. Even the most superficial description of the extant scholarship on Unamuno could take up the entirety of this volume; hence this section will focus on book-length studies in order to provide the most illustrative—and, whenever possible, most recent—examples of the various critical approaches applied to Unamuno's works. Before the arrival of electronic bibliographies and full-text databases, instructors seeking an entry point into Unamuno's vast critical literature had to resort to print compilations such as *Bibliografía crítica de Miguel de Unamuno* ("Critical Bibliography of Miguel de Unamuno"), prepared by Pelayo H. Fernández, and Leticia Gossdenovich Feldman's *Un primer intento de bibliografía crítica de Miguel de Unamuno* ("A First Attempt at a Critical Bibliography of Miguel de Unamuno"). The rapid growth of scholarship on Unamuno, however, has rendered these printed tools rather inadequate. Within the realm of bibliographical studies, one title stands out: *An Unamuno Source Book: A Catalogue of Readings and Acquisitions with an Introductory Essay on Unamuno's Dialectical Enquiry*, wherein Mario J. Valdés and María Elena de Valdés describe the contents of Unamuno's personal library with particular attention to the annotations that he made on his books.

For a comprehensive overview of diverse interpretive perspectives on Unamuno's writings, various conference proceedings published by Ediciones Universidad de Salamanca are quite useful: *Actas del congreso internacional cincuentenario de Unamuno*, edited by Dolores Gómez Molleda ("Proceedings of the Semicentennial International Conference on Unamuno"); *Tu mano es mi destino* ("Your Hand Is My Destiny"), edited by Cirilo Flórez Miguel; and the four-volume (to date) *Miguel de Unamuno: Estudios sobre su obra* ("Studies on Miguel de Unamuno's Works"), edited by Ana Chaguaceda Toledano. Other valuable collections include *Unamuno: Centennial Studies*, edited by Ramón Martínez-López; *Miguel de Unamuno: El escritor y la crítica* ("Miguel de Unamuno: The Writer and the Criticism"), edited by Antonio Sánchez Barbudo; *Volumen-Homenaje Miguel de Unamuno* ("Homage Volume, Miguel de Unamuno"), edited by Dolores Gómez Molleda; and *Re-reading Unamuno*, edited by Nicholas G. Round. The two collections published in Spain around 1986, on the occasion of Unamuno's semicentennial, *Actas del congreso internacional cincuentenario de Unamuno* and *Volumen-Homenaje Miguel de Unamuno* (both edited by Gómez Molleda), liberated Unamuno's scholarship from the ideological constraints of the Francoist period. Likewise, three recent collections are highly recommended for the latest developments in the criticism on Unamuno as applied to a variety of literary genres: *El Unamuno eterno* ("Eternal Unamuno"), edited by J. A. Garrido Ardila; *A Companion to Miguel de Unamuno*, edited by Julia Biggane and John Macklin; and *Unamuno: El poeta del pensamiento* ("Unamuno: Poet of Thought"), edited by Francisco de Jesús Ángeles Cerón.

Akin to conference proceedings and collections in their broad thematic scope, single-authored anthologies of previously published essays can be useful resources. This category includes Juan Marichal's *El designio de Unamuno* ("Unamuno's Scheme"); Ciriaco Morón Arroyo's *Hacia el sistema de Unamuno: Estudios sobre su pensamiento y creación literaria* ("Toward Unamuno's System: Studies on His Thought and Literature"); and Rosendo Díaz-Peterson's *Estudios sobre Unamuno* ("Studies on Unamuno"). A large repository of Unamuno criticism can be found in *Cuadernos de la Cátedra Miguel de Unamuno*, a journal entirely devoted to Unamuno that the Universidad de Salamanca has published since 1948. Three classic, comprehensive studies remain valuable resources: Julián Marías's groundbreaking monograph, *Miguel de Unamuno* (available also in English under the same title); Ricardo Gullón's *Autobiografías de Unamuno* ("Unamuno's Autobiographies"); and Martin Nozick's *Miguel de Unamuno: The Agony of Belief*.

The Biblioteca Unamuno published by Ediciones Universidad de Salamanca has released more than forty volumes comprising both annotated editions of Unamuno's works as well as critical studies on his writings. Various aspects of Unamuno's literary theory are examined in *La teoría poética de Miguel de Unamuno* ("Miguel de Unamuno's Poetics"), by Teresa Imízcoz Beunza; *La palabra y el ser en la teoría literaria de Unamuno* ("Word and Being in Unamuno's Literary Theory"), by Luis Álvarez-Castro; and *Unamuno's Theory of the Novel*, by C. A. Longhurst. Unamuno's ideas on language, crucial for understanding both his literature and his philosophy, have not merited book-length studies in recent years, but instructors can benefit from older works such as Carlos Blanco Aguinaga's *Unamuno, teórico del lenguaje* ("Unamuno, a Theorist of Language"); Adolfo Jiménez Hernández's *Unamuno y la filosofía del lenguaje* ("Unamuno and the Philosophy of Language"); and Thomas Franz's *The Word in the World: Unamuno's Tragic Sense of Language*.

As for genre-specific studies, Ricardo Díez's *El desarrollo estético de la novela de Unamuno* ("The Aesthetic Development of Unamuno's Fiction"); Isabel Criado Miguel's *Las novelas de Miguel de Unamuno* ("Miguel de Unamuno's

Novels"); and Robert L. Nicholas's *Unamuno narrador* ("Unamuno, Fiction Writer") provide useful, descriptive introductions to Unamuno's fiction, while more specific critical approaches can be found in Ronald E. Batchelor's *Unamuno, Novelist: A European Perspective*; Roberta Johnson's *Crossfire: Philosophy and the Novel in Spain, 1900–1934* (also available in Spanish, as *Fuego cruzado*); Francisco LaRubia-Prado's *Alegorías de la voluntad: Pensamiento orgánico, retórica y deconstrucción en la obra de Miguel de Unamuno* ("Allegories of the Will: Organic Thought, Rhetoric and Deconstruction in Miguel de Unamuno's Works") and his *Unamuno y la vida como ficción* ("Unamuno: Life as Fiction"); Paul R. Olson's *The Great Chiasmus: Word and Flesh in the Novels of Unamuno*; and Bénédicte Vauthier's *Arte de escribir e ironía en la obra narrativa de Miguel de Unamuno* ("Irony and the Art of Writing in Miguel de Unamuno's Fiction"). Although somewhat dated, another valuable resource for the teaching of Unamuno's fiction is the short monograph *Unamuno and the Novel as Expressionistic Conceit*, by David William Foster, which offers an accessible overview for students of various backgrounds. While book-length studies on Unamuno's theater and poetry are relatively scarce, recommended titles include *El teatro de Unamuno* ("Unamuno's Theater"), by Andrés Franco; the collections *El teatro de Unamuno* ("Unamuno's Theater") and *La poesía de Miguel de Unamuno* ("Miguel de Unamuno's Poetry"), edited, respectively, by Jesús María Lasagabaster and by José Ángel Ascunce Arrieta; and *Miguel de Unamuno, poeta* ("Miguel de Unamuno, Poet"), by Javier Blasco, M. Pilar Celma, and Ramón González.

For more theoretical approaches, Iris M. Zavala's *Unamuno y el pensamiento dialógico: M. de Unamuno y M. Bajtin* ("Unamuno and Dialogic Thought: M. de Unamuno and M. Bajtin") and Gonzalo Navajas's *Unamuno desde la posmodernidad: Antinomia y síntesis ontológica* ("Postmodern Unamuno: Antinomy and Ontological Synthesis") explore the modernity of Unamuno's writing with particular attention to its foreshadowing of contemporary literary theories. One of Unamuno's most defining stylistic traits, the metafictional experimentation, is examined in Luis Álvarez-Castro's *Los espejos del yo: Existencialismo y metaficción en la narrativa de Unamuno* ("Mirrors of the Self: Existentialism and Metafiction in Unamuno's Fiction"). Javier Krauel's *Imperial Emotions: Cultural Responses to Myths of Empire in Fin-de-Siècle Spain* studies Unamuno's *En torno al casticismo*, among other contemporaneous essays about Spain's identity, from the perspective of postcolonial and affective criticism. Roberta Johnson takes a feminist approach to Unamuno's literature in the context of Spanish modernist fiction in *Gender and Nation in Spanish Modernist Novel*. Victor Ouimette's *Reason Aflame: Unamuno and the Heroic Will* offers an outstanding psychological interpretation of Unamuno's literature, while Gayana Jurkevich's *The Elusive Self: Archetypal Approaches to the Novels of Miguel de Unamuno* and Alison Sinclair's *Uncovering the Mind: Unamuno, the Unknown, and the Vicissitudes of Self* provide, respectively, Jungian and Lacanian readings of some of the Spanish author's major works.

Combining philosophical and literary approaches has been common practice in Unamuno scholarship since its inception. Examples include Mario J. Valdés's *Death in the Literature of Unamuno*; David G. Turner's *Unamuno's Webs of Fatality*; and Frances Wyers's *Miguel de Unamuno: The Contrary Self*. For more philosophy-oriented studies, Carlos París's *Unamuno: Estructura de su mundo intelectual* ("The Structure of Unamuno's Intellectual World") and Pedro Cerezo Galán's *Las máscaras de lo trágico: Filosofía y tragedia en Miguel de Unamuno* ("Masks of the Tragic: Philosophy and Tragedy in Miguel de Unamuno") offer thorough analyses of Unamuno's thought. María Zambrano's *Unamuno*, written in exile and only recently published, is a remarkable study on Unamuno's philosophy by a fellow philosopher (and direct disciple of José Ortega y Gasset). Other recommended readings on this subject include the classic *El pensamiento de Unamuno* ("Unamuno's Thought"), by Segundo Serrano Poncela, and books by François Meyer and by Esteban Tollinchi, each entitled *La ontología de Unamuno* ("Unamuno's Ontology"), which provide excellent introductions to Unamuno's take on the question of being. Comparativist studies of his philosophy can be found in *The Tragic Pursuit of Being: Unamuno and Sartre*, by Robert Richmond Ellis; *Tragic Lucidity: Discourse of Recuperation in Unamuno and Camus*, by Keith W. Hansen; *Unamuno y Ortega: La búsqueda azarosa de la verdad* ("Unamuno and Ortega: The Hazardous Pursuit of Truth"), by Mariano Álvarez Gómez; *Unamuno and Kierkegaard: Paths to Selfhood in Fiction*, by Jan E. Evans; *The Uncertainties in Twentieth- and Twenty-First-Century Analytic Thought: Miguel de Unamuno the Precursor*, by Barry J. Luby; and *Cultural Hermeneutics: Essays after Unamuno and Ricoeur*, by Mario J. Valdés. On Unamuno and theology, Enrique Rivera de Ventosa's *Unamuno y Dios* ("Unamuno and God"); María José Abella Maeso's *Dios y la inmortalidad: El mundo religioso de Unamuno* ("God and Immortality: Unamuno's Religious World"); and Alfonso García Nuño's *El problema del sobrenatural en Miguel de Unamuno* ("The Problem of the Supernatural in Miguel de Unamuno") examine Unamuno's ideas on God and immortality from a religious, not merely an intellectual, angle.

Regarding Unamuno's political ideas and public involvement, Manuel M.ª Urrutia León provides a comprehensive overview in *Evolución del pensamiento político de Unamuno* ("The Development of Unamuno's Political Thought"), and Stephen G. H. Roberts outlines the author's role as an intellectual in *Miguel de Unamuno o la creación del intelectual español moderno* ("Miguel de Unamuno; or, The Creation of the Modern Spanish Intellectual"). Jean-Claude Rabaté's *Guerra de ideas en el joven Unamuno, 1880–1900* ("War of Ideas in the Young Unamuno, 1880–1900") and Eduardo Pascual Mezquita's *La política del último Unamuno* ("The Politics of Unamuno's Last Years") respectively trace the early formation and last stances of Unamuno's ideology, while Colette Rabaté and Jean-Claude Rabaté's *En el torbellino: Unamuno en la Guerra Civil* ("In the Whirlwind: Unamuno in the Spanish Civil War") presents a detailed account of Unamuno's public position during the events leading to the Spanish Civil War.

Francisco Blanco Prieto reviews Unamuno's forty-five-year career as an academic as well as his role in the drafting of the constitution of the Second Spanish Republic in *Unamuno, profesor y rector en la Universidad de Salamanca* ("Unamuno, Professor and President of the University of Salamanca") and in *Unamuno en las Cortes Republicanas* ("Unamuno in the Republican Congress"). As for the connection between politics and literature, Ana Urrutia-Jordana examines Unamuno's politically inspired poetry in *La poetización de la política en el Unamuno exiliado:* De Fuerteventura a París *y* Romancero del destierro ("Politics Turned Poetry in Unamuno's Exile: *De Fuerteventura a París* and *Romancero del destierro*"), while Virginia Santos-Rivero delineates the author's notion of hispanidad as well as his views on language and national identity in *Unamuno y el sueño colonial* ("Unamuno and the Colonial Dream").

For Unamuno and Latin America—a recurrent subject in Unamuno's press articles, including political, linguistic, and literary matters—Manuel García Blanco's classic *América y Unamuno* ("America and Unamuno") remains the most informative resource. Other international influences are explored in Julio García Morejón's *Unamuno y Portugal* ("Unamuno and Portugal"); Vicente González Martín's *La cultura italiana en Miguel de Unamuno* ("Italian Culture in Miguel de Unamuno"); and María de la Concepción de Unamuno Pérez's *Miguel de Unamuno y la cultura francesa* ("Miguel de Unamuno and French Culture"). In *Spanish Modernism and the Poetics of Youth: From Miguel de Unamuno to "La Joven Literatura,"* Leslie J. Harkema studies Unamuno's influence on a younger generation of Spanish writers and intellectuals, while Mario Martín Gijón's *Un segundo destierro: La sombra de Unamuno en el exilio español* ("A Second Banishment: The Shadow of Unamuno on Spanish Exiles") examines Unamuno's intellectual influence on the most prominent Spanish exiles (both writers and thinkers) following the Spanish Civil War. The essays (some of them previously published) that compose Pedro Cerezo Galán's *Miguel de Unamuno: Ecce homo: La existencia y la palabra* ("Miguel de Unamuno: Ecce Homo: Being and Word") provide a valuable picture of the richness of Unamuno's works, with attention to their linguistic, literary, philosophical, religious, and political facets.

From a pedagogical standpoint, reading guides can prove more effective than research-oriented studies. The Critical Guides to Spanish Text series, published by Grant and Cutler, includes volumes on *Abel Sánchez* (by Nicholas G. Round), *San Manuel Bueno, mártir* (by John Butt), and *Niebla* (by Paul Olson). Also akin to a reading guide is Pedro Ribas's *Para leer a Unamuno* ("In Order to Read Unamuno"), a comprehensive yet approachable introduction to Unamuno's literature and thought. Lastly, instructors interested in Unamuno's rather remarkable life have access to two recent biographies—both entitled *Miguel de Unamuno*—by Colette Rabaté and Jean-Claude Rabaté and by Jon Juaristi, in addition to the classic *The Lone Heretic: A Biography of Miguel de Unamuno y Jugo*, by Margaret Rudd, and *Vida de don Miguel* ("Life of Don Miguel"), by Miguel Salcedo. Luis S. Granjel applies a clinical methodology to Unamuno's biography in *Psicobiografía de Unamuno: Un ensayo de interpretación* ("Unamuno's Psychobiography: An Interpretative Attempt"). An excellent complement to these biographical works is the richly edited catalog of the exhibition *Miguel de Unamuno y la fotografía* ("Miguel de Unamuno and Photography"), which compiles all available photographic material related to Unamuno's life and works.

Internet and Audiovisual Resources

Unamuno's works became public domain on 1 January 2017, along with those by all Spanish writers who died in 1936. As a result, his original publications are now available online at the Spanish National Library's digital collection, dubbed *Biblioteca Digital Hispánica* (bdh.bne.es). Another useful digital archive is the Fondo Miguel de Unamuno at the *Repositorio Documental Gredos*, maintained by the Universidad de Salamanca, which contains more than four thousand items including press articles, correspondence with Latin American writers, and drawings and photographs (gredos.usal.es/jspui/handle/10366/3701). The *Biblioteca Virtual Miguel de Cervantes* (cervantesvirtual.com) holds more than fifty items by Unamuno, ranging from letters and articles to several of his major titles, as well as some critical essays on his literature. In addition to these institutional resources, a number of first editions of Unamuno's works (*Amor y pedagogía*, *Niebla*, *Abel Sánchez*, and *La tía Tula*) plus Crawford Flitch's translation *The Tragic Sense of Life in Men and in Peoples* can be read online or downloaded as free e-books at *Project Gutenberg* (gutenberg.org). Translations of *San Manuel Bueno, mártir* and some of Unamuno's religious poetry, including the entire book *El Cristo de Velázquez*, are available for download on Armand F. Baker's Web site (www.armandfbaker.com/unamuno.html). Instructors who wish to bring Unamuno's own voice into the classroom can play a 1931 recording of his extemporaneous lecture "El poder de la palabra" ("On the Power of Words"), which is available online at the *Biblioteca Digital Hispánica*. Also available online (on *YouTube*), part 13 of the series "La aventura del pensamiento" ("Thought's Adventure"), produced by the Argentinean educational television channel Canal Encuentro and hosted by the Spanish philosopher Fernando Savater, presents a twenty-minute commentary on Unamuno's life and works (in Spanish, with Spanish subtitles) that can be used as an introduction to the Basque writer and as a listening-comprehension exercise.

Some survey participants incorporate film into the teaching of Unamuno's fiction. For instance, Woody Allen's *The Purple Rose of Cairo* and Marc Forster's *Stranger than Fiction* may facilitate the understanding of *Niebla*'s metafictional experimentation, while the film *Los girasoles ciegos* ("The Blind Sun Flowers"), José Luis Cuerda's adaptation of the homonymous novel by Alberto Méndez, offers interesting points of comparison with *San Manuel Bueno, mártir* in the portrayal of a priest in crisis. Instructors can make use of film adaptations of Unamuno's works. Two versions of *Niebla* produced by RTVE (Spanish national television and radio) are accessible online: a five-episode series was directed by Pedro Amalio López as filmed theater and is stored in the "A la carta" section of RTVE's Web site, while a one-hour version, directed by Fernando Méndez-Leite, aired as part of the series *Los libros* and is available on the RTVE site (*Los libros: Niebla*), on *YouTube*, and on DVD. *Niebla* was also adapted in José Jara's 1975 film *Las cuatro novias de Augusto Pérez* ("Augusto Pérez's Four Girlfriends"), an original "versión libre," or free adaptation—as the opening titles disclaim—that combines eroticism and psychoanalysis in a somewhat surrealist style. Two other film adaptations are Miguel Picazo's critically acclaimed version of *La tía Tula* and *Nada menos que todo un hombre*, a version of the novella of the same title directed by Rafael Gil, both of which are available on DVD. In an unconventional adaptation, the Mexican dark comedy *Estar o no estar* ("Being or Not Being"), directed by Marcelo González, brings together the female protagonist of Dostoyevsky's short story "White Nights" and the male protagonist of Unamuno's *Niebla*.

Biographical films on Unamuno include Basilio Martín Patiño's documentary *Caudillo* ("Leader"), available on DVD as well as on *YouTube* and *Vimeo*, which pays homage to Unamuno's confrontation with General José Millán-Astray on 12 October 1936 and features a monologue composed of various quotations by the Basque writer (at 58:00). Manuel Menchón's *La isla del viento* ("The Island of the Wind") was the first feature film devoted to Unamuno. This biopic, available on DVD, is set on the island of Fuerteventura, where Unamuno was exiled in 1924, although it covers other significant periods of his life, including the clash with Millán-Astray. At the time of this writing, the Academy Award–winning director Alejandro Amenábar is about to release *Mientras dure la guerra* ("While the War Lasts"), a historical film based on the last six months of the writer's life.

NOTE

[1] For more on the editorial history of Unamuno's complete works, see Stephen G. H. Robert's essay in this volume.

Part Two

APPROACHES

Introduction

Luis Álvarez-Castro

Miguel de Unamuno: A Biographical and Literary Overview

Born in 1864 in Bilbao, the largest city in the Basque Country, Miguel de Unamuno would become the embodiment of a Castile-centric interpretation of Spain, from his cherished retreat of Salamanca, a provincial town that is home to the nation's oldest university, where he served as professor of Greek and eventually as president. An ardent detractor of the literary use of any Spanish languages other than Castilian, he was nonetheless a great admirer of Catalan culture. And his insistence on Spain's role as a spiritual colonizer of both Europe and Latin America—he was a key figure in the development of the concepts of Euroscepticism and hispanidad—was no obstacle for his deep knowledge of the literature and philosophy of those lands, including his heartfelt appreciation for Portuguese history and letters along with his celebration—though mostly rhetorical (Witthaus)—of Spain's cultural ties to Africa. Unamuno was not afraid of maintaining unpopular positions, as long as they reflected his inner convictions, and he was always willing to correct his ideas as they evolved. He stands as one of the most political and religious Spanish writers of the first third of the twentieth century, while he suffered retributions by monarchic, republican, and dictatorial regimes along with the Vatican, which condemned some of his works. Above all, Unamuno is a captivating thinker who resorted to every literary genre in a quest for answers to the following question: how can I know who I am and whether I will be forever? In the process, he developed a highly original body of work that constitutes one of Spain's major contributions to modernist literature and existentialist philosophy.

Within the academic field of hispanism, Unamuno has been traditionally associated with the so-called Generation of 1898. This historiographical term, popularized by José Martínez Ruiz (known as Azorín) and later applied to the criticism of Spanish literature by Pedro Salinas, defines a small group of writers—all of them male, most of them prose writers—purportedly influenced by the crisis of national identity that followed the sudden and calamitous demise of the last remnants of the Spanish Empire in 1898. Unamuno himself rejected the existence of such a generation on several occasions. Moreover, countless critics—beginning with Ricardo Gullón in his 1969 essay "La invención del 98" ("The 98 Invention")—have exposed the weaknesses of this concept. Let us consider just three of them. First, the stylistic features customarily attributed to the Generation of 1898 writers may only apply, at best, to their earlier works, and thus misrepresent the rich variety of their later productions. Second, defining these writers within an exclusively Spanish literary movement seemed to artificially detach them from European cultural trends. Third, and perhaps most significant, the concept distorted the literary landscape of early-twentieth-century Spain by excluding from consideration many worthy writers—every female one, to begin with—whose supposed lack of engagement with the ideals of 1898 was interpreted as unmanly and unpatriotic during Francisco Franco's dictatorship. Notwithstanding these shortcomings and the term's lack of relevance to instructors in fields outside hispanism, some scholars still endorse the notion of a Generation of 1898. Instructors and students alike are bound to encounter this critical label in virtually every textbook of Spanish literature: it is a worthy subject of discussion whether an instructor embraces it or teaches the controversy surrounding it.

But to label Unamuno a modernist instead of a Generation of 1898 writer poses a different terminological and conceptual challenge, for *modernismo* in Spanish studies has historically been used to name the literary movement initiated by the Nicaraguan poet Rubén Darío in the 1880s. Ascribing Unamuno to European modernism, however, does not mean to completely detach his works from the developments of Spanish and Latin American literatures. It is quite revealing that references to Europe in Spanish literary criticism seem to cast Europe as foreign, as if Spain did not participate in the artistic processes taking place in countries like France, the United Kingdom, or Italy in the early twentieth century—on the contrary, Unamuno's writings prove otherwise.

Unamuno's literary production spans from the 1890s to the 1930s, during which every literary genre underwent a radical evolution. Unamuno certainly left his imprint on all of them. His fictional prose is characterized by a deliberate departure from the narrative conventions of realism. Such experimentation is apparent in his invention of the *nivola*, a somewhat ironic term that he put on the cover of his celebrated novel *Niebla* (1914; "Mist") and later was used by critics to describe all of his nonconventional narratives, from *Amor y pedagogía* (1902; "Love and Pedagogy") to *La novela de don Sandalio, jugador de ajedrez* (1933; "The Novel of Don Sandalio, Chess Player"). In fact, *Amor y pedagogía* is part of a selective group of groundbreaking novels—all published in 1902—that was heralded as the inception of Spanish modernist fiction.[1] Recurrent traits in Unamuno's fiction are a focus on psychological and existential conflicts, the primacy of the characters' dialogues over the narrator's discourse, a lack of external descriptions, and a disregard for orderly narrative plots. However, even his first novel, *Paz en la guerra* (1897; "Peace in War"), often dismissed by critics who consider it excessively traditional—that is, dependent on the realist model—and therefore unrelated to Unamuno's ulterior experimentation, attempts to broaden the expressive limits of realist-naturalist fiction by infusing a historical plot with spiritual themes and symbolist techniques. Another distinctive feature of Unamuno's narrative is the use of metafictional devices, be they autonomous characters who rebel against their creators (such as the protagonist in *Niebla*) or narrators who involve the reader in their creative process, as in *Abel Sánchez* (1917), *San Manuel Bueno, mártir* (1930; "Saint Manuel Bueno, Martyr"), or *La novela de Don Sandalio*. This metafictional style blurs the boundaries between reality and fiction and imposes a sophisticated hermeneutical demand on the reader. Indeed, Unamuno's concern with the reader as the ultimate agent in the creation of literary meaning makes him a precursor of reader-response theories developed from the 1960s onward. He stated on several occasions that the main purpose of his writings—not only his narrative—was to unsettle his readers' belief systems in order to make them doubt their own existence. In the prologue to his last book of fiction, *San Manuel Bueno, mártir y dos historias más* (1932; "Saint Manuel Bueno, Martyr, and Two Other Novellas"), Unamuno explains that the underlying topic of the novellas is "el pavoroso problema de la personalidad" 'the dreadful question of personality' (*Obras completas* [García Blanco] 2: 1122; my trans.)—a concern that extends to most of his works. Another defining quality of Unamuno's fiction consistently recognized by critics is its highly philosophical content.[2]

In addition to literary issues such as the purpose and methods of fiction, Unamuno's narrative explores themes related to ontology, epistemology, philosophy of language, religion, ethics, psychology, and existentialism. These are the same subjects that he discussed in his nonfiction. Unamuno's most consequential essay is *Del sentimiento trágico de la vida* (1913; "On the Tragic Sense of Life"), a twelve-part work in which he combines philosophical inquiry with poetic vision in order to analyze the sources, contradictions, and corollaries of religious beliefs and, more specifically, what he refers to as humans' hunger for immortality. Unamuno's focus on the flesh-and-blood individual as the object of his meditations, in contrast to the abstractions of earlier philosophers, represents a major contribution to the new thought movement that would later be known as existentialism. Critics of this essay have studied its philosophical and religious sources (with special attention to Protestantism), its impact in the development of European existentialism, and the intertextual connections between it and other works by Unamuno. Some of Unamuno's major essays can be linked to fictional works that delve into similar topics. For example, his 1895 essay *En torno al casticismo* ("On Authentic Tradition") shares with his novel *Paz en la guerra* a concern for the role of the common people in the making of a nation's history, an idea for which Unamuno coined the term "intrahistoria" 'intrahistory.' The protagonist of *Niebla* seems to be afflicted by the same hunger for immortality described in *Del sentimiento trágico* when he rebels against his creator after discovering that he is a literary character destined to die. And *La agonía del cristianismo* (1931; "The Agony of Christianity"), an essay written during Unamuno's exile prompted by his political opposition to the military dictatorship of Miguel Primo de Rivera, offers a conflicted assessment of the importance of doubt in the experience of Christian faith that is also embodied by the tormented protagonist of *San Manuel Bueno, mártir*.

This fluidity of ideas among Unamuno's works and across different genres, which renders every individual text provisional and incomplete, as if dependent on a broader, all-encompassing text, seems to prefigure the kind of literary discourse described by poststructuralist and deconstructionist thinkers such as Julia Kristeva, Roland Barthes, and Jacques Derrida. In addition to the intertextual dialogue among his works, Unamuno also experimented with a hybrid writing in *Cómo se hace una novela* (1927; "How to Make a Novel"[3]), a hard-to-classify text that blends fictional narrative, metafictional essay, and autobiography, heralding later literary innovations such as Serge Doubrovsky's concept of autofiction.[4] Unamuno's essay production includes other modalities. His "sermones laicos" 'secular sermons,' like the ones included in *Tres ensayos* (1900; "Three Essays"), present existential meditations through a discourse that combines the intimacy of the public lecture with the conceptual density of the philosophical treatise. He assiduously cultivated travel literature in collections of articles such as *Paisajes* (1902; "Landscapes"), *Por tierras de Portugal y de España* (1911; "Through the Lands of Portugal and Spain"), and *Andanzas y visiones españolas* (1922; "Spanish Adventures and Visions"). In these works, written in an evocative, lyrical prose, he applies his notion of *intrahistoria* to the construction of the landscape's spiritual and cultural meaning. Finally, in addition to an abundant body of literary criticism—mainly of works by Latin American authors—some of his extended essays are devoted to literary issues. For instance, in *Vida de Don Quijote y Sancho* (1905; "Life of Don Quixote and Sancho") and the collection of articles *Alrededor del estilo* (1924; "On Style"), Unamuno develops a highly idiosyncratic literary theory in which the reflection about literature is part of a larger meditation on ontological and metaphysical questions as well as issues of national identity.

While a handful of Unamuno's fictions and essays have sparked a sustained critical interest and enjoy considerable popularity in the classroom, his poetry and theater are still poorly known and seldom taught. Unamuno's contributions to these two genres may have suffered from the constraining effects of the Generation of 1898 label precisely because their originality and modernity could not be reconciled with the conventional understanding of this literary group. Indeed, it could be argued that Unamuno's experimentation in poetry and drama was even bolder than that in his narrative. His *Rosario de sonetos líricos* (1911; "Rosary of Lyrical Sonnets") brought renewed attention to this classical form several years before it was adopted by the poets of the Generation of 1927. Likewise, the fictional author to whom he attributed his poetry collection *Teresa: Rimas de un poeta desconocido* (1924; "Teresa: Rhymes by an Unknown Poet"), which was presented as a neo-Romantic response to the dehumanization—to use Ortega y Gasset's term (*La deshumanización*)—of poetry brought about by the avant-garde, can be linked to Fernando Pessoa's heteronyms and is suggestive of future developments in the figure of the lyrical subject and of the return to sentimentality in Spanish poetry in the years preceding the Civil War. Unamuno penned radically different styles of poetry, ranging from the transcendent, solemn religiosity of *El Cristo de Velázquez* (1920; "Velázquez's Christ") to the enraged, politically driven verses of *De Fuerteventura a París* (1925; "From Fuerteventura to Paris") and *Romancero del destierro* (1928; "Exile Ballads"). Unamuno declared that his most ardent desire was to be remembered as a poet and confessed that much of his prose was but aborted poetry. This helps explain the monumental lyrical project in which he embarked in 1928—*Cancionero poético* ("Songbook"), a collection of more than 1,750 poems that he wrote during the last nine years of his life (the last dated only three days before he died).

Unamuno's first attempt at dramatic writing predates his first book of poetry by almost a decade. He went on to write nine dramas, all but the last of which were staged in his lifetime, although in all cases several years after they were written. (Further references to these plays will include both their composition and first staging dates.) The critical and public response to Unamuno's plays was not so favorable. At a time when Spanish theater was still dominated by a combination of neo-Romantic and realist aesthetics—best represented by the melodramas of José Echegaray and the *alta comedia* ("highbrow comedy") of Jacinto Benavente, both of whom were awarded the Nobel Prize for Literature—Unamuno set out to create a new dramatic style that focused on neither the wit of the dialogues nor the excitement of the plot or the spectacle. His was a "teatro desnudo" 'naked drama,' a highly symbolic theater of ideas predicated upon the exposition of the characters' inner conflicts. Nelson Orringer has concluded that, because of this approach to drama, "all the plays of Unamuno could be added to the list of his philosophical works" ("Philosophy" 562–63). The same could be said about Unamuno's entire literary production. In Unamuno's writing a series of recurrent themes appear across different genres (including personal correspondence). He approached literary genres not as sets of discursive conventions but rather as alternative avenues for the expression of human conflicts and desires, thus bringing together philosophy and literature under the guise of fiction, essay, poetry, or drama. If we accept that Unamuno's literary production as a whole constitutes, to some degree, a single text, it is possible then to establish thematic similarities between his plays and the rest of his works. For instance, the symbolism of the blindness-sight dichotomy in *La venda* (1899, 1921; "The Blindfold") is an early formulation of the faith-reason conflict that permeates many of Unamuno's works, most notably *Amor y pedagogía*, *Del sentimiento trágico de la vida*, and *San Manuel Bueno, mártir*. Likewise, the irreconcilability of the inner, authentic self with the public persona, conveyed in dramas such as *La esfinge* (1898, 1909; "The Sphinx"), *Soledad* (1921, 1953; a female name that also means "loneliness"), and *Sombras de sueño* (1926, 1930; "Shadows of a Dream"), is also the basis for *Abel Sánchez*, *Cómo se hace una novela*, and *La novela de Don Sandalio*. Unamuno's exploration of this conflicted, split personality in *El otro* (1926, 1932; "The Other") and *El hermano Juan* (1929; "Brother Juan") leads to a radical ontological insecurity akin to the one experienced by the protagonist in *Niebla*. Lastly, the struggle over an unfulfilled maternal drive in *Raquel encadenada* (1921, 1926; "Raquel in Chains") relates to the protagonist of the novel *La tía Tula* (1921; "Aunt Tula"). Critics of Unamuno's theater commonly point out shortcomings in the plays' dramatic structures, which render them more suitable for reading than for performing. At the same time, critics acknowledge the plays' original assimilation of new dramatic paradigms such as Ibsen's symbolism. Ultimately, Unamuno's efforts to renew the rather dull Spanish theater of his time—including the adaptation of classics like *Fedra* (1911, 1918; "Phaedra")—represent a significant step in the evolution of the genre in Spain, inspired by the same spirit of experimentation behind modernist masterpieces such as Ramón del Valle Inclán's "esperpentos" 'grotesque dramas' and Federico García Lorca's lyrical tragedies.

An overview of Unamuno's cultural significance would be incomplete without addressing his role as a public intellectual. When Unamuno died in 1936, just months after the outbreak of the Spanish Civil War, José Ortega y Gasset mourned the loss of his voice, fearing that "una era de atroz silencio" 'a period of dreadful silence' (qtd. in S. Roberts, *Miguel de Unamuno* 234) would afflict the nation for many years to come. That civic voice had begun resonating with distinct intensity in 1914. Unamuno was elected president of the University of Salamanca in 1901, only to be swiftly removed from that position as a reprisal for his outspoken criticism of the government. This cowardly retribution effectively launched him on a path of political involvement that endured until his death. Unamuno's relentless denunciation of both King Alfonso XIII and the military dictatorship of Miguel Primo de Rivera led to his exile in France from 1924 to 1930. Back in Spain, he held prominent positions in the early years of the Second Republic, including as congressman for Salamanca within the Socialist Party; representative to the Constitutional Congress; and president of the Council for Public Education. Additionally, the city council of Salamanca appointed him as honorary mayor, and he was elected to the Spanish Royal Academy. The official recognitions proliferated upon his retirement as professor in 1934, when he was named citizen of honor of the republic and perpetual president of the University of Salamanca, at the same time that his name surfaced as a possible candidate for the Nobel Prize in Literature. In 1936 he traveled to England to receive an honorary degree at Oxford University.

His open criticism of the policies of the republican administrations, however, led once again to his fall into political disgrace, just as the nation was about to enter a devastating civil war. Following the military coup that prompted the war, Unamuno tentatively expressed support for General Franco, whom he initially considered a fighter for democracy and true republican ideals. This ephemeral sentiment was construed as treason by the republican government. Notwithstanding that resentment, which transpires in early studies of Unamuno's works by left-wing critics writing in exile, the writer's final public appearance represented an act of extraordinary courage that would define him as one of the most distinguished Spanish intellectuals of all times. In 1936 the celebration of the Día de la Raza, or Columbus Day, took place in Salamanca, which had become the headquarters of Franco's army. During an academic ceremony held at the University of Salamanca on 12 October, in front of General José Millán-Astray, founder of the Spanish foreign legion, and others who had disparaged cultural minorities and praised a cult of death, Unamuno declared, "This is the temple of intellect. And I am its high priest. It is you who are profaning its sacred domain. You will win, because you possess more than enough brute force, but you will not convince" (qtd. in Rudd 301). The Fascists had killed Federico García Lorca two months earlier in Granada. Only weeks later Republican militiamen would shoot Ramiro de Maeztu in Madrid. After this episode Unamuno was escorted home, where he spent the rest of his days under house arrest. Just as his literature offers an unparalleled view of a half century of aesthetic experimentation, his own life had become an essential chapter in Spain's history.

Some recent biographers have convincingly argued that the details surrounding the confrontation between Unamuno and General Millán-Astray are mainly fictional, as no transcription of the speeches delivered during that ceremony has survived (Juaristi, *Miguel de Unamuno* 440–42; Rabaté and Rabaté, *En el torbellino* 216–22). The confrontation itself did take place, however, which explains why, in the days that followed, Unamuno was stripped of the honorary titles the Francoist authorities had recently bestowed on him. Whether reality or fiction, this instance of cultural—if not ideological—mythification is indicative of Unamuno's prominent status within modern Spain's symbolic heritage.[5] Yet Unamuno is usually brought into the classroom as a literary author; less so is he taught as a philosopher and even more rarely as an intellectual. A number of critics, however, have recently tried to foreground Unamuno's role as an intellectual by offering new interpretations of the Generation of 1898 that pay less attention to its members' literary aesthetics and instead highlight the actual political content of their writings, particularly in regard to imperialistic sentiments. As Christopher Britt-Arredondo claims, Unamuno "represents as few other thinkers of his time do the tense intellectual, cultural, and political life of Spain as it began its first century without empire" (79). This state of national crisis reveals itself in works such as *En torno al casticismo*, which Javier Krauel describes as "a failed attempt to mourn the imperial ideals that had been a crucial element of Spanish national identity" (36), but it can also be identified in ideological positions that Unamuno maintained throughout his writings. For instance, Joan Ramon Resina contends that Unamuno's animosity toward Spain's languages other than Castilian and his treatment of the concept of hispanidad are intimately related, as both stem from the writer's consideration of language as a nationalistic tool in the context of Spain's demise as an imperial power (110–15).

Similarly, Unamuno's conflicting attitudes toward Europe and Africa provide insights on the development of a contemporary Spanish national identity. As Luis Martín-Estudillo argues, Unamuno "may be considered the founder of Spain's own modern tradition of Euroskepticism" (10), while Susana Martín-Márquez points out that Unamuno equally rejects a European or Latin American kinship in essays like "Sobre la europeización (arbitrariedades)" (1906; "On Europeanization—Arbitrary Notes") and in the poem "Salutación a los Rifeños" (1909; "Greeting to the Riffians") in order to proclaim "the brotherhood of North Africans and Spaniards" (61). With their emphasis on history, politics, and empire, it would appear that such revisions of the Generation of 1898 are to some extent reviving the old patriotic interpretations by critics from the Francoist period, thus bypassing the more literary and comparativist approaches of the last decades. Quite the contrary, these studies seek to expose the counter-democratic drives still latent in nationalist discourses traditionally associated with the Generation of 1898 writers. In so doing, this latest criticism underlines Unamuno's lasting presence in contemporary Spanish public discourse as well as his imprint on historical controversies regarding the role of culture and language in Spain's national identity.

Organization and Scope of the Essays

Participants in the MLA survey of members about teaching Unamuno—whose experiences reflected a diversity of academic settings ranging from small liberal arts colleges to research-oriented institutions—focused almost exclusively on approaches to teaching him to undergraduates. While instructors typically find themselves teaching Unamuno's works to undergraduate students who are not literature specialists, extant scholarship is more readily adaptable to graduate-level classrooms. This volume therefore aspires to provide an alternative, not a mere addition, to Unamuno's critical bibliography by presenting a range of teaching and interpretive resources tailored to undergraduate courses in four major disciplines: Spanish literature and culture, comparative literature, philosophy, and religion studies. This orientation, however, does not preclude occasional references to graduate-level instruction, as in the essays by Nelson R. Orringer ("Teaching Unamuno in Seven Contexts"), Tracie Amend, and Brian Cope, for instance. Ultimately, the goal of this volume is to divulge the pedagogical value of Unamuno's works to instructors who have never taught them while providing new insights to those who regularly do. With this twofold purpose in mind, the essays in part 2 encompass much of Unamuno's literary production: both major titles and lesser-known texts, including poetry, drama, fiction, and essay.

Taking into account the magnitude and diversity of Unamuno's literary production, neither a thematic organization nor one centered on individual works seemed to afford a suitable structure. Instead, a functional, goal-based arrangement was chosen, corresponding to four basic pedagogical approaches: the teaching of Unamuno's works as historical documents, as literary objects, as philosophical and religious inquiries, or as foreign language learning tools. Within that overarching structure, the five sections in part 2 refer to different instructional scenarios, as described next: following the introductory essays in section 1, which offer an overview of the possible pedagogical applications of Unamuno's works, the primary academic setting of the essays in sections 2 and 3 is the Spanish literature class (with an emphasis on the historical and present relevance of his writings, respectively), while the essays in section 4 are intended for the fields of comparative literature, philosophy, and religion, with particular attention placed on the metafictional and existentialist elements in Unamuno's works and their links to other European and Latin American writers. Finally, the fifth section is devoted to pedagogical methodologies that aim to blur the distinction between foreign language teaching and so-called content instruction, as applied to Unamuno's most widely taught title, *San Manuel Bueno, mártir*.

The opening section, "Teaching Unamuno," encompasses the four pedagogical approaches of the volume. Its essays function as a collective preface to part 2, offering a number of compelling reasons why Unamuno's works are still worth reading and teaching (Gonzalo Navajas), a comprehensive survey of teaching settings where they can be introduced (Orringer), and a detailed account of the development and implementation of a semester-long undergraduate-level course on Unamuno (Leslie J. Harkema).

Unamuno's works can be examined as historical documents that provide readers with both a window onto the socioeconomic dynamics, cultural environments, and ideological conditions in which those texts were created and a better understanding of the works' own literary and aesthetic circumstances. The essays by Salvador Oropesa, Amend, Stephen J. Summerhill, Juan Francisco Maura, Edward H. Friedman, Ana Urrutia-Jordana, and Stephen G. H. Roberts, which compose the section entitled "Literary and Historical Milieu," take such a perspective. This approach does not entail an oversimplistic recourse to the text-context dichotomy, inasmuch as Unamuno's works can equally be treated as context for the themes that they verbalize. In fact, Unamuno argued that poetry—by which he meant genuine literature—was more effective than history in the expression of the past, thanks to its superior ability to convey the individual's inner self ("Discurso en la velada" 145–46).

Unamuno's works can be analyzed on the grounds of the originality of their literary topics and techniques, which in some cases had an impact on later generations of writers, as the essays by Cristina Carrasco and by Adam Morris show. This is the unifying perspective of the section "Critical and Theoretical Approaches," whose essays adopt various interpretive frameworks such as psychology (Francisco LaRubia-Prado, Mark Mascia), mobility and science fiction studies (Benjamin Fraser), metafiction (Craig Bergeson, Carrasco), reader response (Thomas Franz, Cope), and gender and film studies (Diana Roxana Jorza) in order to propose new readings of some of Unamuno's most popular literary works and lesser-known titles.

Unamuno's works can also be discussed in relation to their philosophical and theological themes and, more specifically, as prime examples—if not foundational texts—of the existentialist movement. C. A. Longhurst, Tom Dolack, Robert Richmond Ellis, Jan Evans, and Orringer share this view in the section "Comparative Literature, Philosophy, and Religion Classrooms." Of course, the boundaries separating the disciplines featured in these three sections are rather porous, as shown in the essays by Juan Herrero-Senés and Morris, where literature, history, and philosophy are organically intertwined (as they often are in Unamuno's own writing).

In the section "*San Manuel Bueno, mártir* in an Integrated Spanish Major," Dawn Smith-Sherwood and Emily Joy Clark present Unamuno's novella *San Manuel Bueno, mártir* as a useful learning tool in the context of a foreign language education that equally values linguistic proficiency and cultural competence. *San Manuel* has become so customary in Spanish literature classes that it may be surprising to recall the stern condemnations that it received from the Spanish Catholic Church as a result of its controversial—if not heretical—content, which in 1956 led to its inclusion in the Vatican's Index of Forbidden Books along with Unamuno's essays *Del sentimiento trágico de la vida* and *La agonía del cristianismo* (Torrealdai 30). *San Manuel* is a staple in Spanish literature courses across the United States thanks to its availability—it is included in several anthologies and textbooks of Spanish literature—as well as its brevity, clarity of expression, and conceptual depth. As several survey participants pointed out, it is often the first complete novel that students of Spanish read in the target language and their first experience with literary analysis of a foreign language text at the college level.

Within each section, essays follow the chronological order of the works under study. The rationale for this arrangement—approximate as it is, for several essays cover multiple works—is to facilitate a sequential reading for those instructors interested in Unamuno's literary production as a whole. Lastly, though there is only one section explicitly devoted to disciplines other than Spanish studies, the insights provided by all the essays are meant to be relevant to the teaching practices of instructors of Spanish and other modern languages (including English) as well as those of comparative literature, religion, and philosophy.

NOTES

[1] The other novels included in this group are Ramón del Valle Inclán's *Sonata de Otoño* ("Autumn Sonata"), Azorín's *La voluntad* ("Will"), and Pío Baroja's *Camino de perfección* ("The Road to Perfection").

[2] For more on Unamuno's modernist poetics of fiction, see my "La novela modernista de Miguel de Unamuno."

[3] I use Kerrigan's translation of this title, which admits several variations in English (Unamuno, *Selected Works* 6: xii–xiii).

[4] Doubrovsky first used this term on the back cover of his 1977 novel *Fils* ("Son"): "Fiction, from strictly real events and facts; *autofiction* if you like, from having entrusted the language of an adventure to the adventure of language, outside the wisdom and outside the syntax of the novel, be it traditional or new novel" (Boulé 9).

[5] The public clash between Unamuno and Millán-Astray provides the inspiration for Alejandro Amenábar's latest film, *Mientras dure la guerra* ("While the War Lasts"), in addition to having sparked a recent polemic in the Spanish press, as Leslie J. Harkema documents in her essay in this volume.

Unamuno for the Twenty-First Century

Gonzalo Navajas

The Challenge of Reading and Teaching Unamuno Today

From the beginning of the long career of Miguel de Unamuno, the often undefinable and even contradictory nature of his work as a writer, thinker, and public intellectual has been universally recognized. For his contemporary fellow writer and intellectual antagonist, José Ortega y Gasset, Unamuno was an untrained philosopher who lacked the professional discipline that Ortega y Gasset thought must belong to those practicing rigorous philosophical thinking.[1] For other writers and readers, Unamuno was a source of highly insightful and trailblazing ideas that were decisive in renovating the stagnant Spanish cultural life of his time. For today's critics and scholars in particular, Unamuno's achievements and position in the literary paradigm are firmly established: he questioned the worn, repetitive modes of the realist novel and replaced them with bold narrative proposals; he unmasked major fallacies of nineteenth-century philosophical dogmas and aesthetic models; and he opened up new concepts and paths for fictional, poetic, and dramatic texts.[2] Unamuno encompasses all these versions of his multifaceted and complex intellectual personality, but he cannot be defined merely as an accumulation of these separate views because his vast and diverse production as well as his image in the intellectual life of his time cannot be simplified to a reductive whole. The challenge to understand and teach Unamuno today is to preserve the contradictory and often disconcerting nature of his work and public persona while making him not only accessible but also relevant and meaningful to a contemporary audience and especially to our students. To achieve this goal we need to place Unamuno within the parameters of his historically conditioned context and at the same time show that his indeterminate, iconoclastic, and provocative proposals connect with some of the most vibrant currents of philosophical, literary, and social knowledge today.

Unamuno's repertoire of interests and topics is extensive and diverse, reaching from modern philosophy, with an emphasis in Kantian and Hegelian thought, to theology and European intellectual and political history and to a unique hermeneutics of reading written and visual texts. At first sight, some of Unamuno's ideas, such as his views on God, the nation, and gender, may seem somewhat odd and removed from the prevailing cultural trends of our time, especially for young readers lacking familiarity with Spanish and European history of the nineteenth and twentieth centuries. Unamuno's texts elicit opposing and multifaceted interpretive views that may seem difficult to reconcile with prevailing cultural discourses, but their complexity and indeterminacy are what render them conceptually inspiring.

Like his philosophically akin predecessors Søren Kierkegaard and Friedrich Nietzsche, and a later author with whom he shares significant intellectual traits, Jean-Paul Sartre, Unamuno is an author for whom work and personal life are inextricably intertwined.[3] Unamuno's vital and compelling work and life provide profoundly personal but also highly powerful approximations to key philosophical, literary, and historical issues that continue to attract our interest today and are of special significance to students of literature and philosophy. Unamuno is a plentiful source of concepts and insights for discussion in the classroom as well as for topics for papers, theses, and dissertations that can shape academic discourse.

The nature and identity of the self, the power of fictions to define our conscience, the need for a transcendental and spiritual horizon of expectations to counter the contingency of human existence, the role of culture to develop national cohesiveness, and the evolving character of gender relations are some of the fundamental topics that Unamuno addresses in a passionate ("blutig," 'bloody,' in Nietzschean terms [Navajas, *El paradigma* 19]) and often controversial manner. These topics are objects not only of historical study but also of existential inquiry. The internal dialectics of his work help us come to understand the complexity and difficulty of the subjects he considers and at the same time motivate us to (humbly) consider our own views on absolute cultural truths.

On the one hand, Unamuno's work is a response to the specific circumstances of his time, and his statements regarding scientific and humanistic knowledge and his religious and literary views should be studied from the perspective of the ideas of the past. On the other hand, Unamuno's positions regarding fundamental subjects related to epistemology, ethics, aesthetics, and the concept of the nation are still highly relevant to our present situation. To teach Unamuno more effectively to current students we must animate the elements that connect him to the present.

At the same time, the obstacles to interpreting and teaching Unamuno are readily apparent and should be openly acknowledged: his antagonistic position vis-à-vis modernity and the modern project that he subsumes to a subliminally induced return to a medieval order; his theologically bound metaphysics in contrast with our postmetaphysical world; his single-minded search for a reliable ground to which to secure the immortality of the soul in contrast with today's fostering of the ephemeral; his promotion of a centralized, Castilian-based view of Spanish national identity as opposed to the present promotion of the peripheral within the Peninsula and cooperation of international relations within the context of European integration. Unamuno's views on such issues may surprise our students, but because they are presented with depth and principled conviction they don't appear as fruitless gestures of the past. On the contrary, Unamuno's assertions help us view our well-established notions in a different light. Unamuno constantly defies normative thinking; he disrupts the comfort zone of the intellectual status quo and can make our students reopen some of their assumed positions and parti pris, inciting them to assume risks that allow them to reexamine their conventional beliefs. Unamuno banished the terms *peace*, *tranquility*, and *bliss* from his conceptual repertoire because he saw them as tantamount to complacency and inertia, a capitulation to time and death, and he proposed instead a perpetual intellectual and ethical confrontation with established rules and canonical categories and notions. The study of Unamuno should have for our students a corrective role in countering some of the commonplaces and predictable tendencies of culture and thought in our time. The remainder of this essay briefly addresses the epistemological, ethical, and political dimensions of his work that should especially motivate our students.

A Will-Centered World

My initial presupposition is that, although Unamuno's work spans the last decade of the nineteenth century and the first decades of the twentieth and addresses some key issues of that period, it is nevertheless interconnected with a good number of the ideas and cultural orientations of the present. In this respect, Unamuno can be approached not only as a major author of modern Spanish thought and literature but also as a thinker whose conceptual themes and intellectual and aesthetic proposals and methodology are very much alive today and directly relevant to our philosophical and literary context.

Unamuno has an intense mistrust of abstract rational thought, which he views as a clumsy and deceptive way to understand what, for him, are the imperative central issues of all philosophical and intellectual activity: the survival of the physical and spiritual self, the problematics of the insertion of that self in history, and the configuration of the self's autonomy vis-à-vis the other. The definition and characterization of this personal self, his integral "ser de carne y hueso" 'being of flesh and blood' (*Del sentimiento* 20), are the pillars of his philosophical and literary orientation.[4] Unamuno claims that traditional analytical and empirical methodologies are poorly equipped to address questions of the self because they consider them irrelevant compared with the more reliable mode of scientific knowledge (*Del sentimiento* 102–03). Against Hegelian and positivist trends predominant in his time, Unamuno compellingly argues in *Del sentimiento trágico de la vida* ("The Tragic Sense of Life") that primordial existential experiences, such as angst, pathos, and above all the compulsive urge for immortality, are more effective epistemological methods by which to study and comprehend the human condition than those proposed by positivist paradigms of knowledge. Thus, an effective teaching approach to Unamuno should focus on the nature and the extent of the antagonism that exists between him and the predominant scientific concepts and tools of knowledge—rational and logical analysis, experimental verification—as well as on the concomitant methodologies that those concepts propound, which Unamuno considers rigid.

Unamuno's antagonism toward narrowness in logical and empirical thought can be shown to resonate strongly in the present divide that separates the hard sciences and the humanities. That resonance should be qualified, however; rather than being concerned with the place of humanistic studies within the framework of knowledge, Unamuno focuses on the insufficiencies of empirical methodologies to address the existential and spiritual predicament of a vulnerable and isolated self. Instead of a strictly rational and linear argumentation and thought, Unamuno employs a wide repertoire of rhetorical tools such as self-irony, parody, and exclamatory and interrogative language to explore this new path to knowledge. *Del sentimiento trágico de la vida*, his major philosophical book, critically exposes the ostensible indifference of science toward existentially based questions, which for Unamuno should be paramount in our search for knowledge.[5]

Another fundamental task in teaching Unamuno is to delimit the epistemological and philosophical background that shapes his thought. Like his intellectual contemporaries such as Marcelino Menéndez y Pelayo, Ortega y Gasset, and Eugeni d'Ors, Unamuno had an encyclopedic mind that aspired to universal knowledge.[6] He was a professor of classical languages, but his interests also included philosophy, theology, history, and aesthetic theory. Within this vast cognitive field, Hegel's and Comte's systems of knowledge are important referents for Unamuno. He makes his opposition to those systems the centerpiece of his philosophical thought. Like Kierkegaard, Unamuno focuses critically on the Hegelian notion of historical evolution and thought because, in his view, it conflates being, the external world, and the individual conscience into one single entity—the absolute—within which the identity and worth of the self are lost. The existence of the self is absorbed into the superstructural category of history, which advances according to its own rules, obviating the needs of the individual subject and in particular the individual's urge for perpetuation.

Countering that abstract synthesis, Unamuno asserts the rights of the individual subject to define itself according not to a predetermined universal essence but to its own indivisible and nontransferable singularity. Highlighting the links between Kierkegaard and Unamuno vis-à-vis the abstract view of time and history help trace the filiation of Unamuno's epistemology: "Cuando se lee en sus escritos [de Hegel] que el pensar y el ser son una misma cosa, se piensa, pensando en su vida, que ese ser que es idéntico al pensar, no es precisamente ser hombre" 'When one reads in [Hegel's] writings that thought and being are the same thing, one thinks, thinking about one's life, that that being that is identical to thought is not precisely being a man' (*Del sentimiento* 116). Unamuno is referring here to Hegel through a quotation by "hermano Kierkegaard" 'brother Kierkegaard' (115) to highlight their mutual rejection of the reductionism of the absolute rationalism of Hegelian thought. Unamuno additionally dismisses the utopian political and social constructions that proliferated in the second half of the nineteenth century and became a practical reality with the totalitarian political and social systems of the twentieth century. Unamuno can be presented in the classroom as an early debunker of absolute systematic constructions, in particular of Western-centered versions of the modern project and the various forms of totalitarianism.

Unamuno likewise opposes positivistic thought, more specifically, Auguste Comte's narrow, empirical notion of historical progress as an unstoppable march of scientific reason over religious and nonscientific views.[7] In Unamuno's view, empirical methodologies deny individuals the strong need for spiritual pursuits. For Unamuno, the trajectory of truth is not logical and rationally consistent but profoundly personal and individual. The ultimate justification is the process itself, the path we follow to acquire a better knowledge of our conscience and spiritual aspirations.

The Religion of the Temporal Absurd

The self-centered view of temporality allows Unamuno to define the meaning of the absurd, a notion that will acquire a central relevance in the existentialist movement and, in particular, in the work of Albert Camus and Sartre. Students should be made aware of Unamuno's distinctive views and their ramifications for existentialist philosophy. For Unamuno, the absurd consists in the self's condition of finitude, and he asserts against the inexorability of this condition. He rewrites Tertullian's apothegm *credo quia absurdum* ("I believe because it is absurd") as the more pragmatic *credo quia consolans* ("I believe because it consoles"); that is, my belief is cemented on that which legitimizes my struggle against the destruction of time.

This epistemological approach has religious implications as well. God may be a personal creation and thus may function as a fictional character akin to the fictional figures that Unamuno creates, such as the protagonist of *San Manuel Bueno, mártir* ("Saint Manuel Bueno, Martyr"), in order to actualize his controversial ideas. However, like the author's fictional characters, this created God may become separate from his creator and act as the guarantor of the subject's immortality. The ambivalence between a created God that is dependent on his creator's will and a transtemporal God that is autonomous from his creator is left unresolved because the dialectical vitality of the antinomy is the impulse that feeds Unamuno's drive to immortality.

Unamuno's belief in a God that guarantees immortality must be unquestioned, a matter of faith rather than the product of a "razón raciocinante" 'reasoning reason' (*Del sentimiento* 111). This notion can be connected for students with the Nietzschean position that the most powerful ideas are those that are the product of an intense experience that requires the complete involvement of our psyche. Those ideas can be adequately defined not through analytical means but through the indirect and approximate language of metaphors and mythology. Logical reason skirts the issues that are more urgent for Unamuno and, for him, reduces the possibilities of human experience.

Technology and National Identity

Within the parameters of an affective and emotive rather than rational and empiric version of truth, Unamuno addresses the question of *techne* in connection with modernity and the concomitant economic and social progress. Unlike Martin Heidegger, Walter Benjamin, and Ortega y Gasset, who consider the topic primarily from ontological or sociological premises, Unamuno considers the role of scientific discoveries and their technological applications in conditioning the theoretical presuppositions underlying the differing cultural and political discourses of northern and southern Europe that existed in his time. Unamuno insists on studying that seemingly insurmountable opposition from the position predominant in national cultures vis-à-vis scientific research and technological progress. The relevance of Unamuno's views to the present day is apparent in the divide between northern and southern cultures in the actualization of the European Union. Unamuno's views can be discussed in the light of how southern European nations and Spain in particular have approached various components of the modern project differently from the nations of northern and central Europe.

Unamuno's views evolve from seeing Spain's adherence to the conventional paradigm of European modernity as unavoidable to opposing it. Unamuno transitions from the conventional liberal Spanish view, which assumed the complete integration of Spanish culture into the progressive and more technologically advanced European culture, to a more nuanced view, which, without abiding by the strict tenets of traditionalism, foregrounded the singularity of the Spanish *Lebensphilosophie* (philosophy of individual life) centered on the spiritual dimension of Spanish cultural production. To what he considers the prevailing European thought, which he subsumes under the comprehensive category of Kantian *Vernunft*, or abstract and systematic reason, Unamuno counterpoises a new approach that he identifies with a personal rendition of quixotism in which Don Quixote becomes the redeemer of the forgotten immaterial values of the

European tradition. In addition to Don Quixote, Unamuno finds other emblematic figures of this spiritual élan in various mystic authors, in particular Saint Teresa of Jesus.

Unamuno rejects the humanistic and rationalist values of Spanish Renaissance figures like Juan Luis Vives and instead promotes a view of medieval spirituality in which the preservation of the soul and the devotion of that soul to the ultimate fusion with an omnipresent God are the only worthy human enterprises. Students should not be led to believe, however, that Unamuno assumes a regressive position regarding modernity. He doesn't reject modernity, but he perceptively points out that when positivist and materialist methodologies become all-encompassing frameworks they tend to restrict alternative intellectual discourses.

A Hermeneutic Unamuno

Unamuno is attractive to students today because the conceptual framework of today's cultural condition is still defined by some of the premises that motivated Unamuno. A literal reading of Unamuno is unproductive today. To judge him from a narrow, ideologically based perspective deprives him of his most vital and dynamic qualities. It is more creative and effective to consider him from a hermeneutic perspective that lets him converse with us—in an agonistic and pugnacious way—about his perpetual combat with time and the obliteration of the self.

NOTES

[1]While Ortega y Gasset's judgments of Unamuno can be harsh, he also praises Unamuno's moral integrity and political acumen (Ortega y Gasset, *Ensayos* 37).

[2]Of the extensive bibliography on Unamuno, I highlight three titles: LaRubia-Prado's *Unamuno y la vida como ficción*; Olson's *The Great Chiasmus*; and Álvarez-Castro's *Los espejos del yo*.

[3]Despite their philosophical and ideological differences, these authors share a common view of the intimate identification of their life and work, and they make that identification the deciding criterion to determine the ethical legitimacy of both (Navajas, *El paradigma* 59).

[4]This essay quotes from the Alianza edition of *Del sentimiento trágico de la vida*. English translations are mine.

[5]Other significant texts are *La agonía del cristianismo* ("The Agony of Christianity") and the first part of *Vida de Don Quijote y Sancho* ("Life of Don Quixote and Sancho").

[6]Ernest Renan, Benedetto Croce, and Thomas Mann, among others, are comparable figures in the European context of this integrative view of the arts and thought.

[7]In this respect Unamuno can be studied as a precursor of the poststructuralist and postmodernist critique of modernity as envisioned by Paul de Man, Jacques Derrida, and Gianni Vattimo, among others (Navajas, *Unamuno* 185).

Teaching Unamuno in Seven Contexts

Nelson R. Orringer

Some authors invite their works to be taught, while other writers keep the learner at bay. Miguel de Unamuno and Federico García Lorca call to inexperienced readers, while Luis de Góngora and his admirer Stéphane Mallarmé are less accessible. Thirty-six years of teaching Unamuno in seven different contexts have proved to me his openness for students, a result of his basic vocabulary and universal expressiveness. The contexts in which I've taught Unamuno include intermediate Spanish language, intermediate Spanish conversation, undergraduate survey of twentieth-century Spanish literature, monographic undergraduate courses, comparative literature graduate courses, Spanish graduate courses on special topics, and postdoctoral courses. The last four emerged out of my research on Unamuno performed at his archives at the Universidad de Salamanca. This essay discusses each context by briefly describing course aims and content.

Intermediate Spanish Language

Foreign language skills include understanding, reading, speaking, and writing. To reinforce the first three through literature, instructors can use what is arguably the plainest Unamuno text available: *Nada menos que todo un hombre* ("Every Inch a Man"), published in *Dos novelas cortas* ("Two Short Novels"; 45–90) along with study questions and Spanish-English vocabulary.

Intermediate Spanish Conversation

For honing students' conversational skills, few fictions surpass *San Manuel Bueno, mártir* ("Saint Manuel Bueno, Martyr"), the other novella in *Dos novelas cortas* (1–43). Classes can revolve around discussions in Spanish on faith, hypocrisy, and religion in politics. Unamuno's novella *Dos madres* ("Two Mothers") allows for exchanges about family relations and parental authority. The 1920 edition, published in *Tres novelas ejemplares y un prólogo* ("Three Exemplary Novels and a Prologue"; 31–80), appears online as well.

Undergraduate Survey of Twentieth-Century Spanish Literature

To introduce Spanish letters to intermediate or advanced undergraduates, the novels *Niebla* ("Mist") and *Abel Sánchez* hit the mark. *Niebla* early establishes its primary question, that of free will versus determinism, and leaves the answer open-ended. Whatever students argue with regard to this question, the instructor can maintain the opposite position. For interpretive depth, students and instructor can reconstruct a web of creators and creatures, including readers, the author Unamuno, his self-caricature, the protagonist Augusto, and characters Augusto imagines. However, in times when social uncertainties overtake more abstract concerns, *Abel Sánchez* exemplifies the channeling of negative passions into creative pursuits. Two views of envy or hate here emerge, orthodox negativity and modern positivity. The novel also teaches different forms of achieving immortality, or making life worthwhile: family formation, immortalization of artists and models, scientific prestige through discovery, literary fame, and religious salvation.

Monographic Courses for Advanced Undergraduates

Instructors moving from period-based surveys to more specific, theme- or genre-based courses, usually taught as senior seminars, can include Unamuno in offerings such as the following courses.

The Generation of 1898

No matter how loudly scholars protest the narrowness of the concept and the greater relevance of broader, pan-Western notions like modernism, the idea of the Generation of 1898 persists in hispanism for pedagogical purposes, easing comparisons at the undergraduate level between diverse authors like Unamuno, Ángel Ganivet, Pío Baroja, Azorín (José Martínez Ruiz), Ramón del Valle-Inclán, and Antonio Machado. All have two major themes: the problem of Spanish decadence and the conservation of identity. Unamuno's *En torno al casticismo* ("On Authentic Tradition") forms his most comprehensive statement on national decline. *Del sentimiento trágico de la vida* ("The Tragic Sense of Life") constitutes his most complete thoughts on personal immortality. Its erudition may seem daunting, but its basic ideas are thought-provoking:

The will to persist forever is the starting point and goal of all human acts.

Reason denies self-perpetuation, while religious faith affirms it. The clash between faith and reason, religion and science, defines the tragic sense of life.

Faith, surmounting reason, unveils universal truth.

That truth is a God with personality, love, and the will to immortalize believers.

This God is inseparable from questioning faith in God, questionable hope in salvation, and suffering love on which salvation is grounded.

All human history moves toward universal salvation: the apocatastasis, or restoration of all creatures to God, with all in God and God in all.

> People should live each day progressing toward the apocatastasis and, if immortality is not granted, daily living should make our annihilation seem unjust. (59–60)[1]

When *Del sentimiento trágico* does not fit into undergraduate syllabi, an alternative exists. An earlier version of *Del sentimiento trágico*, previously unpublished, appeared in 2005, with an English translation appearing in 2007: *Tratado del amor de Dios* ("Treatise on Love of God"). Easier to read than *Del sentimiento* while including most of its main ideas, its chapters identify Unamuno's stances on love as well as knowledge of God, faith, truth, the mystery of mortality, charity, religion, and Christianity.

Other works of the Generation of 1898 cohere with Unamuno's works, suitable in a monographic course. Baroja's *El árbol de la ciencia* ("The Tree of Knowledge"), Azorín's *Castilla* ("Castile"), and Valle-Inclán's *Luces de bohemia* ("Lights of Bohemia") all deal with the problems of national decline and of individual personality. Machado's *Soledades, galerías y otros poemas* ("Solitudes, Galleries, and Other Poems") address individual identity and its persistence in time, while his *Campos de Castilla* ("Castilian Countryside") contemplates national identity.

Genre- and Gender-Based Courses on Modern Hispanic Literature

A course on Hispanic modernist poetry can include Unamuno's *Antología poética* ("Poetic Anthology"), focusing on themes shared with his essays and coinciding with themes from José Martí's *Ismaelillo*, José Asunción Silva's *Poesías completas* ("Complete Poetic Works"), Rubén Darío's *Cantos de vida y esperanza* ("Songs of Life and Hope"), Juan Ramón Jiménez's *Arias tristes* ("Sad Arias"), and Machado's *Soledades* and *Campos de Castilla*.

A course on strong mother figures invites study of *Dos madres* and *La tía Tula* ("Aunt Tula"), which can be read alongside Gregorio Martínez Sierra's *Canción de cuna* ("Cradle Song"), Jacinto Benavente's *La malquerida* ("The Unloved Woman"), and García Lorca's *Yerma* and *La casa de Bernarda Alba* ("The House of Bernarda Alba").

Comparative Literature Graduate Course in Translation

The course Don Quixote and His Literary Children explores the many respects in which Unamuno accentuated *Niebla*'s kinship to *Don Quixote*, especially both novels' handling of character independence in prologues, epilogues, and intercalated novels. Other novels have imitated Cervantes's, calling for comparisons: Henry Fielding's *Joseph Andrews*, Laurence Sterne's *Tristram Shandy*, Mark Twain's *A Connecticut Yankee in King Author's Court*, and Gustave Flaubert's *Madame Bovary*.

Graduate Courses on Twentieth-Century Spanish Literature

Graduate courses may focus on periods and genres (e.g., twentieth-century prose and poetry) or on special topics in Peninsular literature. Here follow two examples of special topics courses.

The Human Body: Mirror of Culture from the Renaissance to Unamuno

Thomas Kuhn posits shifts in ruling paradigms in the material sciences throughout Western history. Analogously, the medical historian Pedro Laín Entralgo discovers different paradigms of the human body shaping culture by affecting corporeal representation in multiple media, including painting and literature. The ancient Greek physician Galen thought the human body was a piece of nature (Laín Entralgo 19). In the Renaissance, Vesalius viewed it as architecture. In the baroque period, the architectural paradigm was dynamized, and the body was conceived alternatively as a machine or as a great organism. In the politicized mid-nineteenth century, the German physician Rudolf Ludwig Carl Virchow regarded the body as a republic of cells, while post-Darwinian Europe adjudged the body a product of evolution (20). The twentieth century recapitulated earlier paradigms of the body (26). A lyric poetry course can show that representations of the human body precisely follow paradigms distinguished by Laín Entralgo and offer a key to poets' worldviews. The Renaissance poet Garcilaso de la Vega's bucolic portraits of the beloved Elisa exemplify Vesalius's paradigm. The baroque poet Góngora's word-paintings of Polyphemus represent the Cyclops as the archetypal organism. Unamuno, a modern poet, in *El Cristo de Velázquez* ("Velázquez's Christ"), represents Christ's body as the recapitulation of all bodily paradigms, just as Christ seeks the recapitulation of all mankind in himself at the end of history (Unamuno, *Del sentimiento* 409).

Science and Literature in Modern Spain

This course exposes varied ways in which science forms a theme in twentieth-century Spanish literature and is treatable as scientific cognition. The physician-protagonist provides moral, social, and scientific perspectives in Unamuno's *Abel Sánchez*, Baroja's *El árbol de la ciencia*, and Luis Martín-Santos's *Tiempo de silencio* ("Time of Silence"). A physician's exemplary professional development appears in the autobiography of the eminent neuroscientist Santiago Ramón y Cajal's *Recuerdos de mi vida* ("Memories of My Life"). Associations between illness and sinning dominate Laín Entralgo's essay *Enfermedad y pecado* ("Sickness and Sin") and Gabriel Miró's novel *El obispo leproso* ("The Leprous Bishop"). Finally, psychoanalytic techniques elucidate surrealist or surrealist-style texts such as García Lorca's *Poeta en Nueva York* ("Poet in New York") and Vicente Aleixandre's

La destrucción o el amor ("Destruction or Love"). These techniques are also useful for clarifying the insanity of Unamuno's protagonist in *El Otro* ("The Other").

Postgraduate Courses

To condense Unamuno's vast production into nine hours of lectures for philosophy professors in Spain, I present Unamuno as a poet-philosopher of Spain's Silver Age (ca. 1868–1939). Concerned about national decadence culminating in defeat in the Spanish-American War, Spanish intellectuals generated an era of creativity in Spain rivaled only by its Golden Age (1550–1650). The creative production of the Silver Age—a critical term that has gained acceptance thanks to José-Carlos Mainer—displays four characteristics: awareness of national decadence, experienced as pain; the wish to elevate Spain to the perceived height of Western Europe; the ambition to surpass the achievements of the Golden Age; and the desire to delve into Spain's Greco-Latin substratum.

The first lecture defines the Silver Age and relates Unamuno to his rival philosopher José Ortega y Gasset, while the remaining eight lectures link some of Unamuno's major works to the Silver Age. *En torno al casticismo* offers five key ideas: the inner history ("intrahistoria"), that is, the permanent component of history at every moment; the eternal tradition ("tradición eterna"), or inner history extended through time; the contrast between the Castilian historical caste ("casta histórica") and the eternal caste, or generically human Spaniards from the provinces ("casta eterna"); humanistic mysticism ("misticismo humanista"); and Spanish stagnation ("marasmo"). All these ideas employ the empirical observations of the British positivist Herbert Spencer to corroborate the metaphysical speculations of the Spanish Krausists Julián Sanz del Río and Francisco Giner de los Ríos.

In *Vida de Don Quijote y Sancho* ("Life of Don Quixote and Sancho"), Unamuno follows the French critic Paul Stapfer's idea that some works become bibles for their nations (197) and attempts to make *Don Quixote* the new gospel for Spanish Christianity. *Del sentimiento trágico de la vida* represents Unamuno's systematic reworking of the basic principles of Albrecht Ritschl's theological system. In *Fedra* ("Phaedra"), Unamuno modernizes Euripides's tragedy *Hippolytus*, wherein Phaedra falls in love with her stepson. *El Cristo de Velázquez*, a long devotional poem regarded as Unamuno's best poetic work, seeks to relate the Golden Age painter Diego Velázquez's *Christ Crucified* to the faith of the Spanish people, coinciding with Unamuno's own tragic sense of life. Aside from its connections to *Don Quixote*, *Niebla* is Unamuno's protest against the notion of William James that God planned the world as a chess game between himself and his human creation, with God the expert inevitably winning against the human novice (James 181). In *Abel Sánchez*, Unamuno offers a literary means for repentance and redemption. To arouse terror and contrition, he posited a civil war between two opposing outlooks, the traditional and the modern, in the protagonist's spirit. Lastly, *San Manuel Bueno, mártir* represents a synthesis of *Del sentimiento trágico* and *La agonía del cristianismo* ("The Agony of Christianity"), a brief, intense, essayistic work penned in exile in France.

NOTE

[1] This essay cites my edition of *Del sentimiento trágico de la vida* and *Tratado del amor de Dios*, published by Tecnos.

Teaching the Multifaceted Unamuno in a Semester-Long Undergraduate Course

Leslie J. Harkema

Many undergraduate students of Spanish language and literature in the United States encounter Miguel de Unamuno early on in their studies, usually by reading a short story or novel in an introductory literature course. Some arrive at college having studied *San Manuel Bueno, mártir* ("Saint Manuel Bueno, Martyr") in an advanced placement course in high school; a few have had the opportunity to read *Niebla* ("Mist") or *Abel Sánchez*. College-level surveys of modern Peninsular literature often include one of these texts, or a novella like *Nada menos que todo un hombre* ("Every Inch a Man"). As a result of this exposure to his work, today Unamuno is familiar to undergraduate students of Hispanic literatures and cultures as a writer of fiction. Rarely, however, do these students have the chance to explore the wide range of his literary production in poetry, drama, or the essay; nor do they learn about Unamuno's life and work in historical context, beyond a passing reference to the Generation of 1898. Reception and adaptation of Unamuno's work in Spain and in other countries are rarely discussed. Given the sweeping breadth of this author's writing in generic terms, not to mention his prominence as a public figure in pre–Civil War Spain, to limit students' exposure to him to even so rich a text as *San Manuel Bueno, mártir* is to exclude a great deal of Unamuno. Such limitation, though unavoidable in the context of a survey course, obscures the polyvalence that is central to the Unamunian conception of the self as a composite and succession of *yo*'s ("selves"). Curiously, the presentation of this Spaniard as first and foremost a novelist whose fictions perform the Barthesian "death of the author" has reinforced a fixed vision of Unamuno *as* author, flattening the dynamic heterogeneity that characterizes his writing.

In an effort to challenge this state of affairs, this essay proposes that the many facets of Unamuno's work provide a compelling body of material for an upper-level undergraduate seminar. A course dedicated solely to this writer creates opportunities for students to compare different literary genres and think critically about the nature, capacities, and limitations of each—this especially because Unamuno's work constantly questions and subverts the boundaries of genre. Furthermore, such a course allows instructors and students to look beyond the literary, to consider historical context and recognize the multiple ways in which Unamuno's writing challenges the division between art and life. This move from questions of literary genre to Unamuno's biography allows class participants to reflect on the relationship between literature and history—a topic that itself appears repeatedly in the writing of this poet, dramatist, essayist, novelist, and professor.

The ways we teach Unamuno today are rooted in history. His rise to prominence as a writer, cultural critic, and public figure in Spain coincided with the period in North American history that Richard Kagan has referred to as the "Spanish Craze"—a time when, among other reflections of the fascination with all things "Spanish," the teaching of the Spanish language expanded notably and began to eclipse that of French and German. Unamuno's was one of the contemporary Spanish voices to which educators in the United States attended in the 1910s and 1920s, thanks to individuals like Federico de Onís, the influential chair of Hispanic studies at Columbia University who had studied with "Don Miguel" in Salamanca. In the first issue of the North American journal *Hispania*, Onís referred to the collection and republication of Unamuno's *Ensayos* ("Essays") by the Residencia de Estudiantes as "el hecho más importante" 'the most important occurrence' in the world of Hispanic letters in 1918 ("Crónica" 48). In keeping with Onís's statement, over the next decade contributors to the journal characterized Unamuno primarily as a writer of essays and short stories. Additionally, in the early 1930s the journal published at least one personal account of the writer, a vivid description of Unamuno's interactions with North American students at the Residencia during the summer of 1932 (see Hay).

This decade also saw the first uses of the term "Generation of 1898" in *Hispania*. As in the realm of scholarship (see especially Díaz-Plaja), the critical framework that this concept brought with it shaped the teaching of Unamuno's work decisively in subsequent decades, reinforcing a focus on his work in prose. The effort to present Unamuno as a representative member of the Generation of 1898 has forced imprecisions and anachronisms. For example, the widely used anthology *Aproximaciones al estudio de la literatura hispánica* ("Approaches to the Study of Hispanic Literature") aligns *San Manuel Bueno, mártir* with "generational" concerns, despite the fact that Unamuno wrote this novella more than three decades after 1898. In recent years, with the accumulation of critical voices that cast the generational framework as part of a literary historiography that emphasizes Spanish national particularity and "difference" (see, inter alia, R. Gullón, "La invención"; Fox; and Soufas), the Generation of 1898 label has begun to seem cumbersome. While it may still serve as a topic for fruitful classroom discussion and collective critical reflection, the shift away from generation-based historiography in the field of Hispanic studies creates an opportunity for thinking about and teaching Unamuno in new—or never fully explored—ways.

Here it is worth briefly considering the pedagogical vision that one of Unamuno's successors developed while teaching Spanish literature in exile in the United States. In 1951, the last year of his life, Pedro Salinas made a series of notes toward the creation of a course on Unamuno. Held today among Salinas's papers at Harvard University's Houghton Library, these notes trace the contours of a corpus and reflect on a life; as both poet and expatriate, Salinas was heir to more than one of Unamuno's legacies. While multiple critics have highlighted Salinas's role in shaping and perpetuating the notion of the Generation of 1898 as a critical category, his writing on Unamuno testifies to the diversity of a body of work that defies easy categorization. Toward the end of his notes from 1951—after carrying out an exhaustive survey of his predecessor's poetry, novels, and philosophical works—Salinas remarks,

> Los géneros literarios Unamuno los toca todos. ¿Por virtuosismo? ¿Por versatilidad? No. Porque cada uno es un punto de vista para iluminar el mismo tema. Unamuno da vueltas alrededor de su tema. Pero un mismo tema tratado en lírica, en teatro o novela, dará resultados diferentes.
>
> Unamuno touches all of the literary genres. Out of virtuosity? Out of versatility? No. Because each one is a point of view from which to illuminate a single theme. Unamuno moves in circles around his theme. But a single theme addressed in lyric, in drama, or in the novel will produce different results.

Salinas's observation that different genres produce different results highlights how Unamuno's work lends itself to a semester-long examination that need not become tedious or overly repetitive. In reading a number of his writings over the course of a single semester, students will inevitably encounter echoes and reprisals of key themes. Yet if they are asked to pay attention to how the treatment of these themes changes from one text to another and from one genre to the next, undergraduates can refine their understanding of what each text and form achieves. I have found that incorporating a discussion of Unamuno's role in early-twentieth-century Spanish history into the semester further diversifies the course material, while also placing the themes developed in the literary texts in a new light. Through this inclusion, students have the chance to examine areas of Unamuno's writing where politics and poetics intertwine and to rethink the blurring of the boundaries between art and reality that they find in the metafiction of a novel like *Niebla*. Indeed, it is difficult to avoid history and biography very long when one contemplates Unamuno's work. Salinas attests to this too, as he fills the last pages of his notes with memories of the writer's return from exile in 1930, passages from newspaper articles about his death in 1936, and a transcribed account of his last days. For Salinas, an exiled poet who had known Unamuno and interacted with him, the "hombre de carne y hueso" 'man of flesh and bone' cannot but appear alongside the poetry, fiction, drama, and essays that—equally, differently—incarnate his thought and his being.

If Salinas's notes provide some indications toward what a monographic course on Unamuno might look like, they also inadvertently suggest why such a course is a worthwhile undertaking at the undergraduate level. As it happens, some of these notes are written on the reverse side of curriculum-related memoranda sent from the administration of Johns Hopkins University, where Salinas taught. One memorandum, dated 9 May 1951, outlines new guidelines and requirements for students studying the humanities. The document states that these students ought to acquire a "reading knowledge of a foreign language," the "ability to write English clearly and correctly," a "broad knowledge of occidental civilization," and familiarity with "the discipline of Logic" and "the methods of literary analysis." Although we frame them differently today, these basic categories—foreign languages, written composition, history, philosophy, and literary analysis—continue to be pillars of a humanities education. One of the greatest strengths of a course on Unamuno is that it can deal meaningfully with all of them, integrating learning as it encourages students to consider multiple approaches to a single author and a single—if multifaceted—body of work.

In the spring of 2016, I taught a course titled The Many Faces of Miguel de Unamuno. I had envisioned the class as giving students the opportunity to engage with a variety of texts by and about Unamuno and to develop their own critical perspectives on his work. In what follows, I offer a summary of the course and its strengths and reflect on how it can be adapted for future implementation.

Over the course of thirteen weeks, my students and I studied Unamuno in numerous guises: the novelist, the philosopher, the (heterodox) believer, the dramatist, the poet, the public intellectual, and the political exile. During the first half of the term, each student selected one of these "faces" and prepared a short report on the corresponding aspect of Unamuno's life and work. While in my class I instructed the students to carry out independent research on their assigned topic, offering guidance about secondary sources when necessary, such reports might also take the form of summaries of critical essays selected by the professor. (The recent collection *El Unamuno eterno* ["The Eternal Unamuno"], edited by J. A. Garrido Ardila, includes several essays that might serve this purpose.) During this first part of the course I also assigned two short reflection papers: a response to one of the two novels we read in class, and an analysis of Unamuno's concept of philosophy, religion, or art as evidenced in later course readings. Cumulatively, this coursework prepared the students for their final research project: the identification and analysis of a new "face" of Unamuno, one not explicitly named in the syllabus but that they were able to discern through their own reading, interpretation, and investigation. The semester was thus oriented toward the development of the students' own critical perspectives on the body of work to which they were exposed.

We began the term with a discussion of the best-known area of Unamuno's work, narrative fiction. Our first reading was the short story "Y va de cuento" ("So the Story Goes"), which provides an introduction to several recurring elements in Unamunian writing: intertextuality; etymological play; the notions of paradox, orthodoxy, and heresy; and the writer's tendency to construct himself as a character within his own fictions. We then proceeded to read two novels: *Niebla* and *La tía Tula* ("Aunt Tula"). Our analysis of the role of the multiple paratexts in the first novel, Unamuno's coinage of the term *nivola*, and his treatment of protagonist Augusto Pérez took on new dimensions when we turned to *La tía Tula*, where prologue, neologisms, and characterization all center on questions of gender. As we debated whether this novel challenges or reifies essentialist notions of masculinity and femininity, and whether it successfully reconstrues the place of women in Spanish society, the students were asked to ponder whether Unamuno might have a "feminist" or a "misogynist" face and to what extent these labels are appropriate or useful.

By this point in the term, about the fifth week, the class had dealt with some of the key philosophical problems that appear in Unamuno's writing: the problem of free will; the desire for immortality; the tensions between reason, will, and desire; and the nature of belief. In the next section of the course, we studied these topics in more depth, beginning with a discussion of the first chapter of *Del sentimiento trágico de la vida* ("On the Tragic Sense of Life"), "El hombre de carne y hueso" ("The Man of Flesh and Bone"). A dense read for undergraduates, this text can intimidate students with its discussion of several philosophers with whom they may or may not be familiar. I found it helpful to provide a glossary of the names that appear (one is provided in an appendix in Nelson Orringer's 2005 edition of *Del sentimiento trágico*) and to instruct students to read the text with attention to Unamuno's overarching argument, identifying his own authorial assertions and focusing especially on the opening and closing passages. In class, we centered our discussion on how Unamuno defines the terms *hombre* and *humano* in this text and asked how these definitions shape his thought.

Next we read the essay "Mi religión" ("My Religion"), accompanied by the poems "Salmo I" and "Salmo II" ("Psalm I" and "Psalm II"), "La oración del ateo" ("The Atheist's Prayer"), and "Razón y fe" ("Reason and Faith"). Here I placed emphasis on the connectedness of faith and poetic creation in Unamuno's thought, drawing on his declaration in the essay that the "Salmos" *are* his religion (Unamuno, *Obras completas* [Senabre] 8: 55). Several students found this statement intriguing, and this provided an opportunity to discuss Unamuno's well-known juxtaposition (and equation) of the verbs *creer* ("to believe") and *crear* ("to create").

Finally, we explored the dialectic relationship between reason and faith in the context of Unamuno's play *La venda* ("The Blindfold"). I found that studying a dramatic work at this point in the semester afforded the students an opportunity to participate in a truly creative act of interpretation. In my class we staged scenes and read dialogues aloud, but this type of engagement with the text could extend much further, from considerations of the use of props (in this case, the blindfold) and lighting (juxtaposing darkness and light, blindness and sight) to a full-fledged performance of the work.

The next several classes presented a broader survey of Unamuno's poetry. In order to refine our understanding of the writer's poetics, I selected poems in the *ars poetica* vein such as "Credo poético" ("Poetic Creed") and "Denso, denso" ("Dense, dense") from the collection *Poesías* ("Poems") as well as "Caña salvaje" ("Wild Reed") from *Rimas de dentro* ("Rhymes from Within"). Other choices, such as "Elegía en la muerte de un perro" ("Elegy upon the Death of a Dog") (*Poesías*) and "Aldebarán" (*Rimas de dentro*), picked up on the themes of existential questioning and longing for immortality that we had talked about in relation to *Niebla* and "El hombre de carne y hueso." As we read these poems, I asked my students to reflect on how Unamuno makes use of lyric form. How does the experience of reading Unamuno's poetry compare with reading his novels? What formal choices does the writer make in this genre? The students were able to identify the relative flexibility of the forms Unamuno employs (such as the *silva modernista*, a form characterized by assonant rhyme and the free combination of seven-, nine-, and eleven-syllable lines) without a need for detailed discussions of versification. These observations fueled our ongoing discussion of Unamuno as a modernist in the broadest sense—an artist and thinker who pursues novelty by breaking with and revising traditional forms, whether literary forms or forms of thought, genre, or dogma.

In closing our discussion of poetry, we turned to texts Unamuno produced during his exile. A selection of poems from this period served as an introduction to the final unit in the course, which dealt with Unamuno's status as a public figure in the later portion of his life. We read selections from *De Fuerteventura a París* ("From Fuerteventura to Paris"), *Romancero del destierro* ("Ballads of Exile"), and *Cancionero* ("Songbook")—in the last case, poem 828, "Me destierro a la memoria . . ." ("I'm exiling myself to memory . . ."), was a key inclusion. As I stressed to my students, each of these poems bears a date that ties it to a particular day, month, and year. As Ana Urrutia-Jordana has demonstrated at length, the writings of this period in Unamuno's life foreground the intertwining of poetry and the political circumstances that had forced his exile. Through our analysis of these texts, poetry became a bridge to a consideration of the relationship between literature and history. In subsequent classes we read historical documents: letters that Unamuno wrote from Fuerteventura to his wife, Concha, and from Hendaye to the university students of Spain (Unamuno, *Cartas del destierro*); selections from the clandestine journal *Hojas libres* ("Free Pages"), to which he contributed assiduously (see Martínez-Nadal); and accounts of his return from exile that appeared in the Spanish press in February 1930. Confronted with these documents, the students expressed surprise at finding such direct evidence of Unamuno's fame and public status in early-twentieth-century Spain, and this moment of discovery provided useful context for our next topic: the events of the last months of the writer's life and, in particular, his clash with General José Millán-Astray on 12 October 1936. As an introduction to this storied confrontation, I assigned two accounts of the event, one taken from Andrés Trapiello's *Las armas y las letras* ("Arms and Letters") and the other from Carlos Rojas's *¡Muera la inteligencia! ¡Viva la muerte!: Salamanca, 1936, Unamuno y Millán Astray frente a frente* ("Death to the Intellectuals! Long Live Death!: Salamanca, 1936, Unamuno and Millán Astray Face to Face"). Comparing two distinct records of this clash helped students to recognize the constructed nature of each, as they identified discrepancies between the two texts and talked about the different framing strategies Trapiello and Rojas employ. In the future, class discussion could also engage with the debate about the historical veracity of the encounter that broke out in the Spanish press in the late spring of 2018 (see del Molino; Rabaté and Rabaté, "Enfrentamiento"). Analyzing texts like these allows class participants to think together about the mediated nature of our reception of history and to debate the merits of an assertion that Unamuno makes often in his work: that it is his writing, and not his biography, that encapsulates his true self.

Ultimately, a semester-long course on Unamuno must confront the question of authenticity, so central to the existentialist tradition from which this writer draws and to which he contributes. Among so many "faces" of Unamuno, are some "truer" than others? What do we mean when we say that? Do we refer to a Romantic notion of literary self-expression, to historical accuracy, or to the reception of the reader? In this first iteration of The Many Faces of Miguel de Unamuno, we closed our semester by reading a text that lends itself to discussions of these questions, the novella *Don Sandalio, jugador de ajedrez* ("Don Sandalio, Chess Player"). Another approach might make use of the final weeks of the semester to consider Unamuno's later legacy in film and literature. Students might compare the multiple movie adaptations of *Niebla* (see Álvarez-Castro, "De la metaficción"), discuss Miguel Picazo's 1964 adaptation of *La tía Tula* (see Diana Jorza's essay in this volume), or even consider Unamuno's recent reappearance in Spanish film, in Manuel Menchón's *La isla del viento* ("The Island of the Wind") and Alejandro Amenábar's *Mientras dure la guerra* ("While the War Lasts"). A discussion of Unamuno's legacy today might further be informed by a critical examination of his online presence, in Spanish and English. Indeed, one aspect of my course involved engaging this digital presence through the development of a course Web site.

My central goal for this course was for my students to become invested in their own approach to Unamuno and thus find themselves equipped to enter into the ongoing debates about his work and legacy. Furthermore, after thirteen weeks spent with this multifaceted Spaniard, I hoped that they would not only refine their own vision of Unamuno—*their* Unamuno—but also, in the process, come to understand better the prismatic value of the literary in relation to broader humanistic study. The feedback I received suggested that a semester-long course dedicated to Unamuno can achieve these goals. Multiple students enjoyed discovering "faces" of the writer that had been unknown to them previously and identifying which ones they "liked" best. Others expressed surprise that the class did not become repetitive or boring. More than one student observed that the course involved more in-depth literary analysis than other literature classes they had taken—a view that may or may not be accurate but that in any case attests to the conscious reflection on literary genres (and the nature of the literary itself) that a course solely dedicated to Unamuno can facilitate.

NOTE

I am exceedingly grateful to the group of students who took the course and collaborated with me in this endeavor. Though I do not quote them or their work directly here, their enthusiastic participation and input throughout that semester have shaped my reflections a great deal. Unless noted, translations of quotations are mine.

LITERARY AND HISTORICAL MILIEU

Toward a Twentieth-Century Modernity: Unamuno's *Paz en la guerra*

Salvador Oropesa

Miguel de Unamuno's opera prima contains his first systematic analysis of Spain's problems. Bilbao, which experienced the most radical demographic changes of the entire nation between 1850 and 1900, plays a central role. During those years, the city tripled its population, and surrounding villages became industrial hubs, primarily of steel mills, and lost their rural identity. The liberal government's 1876 abolition of *fueros*, or legal privileges granted to particular territories, opened the door to redirecting local capital from mining to steel mills. Facilitated by the growing railway system and shipping lines, commerce from northern Europe brought access to new goods and transformed the city and its participation in the national economy.

Paz en la guerra ("Peace in War") is a true masterpiece that provides today's students and scholars different readings and a variety of teaching options. Given its length and complexity, this is a novel best imparted in a graduate seminar or a capstone undergraduate literature class. I recommend four uses of the novel in class, although the versatility of this text allows for other possibilities.

A first reading is as a historical novel that contains the details of the last *carlista* war: troop movements, weaponry, Bilbao's defenses, effects of the attack on the civilian population, and the presence of historical figures. In this context students can learn how the novel cunningly embeds *costumbrismo*—the artistic interpretation of local everyday life, especially customs in the process of disappearing—in the frame of the realist novel; *costumbrismo* adds an element of nostalgia and resistance to modernity. In this regard, critics agree, Unamuno's novel is indebted to Pérez Galdós's *Episodios nacionales* ("National Episodes").

The historical context of *Paz en la guerra* begins with *carlistas*, political traditionalists who opposed parliamentarism and secularism and sought to establish an alternative branch of the Bourbon dynasty on the Spanish throne. *Carlismo* was a heterogeneous social movement that had the support of regular clergy (religious orders had lost most of their real estate holdings under the liberal government's privatization efforts), rural nobility, reactionary intellectuals, bureaucrats, and members of the military. However, the most ardent supporters were Catholic farmers overwhelmed by modernity, new international market forces in agriculture and manufacturing, the loss of newly privatized communal lands, and the taxes imposed by liberal administrations. Many such farmers had lost their farms to moneylenders and land speculators. Their ultimate goal—to return to a preindustrial, premodern past—represented an impossible utopia. *Carlismo* paralleled similar counterrevolutionary movements, like *Action française* in France. The *carlista* leader Carlos VII entered Spain on 16 July 1873, swore allegiance to traditional Basque laws under the sacred oak tree of Guernica, and visited Loyola sanctuary, birthplace of Saint Ignatius of Loyola, where he was anointed king of Spain. He also recognized the traditional laws of Catalonia. During the war *carlistas* attacked trains and other symbols of modernity and burned property registries of the liberal state; historians discern a deep anticapitalist bias in these facts. All these actions are present in *Paz en la guerra*.

The core of the novel is the unsuccessful siege of Bilbao between 21 February and 2 May 1874.[1] It lasted 124 days, and for over two months the city was bombed continuously. *Carlistas* surrounded the city with six battalions totaling 4,000–5,000 soldiers and twenty heavy weapons (cannons and mortars). Bilbao was ready for the attack; its garrison had 4,500 government soldiers plus 1,000 civilian volunteer combatants. Trenches were also built for fortification outside city walls. As in most blockades, Bilbao's weak point was food scarcity, but the train from Santander and western ports of Cantabria allowed access to fresh troops and weaponry. After one failed attempt to break the siege, General Manuel Gutiérrez de la Concha deployed three divisions comprising fourteen battalions of infantry with 18,000 soldiers, a cavalry of 1,000 additional men, and twenty-four pieces of artillery. This time he freed the city.

Unamuno created an eyewitness-like portrayal of events via exhaustive research. In addition to methodical archival reading of newspapers, memoirs, and official documents, he interviewed many witnesses and protagonists of the war and spent several days at different stages of writing exploring battle scenarios on horseback. He included his own memories as a ten-year-old during the war. Reading the novel, we learn that between the start of the assault and the first city bombing there were thirty dances; that on a single day eighty-three bombs fell in Bilbao and their destructive effect was magnified by winds from the south. These historical facts add to the immediacy of the novel. Unamuno spent over ten years writing the work and it evolved over time, moving from a traditional historical novel like Leo Tolstoy's *War and Peace* to a more psychological account. Students can follow the novel's genesis by reading the many letters Unamuno sent to fellow writers and scholars explaining his progress on the project. Another genre at play is modern journalism, seen in conflict descriptions that sound as if the narrator were a war correspondent.

The second option is to use *Paz en la guerra* in a class on late-nineteenth-century Spanish realism. Students can explore how the novel represents modernity and the anxiety produced by the homogenization imposed by the liberal nation-state as debated and developed during the *sexenio revolucionario* (the six-year democratic period between 1868 and 1874), exemplified in the novel by the trauma of the loss of *fueros*. This anxiety is depicted in the intense intellectual effort needed to represent a new "imagined community," using the concept developed by the political scientist Benedict Anderson. Students can research how representation becomes reality; for instance, Unamuno distorts the composition of the combatants defending Bilbao, overvaluing the civil component of the defendants of the city. The narration emphasizes the viewpoint of modernity's losers, who, against their will, were incorporated in the Spanish liberal project. Unamuno also analyzes the political climate with emphasis on the tensions between Spain's traditional ancien régime (strong public role of the Catholic Church, an absolute king, restrictions to free trade, defense of *fueros*) and liberalism (free trade; the nation-state as a unique market; disentailment, or "privatization," of religious property, rural communal lands, and the national railroad and telegraph networks; constitutional law). Unamuno witnessed the breakdown of Bilbao's traditional social contract, whose challenge was to reconcile incompatible political models from traditionalism, socialism, and incipient nationalism within a constitutional framework. In private letters Unamuno indicated that his goal was to write a novel that both liberals and *carlistas* would dislike. He also aimed to criticize the demagogue, the *jebo* ("bumpkin"), and the *bilbaíno* ("Bilbao dweller").

End-of-century realist novelists were obsessed with the *sexenio revolucionario*. Students can compare how different novels represented Spain's traumatic entry to modernity. *Paz en la guerra*, like Benito Pérez Galdós's *Fortunata y Jacinta*, explores two of the main ideologies of this period, republic and absolute monarchy, which were reconciled with the constitutional monarchy of Alfonso XII, who was restored as king of Spain on 19 December 1874, putting an end to *carlista* aspirations to the Spanish throne. Alfonso XII represented a moderate rule between the reactionary forces of *carlismo*, the liberal aspirations of the republic, and the Saboya monarchy. His ascent to the throne marked the beginning of the period known as Restauración (Restoration), which ended in 1930.

Other *sexenio revolucionario* novels emphasized the need to incorporate regional diversity in the new order, like *Pepita Jiménez*, by Juan Valera; *Los pazos de Ulloa* ("The House of Ulloa"), by Emilia Pardo Bazán; and *Peñas arriba* ("Up in the Mountains"), by José María de Pereda. The last denounces the overcentralization of the liberal nation-state. All these masterpieces of Spanish realism allow a centralist and a regional reading, as well as a conservative and a liberal reading. Students can investigate the representation of the free market in these novels: the presence of diverse stores and forms of commerce in *Fortunata y Jacinta*; the production of olive oil and wine—commodities that were freely traded without tariffs—in *Pepita Jiménez*; and the import of new goods from the city in order to civilize the countryside in all of them. In *Paz en la guerra* Unamuno depicts the free-market tensions using two stores and two nuclear families: a modest chocolate mill managed by the former *carlista* soldier Pedro Antonio Iturriondo, and a modern textile store owned by the liberal free trader Don José María Arana. One character possesses the title of "don" 'mister' (indicating secondary or university studies), while the other one lacks it. The novel locates both shops in the historical center of Bilbao, known as the *siete calles*, or seven streets. The chocolate store is a premodern store, barely an open counter and without windows. The novel lacks description of the textile store, but it is a modern store: it receives goods from different countries via Bilbao's port. One store does not seek growth while the other is immersed in global commerce.

More important than the commercial revenue of the chocolate store, as summarized by weekly purchases by family maids, is the *tertulia*, or regular meetings, of certain clients at the business. Pedro Antonio's *tertulia* in the chocolate store represents *carlismo* and links the second *carlista* war to the first one. Except for the owner, all members of the *tertulia* belong to nonproductive classes who are nostalgic for the final decade of Fernando VII's reign, the (according to them) peaceful period from 1823 to 1833. One character, the conspirator Gambelu, presents the war as a conflict between rich and poor; he represents the anarchist and populist wing of *carlismo* and supports the destruction of the liberal state. Juan José, a young future *carlista* volunteer, represents *fuerismo* (the political doctrine seeking to restore former territorial privileges). Don Eustaquio, as a *carlista* officer of the previous war, receives a pension from the liberal government and favors an understanding between the government in Madrid and the *carlistas*. Don Pascual, a priest and a first cousin of Pedro Antonio, is a flat character who advocates destruction of the enemy. The ultraconservative, intransigent priest is a staple figure of the realist novel. Don José María, the official representative member of the party, consistently spouts the party line. Don Braulio, the immigrant returned from the Americas, advocates resignation. Pedro Antonio, the only one who fought in the previous war, is a pacifist who accepts that his son will volunteer to go to war; the son's subsequent death will devastate him. Clearly, each *carlista* is different, and together they represent the intricacies and contradictions of this political movement.

The textile store belongs to the Arana brothers, well-known liberals. José María Arana started as a tailor working for others until he opened his own store. His brother, Juan, is the accountant, in charge of receiving imported merchandise and writing commercial letters in different languages all over the world. Don Juan affirms that "¡El comercio matará a la guerra y a la barbarie!" 'Commerce will do away with war and barbarism' (148, 21).[2] While the Iturriondos speak Spanish and Basque, the Aranas speak Spanish and French. José María reads French economic magazines and becomes familiar with the ideas of Adam

Smith, Jean-Baptiste Say, and Frédéric Bastiat, defenders of free trade and the self-regulation of markets. The Aranas are Catholic and moderate.

The *sexenio revolucionario*'s aim was to make all inhabitants of Spain citizens of the nation. Students can observe how people of Bilbao were already citizens, but the novel illustrates the challenges of incorporating the peasants of rural Biscay into the new nation-state. They can also study how the same problem is undertaken in *Pepita Jiménez* with rural Andalusians, in *Los pazos de Ulloa* with rural Galicians, and in *Peñas arriba* with Cantabrians. Other concepts that can be developed in class are the problematization of what is "natural," based on the dominant Krausist ideology among fin de siècle intellectuals that there was no divide between the social and the natural, and the use of "natural" to legitimize social practices like patriarchy. All these novels challenge the naturalness of what constitutes the feminine and the masculine. They are also infused with discourses on social control and the institutional presences that enforce it. Also prevalent is the equation of freedom and private property.

A third and challenging reading of the novel is as a modernist novel; others use the term "impressionist." The key difference from realism is characters are more developed psychologically than those of most realist novels. Characters show their inner self via stream of consciousness. Students will notice how the novel lacks the clear beginning, middle, and end of the realist novel and the chapters are unequal in length. Realism and modernism coincide in that reality has become representation; the difference is that the latter intensifies how problematic this relationship is. Unamuno seeks an active presence in his writing, and in *Paz en la guerra* he inserts himself in the omniscient narration and through the character Pachico Zabalbide. Pachico's role is not protagonic but rather editorial; he has the final word in the novel. (Critics have also seen Unamuno in the commonsensical, chaste, and strong Rafaela Arana.) Unamuno uses the narrator and Pachico to eulogize rural Biscay, centuries of tradition, resistance to centralist forces, the dynamism of modern cities, and commerce. As a polyhedral, implied author, Unamuno is torn between two incompatible philosophies of life. The narrator feels empathy for rural life and traditions and the Basque language but understands the inevitable triumph of urban culture and capitalism.

Paz en la guerra also starts developing the concept of *intrahistoria*, a device used to cope with fears of modernity that Unamuno would fully develop in his collection of essays *En torno al casticismo* ("On the Essence of Spanishness"). Students can question if this is a modernist device and explore the techniques used to implement it and the ideological implications of its use. Unamuno centers his text on the everyday lives of ordinary people, who are the true protagonists (rather than historical figures like generals and politicians who make decisions affecting the lives of others) but have no voice in the novel. *Intrahistoria* also emerges in Unamuno's portrayal of the civil war as a fraternal conflict devoid of intervention by the state or the government army and fought by civilian combatants, liberal militia, and *carlista* volunteers. In reality, most military actions were carried out by professional troops, and it is a stretch of the imagination to consider as civilians the liberal and *carlista* volunteers who served under military discipline. In this way Unamuno creates the myth of a neighborhood-based Bilbao, seed of the new liberal Spain. Tied to this idea is Unamuno's invention and use of a Bilbao dialect in *Paz en la guerra*, seen also in *Recuerdos de mi niñez y mocedad* ("Memories of My Childhood and Youth"). In these texts only children use the dialect; adult characters speak conventional Spanish. According to the literary critic and historian Jon Juaristi, the invention of this dialect played some role in developing nationalist theories and literature, because the dialect marked the difference between true *bilbaínos* and, by extension, Basques and *maquetos*, the dysphemism used by Basques to refer to Spaniards from other regions who migrated to Bilbao (*El chimbo*).

Any of the first three readings should take into account the structure of the novel. Each of the novel's five chapters is divided into brief scenes marked with dialogues and apparently disconnected events. Critics regularly use the term "fragmented" to describe this technique, which, like impressionism in painting and modernism in literature, creates a new reality that provides the reader with a keen sense of immediacy. Students can observe how rural realist novels depict the landscape through subjective focalization like in impressionist painting.

Paz en la guerra follows a lineal structure capped by an epilogue that preludes later novels. The first chapter introduces the reader to Spain's most important prewar events and the main characters and is centered on the private and public life of Pedro Antonio Iturriondo and his son, Ignacio. The Basque meaning of Iturriondo is "by the water spring." Chapter 2 depicts the war's onset. The narration takes the reader through different stages leading to the *carlista* military coup d'état, the rebel troop occupation of parts of Biscay, and the siege of Bilbao. Chapters 2 and 4 focus on Ignacio, who enlists in the army in April 1873; during this period the *carlistas* move from place to place, engaging in skirmishes but not directly confronting government troops. Chapter 3, the novelistic center, concentrates on the city siege and resistance from late 1873 to 2 May 1874. It features the family life of Don Juan de Arana and the spiritual and intellectual life of Pachico Zabalbide, whose surname means "wide trail" in Basque. Chapter 4 describes the war in Biscay province and the liberation of Bilbao. According to Birutė Ciplijauskaitė, this chapter contains two of the most interesting psychological portrayals in the work: during one attack, Ignacio becomes simultaneously an actor and a spectator; later, his mind flashes back to childhood just before his death (151). Ignacio dies when hit by a stray bullet, but his presence continues through references to him by his parents, his friend Pachico Zabalbide, and Rafaela Arana, the girlfriend he never had. Ignacio's death stresses the contingency of history. Neither hero nor antihero, he simply lived a short, anonymous life, and the sum of all such lives constitutes *intrahistoria*, which Unamuno deems more relevant than any history sanctioned by society or academe. This chapter is deeply antimilitarist.

Chapter 5 recounts the end of military operations and reflects on the war's consequences. As in chapter 1, Ignacio's point of view dominates, as he lives on in other characters' memories. Paul Olson notes how his presence is "consuetudinaria" 'customary' ("Sobre el arte" 323). The narration paradoxically associates his death with dawn. The final word is given to the mythical, pantheistic vision of Unamuno's alter ego Pachico Zabalbide, who is determined to fight for progress and social welfare:

> Así es como allí arriba, vencido el tiempo, toma gusto a las cosas eternas, ganando bríos para lanzarse luego al torrente incoercible del progreso, en que rueda lo pasajero sobre lo permanente. Allí arriba, la contemplación serena le da resignación trascendente y eterna, madre de la irresignación temporal, del no contentarse jamás aquí abajo, del pedir siempre mayor salario, y baja decidido a provocar en los demás el descontento, primer motor de todo progreso y de todo bien. (510)

> Up there on those heights time was vanquished for Pachico, and thus it is that he finds a taste for things of eternity and gains the determination to throw himself into the unrestrainable torrent of progress, in which fleeting things roll over permanent ones. Up there on the height, peaceful contemplation gave him an eternal sense of resignation which will never allow him to resign himself in temporal matters nor to be contented here below with endlessly seeking a larger salary. He has come down from the height determined to arouse in other men the discontent which is the prime mover of all progress and all good. (383)

The epilogue's main purpose is to break the cyclical idea of history that the structure of chapters 1 through 5 could imply. As seen in the quotation, Unamuno is tempted by metaphysical closure but at the end he remains consistent and declares that history is open, that we do not know what the future will bring. Pachico moves from history to *intrahistoria* to give voice to the people, defined as the sum of all individual lives and aspirations. In one of many comments about his novel, Unamuno indicated that, unlike a historical novel, in his text history adapts forms from the novel (G. Gullón 43). After the choral novel and its polyphony, it is Unamuno's voice that pervades. This ending recalls the speech that Don Manuel gives to Ángela Carballino when they see the female goat herder in *San Manuel Bueno, mártir* (Caudet, Introduction 62).

A fourth and thought-provoking reading of the novel treats it as the political text that led to the evolution of *carlismo* to modern Basque nationalism based on the new post-*fueros* political and economic reality in the Basque Country. This nationalism oscillated between linguistic and ethnic difference, according to Juaristi in *El chimbo expiatorio* and subsequent books on Basque nationalism. By 1887 Galdós had already developed two characters in *Fortunata y*

Jacinta, Juan Pablo Rubín and José Izquierdo, who fluctuate between *carlismo* and republicanism (Labanyi, *Gender* 177).

Any seminar on literature and cinema of the violence in the Basque Country should include parts of *Paz en la guerra* and Juaristi's reflections on how the seed of future conflicts is present in this novel. Another text that could be considered for a class about terrorist violence is the novel *Patria* ("Country"), by Fernando Aramburu. This novel has had the same effect as *Soldados de Salamina* ("Soldiers of Salamis"), by Javier Cercas, had on the Civil War novel. It opened the door to new representations of violence and social conflict in the Basque Country. One example is Edurne Portela, who followed her book *El eco de los disparos: Cultura y memoria de la violencia* ("The Echo of the Shots: Culture and Memory of Violence") with the critically acclaimed novel *Mejor la ausencia* ("Better the Absence"). The Basque separatist group Euskadi Ta Askatasuna (ETA) has, through its terrorist actions, already inspired important works like the documentaries *La pelota vasca: La piel contra la piedra* ("Basque Pelota: Skin against Stone"), directed by Julio Medem, and *Asier eta Biok* ("Asier and I"), by Amaia Merino and Aitor Merino. Relevant fictional films about ETA are *Días contados* ("Numbered Days"), by Imanol Uribe, and *La casa de mi padre* ("The House of My Father"), by Gorka Merchán. Other possibilities for texts to study in class are essays like *Polvo de ETA* ("ETA's Dust"), by Joseba Zulaika, and testimonies of victims like *Sangre, sudor y paz* ("Blood, Sweat and Peace"), by Lorenzo Silva, Gonzalo Araluce, and Manuel Sánchez.

Paz en la guerra is the last key novel of the nineteenth century in Spain and the first one of the twentieth century. It put Miguel de Unamuno on the Spanish literary map and was followed by forty more years of superb literature.

NOTES

[1] In the past, historians counted three *carlista* wars, but the second war (1846–49), which consisted of local insurrections, is no longer considered as such (Fontana 375).

[2] The text of *Paz en la guerra* used in this essay is Francisco Caudet's edition, published by Cátedra. English translations are from *Peace and War*, a translation by Allen Lacy, Martin Nozick, and Anthony Kerrigan.

Dressing Up Unamuno's *Naked Theater*: Contextualizing Unamuno's Drama in the Classroom

Tracie Amend

Thematically, Miguel de Unamuno's dramas lend themselves to a number of frameworks and courses. The quintessential hallmarks of Unamunian narrative also appear in his drama: from the abulic male soul disillusioned with Spanish society to the infertile wife succumbing to either illicit desire or the madness of her environment. Several of Unamuno's dramas constitute nice companion pieces to narrative works: *Raquel encadenada* ("Raquel in Chains") pairs well with *La tía Tula* ("Aunt Tula"), as both concern the nearly hysteric obsession of an aunt with her nieces and nephews. So too could the schizophrenic, murderous protagonist of *El otro* ("The Other") provide a foil to the fratricide in *Abel Sánchez*. Unamuno's *El hermano Juan o el mundo es teatro* ("Brother Juan or the World Is Theater") is one of many Generation of 1898 parodies of the Don Juan myth and, as such, speaks to the Spanish modernists' love-hate relationship with the Spanish Romantic tradition. In effect, nearly any dramatic work of Unamuno's may be gleaned for its contribution to the Unamunian oeuvre, its characterization of the philosophical angst in fin de siècle Spain, or its dialogue with the disparate theatrical movements that captivated European stages in the late nineteenth and early twentieth centuries. While I intend to comment briefly on the general use of Unamunian drama in survey or topics courses, the majority of this essay is dedicated to a focused textual and theatrical analysis of Unamuno's *teatro desnudo*, or naked theater, using *La venda* ("The Blindfold") and *El otro* as teaching templates for the undergraduate and graduate classroom, respectively.

When considering Unamuno's dramas within a European context, one can interpret his naked dramas as a reaction against Romantic melodramas as well as naturalism onstage.[1] Unamuno's sympathy with symbolist dramatists suggests that he participated in early avant-garde movements, particularly those spearheaded by Maurice Maeterlinck, August Strindberg, and Vyacheslav Ivanovich Ivanov, among others. While Unamuno did not seek to create a dream state onstage, his minimalist approach to visual sign systems parallels the symbolists' eschewal of realistic sets (Sprinchorn 641). Thematically, an instructor might juxtapose *La venda* with Maeterlinck's *The Intruder* or *The Blind*, both of which likewise explore the allegorical blindness of humanity and man's existential crisis. In this way, the study of Unamunian drama could contribute to a course on proto-avant-garde movements in Europe.

If the instructor wishes to give students a panoramic view of Spanish literary movements and techniques onstage, Unamuno's drama provides a helpful bridge between hyperbolic tragic melodramas (also known as neoromanticism) and the early-twentieth-century realists like Jacinto Benavente. More specifically, assigning a trio of dramas such as *El gran Galeoto* ("The Great Galeoto"), by José Echegaray; *Fedra* ("Phaedra"), by Unamuno; and *La malquerida* ("The Disliked Girl"), by Benavente as an "adulteress / illicit desire" unit is an effective way of discussing the disparate theatrical movements that characterized Spanish theater from 1880 to 1920.

In a more general sense, Unamuno's dramas are perfect launching pads for discussing the nature and elements of tragedy. Many of Unamuno's dramas are adaptations or variations on Greek myth and, as such, provide a fruitful basis for the discussion of Aristotelian form and practice. In his *exordio* (introduction) to *Fedra*, Unamuno defines *teatro desnudo*, at least in part, as a tragedy laid bare: "llamo desnudo en la tragedia o desnudez trágica al efecto que se obtiene presentando la tragedia en toda su augusta y solemne majestad" 'I call that which is naked in tragedy or tragic nudity the effect that one obtains while presenting the tragedy in all of its august and solemn majesty' (302).[2] He goes on to describe naked theater as prohibitive of any sort of visual or scenic adornment. Each scenic distraction obstructs the message of the work; the literary work as a whole loses its purity to theatricality. In particular, Unamuno characterizes luxurious costumes as a restriction of honesty and clarity of the literary message: "Aspiro a que cuanto diga y exprese Fedra, por ejemplo, sea de tal intensidad trágica, que los espectadores—y sobre todo las espectadoras—no tengan que distraerse mirando como va vestida la actriz que la representa" 'My goal is that everything that Phaedra says and conveys, for example, has such tragic intensity that the spectators—especially the female spectators—do not have to distract themselves paying attention to how the actress playing her [Phaedra] is dressed' (302). In this particular portion of his *exordio*, Unamuno seems to contradict himself. While he resists the theatrical components of the performance, he also seems to admit to the inherent purpose of the drama: its presentation to the public. There remains the potential for a performance, but such a performance must adhere to a severe sense of simplicity.

The fact that Unamuno eschews some performative elements underscores his desire to re-create (at least to some extent) the simplicity and "bare" tragic form of the classical Greek theater. Ironically, this harkening back to the origins of theater also serves to emphasize the necessity of the performance: the public must see and be drawn into action in order to experience a catharsis and, as Angelos Terzakis states, renew the spectators' "love of humanity" (7). This potential contradiction of generic definition is one of many that can incite a healthy discussion in the classroom. The dramas' supposed nakedness lends itself to an exploration of the nature of theater: if a drama is visually minimalist in the text, does that bare textual foundation (along with Unamuno's own proclamation) preclude those dramas from a theatrical categorization?[3] This question can instigate a fruitful discussion among students at various levels of Spanish competency and literary studies.

The study of theater demands that the students make note of and imagine the visual signs within the text. When approaching a typical play in the undergraduate classroom, I underscore the importance of the stage directions (both technical and parenthetical). I often ask students to draw a picture of a set as it is described in the opening stage directions. I stress the importance of theatrical terminology, including, but not limited to, visual production elements such as props, lighting, and costumes. Even if the stage directions fail to mention or describe visual elements, I ask students to imagine what the actors and the stage might look like, given the period and the information that is available in the text. When available, I show pictures of productions from the period, as well as images related to the staging of the play itself. As we analyze the characters, themes, and action, I ask students to describe how the explicit or implied visual elements enhance or expand upon the textual basis for the play, and I remind students that most drama was written to be performed.

If the class includes an analytical essay or a reflective composition, I will include specific references to visual elements as a requirement for their analysis. For example, I will ask students to explain how a symbolic title relates to the central themes of the play. Then, in the body of their composition, the students must cite and describe visual elements that elucidate the play's themes. In this way, students will recognize how dramas or theatrical texts fit into the larger literary field, and they will view theater as a dynamic genre that lives beyond the text.

All of these strategies apply to *teatro desnudo*, but it is also important to underscore the ways in which Unamuno's dramas defy or adhere to theatrical categorization. In most undergraduate settings, *La venda* is an appropriate introduction to Unamuno's dramas. If I were to use *La venda* in the context of a theater course, I would also assign the *exordio* to *Fedra*, in which Unamuno defines and describes the concept of *teatro desnudo*. Rather than reading the introduction first, an instructor might choose to read and discuss *La venda* as its own entity. This postponement allows students to analyze the work before they censure their own observations of its potential "theatricality" or lack thereof. The premise of the play is simple: María, the tragic heroine, pretends to be blind so that she cannot see her father on his deathbed. She wears the title bandage until the other characters force her to remove it, thereby creating a climax in which father and daughter see each other for the first time. Upon looking into his daughter's eyes, Juan is horrified and dies instantaneously.

Along with its short length, *La venda* emphasizes universal themes with straightforward language and relatively easy Spanish vocabulary. The first step is to assess what (if any) visual elements are presented in the text. As we read, we scour the text for visual cues, either explicitly stated in the stage directions or implied. It is helpful to put students in groups, giving each group a specific visual element to discover: props, movement, and gestures, among other elements. In the case of *La venda*, Unamuno provides sparse stage directions. The play consists of only two *cuadros*, or scenes, and Unamuno begins each with a one-sentence description of the setting: "*En una calle de una vieja ciudad provinciana*" '*On a street in an old provincial city*' (223). Later, Unamuno simply states: "*Interior de casa de familia clase media*" '*House interior of a middle-class family'* (230). In a typical play in the realist style, dramatists offer an extended description of the set: the entrances and exits, the placement of the furniture, and the overall style of the living area. All of these visual descriptions are conspicuously absent in *La venda* and, indeed, in most of Unamuno's dramas. Yet the mere mention of a setting, along with the adjectives *old*, *provincial*, and *middle-class*, automatically evokes a visual picture in the reader's mind. The dialogue does not exist in a vacuum but rather is tied to the specific setting.

Although Unamuno does not reference costumes, sets, or lighting in *La venda*, he does employ stage directions indicating entrances, exits, movement onstage, and use of props. In fact, the way in which María moves as a "blind" character becomes an essential element of the drama's thematic context and flow. Her performance of blindness, or innocence, depends upon the movement she creates: stumbling, waving her arms in front of her face, and, of course, securing or taking off the all-important bandage. The actor's performance creates and enhances the play's meaning. Even when there is no realized production, the action indicated in the text alludes to a visual context. By breaking up the visual signs into categories, students can focus on what visual information is provided rather than limiting the play to a nontheatrical category. Moreover, students gain practice in theatrical analysis within and beyond the text: they learn to identify textual and visual elements, be they explicitly stated or implied within a hypothetical production.

Like so many of Unamuno's dramas, the visual information in *La venda* seems to belie Unamuno's description of his dramatic works. This particular play provides an even greater paradox for students to ponder: María and her father cannot "see" the truth, yet the reader's or spectator's understanding of their predicament relies at least partially on the visual presentation of their denial. The readers and spectators see what they do not. Even in the opening scene, Unamuno writes the dialogue around what the other characters see as María walks by them. Their conversation gives us an exposition and status for the world of the play, but it also incites the imagination of the reader to visualize the way in which María walks. This concept of literal and figurative blindness allows students to connect the dots between the drama's overarching themes and unavoidable theatrical elements. María has to remove her bandage to look directly at her father, the other characters are witnesses to this act, and the hypothetical spectators observe the actions onstage. The students realize that the bandage's use as a prop is just as important as its symbolic meaning in the play's title.

After students have had the opportunity to connect the text with movement, space, and technical elements, it is helpful to return to a discussion of the nature of theater. Students can read Unamuno's description of his own dramas and assess to what extent his definition applies to *La venda*. We compare this relative lack of visual elements with other plays, and I pose the question: is this still theater? My hope is the inherent contradictions that I highlighted in *La venda* will provoke a spirited conversation among students, with a number of participants undecided as to whether *teatro desnudo* constitutes "real" theater.

In the case of a graduate course, similar concepts and questions lend themselves to a discussion of genre and theory. Nearly every Unamunian drama is replete with textual allusions, adaptations, and imitations: Greek myth and tragedy, the Bible, baroque and Romantic texts in the Spanish canon, realist novelists from a generation earlier, and his contemporaries throughout Europe. Unamuno often engages with multiple genres and periods through his dramatic form, thereby goading readers, spectators, and scholars to examine his "theater" through an intertextual lens. The extent to which Unamuno alludes to, adapts, imitates, or parodies other texts in his dramas remains a point of critical debate, yet it is clear that Unamunian drama rests its head on a blanket of intertextuality. If one presents *teatro desnudo* as a type of dramatic narrative, then Unamuno's dramas offer a fruitful discussion of hybrid genre and textual analysis apart from visual elements. This sort of approach to Unamuno's dramas could enhance a graduate discussion of Roland Barthes, Mikhail Bakhtin, and performativity, even in classes where theater or drama is not the focus of the course. If one presents Unamunian dramas as minimalist theater and the basis of theatrical production, the intertextuality is still relevant. An instructor may assign the chapter of Marvin Carlson's *The Haunted Stage* that discusses "textual haunting": the process by which the dramatist or the dramatic text provokes the reader's or spectator's memory of past performances or stories (16–51, esp. 5–7). Whichever interpretation of intertextuality the instructor wishes to flesh out, Unamuno's dramas constitute effective models of intertextual complexity.

Although several dramas exemplify Unamunian intertextuality, *El otro* offers the instructor multiple points of departure, particularly in a graduate course. The drama presents a case of possible insanity: Cosme, the main character, has created a sort of evil twin named Damián, whom he has dubbed "the other." Initially, it seems that both brothers existed in the flesh, but one brother has killed the other. Even if there were a literal murder, Cosme, or "the other," embodies both brothers within himself. Cosme's family members and his wife, Laura, have observed both personalities in action, but it has become increasingly difficult to identify which personality embodies Cosme at any given time. In addition, Damián has created his own life apart from Laura: he has seduced, married, and impregnated Damiana. Eventually, Cosme is unable to overcome his internal duality, and he commits suicide. Later Damiana announces that she is pregnant with twins, and the reader/spectator is left with the ominous feeling that the boys will inherit the insanity and fratricidal tendencies of their father.

The philosophical themes of *El otro* have the potential to provoke a meaty discussion in class. An instructor might ask whether Damián truly exists and whether the family members are objective observers or have been contaminated by Cosme's (or the other's) insanity. This sort of thematic dissection might fill a class in and of itself, but *El otro* has so many layers that an instructor could incorporate it into several activities, discussions, and assignments. Whereas some of Unamuno's dramas have received little attention from critics, *El otro* has been interpreted by several esteemed scholars and has even provoked debate among them.[4] Therefore, the ongoing critical discussion can provide graduate students with a context for discussion and analysis.

Unamuno's complex vision of psychological fratricide invites multiple theoretical approaches in the graduate classroom. The incredible amount of references in *El otro* seems to create a boundless sea of intertextuality, and the classical themes of fratricide, duality, and insanity naturally tempt the instructor to apply psychoanalytical readings and theories to its study. The unnerving representation of the schizophrenic hero (or twins) lends itself to a Freudian reading, with students applying such concepts as *unheimlich* and doppelgänger to their interpretations. Moreover, the Lacanian description of fractured subjectivity may also apply to the tragic hero's dual personality and his relationship with the two female foils. In a class that focuses on gender or queer theory, there is the potential to examine the multiple erotic triangles using Eve Kosofsky Sedgwick's definition of homosociality in *Between Men*. In this sense, *El otro* provides a great theoretical flexibility: it fits in multiple contexts and becomes a useful tool for theoretical application.

In addition, I would recommend *El otro* as a basis for examining the nature and definition of theater. Like in *La venda*, Unamuno uses *El otro* to play with generic ambiguity: he combines naked minimalism and narrative philosophy with powerful moments of theatricality. However, the generic ambiguity of *El otro* is subtler than that of *La venda* and therefore provides a more nuanced analytical exercise for advanced students. In the case of *El otro*, there are virtually no stage directions and almost no descriptions of the set, time of day, props, and so forth. At first glance, this play appears to embrace absolute nakedness. However, there are occasional stage directions that indicate movement—particularly the movement of a character's eyes. Unamuno explains on more than one occasion that one character visually assesses the other. The dialogue underscores constantly the imagery of the gaze: who looked, who was the object of the look, and what the characters discovered as they perused each other. Initially, the movement of the gaze is specified briefly in short stage directions, such as "*se pasea silencioso, siguiéndole los otros con la mirada, como a quien discute a solas*" '*he paces silently, with the others' gaze following him, as if he were arguing with himself alone*' (660). In several cases, Unamuno describes the insane or tormented actions of Cosme/Damián, but he also indicates the way in which the other characters observe his actions.

This pattern helps the drama build to a climax in the third *jornada*, or act, in which Unamuno provides a full paragraph of stage directions. It is important to note that while the action is delineated carefully, Unamuno does not offer a description of the room's dimensions, furniture, or entrances and exits. There is an oblique reference to a mirror, but little guidance regarding the space. Nonetheless, the stage directions do indicate how Cosme/Damián moves around the room and, more important, that another character is watching him: "*en este momento aparece Laura, que se le queda observando, se le acerca de puntillas por detrás y le pone una mano en el hombro*" '*in this moment, Laura appears, continues to observe him, approaches him from behind on tiptoe, and places her hand on his shoulder*' (682). The fact that Unamuno specifies when and how one character looks at another suggests a performance. The text may describe what one saw, but the stage directions give instructions as to what the actors should do in the moment. Moreover, the spectators themselves watch the actors watching Cosme/Damián, and the multiple gazes throughout the drama reinforce the interpretation of the tragic hero's insanity.

This particular type of stage direction suggests the potential theatricality of Unamunian drama. More important, it is a tangible visual element that students can analyze and discuss. In order for students to understand the intersection of semiotics and subjectivity onstage, it is helpful to assign the introduction to Stanton Garner's *Bodied Spaces: Phenomenology and Performance in Contemporary Drama*. Garner describes how the body, unlike other sign-objects onstage, has a dual role. On the one hand, it is the central object within the theatrical space (2). All spectators examine the body, and it fulfills its theatrical role by receiving the gaze and allowing the spectator to interpret the stage visually. The actor's body acts as a gauge upon which all the other objects (sets, props, etc.) are measured and understood. For example, a prop does not acquire its significance as theatrical object until the hand of the actor touches it or uses it (47). On the other hand, the body functions as a prop as well as a subject that both receives the audience's gaze and looks back at the audience (49). By emphasizing the body (and, by extension, the actor) as a key object of visual interpretation, the students begin to glimpse the hidden layers of theatricality even in the most naked of dramas. The discussion of the gaze also allows the opportunity to introduce and practice different theoretical approaches, while also debating whether Unamuno's dramas constitute theater or alternative narratives.

Ultimately, Unamuno's dramas offer a plethora of teaching options for both the undergraduate and graduate classroom. At an undergraduate level, Unamunian dramas introduce theater as a genre and provide the opportunity to analyze visual elements of a production. Should an instructor wish to incorporate Unamuno's dramas into a course on European theater, there is the potential to analyze Unamuno's drama through the lens of early avant-garde movements. In a survey or topics in literature course, the addition of Unamunian drama buttresses the study of the Aristotelian form of the tragedy or the modernist movement in Spain. When a course focuses specifically on modern Peninsular theater, Unamuno's *teatro desnudo* offers a minimalist foil to the visually elaborate, melodramatic dramas of his neoromantic contemporaries. At the graduate level, the instructor may use naked drama to initiate a discussion of hybrid genres and apply various theoretical approaches.

NOTES

[1] In his article "La regeneración del teatro español" ("The Regeneration of Spanish Theater") Unamuno eschews the naturalist notion that "scholastic ideology" and "paraphysiology" can create an objective "living reality" onstage (qtd. and trans. in George 484).

[2] Unamuno's dramas are quoted from volume 5 of *Obras completas*, edited by Manuel García Blanco and published by Escelicer. All English translations are my own.

[3] The question of generic categorization continues to be a point of discussion among critics. Marie Barbieri and Lucile Charlebois, among others, characterize Unamuno's dramas as alternative narratives or dramatic essays rather than "actual" theater.

[4] In her article "Yet Another 'Other': Unamuno's *El otro* and the Anxiety for Influence," Julia Biggane outlines the complex intertextuality within *El otro*, as well as the various critical interpretations of the play.

Teaching Unamuno's Poetry: Romanticism and Modernity

Stephen J. Summerhill

Teaching poetry is always difficult, and one suspects that it has become even more so in an era when popular music has overwhelmed the consciousness of young people while perhaps leaving them unacquainted with traditional poetic expression. In a time when Bob Dylan has been awarded the Nobel Prize in Literature—and this writer believes that the award was richly deserved—the idea of reading and studying a traditional poet may well be met with resistance or indifference because the texts appear too difficult or obscure. Nor are there easy solutions to this problem. Poetry, even popular poetry, is never simple. It requires concentration and a willingness to study (or "work") the text in order to elicit as much understanding as possible, with no guarantee of definitively understanding the poem. Such protracted struggle, which in fact is one of the great attractions of poetry, is sometimes not well received by students in an era of short attention spans and easy music that passes as significant.

In the case of Miguel de Unamuno, certain other features may also create obstacles to the enjoyment of his poetry. From 1907 through 1928, Unamuno published eight books of poetry, and then, over the rest of his life, he composed *Cancionero* ("Songbook"), a kind of huge diary containing more than 1,750 poems. These volumes, along with many other texts not included in them, contain more than 2,500 poems. How does any reader sort through all this and make sense of it? In addition, Unamuno seems not to have discarded any of his poems. As a result, his work is very uneven, with strong and less strong texts jumbled together. Can experienced readers even judge what is or is not accomplished in such a huge body of work? Likewise, the themes of the poetry can be forbidding or intimidating in a postmodern world of superficial media. A long meditative poem such as *El Cristo de Velázquez* ("Velázquez's Christ") is unique in modern Spanish poetry because of its intense focus on the meaning of Jesus Christ, but this very intensity within a Roman Catholic perspective, especially from a writer who seems to deny the divinity of Christ, may make it unappealing to a wide readership. (Because it and another poem, *Teresa*, are single works of considerable length, this essay will not consider them. *Cancionero* will also receive minimal attention.) Finally, though Unamuno could write excellent poetry using everyday language, he often chose a more ample rhetoric influenced by a Renaissance diction that can make his style sound very elaborate, perhaps ponderous or antiquated. Accompanying this was his preference for certain difficult poetic styles such as the sonnet, of which he wrote hundreds. All these factors may make Unamuno's poetry seem unattractive.

Against all these difficulties, the goal of this essay is to study a limited range of Unamuno's poetry with an eye to what makes his search for the poetic important and interesting. Scholars agree that Unamuno's poetry is historically important for a variety of reasons. But historical importance is not necessarily readerly interest. Readers have to find more than what literary historians argue is important, because poetry must always speak to a deeper connection within each of us than the historical trends governing an era. Beyond this, the essay will outline the major themes of Unamuno's poetry with examples from a few salient texts, including political poetry that was unfairly censored for more than fifty years (see Urrutia-Jordana's essay in this volume). Unfortunately, limitations of space prevent inclusion of more than a few quotations from a too small number of texts.

First, a word about historical context. Toward the end of the nineteenth century, the major trend in Hispanic poetry was *modernismo*—not to be confused with modernism—which originated in Latin America under the aegis of the Nicaraguan poet Rubén Darío, although it took many of its cues from French symbolism. Essentially, *modernismo* cultivated a highly artificial world of refined, sometimes decadent themes within an aestheticist posture of art for art, a search for beauty for its own sake. By also pursuing a renovation of poetic language and forms, *modernismo* was quite innovative in its diction, imagery, and rhythms. It can also be seen as a rejection of the mediocre, practical world of bourgeois capitalism during the era.

Unamuno was an outspoken critic of *modernismo*, which he saw as excessively exquisite and superficial. In response to such artificiality, he sought poetry of deep feeling and profound ideas. His goal was to write texts with intellectual depth and density of expression:

> Dinos en pocas palabras,
> y sin dejar el sendero,
> lo más que decir se pueda,
> denso, denso. (6: 170)
>
> Tell us the most that can be said,
> In few words,
> Without getting off track,
> Dense, dense.[1]

Or from another angle: "Piensa el sentimiento, siente el pensamiento" 'Feeling thinks and thought feels' (6: 168). In other words, Unamuno's poetry seeks to be thought-provoking rather than beautiful, although many poems reveal great aesthetic achievement. Mostly, his poetry explores a limited number of themes that were important to him personally but were also, he believed, of universal value. It is a "human poetry" grounded in personal experience and the Spain of his era.

Without wishing to be reductive concerning a work as vast as Unamuno's, we might say that his main themes were the existential struggle between death and God and, no less important, his love of nature and the land, which was linked with the first theme. Additional themes include domestic and family life and his experience of exile.

Beginning with the fundamental concern for death and God, it is well known that Unamuno elaborated a personal philosophy of existential struggle between human finitude and the desire for God or transcendence. He believed that in daily life, people exist submerged by what he called "costras," or layers of inauthentic, conventional behavior, which were primarily the world of bodily habits and the intellectual constraints of reason. Unamuno sought to break the chains of the ordinary and "desnudar el alma" 'to strip the soul bare' ("Soledad" 1261) so that his readers might free themselves from superficiality and discover a more profound understanding of life as an irrational struggle between death and the search for a transcendent God. But the journey inward is never easy. Humans who manage to break open the layers of servitude will experience profound anguish at the prospect of their inevitable extinction in death. However, the despair they suffer as a consequence can force them to discover an equally profound wish to live forever. This desire, which is nothing less than the spiritual plenitude of love, if pursued fully, may become a wellspring that awakens them to the power of creativity. From this, poetry, God, and the transcendent can emerge. It does not happen easily, however, for anguish and despair constantly undermine our hope for something meaningful. Such ideas are fully explained in Unamuno's masterful essay *Del sentimiento trágico de la vida* ("The Tragic Sense of Life").

The unresolved dialectic between anguish and hope, time and eternity, death and the desire for transcendence, was the poetic foundation of Unamuno's work and was nurtured by an essentially Romantic theory of creative imagination. Adumbrated most completely in the idealistic philosophy of Immanuel Kant during the late eighteenth century and subsequently elaborated by many later thinkers, especially in early-nineteenth-century Britain (the most influential of these, in Unamuno's case, being Samuel Taylor Coleridge), the theory of creative imagination poses that human beings can acquire the ability to overcome the fear and anguish of death by imagining and ultimately creating a poetic world of desire. The poem thus articulated is not simply an idealized set of dreams but an expression of the inner struggle to overcome loss and achieve value in life. In this, an important element is the *symbol*, which is an image or figure—often a full poem—that expresses a "concrete universal": that is, provokes profound insight in an immediate or concrete form.

In this way, Unamuno drew his fundamental poetic impulse from what critics today call High Romanticism, the literary expression developed mostly in Germany and England at the end of the eighteenth century that explored inner being and subjectivity through symbols drawn from the external world of nature or the built environment. Such an approach, which M. H. Abrams has called "natural supernaturalism," differs strongly from the Romanticism of writers such as the Duke of Rivas and José de Espronceda during the first half of the nineteenth century. These and other poets favored a more popular balladry with nostalgic historical themes drawn from the Middle Ages. Unamuno, in contrast, sought to penetrate the depths of inner being, which in the end is the subjective foundation of modern literature. In this sense, by bringing into Spain the High Romantic tendencies of Coleridge, William Wordsworth, Giacomo Leopardi, and others, Unamuno articulated a new mission for Spanish poetry: a meditative exploration of subjectivity—its struggles, its uncertainties, and even its loss—within a deep sensitivity to nature. It is of course not lost on us that this movement toward the most profound form of Romanticism occurred fully a century later than in its countries of origin, a sign of the "belatedness" of Spanish culture during this period. Nonetheless, the introduction of subjectivity had to occur if Spanish poetry was to become fully modern, and like others of his era—Antonio Machado and Juan Ramón Jiménez, for example—Unamuno contributed centrally to the process.

One of Unamuno's poems within the thematic cluster of death and God, with its turn toward nature and the land, is the well-known ode "Salamanca," an extended paean of 124 lines to the city where Unamuno lived and taught during most of his adult life. Its language is highly rhetorical, with several hyperbatons that are reminiscent of Renaissance poetry. The text begins by extolling the beautiful golden glow of the many church towers in the city at sunset. The imagery specifically alludes to the towers as trees in a grove or forest—"Alto soto de torres" 'High grove of towers'—and it insists that the stone of these towers was wrested from the earth: "bosque de piedras que arrancó la historia / a las entrañas de la tierra madre" 'Forest of stones which history did wrest / from the bowels of Mother Earth' (6: 178; 77). The city's buildings are therefore part of history or civilization, but they carry within them the echoes of something deeper, the unchanging world of nature. Here in the stones of the towers is the poetic desire for permanence that speaks to the search for the transcendent.

The tranquil environment of stone trees leads the speaker to feel that past and future melt away as he finds within himself a sense of "fe, paz y fuerza" 'faith, peace and strength' (6: 179; 79). Looking intensely at the patio of the university, he meditates on poets and writers who preceded him, like Fray Luis de León and Miguel de Cervantes, figures who paid tribute to the city. This in turn leads him to a crucial idea: Salamanca embodies continuity and the desire for eternity: "Sueño de no morir es el que infundes / a los que beben de tu dulce calma" 'The dream of not dying is what you inspire / in those who absorb your sweet calm' (6: 180). Salamanca is a symbol of that dream of immortality that undergirds human creativity. It is in fact a symbol of the divine.

Having uncovered eternity, the speaker now shifts to the fundamental impulse behind this vision, desire or love: "en tus callejas duermen los amores / más furtivos" 'In your streets, the most furtive loves dream' (6: 180; 79–80). The second half of the poem starts with the love of learning experienced by scholars at the University of Salamanca, but it quickly turns to the students who fall in love while in class: "y cuando el maestro calla, aquellos bancos / dicen amores" 'and when the teacher stops talking / those desks speak about love' (6: 181; 111–12). In effect, the poem uncovers the fundamental dynamic that presses existence always forward: love, the origin of creation. The poem now ends with the speaker praising the fertility of the students and of all life in the surrounding fields, with the hope that this world of love will also help him be remembered after death.

Overall, then, it seems possible to say that "Salamanca" stands as an Unamunian variation on what Abrams calls the "greater romantic lyric" ("Structure") by articulating a visionary Romanticism that seeks to capture the ideal of love and creativity in the past and present of the city. Less melancholic than Wordsworth's "Tintern Abbey," for example, it seeks to feel the mystery of the permanence of nature behind the facade of time. The poem is ecstatic or aspirational and wants to be uplifting, a song in praise of Salamanca's truly poetic quality as a locus of hope and belief in the permanent.

Unamuno was not always so confident. A much less positive vision appears in a brief text from the collection *Rosario de sonetos líricos* ("Rosary of Lyrical Sonnets"). "La oración del ateo" ("The Atheist's Prayer") not only addresses the abyss of anguish and despair often found in Unamuno, but it does so with the language of paradox so characteristic of his work. The poem begins: "Oye mi ruego Tú, Dios que no existes / y en tu nada recoge estas mis quejas" 'Listen to my prayer, oh non-existent God, / and in your unreality receive my lamentations' (6: 359; 69). Unamuno here affirms the paradox that he does not believe in God but, at the same time, he cannot live without him. Humanity holds on to the consolation of God and yet cannot see or hear him. Indeed, the more God escapes our apprehension, the more we humans are drawn to a wish that he be real: "Cuando Tú de mi mente más te alejas, / más recuerdo las plácidas consejas, / con que mi ama endulzóme noches tristes" 'as you move away out of my sight / the more my mind recalls the placid tales / with which my nurse lit up those anxious nights' (6: 359; 69). Unamuno was haunted by this mystery of the silence of God.

In the two tercets of the poem, Unamuno drives home his concluding argument that God is merely an idea, a theoretical being that does not really exist. And if that is the case, the reality of the human being is also open to question, because death will extinguish him or her: "pues si Tú existieras / existiría yo también de veras" 'for if you did exist / my own existence would be assuredly true' (6: 639; 69). Without God, the subject is lost, a mere illusion condemned to disappear.

Many other excellent poems express this same haunting anguish about death and God. "Para después de mi muerte" ("After I Cease to Be") is a lamentation on the survival of Unamuno's voice long after he has died: "lector solitario, que así atiendes / la voz de un muerto" 'Lone reader, you who listen / to the voice of a dead man' (6: 173; 55). Unamuno cannot hear himself speak now because he has passed away, but he can remind us of the fate awaiting us as we take on his words:

> ¡Oye la voz que sale de la tumba
> y te dice al oído

este secreto:
"¡Yo ya no soy, hermano!" (6: 173)

Listen to the voice that rises
from the grave to gently whisper
in your ear the secret truth:
"I no longer am my friend." (57)

The final message could not be more disconsolate: "¡Tú también morirás, morirá todo, / y en silencio infinito / dormirá para siempre la esperanza!" 'For you will die, and all will die / and in perpetual quietude / hope will forever dormant lie' (6: 174; 59).

Turning to additional themes in Unamuno's poetry, one of the most interesting appears in a relatively small group of texts from different moments of Unamuno's life: family and domestic life. These are poems that speak in a more simple language to convey his thoughts while alone or while observing his children:

No me mires así a los ojos, hijo mío,
no quiero que me arranques mi secreto,
y cuando yo te falte
sea el veneno de tu pobre vida. (6: 303)

Don't look at me that way, my son,
I don't want you to tear my secret from me,
so that when you no longer have me,
I will be the poison of your poor life.

Sometimes Unamuno is working in his study or is lying in bed thinking about when death will come and take him. Other times he is watching over his children as they sleep:

Y era oración su respiro,
respirando el sueño oraban
. . . .
Eres, sueño, el anticipo
de la vida que no acaba. (6: 298)

their breathing was a prayer,
breathing their dream they prayed
. . . .
You are, Sleep, anticipation
of unending life.

One of the most endearing features of these poems is the tenderness of the language. The aggressive, passionate Unamuno who wages war against death and social mediocrity melts into a warm, loving father or husband thinking about the persons with whom he shares the events of daily life. Among these is the brief but beautiful elegy Unamuno composed after the death of his wife, Concha, in 1934. The aging Unamuno contemplates how Concha maintained an abiding religious faith even as her husband became a famous heretic. With his usual paradox, he believes she lived the eternal in an ephemeral life on earth, and she attained true holiness in silent glory:

> Fue una vida sin historia,
> en lo eterno cimentada,
> por el mundo de pasada
> una vida toda gloria. (6: 1412)
>
> Her life was not a history
> for it belonged to timelessness;
> in transient passage on this earth,
> her life was bathed in godliness. (39)

It is important to note that no matter how ordinary the events depicted in these poems, Unamuno always elicits a profound conclusion at the end. He never abandoned his mission of seeking always to make his poetry articulate meaning.

In 1924 Unamuno was exiled to Fuerteventura in the Canary Islands because he would not soften his harsh criticism of Miguel Primo de Rivera's dictatorial government. He stayed on the island for several months and then was "rescued" by French journalists, who took him to Paris, where he stayed an unhappy year. He then moved to Hendaye on the Spanish border until returning to Spain with the fall of the monarchy in 1930. These six long years of exile were riven by periods of loneliness, self-doubt, worry about his family, and deep boredom. They also led to, among several other works, two new volumes of poetry, *De Fuerteventura a París* ("From Fuerteventura to Paris"), composed entirely of personal and political sonnets that are accompanied by commentaries, and *Romancero del destierro* ("Ballads of Exile"), which combines thirty-seven traditional poems with seventeen fiercely polemical ballads attacking the dictatorship governing Spain. Because both volumes were published outside Spain and then were heavily censored in every edition published during the Franco regime, both volumes never reached their intended audiences and have been largely overlooked. In addition, the few who have read them have found their political dimension too polemical.

However, in spite of the polemics, these books are much more interesting than has been conceded. On the one hand, Unamuno pursues his traditional themes of death, nature, and God in parts of both books (Álvarez-Castro, "Yo"). On the other, he felt such deep anger at the intrusion of falsehood, cruelty, and corruption into the public life of Spain that he could not let things pass without comment. As a result, both books appear split or divided between the calm, eternal world of poetry and the violent, destructive experience of the Spain of that time. It is this political aspect that is the really new dimension of Unamuno's writing in these works. In fact, it constitutes a cry of horror over the disappearance of poetry in the world and appears as a kind of antipoetry constructed on the absence of the poetic in Spanish life.

Interestingly, the political texts of *Romancero del destierro* also embody something else that was new in Unamuno: one of the most time-honored forms of popular poetry in Spain, the "romance" or ballad, which was undergoing a revival among other poets in the era. Unamuno launches into attacks against the major figures of the government, specifically King Alfonso XIII, Primo de Rivera, and the feared strongman behind the scenes, Severiano Martínez Anido. Alfonso is a fool who gave his throne to thugs only to realize later that he is being played as a pawn. For his part, Primo de Rivera likes wine and women too much, and he imposes a "barracks discipline" that considers military honor more important than truth. And Martínez Anido glories in torture:

> No basta ya retorcerles
> los testículos, ¡hay más!,
> en el nervio del dentista
> es en donde hay que operar. (*Poesía completa* 2: 408)
>
> It's not enough to squeeze
> their testicles; we can do more!
> We need to operate
> where the dentist touches the nerve.

The author of these poems feels poisoned by the degradation of his nation, and he cries out to God to give him a voice of fire that his submissive countrymen have lost (2: 414). There is no question that Unamuno does speak with fire in his voice and he achieves his goal well, even if some readers prefer his nonpolitical texts.

The appearance of political poetry in the older Unamuno may signal a shift in the parameters of his work. For example, if his novels and plays show an evolution toward the antirealistic stance of modernism, his poetry always seemed to remain fundamentally Romantic, which is no doubt why it is the least known and studied aspect of his work. But the political poetry of exile develops an opening toward a satirical and sarcastic verse reminiscent of the works of Ramón del Valle Inclán and Francisco de Quevedo. This could be where his poetry finally meets modernism, not exactly in the experimentation of the avant-garde, which Unamuno scorned, but in expressionism, the world of the grotesque, black humor, and a literature of cruelty. For this reason, his social poetry deserves much more attention.

It is also true that Unamuno's Romanticism was not merely nostalgia for a lost past. It heavily influenced the discovery of High Romantic poetry in twentieth-century Spain by Luis Cernuda, Claudio Rodríguez, and others. Unamuno's Romanticism carried much future in it. His poetry is certainly not close to popular music in contemporary culture, but for those who are willing to explore its depths and challenges, it holds many possibilities for profound and lasting appreciation.

NOTE

[1] Unless noted otherwise, Unamuno's poetry is quoted from volume 6 of *Obras completas*, edited by Manuel García Blanco and published by Escelicer. When a reference is provided, translations are from the anthology *Miguel de Unamuno: An Anthology of His Poetry*, edited and translated by C. A. Longhurst. Otherwise the translations are my own.

Unamuno, an Iberian Thinker: Portuguese Culture and Travel Literature in *Por tierras de Portugal y España*

Juan Francisco Maura

> Une más el espíritu que la sangre.
> (The spirit is more binding than blood.)
> —Julio García Morejón, *Unamuno y Portugal*

Miguel de Unamuno, a good connoisseur of the philosopher Francisco Giner de los Ríos's pedagogy, knew that in order to achieve a good and solid education, it was necessary to leave the four walls of the classroom. Giner de los Ríos was the founder of one of the most effective private institutions in Spain in giving a complete education to his students: the Institución Libre de Enseñanza. Students of this institution, besides Unamuno, included Federico García Lorca, Salvador Dalí, Antonio Machado, Luis Buñuel, and José Ortega y Gasset, among others. Unamuno knew that in order to understand a culture it was not enough to study its history and literature in a static and rational way. It was imperative to go one step further—to feel their people, smell their cities, observe their fields, and learn their language. Unamuno traveled to Portugal on several occasions, often in solitude but sometimes in the company of dear friends, who left on him an indelible imprint, both emotionally and intellectually. Unamuno knew by experience that leaving the university cloister to have a vital experience of different languages and cultures enriched and opened the minds of individuals.

Much has been said about the influence of Søren Kierkegaard, Blaise Pascal, and English and German Protestant theologians from the eighteenth and nineteenth centuries on the ideas of Unamuno. Indeed, their doctrines appear in Unamuno's work with relative frequency, and the author himself recognized these preferences. However, if we want to place Unamuno in a tradition of Iberian anguish, his more intimate and direct connection would be with Portuguese authors, especially Antero de Quental. Among Unamuno scholars, perhaps only Julio García Morejón has pointed with all due rigor to this influence.

Unamuno, who was fluent in English, Danish (allowing him to read Kierkegaard), and German (to read Arthur Schopenhauer), was definitely fluent in Portuguese. His favorite author in this language was the Romantic writer Camilo Castelo Branco. Castelo Branco's work is very difficult to read, even for the average Portuguese speaker. It is no secret that Unamuno repeatedly claimed that Castelo Branco was a greater prose writer than José Maria de Eça de Queirós, who is generally regarded, both in Portugal and abroad, as one of the most important Portuguese authors of the last two centuries, along with Fernando Pessoa.[1] Perhaps Unamuno's predilection for Castelo Branco is due to their shared obsession with individual freedom, anticlericalism, Christianity, and the feelings of the people (Unamuno, *Por tierras* 37).[2]

Unamuno's modernity and clairvoyance are truly remarkable. Long before the existence of academic ghettos that strive to transform literary theory and criticism into a science, this Spanish philosopher said that it is very odd that those who have chastised intellectualism are precisely the most intellectualized. Unamuno despised those who have inherited this scholarly concoction that stiffens the innermost longings of the heart into formulas; the terrible architectonic structure that does not grant access to outsiders, who in turn have to resign to blind faith (*Por tierras* 339). The philosopher wrote, "Las voces rudas de los definidores, de los que aseguran no entender ni esto ni lo otro, y como no lo entienden lo declaran vacío y disparatado y retórico, ellos, ellos, hinchados de retórica y de lógica formal, que es cosa peor aún que la retórica" 'The rude voices of the definers, of those who demonstrate a general lack of understanding of things, and due to this very lack of understanding declare things as void, absurd, and rhetorical; those, precisely those who are full of rhetoric and formal logic, which is even worse than rhetoric itself' (340).

One present-day example of such ill-named rhetoric would be the antipedagogical definitions assigned to terms such as *Iberian* or *Hispanic*. Edward Said, the renowned literary critic, starts his book *Orientalism* with the following assertion: "The Orient was almost a European invention, and had been, since antiquity, a place of romance, exotic beings, haunting memories and landscapes, remarkable experiences" (1). Something similar has occurred with the concept of Europe as an invention of Anglo-American critics.[3] In this case, a slightly more malicious tone is present, since those who define what is currently denominated the neocolonial or postcolonial Western world are housed in universities—the hubs of this hegemonic world that they both criticize and speculate about—which, in turn, grant them the freedom of expression to do so.

Unamuno had a different didactic approach when referring to European cultures, particularly Germanic ones. He would be cataloged today as a Eurosceptic. It is difficult to compare the Germanic world with the Mediterranean world, particularly to the Iberian world, in which Islam, Judaism, and Christianity struggled and coexisted within the same areas for almost eight centuries. Furthermore, in the beginning of the first millennium, Al-Andalus was the periphery of the Islamic empire, while the rest of the Peninsula was the colonized world. Cultural expressions such as flamenco and chess are perfect examples of this hybrid world. From the perspective of these critics, speaking about colonization, colonialism, or imperialism is problematic and politically incorrect when referring to non-European cultures. For example, in his essay "The Commitment to Theory," included in the book *The Location of Culture*, Homi K. Bhabha defends himself by saying, "There is a damaging and self-defeating assumption that theory is necessarily the elite language of the socially and culturally privileged. It is said that the place of the academic critic is inevitably within the Eurocentric archives of an imperialist or neo-colonial West" (28). However, if we bear in mind the fact that a single group has access to specialized academic journals, would it not be pointless to deny that literary criticism and theory presently belongs to a minority of theoretical thinkers in a privileged neocolonial or neoimperialist world encompassed by countries that communicate in English or French?

The polemic around the Europeanization of Spain is an outgrowth of the wider polemic around science and religion. For many, the verb *Europeanize* is synonymous with having or not having science. Unamuno used to respond to said polemic by bringing up the "Spainization of Europe," which was referred to by Ortega y Gasset as "an Africanist deviation of the University of Salamanca rector" (Abellán). We must keep in mind that Unamuno self-identified dialectically as African, similar to Saint Augustine and Tertullian, and he referred to the German world as the "red-headed beast" (Abellán). Undeniably, in *Del sentimiento trágico de la vida* ("The Tragic Sense of Life") Unamuno protested against the "scientific orthodoxy" of positivism that was equivalent to European modernity, which he denominated "scientific inquisition," while claiming the superiority of intuitive wisdom over science (*Obras completas* [Senabre] 10: 515). For Unamuno, science seeks life, while wisdom prepares for a good death.

Américo Castro, a disciple of the Generation of 1898, echoed the restlessness of these thinkers and developed—after extensive research and conscientious analysis of the history of the Iberian Peninsula—a different pedagogical approach: the concept of medieval Spanish tolerance serving as the basis of a system molded by the Muslim civilization. Quental, accordingly, defends the Iberian world by devotedly praising the medieval Luso-Hispanic world over its European counterpart. In terms of artistic and social accomplishments, the Iberian Peninsula was comparable to any other culture.

Unamuno had many commonalities with several Portuguese writers, among them some members of the so-called Generation of Coimbra: Joaquim Pedro de Oliveira Martins, Eugénio de Castro, Teixeira de Pascoaes, Fidelino de Figueiredo, Quental, and Eça de Queirós. Quental, just like Unamuno in his time and many Spaniards today, dreamed of establishing an Iberian federative republic. However, his uncertainties, his metaphysical and existential anguish, as well as his proximity with the positivist philosophy—which Unamuno loathed—led Quental to suicide. Unamuno had a different death, perhaps due to his desire to believe, which helped him maintain a spiritual grip until the end of his days and experience a natural death at home, comforted by the warmth of a *brasero* (heater): no more nor less than the death he would have chosen himself. Nonetheless, in spite of his passionate and almost always tormented search for faith, some of Unamuno's writings, such as *Del sentimiento trágico de la vida* and *La agonía del cristianismo* ("The Agony of Christianity") are listed, through a decree of the Vatican, in the Index Librorum Prohibitorum (Index of Forbidden Books) of the Catholic Church. According to Jon Juaristi, the Church also wanted to bring Unamuno's figure into its fiefdom: "La última de tales tentativas fue la del P. Félix García, agustino franquista especializado en recuperaciones de almas de literatos, que prologó la edición del *Diario íntimo*" 'The last of these attempts was made by pro-Franco Augustinian priest Félix García, who specialized in recovering the souls of literati: García prefaced the edition of *Diario íntimo*' (*Miguel de Unamuno* 479).

Unamuno, together with Gil Vicente, Luís de Camões, and Francisco Manuel de Melo, is one of the greatest pedagogical sources for the intellectual dialogue between Spain and Portugal. Also, Unamuno was the only Spaniard of his time to incorporate the psyche of his Portuguese brothers, to such an extent that he was hardly able to escape the spell of that culture during his life (García Morejón 21). He learned from the writer Manuel Laranjeira—as the scholar Marcelino Menéndez y Pelayo also noted—that there is no history of Spain without Portugal and that the history of Spanish literature would be incomplete if it did not embrace Portuguese literature as one of its central components (García Morejón 45, 152).

The reports of Unamuno's travel experiences, which he often carried out solo, offer us a slightly different—a somewhat gentler and more humanized—dimension of Unamuno. Although he was frequently pictured as surly, rude, and hostile, as the protagonist of these trips we see a different side of Unamuno's personality, one that is more dynamic, almost sporty, and close to nature; an adventurous man who nonetheless will not lose his polemical vein when describing his experiences.

Given current nationalist polemics in Spain, Unamuno has things to offer. Although Unamuno's travel writings are closely identified with Castile and display such genuine love for Portugal, its people, and its culture, his work constantly exudes an intense pride of the land where he was born, the Basque Country. However, Unamuno never succumbed to the temptation of embracing Basque nationalism, which was too provincial and rickety for a generous and universal spirit like his; quite the contrary, Unamuno repeatedly attacked it. For this reason, *El Euskalduna*, one of the local newspapers in Bilbao, published a sketch of its countryman, describing him as resentful and unstable. Still, Juaristi questions how a provincial newspaper, read by a bunch of simpletons who believed they belonged to a superior race, could harm Unamuno (*Miguel de Unamuno* 254). In comparing Unamuno's vision of unity in diversity, there is a notable difference from the current situation of Spanish nationalisms, especially the Basque and Catalan. Today we can see that under a mask of national diversity, there are hidden socioeconomic interests of richer regions that do not want to share their benefits in solidarity with the less prosperous regions of the country. Furthermore, the most recalcitrant nationalists often are the children of immigrants, dressed in the flag of a homeland that was not their parents', wielding a victimhood that goes back, in some cases, to an almost mythological past. That creates xenophobia and a false feeling of superiority, with tragic results, as in the case of the Basque Country. Unamuno, on the contrary, teaches us that you can love and be proud of the place where you were born at the same time you love the country where you live.

Unamuno's interest for Portuguese literature and history goes back to the sixteenth-century chroniclers. Francisco de Souza's 1570 work, *Tratado das Ilhas Novas* ("Treatise on the New Islands"), mentions Portuguese travels to the "New Land of Codfish." Much to the surprise of the Portuguese, Basque fishermen had already been to these waters (Unamuno, *Por tierras* 224). Regrettably, many Spanish pedagogues, researchers, historians, and literary critics have failed to acknowledge the Portuguese ideas that served as forerunners of the Generation of 1898, searching for its origins in the neoclassicism of Benito Jerónimo Feijóo y Montenegro and in the early Romanticism of Mariano José de Larra, as if the Generation of Coimbra had never existed. That was the case in works such as *A History of the Iberian Civilization* by Joaquim Pedro de Oliveira Martins. Many of the members of the Generations of Coimbra and of 1898 saw the Iberian decadence in the occurrences of the sixteenth and seventeenth centuries; some, like Oliveira Martins, saw it in the religious politics of the Austrias. It is also undoubtable that at that time, universities did not have the means to make available the sources from which other young students drank. For this reason, self-education among the most advantaged and curious students routinely closed the gaps left unfilled by classes. Hence, writers and thinkers from Germany, France, England, Russia, and other countries were able to penetrate Spain, bringing Spanish writers closer to the Europe of that time (García Morejón 196–98).

Unamuno, similarly to Quental, denounced false patriotism. Both of them adopted a Don Quixotesque style of Christianity, a Christianity of action. Indeed, the 1890 British Ultimatum with regard to Portugal's presence in Africa served as an eye-opener to the Portuguese people, just as the disastrous loss of Cuba, Puerto Rico, and the Philippines affected the Spanish people.[4] As indicated by some authors, the members of the Generation of 1898 supposedly had a stronger influence than those of the Generation of Coimbra on poets such as Quental.

Reading about the peregrine experiences of such an unconventional traveler as Unamuno in the lands of Portugal and Spain will unquestionably increase fondness toward these Iberian nations, enriching criteria and perceptions about the nature of these peoples through a rarely attained perspective. Unamuno's pedagogical skills invite us to learn more about these two Iberian countries from a physical in situ experience on one hand and from readings about their common history from different perspectives on the other.

NOTES

Most of this article was translated into English by Débora de Granville Manço Teixeira. Some translations are mine.

[1] Eça de Queirós's impression of contemporary Portugal is similar to the Generation of 1898 members' impression of Spain.

[2] The text of *Por tierras de Portugal y España* used in this essay is the 1953 Aguilar edition. English translations are mine.

[3] I refer to Anglo-American critics, despite the fact that many of their members are from "ethnic" countries that once were part of the British Empire. *Ethnic* is one of the most condescending, hypocritical, and racist qualifiers found in Anglo-Saxon terminology and is applied to cultures regarded as culturally and racially inferior.

[4] England demanded that Portugal remove its troops from the Portuguese territories located between Angola and Mozambique. The Portuguese people saw this concession as humiliating and blamed the government of Carlos I.

Unamuno's *Niebla*: A Lesson in Paradox, Adaptation, and Innovation

Edward H. Friedman

Miguel de Unamuno was an iconoclast, an unapologetic contrarian. He found comfort in polemics and fostered the taking of sides, at times, it would seem, for the sake of argumentation itself. As a classicist, he celebrated dialogue as an expression of multiple points of view and as a fundamental component of narrative and drama. Unamuno's distinctive style factored into all his creations and meditative commentaries. His ego and his alter egos dominate the writings, but not in an offensive way; rather, they constitute part of his work product and his patterns of reflection. Like Francisco de Goya and Pablo Picasso, among other artistic masters, his corpus evolves from the representational to the abstract, from narrative realism to his particular brand of modernism. *Niebla* ("Mist") is a major achievement in fiction and a superb text for the classroom.

Unamuno was a philosopher, a political commentator, a firm but questioning Catholic, a writer who cultivated an array of genres, a professor of Greek language and literature, a rector of the University of Salamanca—in short, a public intellectual with ideas to share on topics from antiquity to current events. He was the elder statesman of the Generation of 1898, a notable group of Spaniards of assorted stripes who recognized the transitional period in which they lived and who articulated—each in a discrete, moving, and eloquent manner—their concerns about the status of their country in the world. On one plane, it is possible to point to the extraordinary scope of Unamuno's writings, which include short stories, novels, poetry, dramas, and essays, both short and book-length. On another, the collective works display the author's principal interests and, it could be said, not with negative intent, his obsessions. Unamuno demonstrated, through word and deed, his deep devotion to Spain and its people. The nation, the *pueblo*, was unique and dear to him, as were its traditions, legacies, idiosyncrasies, conflicts, and contradictions. He coined the term *intrahistoria* ("intrahistory") to describe the spirit and the character of the country: what remains after decisive moments in history have transpired. His profound concern for the present notwithstanding, the overriding element in Unamuno's worldview is his preoccupation with death and the afterlife. The issue of immortality becomes a thematic center and common denominator of his writings in all genres. The agonizing contemplation, the doubts, and the dialectics of faith and reason mark a search with continual self-examination that takes a diversity of forms and tones. In the case of *Niebla*, the form is innovative and the tone may be classified as deceptively comic.

Niebla recounts the story, and the trials and tribulations, of Augusto Pérez, a refined and introspective gentleman who is often so absorbed in ruminations that he overlooks what is happening around him; the abstract surpasses the concrete. He acknowledges that, to a degree at least, his life is directionless, and he yearns to find a purpose. He chances upon a young woman and is immediately lovestruck, and he follows the lady home. She is Eugenia Domingo del Arco, an orphan who lives with her aunt and eccentric uncle, an "anarquista místico" 'mystical anarchist' (113; 65) and a champion of Esperanto.[1] On learning that Eugenia has inherited the debts of her father, Augusto pays off a substantial mortgage, in the hope that his "acto heroico" 'heroic act' (140; 109) will endear her toward him. The tactic is unsuccessful; Eugenia is insulted and rejects his suit. She has a boyfriend, Mauricio, an uncouth ne'er-do-well who functions as the antithesis of Augusto. The distraught suitor consults his mentor, Don Antolín S. Paparrigópulos, an academic who is completely engaged in the realm of books. Don Antolín advises Augusto to conduct a scientific experiment on women. Psychology, or pseudo-psychology, fails Augusto, who has enmeshed Eugenia, his unworldly laundress Rosario, and his dowdy housekeeper Liduvina in the strategy. Eugenia and Mauricio plot to deceive him, and they leave town. Acknowledging that he is the guinea pig of the experiment, the devastated Augusto resolves to commit suicide. In the climactic moment of the narrative, Augusto visits Don Miguel de Unamuno in Salamanca to announce his decision. A debate ensues. Don Miguel asserts that, as the creator of the work, he controls, in godlike fashion, the fate of his creation. Augusto reminds Don Miguel of his testimony to the contrary, noting that Don Miguel convincingly had declared that Don Quixote invented Cervantes. Both make valid claims, and the debate seems to end in a draw. Augusto, shattered and despondent, returns home. He eats to excess and dies. Whether the cause of death is overeating or the will of Don Miguel is not perfectly clear.

Unamuno inscribes a fictional version of himself into the narrative, without accentuating that there is a separation between the real and fictional selves. He is creator and player, the ultimate authority and interlocutor with Augusto Pérez. By entering the imaginary scheme, Unamuno both aids and compromises his claim to superiority. He ingeniously allows Augusto to refute "Don Miguel" in the debate, but his very presence in chapter 31 is significant. In the "bufo trágico" 'comic-tragic,' as the character Víctor Goti calls it in the prologue of *Niebla* (77; 9), Unamuno puts forth an analog of immortality. A writer may attain a secular variety of immortality by writing—and inserting himself into—a classic text, as he aligns his anxieties and uncertainties with those of his protagonist. Like Cervantes in *Don Quijote*, Unamuno fictionalizes himself while maintaining his identity as director (and administrator) from without. In a stroke of brilliance, he incorporates into the narrative, from the prologue forward, a writer named Víctor Goti, whose work in progress closely resembles the plot of *Niebla*. Víctor labels his opus a *nivola*, to differentiate it from the *novela*, or novel, a reference to nineteenth-century narrative realism and naturalism exemplified in Spain in the novels of writers such as Benito Pérez Galdós, Emilia Pardo Bazán, and Leopoldo Alas (known as Clarín). Víctor is voicing Unamuno's distancing of his model for narrative composition from the conventions of realism; the book should not be deemed a deficient novel but instead should be judged by the criteria of the *nivola*, which has its own set of standards. The juxtaposition of Unamuno and Víctor also produces a layering effect, with the authors adding metadimensions to a narrative whose primary character is an abstraction, already several stages removed from the norms of realism.

Another figure worth noting is Orfeo, a stray dog to which Augusto becomes attached. He designates the canine companion as the recipient of his soliloquies, or, more properly, "monodiálogos" 'monodialogues.' Orfeo summons Cervantes's exemplary novella *El coloquio de los perros* ("The Dogs' Colloquy"), which endows the animals with a breadth of experiences and a rich inner life.

Niebla concludes with Don Miguel's response to the death of Augusto Pérez. In the last numbered chapter (33), the deceased character appears to the author in a dream, and once again Augusto forces his creator to probe his own existence. This is followed by "Funeral Oration by Way of Epilogue," delivered by a wise and compassionate Orfeo, who subsequently is found dead by Augusto's servants. Liduvina's husband, Domingo, weeps for his master and for the loyal confidant. Here, Unamuno anticipates a scene from his novella *San Manuel Bueno, mártir* ("Saint Manuel Bueno, Martyr"), in which the mentally handicapped Blasillo kneels beside his spiritual guide Don Manuel, in repose, and accompanies him in death.

Niebla has been categorized as a philosophical, existential, antirealist, modernist, and metafictional narrative. Possessing a comedic and satirical edge, *Niebla* flaunts its detachment from the goal of objectivity associated with European realism. The narrative is strong on technique and steeped in wit, but its predominant features are, arguably, its ideological aspects and its portrayal of literature and of life, or, stated alternatively, of the movement from signifier to signified—that is, the passage from sign to meaning. The break from realism, the conception of the *nivola* and its ties to metafiction, the formidable intertextuality, the pursuit for originality, and the personal touches correspond to the structural configuration of *Niebla* and to the correlation between the text and the outside world. Guided by Cervantes and other exponents of the meta-arts, Unamuno invites the reader to collaborate, to make connections, to fill in gaps, and to determine the implications and applications of the words on the page. A message of *Niebla*, one might submit, is that the deviation from strict realism does not necessarily denote an escape from the representation of reality or from the interplay of similitude and difference. Cervantes and other predecessors have shown Unamuno that access to reality can be circuitous and that ideas and art—including self-conscious and self-referential art—are hardly incompatible.

As with part 1 of *Don Quijote*, the fiction of *Niebla* begins with the prologue, in which Víctor Goti discusses the "misteriosa muerte" 'strange death' (73; 3) of Augusto Pérez, which he insists is a suicide. Despite allusions to Hamlet and to Víctor's insecurities, the focus of the prologue, not surprisingly, is Unamuno: his perceptions, his opinions, and his peculiarities. Unamuno will merge, in large measure, with his character and with his authorial double. He intercedes, in a post-prologue, to convey to the reader that he is in on the secret of Víctor's existence and that he alone has a hold on the fate of the *nivolista*. The metaphor of the author as God of the artistic creation will dominate throughout the narrative, yet Unamuno obviously realizes—as he has Augusto realize—that he is doing nothing more than posing as a deity; he is as lost, as apprehensive, and as frightened as anyone in either domain, real or fictional. Existential anguish does not easily provide a story in and of itself, and Unamuno takes Augusto on a journey, or on interrelated journeys, that will compose the narrative thrust. As *Niebla* opens, Augusto stands at the doorway of his house, so eager to establish a course of action that he is prepared to let the next dog that passes by define his route. He modifies the plan when Eugenia enters the picture. He is enamored, or, more accurately, in love with love: in love with the mental image of Eugenia as the ultimate metonym of desire. When he informs Víctor of his passion, Augusto has no memory of the physical qualities of the lady, and on one occasion he takes no notice of her when she crosses his path. In line with the general departure from realism, the love story and the love triangle of *Niebla* cast the quest for fulfillment as less emotional than speculative and conjectural. Theory trumps praxis. Realism emphasizes specificity, through detailed descriptions of characters and settings, of times and places, whereas Unamuno seems to delight in vagueness, in a blurred and nebulous vision that befits the book's title. The *nivola*—Unamuno's and Víctor's—prioritizes unfiltered thought, the powers of the mind, and unending discourse.

In *Niebla*, the author writes himself into a story that introduces an additional author, who is writing an almost identical story and likewise fabricating a singular kind of narrative, an intellectualization and a transformation, as it were, of models of realism. A key facet of *Niebla* is its disjunction from the realist and naturalist impulse, a disjunction that is highlighted by Augusto Pérez's conscious or subconscious wish for the leading role in a conventional novel and, commensurately, for a happy ending. Augusto's tentative and distracted nature sets him apart from characters that resemble the flesh-and-blood men and women of narrative realism. Augusto is conspicuously inhibited in his encounters with the earthy Rosario and with the vulgar Mauricio, because their blatant physicality runs counter to his dependence on the intangible; he is adrift, if not in the clouds, in the mist. Unamuno blends comedy, intertextuality, and the deadly serious in equal doses. The mimetic yields to the metaphysical, and Unamuno's rendition of metaphysics never elides writers and readers. *Niebla* honors and reverently strays from the Cervantine template. Although Unamuno never remains humbly in the background, his narrative prescription—a poetics of the *nivola*—is suggestive, compelling, and far-reaching. Ambiguity and a liberal field of potential signifiers reveal the fluidity and flexibility of the narrative, which vacillates freely between fiction and reality, frequently confusing the two or disregarding borders. Cervantes in *Don Quijote* and Unamuno in *Niebla* are, simultaneously, inside and outside the text, as fictional entities and implied authors, as puppets and puppeteers. Metafiction is a means to myriad ends and frames, and thus *Niebla* lends itself to scrutiny within a range of contexts: analysis of the metaliterary commentary, the parameters of art, the symbolic value of writing, the exploration of this life and of what may lie beyond, the evocative Unamuno-centric universe, the bidirectional intertextuality of the narrative, and so forth.

In a classroom setting, I would propose offering background materials on the life, works, and worldview of Unamuno; on narrative realism, as illustrated in the sixteenth and early seventeenth centuries and in the eighteenth and nineteenth centuries; on the Generation of 1898, with a look at major writers such as José Martínez Ruiz (known as Azorín), Ramón del Valle Inclán, Antonio Machado, and Pío Baroja; on the mimetic versus the antimimetic; on metafiction and the *meta* prefix; on intertextuality; on modernism, as compared with postmodernism; on the basic concepts and lexicon of narrative theory; on Cervantes and Unamuno; and on the notion of *niebla* and approaches to the *nivola*. I would include brief readings and examples within the individual sections; the precise choices would depend on the topic and the level of the course. With respect to the Cervantine intertext, I would stress the prologue to part 1 of *Don Quijote*: the process of gathering data for the true history, the discovery of the manuscript by the historian Cide Hamete Benengeli and its translation from the Arabic, the foregrounding of reading and writing, the metaliterary references, the linking of process and product, the intercalated stories, and the pervasive and shifting irony. Cervantes seems to be on Unamuno's mind as he composes *Niebla*. Under no circumstances does Unamuno strive to imitate his artistic idol and soul mate, but he steers the reader—in this and other texts—to indisputable, and unsubtle, correspondences between the two writers.

The initial discussion is based on student responses to questions on the readings. At the end of the class dialogue, I have assigned essays on one or more of the following topics: an exploration of the term *nivola*; the characterization of Augusto Pérez; the female characters of *Niebla*; the symbolism of the debate between the author and Augusto Pérez; and the representation of reality in *Niebla*.

The bibliography on Unamuno and *Niebla* is extensive, and there are outstanding critical studies for graduate and undergraduate students. I would recommend, among numerous alternate choices, essays by Luis Álvarez-Castro ("¿Quién mató?"), Roland Batchelor ("Form"), Carlos Blanco Aguinaga ("Unamuno's *Niebla*), Ignacio Galbis, J. A. Garrido Ardila ("La génesis"; "Origin"; and "Unamuno"), Willard King, Francisco LaRubia-Prado ("Deconstrucción"), Carlos Longhurst ("Unamuno"), Paul Olson ("Unamuno's Break"), Alexander Parker, Janet Pérez, Geoffrey Ribbans ("Structure"), Rachel Schmidt, Antonio Vilanova, Frances Weber, and Iris Zavala ("*Niebla*"), together with book-length studies by Álvarez-Castro (*La palabra*), Basdekis, Julia Biggane and John Macklin, Thomas Franz (Niebla *inexplorada*), Garrido Ardila (*La construcción*), Roberta Johnson (*Crossfire*), Gayana Jurkevich, Olson (*Great Chiasmus* and *Unamuno*), Ribbans (*Niebla*), and Armando Zubizarreta. My study *Cervantes in the Middle* contains chapters on *Amor y pedagogía* ("Love and Pedagogy") and *Niebla* (177–234, 235–307).

Niebla could be used in a number of classes in Spanish and comparative literature, courses with titles such as *Don Quijote* and Metafiction; *Don Quijote* and the Experimental Novel; Spanish Realism and Modernism; The Genres of Unamuno; Cervantes, Unamuno, Borges, and Company; Self-Fashioning in the Spanish Novel; and Contemporary Metafiction and Metatheater. The primary texts for *Don Quijote* and Metafiction, for example, could consist of *Don Quijote*; *Niebla*; Paul Auster's *City of Glass*; Javier Cercas's *Soldados de Salamina* ("Soldiers of Salamis"); and Mark Haddon's *The Curious Incident of the Dog in the Night-time*. Each work interrogates the making of narrative from a distinct and intriguing angle of vision. *Don Quijote* and the Experimental Novel, in turn, could include the anonymous picaresque narrative *Lazarillo de Tormes*; *Don Quijote*; Charlotte Lennox's *The Female Quixote*; *Niebla*; and Mario Vargas Llosa's *La tía Julia y el escribidor* ("Aunt Julia and the Scriptwriter"). These works are memorable for their confrontation with—and perhaps deconstruction of—the intertext. Spanish Realism and Modernism could examine *Niebla* as a rejoinder to the realism of such novels as Galdós's *La de Bringas* ("That Bringas Woman"); Pardo Bazán's *Los pazos de Ulloa* ("The House of Ulloa"); Clarín's *Su único hijo* ("His Only Son"); and Unamuno's *Paz en la guerra* ("Peace in War"). The Genres of Unamuno could concentrate on the essay *En torno al casticismo* ("About Tradition and Authenticity"); the short story collection *El espejo de la muerte* ("The Mirror of Death"); the novels *Amor y pedagogía* and *La tía Tula* ("Aunt Tula"); the novella *San Manuel Bueno, mártir*; the plays *El otro* ("The Other") and *El hermano Juan* ("Brother Juan"); and selected poetry. For Cervantes, Unamuno, Borges, and Company, clear choices would be *Don Quijote*; *Niebla*; Jorge Luis Borges's *El Aleph*; and selected short stories by Julio Cortázar, Marco Denevi, and other Latin American writers. Self-Fashioning in the Spanish Novel could survey character-building from the picaresque tradition onward, in texts such as *Lazarillo de Tormes*; Cervantes's *El licenciado Vidriera* ("The Glass Lawyer") and *La gitanilla* ("The Little Gypsy Girl"), available in the collection *Novelas ejemplares* ("Exemplary Novels"); Galdós's *Tristana*; *Niebla*; Camilo José Cela's *La familia de Pascual Duarte* ("The Family of Pascual Duarte"); and Carmen Martín Gaite's *El cuarto de atrás* ("The Back Room"). Options for Contemporary Metafiction and Metatheater could include *Niebla*; Toni Morrison's *The Bluest Eye*; Clarice Lispector's *The Hour of the Star*; Italo Calvino's *If on a Winter's Night a Traveler*; Michael Cunningham's *The Hours*; Luigi Pirandello's *Six Characters in Search of an Author*; Tom Stoppard's *Rosencrantz and Guildenstern Are Dead*; Doug Wright's *I Am My Own Wife*; and David Henry Hwang's *Yellow Face*. In 2011 I published an adaption for the stage of *Niebla* titled *Into the Mist*, and I have spoken, very briefly, with students on adaption as a textual reading and on the challenges involved in the new medium.

In *Del sentimiento trágico de la vida* ("The Tragic Sense of Life"), Unamuno confesses his doubts about eternal life. His soul-searching and, finally, his argumentation lead him to gain a paradoxical satisfaction by using reason to validate the superiority of faith over reason. Philosophy assists theology; one could contend that logic helps Unamuno to keep the faith. In *Niebla*, Unamuno begets a fictional entity—*un ente de ficción*—Augusto Pérez, who serves as co-protagonist of an existentialist allegory in which fiction and reality spar most grippingly. In *San Manuel Bueno, mártir*, Unamuno reprises the theme in the story of an adored priest who begins to question immortality, yet who encourages his parishioners to embrace the promise of eternal life. The narrator of the novella is Ángela Carballino, a villager who knows Don Manuel's secret and who deduces that the priest could not have been so vigorous and persuasive a guide had he not truly believed, even while fearing that he had challenged his convictions. Like Unamuno, Ángela rationalizes her conclusion. Unamuno makes an appearance at the end of the narrative to state that he agrees with the narrator, that he believes in her more than in his own reality, and that it is conceivable that Augusto Pérez, in *Niebla*, might have been correct, upon review, in claiming that he was more real and more objective than the man who thought he had invented a character. *Don Quijote* may be the product of an intricate comic vision, but Cervantes considers infinite themes, many of which are serious, weighty, and all-encompassing. Literature becomes the macrocosm and everything else the microcosm. *Niebla* is, likewise, a human comedy, but much more. As he develops a *mise en abyme* of impressive proportions, Unamuno brings theology, specifically, his preoccupation with the afterlife, into the *nivola*. Reality and the beyond are encrypted into the fiction, into the metafiction, as the writer and the thinker—and literature, life, and eternity—unite. It seems poetically just that Unamuno has devised a new name for this fiction that is never pure fiction and whose points of reference, and lessons, may be limitless. In a review of a recent biography of Gustave Flaubert by Michel Winock, Peter Brooks cites an 1852 letter from Flaubert to Louise Colet, at the time that Flaubert was writing *Madame Bovary*, in which he says, "The author in his work should be like God in the universe, present everywhere and visible nowhere" (24). *Madame Bovary* moves in one direction, *Niebla* in another. The contrast is striking, because Unamuno the polemicist and purveyor of polysemy is rarely, if ever, invisible.

NOTE

[1] The text of *Niebla* used in this essay is Mario J. Valdés's edition, published by Cátedra. English translations are by Warner Fite in the edition published by the U of Illinois P in 2000.

The Perversion of Genius: Unamuno's Exile and the Censors

Ana Urrutia-Jordana

These days it is increasingly difficult for undergraduates to imagine a world without the Internet, much less a fading and outdated world where instant access to news and people is simply not a part of one's daily life. For our students, snail mail, printed newspapers, and even personal phone calls are quickly becoming relics of a curious past that is understandably often viewed as somehow foreign, almost alien. Instead, images (video, photos, some with captions) seem to be the preferred way of communication among millennials; sharing how they dress, what they eat, who they see, and where they are at all times has become a way of life—virtual reality that today is nonetheless quite real. With such a brave new world at their fingertips, they have the sense of being in touch with what is happening everywhere and at all times. Human history is as close as the next *Google* search. Curiously, such access to the past is often taken for granted by students, since they struggle to see the black-and-white country of the past as relevant to their high-tech lives. So the idea of reading literature from another time, culture, and language, especially the poems of a writer (another dead white man, no less) famous for his dense and dark religious dilemmas and philosophical approach to life, is usually greeted with a healthy dose of skepticism: another mysterious and probably pointless academic exercise?

With this in mind, I always look forward to teaching Miguel de Unamuno's poetry of exile as a kind of pedagogical ambush. The outrageous language of some of his best lines tends to shock my students quickly out of their apathy toward another place and time, which then paves the way for a more in-depth reading of a challenging artist and text. Our discussion begins with the obvious complexities of modern poetry and the subject matter of these poems—ideas of dislocation, anger, fear, and loneliness associated with exile—and students soon discover the timelessness and universality of the work. In this respect, literature becomes both more intimate and vivid for any reader willing to engage with difficult experience and see the world of a very public figure turned upside down. Our examination of the writing also includes a key question: why is this poetry of exile a perfect example of the fragility of art within the wider context of dictatorial Spain? Students are confronted with the harsh fact of General Franco's many censors and the edicts they imposed throughout the culture. In the bitterest of ironies, Unamuno's political poems—which he tirelessly used to fight against the injustices and abuses of Miguel Primo de Rivera's dictatorship—not to mention his personal and artistic reputation, would be subjected to a series of distortions as the result of *franquista* censorship over the next four decades. Their calculated cleansing of Unamuno's work during the period resulted in a far longer and more damaging banishment than the poet could have initially imagined. Such a perversion of the writer's literary and intellectual intentions becomes a cautionary tale in twentieth-century literature. This most famous of men in modern Spanish letters was posthumously seen, for almost half the century, as someone far different (through both malice of editorial design and propaganda) than he ever would have believed possible in life: the ultimate identity theft.

For Unamuno in exile, tone often was the favorite weapon of choice against dictatorship. What grabs the attention of upper-division students first is the clear rhetorical strategy of attack. In the political sonnets of *De Fuerteventura a París* ("From Fuerteventura to Paris") and the *romances* (ballads) of *Romancero del destierro* ("Ballads of Exile"), neither published in Spain—unexpurgated—until the 1980s, time and again the Basque intellectual is edging for a fight: anger, moral outrage, a deliberate and surprising irreverence that continually appears side by side with the vicious political (very personal, even ad hominem) insults of so many of his countrymen. Unamuno never suffers fools, but it is the mindlessness of the public thug—and the indifference of Spanish liberals who allow such abuses of power—that gets his close attention. He picks on and ridicules tyrannical figures, using his art to savage their corruption of Spain. Primo de Rivera is accused of mistreating Spain like just another of his prostitutes (and not even one of his favorites). College students today are quite familiar with such attacks and political satire; late-night TV has become prime comic relief, especially during election years, with skits, jokes, and spoofs that can be constantly replayed day and night on their electronic devices. As a result, Unamuno's strategy of using words to wound and humiliate makes instant sense; in fact, the element of surprise is part of what works best. I want my students in the early stages of our conversation to be a bit off-balance. Unamuno's merciless ridicule of his enemies does just that job. In this context of the darkest sort of humor, I find that students are more receptive, once they are clear about the rhetorical point, to delving into the historical circumstances of these verbal aggressions. We start with the official decree, ordered by Primo de Rivera, banishing the writer to the island of Fuerteventura in February 1924. The second sonnet in *De Fuerteventura*, which includes an explanatory note about a few of the dictator's most reprehensible habits (that also served as inspiration for the poem), illustrates the tone and content of this type of broadside:

> ¿Conque iban a barrerte? Pura coba.
> Lo que hacen es ponerte roja y gualda
> de rubor y de bilis, que en la espalda
> te están, España, dando la gran soba.
>
> Y si fueses al menos la Caoba
> con su gobierno de bajo la falda,
> harías que pusieran por guirnalda
> en tu sombrero de guión la escoba.

Nada de aquellas recomendaciones
del régimen antiguo, el del embudo;
ved al macho, señor de las legiones,

como bajo un fanal ríe desnudo
y ante el pueblo se rasca los calzones[1]
y el pueblo mira, por mordaza, mudo. (15)[2]

They were just going to sweep you away? Pure flattery.
What they're doing, turning you red and then yellow
blushing, and then the bile, on your back
from behind, Spain, they're groping you

And at least if you were "la Gaoba"
with the government under her skirt
you might ask for the broom as a garland
to trim your flagbearer's hat.

Nothing from those recommendations
of the old regime, that one-sided law;
observe the macho man, lord of those legions,

how he laughs naked under a streetlight
and in front of the nation he scratches his balls
while the nation stares, gagged, speechless.

In these four stanzas, Unamuno pities Spain, a country full of bile and ire, being lied to and "groped," victimized by a despot, a shameless pimp who will scratch himself grinning and naked in public, while his citizens can only stare at such crassness, speechless. The note that follows the sonnet details the infamous case of La Caoba, a drug-dealing prostitute whom the dictator—a self-appointed (as Unamuno viciously discloses) "protector de las jóvenes alegres" 'protector of cheerful girls' (16)—got out of jail by forcing the judge in this case to dismiss all charges and order her immediate release. Still unhappy with the outcome, Primo de Rivera proceeded to berate the judge publicly in a series of *notas oficiosas* ("press notes").

This deluge of rage gives us an effective opening to discuss the shaky correlation between poetry and politics. Should these poems be considered versified pamphleteering rather than art? Are these lines unnecessarily vulgar, unpoetic, and therefore unworthy of study? In other words, can such poetry aesthetically stand on its own merits? And if so, how? Our debate often spills over into the realm of music, especially rap, which is always a welcome reference point of interest for my undergraduates. Inevitably, another question is posed: what if the book that includes this poem was designed to serve as a diary as well? Would our reaction to the writing change? In the same way that the entries of a diary could never really make complete sense if examined in isolation from one another, we soon end up exploring the idea of whether poetic compositions are always read best within a stricter context—particularly in this case, when each book can be seen as a series of emotional responses to the poet's day-to-day life in exile, a context that is undeniably a consequence of the politics of his time. The subtitle of *De Fuerteventura—Diario íntimo de confinamiento y exilio vertido en sonetos* ("Intimate Diary of Confinement and Exile Poured Out in Sonnets")—confirms the intention of the author in crafting a book with three objectives in mind: to chronicle the events of the day (much like a *diario* or newspaper would, if censorship were not a constant issue); to reflect both the mood and intimate thoughts triggered by particular moments; and to create a popular conscience by shaking the audience into action through the art of poetry. For Unamuno the artistic process was inescapably connected to the historical and the political, since his reactions to such ephemeral experience served as the inspiration for these poems, which in turn attempted to resist the passage of time. Politics always influenced his life, and this life in exile certainly influenced his verse. Sonnet 89 (again with commentary), written after his escape from Fuerteventura and settling in Paris, is yet another example of this artistic purpose. Here are the first two stanzas:

> ¡Ay triste España de Caín, la roja
> de sangre hermana y por la bilis gualda,
> muerdes porque no comes, y en la espalda
> llevas carga de siglos de congoja!
>
> Medra machorra envidia en mente floja
> —te enseñó a no pensar Padre Ripalda—
> rezagada y vacía está tu falda
> e insulto el bien ajeno se te antoja. (138–39)
>
> O forlorn Spain of Cain, red
> with sibling blood and yellow with bile,
> you bite with nothing to eat and carry
> on your back centuries of angst!
>
> A fruitless envy grows within slow minds
> —taught not to think by Father Ripalda—
> lagging behind, your skirt is empty
> as you see insults in the luck of others.

Apart from showcasing this very public side of Unamuno, the sonnet encompasses many of the subtopics and stylistic characteristics of his uniquely combative stance: while accepting the existence of more than one Spain, he denounces yet again the disastrous predicament of the country under Primo de Rivera and communicates the quixotic spirit of his own political campaign, grounded on principle and resistance. Unamuno does so with the verbal aggressiveness of someone who is forced to witness from afar the collapse of a culture, not to mention of a sovereign nation. In essence, this sonnet becomes a form of creative politics, or a "poetization of politics" as I have written elsewhere. Unamuno impugns Spain's violent and fratricidal past, with its history of civil wars and even that lurking spirit of the Inquisition, so damning for so many and for so long. His opening, "triste España de Caín," which plays off a famous line by Antonio Machado,[3] underscores the idea of *las dos Españas* ("the two Spains"), along with the hope for a better future—at least among the civilized in society who have yet to react but might once they realize the abuses perpetrated by those in power. Also worth noting is the animalization of the masses (through adjectives such as *machorra*) under these dehumanized dictatorial rulers and the personification of his degraded homeland.

Like so many other writers from the Generation of 1898, Unamuno believed that his art should serve a social obligation, which explains the didactic nature of much of this poetry of exile. For the Basque, precision of logic, verbal clarity, and directness of expression were essential qualities for any verse, a point we talk about at some length. Moreover, the selection of the Petrarchan sonnet as the form of choice for *De Fuerteventura* and the ballad for the key section of *Romancero del destierro* should not be overlooked (we have already considered these poetic forms before ever tackling these two collections). And since our students are so comfortable communicating through pictures, for them visual metaphors can have an extremely powerful effect. For example, in the letter Unamuno uses to preface the first set of poems in *De Fuerteventura*, the poet provides his rationale for using the Italian sonnet, with its taut rhyme scheme and metrics. In such a formal arrangement, Unamuno argues that emotion becomes more forceful if expressed with the intensity of poetic compression. Human feeling and experience in general—whether disdain for the dictator and his acolytes; disgust at the corruption of those itching for power; scorn for the apathetic who mindlessly allow it all; or high praise for the enduring truth symbolized by the island and its sea—is the raw material to compress. He speaks of the possibilities for a "diamond of words": fourteen smooth and "polished facets," cut with very sharp and defined edges (11). This process of compression, he argues, is one way to think through the Petrarchan form to give both resistance and permanence to such public thoughts. (A comparison for students about why certain tunes are just catchier than others helps underscore his artistic tactics.) The choice of the *romance* is equally meaningful. This poetic tradition—the oldest and most common in popular Spanish verse—grants the ensemble of poems in his second book an unequivocally political character as well as perfectly fits Unamuno's didactic purpose: a writing that is easy to memorize and disseminate and that is patriotic in the sense of reflecting the national Spanish spirit, with unmistakable narrative qualities. Not surprisingly, this poetic form would resurface during the Spanish Civil War, and *romances* by writers from the Generation of 1927, especially those by José Bergamín and Rafael Alberti attacking Franco and his generals, could also be used to show this point.[4]

Within this context, students do come to appreciate exactly why Unamuno's controversial stands—before and after Primo de Rivera proclaimed himself dictator—only intensified an already overzealous and reactionary censorship of his work. No doubt harder to discern is the manipulation of Unamuno's image throughout Spain as a liberal who somehow reformed under the long shadow of the Franco regime: decades of state propaganda, along with calculated censorial cleansing, especially of the political poems within these books, distorted the writer's reputation and literary legacy for much of the twentieth century. For example, most of the prose commentaries that follow many of his sonnets—a vital complement to these poems as can be seen in the two examples quoted here—as well as the majority of the *romances* (thirteen out of eighteen) were deliberately omitted from the first reprints of *De Fuerteventura* and *Romancero del destierro* that appeared in Unamuno's *Obras completas*, published posthumously in Spain. Needless to say, the mutilation of his overtly politicized writing made an accurate reading of these texts impossible until the 1980s, almost fifty years after Unamuno's death. It is worth emphasizing (possibly as a subject for further study) that the most revered poets of the left and the republican cause, including Federico García Lorca and Machado, admired Unamuno and were influenced by his artistry. In this way, Unamuno becomes a symbol, almost a metaphor: a major writer trying to create political change through his words and personal sacrifice, only to have his reputation drastically perverted by the political hacks he so thoroughly loathed.

My hope always is that by the end of our study, my students will see the universal relevance of Unamuno's trials and, of course, his political poetry. These poems are an essential part of the poet's corpus and of the harsh realities of exile (an isolation that nearly drove him to suicide), and they surely can stand the test of time as documents of political dictatorship and artistic repression, of a writer's conscience and a remarkable poetization of politics and revolt.

NOTES

1 "Cojones" 'balls' in the original manuscript.

2 The text of *De Fuerteventura a París* used in this essay is the edition published by El Sitio. English translations are mine.

3 Machado's lines, which Unamuno chooses for an epigraph, read, "Un trozo de planeta / por donde cruza errante la sombra de Caín" 'A piece of planet / crossed by the wandering shadow of Cain' (Machado 140).

4 See Caudet, *Romancero* 114–17.

Unamuno's Press Articles: The Badge of Identity of the Unamunian Intellectual

Stephen G. H. Roberts

When it comes to academic curricula, Miguel de Unamuno's press articles feature low down in the order of priority, most probably running in last after his prose fiction, poetry, essays, and drama (more or less in that order). One of the probable reasons for this situation lies in the fact that it may seem easier, at least at first sight, to establish a relationship between Unamuno's imaginative literature and his philosophical, theological, and literary essays than one between that literature and his press articles. However, it is clear too that we are still suffering from a certain historical bias in this respect. The image of Unamuno that was packaged and sold in Spain in the immediate aftermath of his death and through the first decades of the Franco regime was that of a patriotic writer who was devoted to the noble task of seeking out the true values of the nation. There was no place in this image for the combative and often subversive journalist who, from the start of his career in the 1880s until the outbreak of the Civil War, had written thousands of articles on current affairs for the national and regional newspapers of Spain and Latin America. Indeed, Manuel García Blanco, the editor of the first serious attempt to create an Unamunian *Obras completas* ("Complete Works"), those published by Vergara (under the permission of Afrodisio Aguado) between 1958 and 1964, in his introduction to the seventh volume made use of what he called Unamuno's own distinction "entre lo que pasa y lo que queda, entre la historia que permanece y la que se olvida" 'between what passes away and what stays, between the history that remains and the one that is forgotten' in order to justify his omission of some of Unamuno's more overtly political writings and speeches (7: 112).[1]

This situation was not challenged until the mid-1960s, when a series of courageous researchers started to recuperate Unamuno's journalism and, with it, the political dimension of this figure and his work. Foremost among these were Elías Díaz (*El pensamiento político de Unamuno* ["Unamuno's Political Thought"] and *Revisión de Unamuno* ["Reexamining Unamuno"]), Rafael Pérez de la Dehesa (*Política y sociedad en el primer Unamuno* ["Politics and Society in Early Unamuno"]), and Carlos Blanco Aguinaga ("El socialismo de Unamuno" ["Unamuno's Socialism"] and "De nuevo: El socialismo de Unamuno" ["Revisiting Unamuno's Socialism"]), whose collections and analyses of, above all, Unamuno's early press articles drew attention to Unamuno's youthful commitment to socialism and thus helped to forge a new image of the Basque writer that was more in tune with the radical zeitgeist of the 1960s and even helped to transform him into a symbol of opposition to the Franco regime. Then, in 1971, in a truly breakthrough moment, Manuel García Blanco, editor of the new official

Unamunian *Obras completas*, published by Escelicer, brought out a ninth and final volume that, for the first time in the history of Unamuno's collected works, contained press articles—360 in all—in two special sections entitled "Escritos dispersos" ("Scattered Writings"; 469–1237) and "Otros artículos" ("Other Articles"; 1241–1604), which were compiled and introduced by Pérez de la Dehesa. The former section featured articles written between 1889 and 1934, with most belonging to the period of Unamuno's greatest involvement with socialism (1895–1905), while the latter contained some of the articles that Unamuno published in the Buenos Aires newspaper *La Nación* during World War I. Since then, several generations of researchers (many of whom are mentioned below) have continued the painstaking task of seeking out Unamuno's thousands of press articles in the newspaper libraries of Spain, the rest of Europe, and the Americas.

At the end of his prologue to the articles reproduced in *Obras completas*, Pérez de la Dehesa expressed the wish that this compilation would help the reader to get closer to "un Unamuno cada vez más completo" 'an ever completer Unamuno' (9: 468).[2] While this has undoubtedly been the case, there is still a tendency in Unamuno studies to separate his press articles from his supposedly more significant (and certainly more studied) literary and philosophical works, a tendency that, in my opinion, has helped to obscure the richness and complexity of Unamuno's role as a writer and as a public intellectual. I endeavored to address this issue in *Miguel de Unamuno o la creación del intelectual español moderno* ("Miguel de Unamuno; or, The Creation of the Modern Spanish Intellectual") by suggesting that it is in fact Unamuno's mission as a regenerating intellectual that informs and animates his writings in each and every genre that he cultivated, from essays to novels and from drama and poetry to press articles, and therefore endows those multiple writings with coherence and meaning. Such an emphasis on Unamuno's role as an intellectual allows for a new periodization of Unamuno's work: the earliest writings (1879–97), where he gives expression mainly to his search for a community that he can serve; the years between 1897 and 1900, when his main concern is to bring his new role as a public intellectual into focus; the period between 1900 and 1913, when he seeks out the values that will inform both the community he will serve and the role he will play in order to do so; and, finally, the last two decades of his career, when Unamuno endeavors to carry out his role in the most direct fashion possible, which means, among other things, becoming fully involved in the res publica and the world of politics. And Unamuno created his role as a public intellectual by inventing new genres through which he could express himself and reach out to and influence the readers who represented the inhabitants of his ideal nation: a new sort of autobiographical and even confessional essay in which he could present his struggle with the complexities of life and the modern world as an example to be followed; innovative plays, poetry, and, above all, novels through which he could undermine the intellectual, moral, and religious certainties of his readers; and, of course, a new type of press article through which he could engage with the most pressing problems of the day.

Although Unamuno had been writing press articles since the very beginning of his career, it was only after 1914 that he truly started to fashion the genre in his own image. There are several reasons for this. On the one hand, he had by then brought his role as an intellectual fully into focus in his most important philosophical work, *Del sentimiento trágico de la vida* ("On the Tragic Sense of Life"), much of which, especially chapters 7 and 11, centers on the issue of how an individual should act upon and influence those around him or her. On the other hand, 1914 saw two events that would radically affect Unamuno's relationship with the world of politics: first, the loss of his influential public role as rector of the University of Salamanca, and second, the start of World War I.[3] Unamuno's dismissal from the rectorship, which came about because of his campaigns for agrarian reform and his opposition to certain policies of the liberal and conservative governments of the Count of Romanones and Eduardo Dato, respectively, caused him to become more outspoken in his criticisms of the powers that be and to turn increasingly to the press as his new public tribune and source of influence and prestige in the country. Meanwhile, despite Spain's official position of neutrality, World War I served, according to Unamuno, to bring a more authoritarian strain into Spanish public life, especially among certain key figures in the worlds of politics, the military, and big business, many of whom started to group themselves around King Alfonso XIII. The combination of these personal and political factors led Unamuno not only to transform the periodical press into his main publishing outlet (and means of reaching an ever-larger readership) but also gradually to forge a new sort of press article that could give expression both to his righteous anger at the state of Spain and to his mission to educate the Spanish people and thereby regenerate the country. The Unamunian article will share with the Unamunian essay its deployment of an all-powerful and authoritative *yo*, but that "I" is now responding to and interacting with current events (*actualidad*) and doing so in such a way as to reveal their underlying significance for the life both of the nation and of each and every one of his readers (who, of course, represent for Unamuno the inhabitants of that nation).

The origins and nature of the Unamunian press article help to reveal the multiple ways in which this genre can be used and enjoyed in the classroom. The rest of this essay will provide several suggestions, each of them related to the different kinds of collections and compilations that have appeared over the past half century.

First, there is no doubt that Unamuno's articles can be used to shed light on some of the most important events affecting Spain and the world over the final years of the nineteenth century and the first four decades of the twentieth. Some of the compilations focus on the articles that Unamuno produced at, and in response to, a specific historical moment and therefore provide insight into both the events of that particular time and Unamuno's own personal reading of them. Christopher Cobb's edition of Unamuno's *Artículos olvidados sobre España y la Primera Guerra Mundial* ("Forgotten Articles on Spain and the First World War"), for instance, reveals how Unamuno became one of the most outspoken *aliadófilos* (supporters of the Allied Powers) in Spain during World War I and also how he came to identify a fundamental *germanofilia* (support for Germany and the Central Powers) among the authoritarian factions that were starting to dominate the political scene within the country. The articles reproduced in Unamuno's *Political Speeches and Journalism, 1923–1929* and Manuel M.ª Urrutia León's "Miguel de Unamuno y *España con Honra* (1924–1925)" shed light on the reasons for his opposition to the military dictatorship of General Miguel Primo de Rivera and on the evolution of his political position and rhetoric during his exile in Fuerteventura, Paris, and Hendaye. And *República española y España republicana* ("Spanish Republic and Republican Spain"), edited by Vicente González Martín; *Ensueño de una patria: Periodismo republicano, 1931–1936* ("Dream of a Homeland: Republican Journalism, 1931–1936"), edited by Victor Ouimette; and Eduardo Pascual Mezquita's *La política del último Unamuno* ("The Politics of Unamuno's Last Years") all help to tell the story of Unamuno's initial support for and then growing disaffection with the Second Spanish Republic.

Second, those compilations that focus on Unamuno's collaboration with a particular newspaper or periodical serve to illuminate certain aspects of his political or ideological evolution and also the character and outlook of the publication itself. The works by Díaz, Pérez de la Dehesa, and Blanco Aguinaga mentioned above, together with Pedro Ribas's edition of Unamuno's *Escritos socialistas* ("Socialist Writings") and José Antonio Ereño Altuna's *Artículos inéditos de Unamuno* ("Uncollected Articles by Unamuno"), all include articles that Unamuno published in the Bilbao periodical *La Lucha de Clases* during his militancy in the Socialist Party in the 1890s and enable us to understand his evolving and idiosyncratic relationship with Marxism at this time. Ribas, working with Diego Núñez, later brought out *Unamuno y el socialismo* ("Unamuno and Socialism"), a selection of the many and varied articles that Unamuno wrote about socialism between 1886 and 1928, and the latter part of this selection reveals a good deal about Unamuno's relationship with the main socialist newspaper *El Socialista* between the end of World War I and his banishment to Fuerteventura in February 1924. In these articles, one can see how Unamuno espouses what he calls an essentially political, democratic, or liberal form of socialism that he offers as an antidote to the syndicalist or revolutionary strain that he fears in the late 1910s and early 1920s might be about to take over the Socialist Party (see Núñez and Ribas 247, 276–78, 298–301, 442–44, 463–96). It is a sign both of the moderation of the editors of *El Socialista* and of Unamuno's power and influence as a public intellectual that the former added a note to his article "Sin color ni grito" ("With No Color or Shout"), published in the newspaper on 18 December 1923, in order to express their support for his assertion that "los socialistas somos antes que nada liberales" 'we socialists are liberals above everything else' (qtd. in S. Roberts, "Unamuno" 96–98).[4] *Artículos desconocidos en "El Mercantil Valenciano," 1917–1923* ("Unknown Articles in *El Mercantil Valenciano*, 1917–1923"), edited by Laureano Robles Carcedo and Urrutia León, focuses on Unamuno's collaboration over the same years with a liberal newspaper that allowed him freely to express his extreme and sometimes libelous opinions about the royal family and the conservative and liberal governments of Spain—opinions which saw him end up in court on a couple of occasions in the early 1920s.

Third, Cobb's, Núñez and Ribas's, and Robles Carcedo and Urrutia León's compilations mentioned above, together with some of the articles reproduced in volume 9 of the Unamunian *Obras completas* published by Escelicer and the 587 articles contained in G. D. Robertson's three-volume *Political Writings, 1918–1924*, reveal not only how Unamuno responded to the national and international events that took place between 1914 and 1924 but also how he went about fashioning both his role as a politically committed intellectual and the very vehicle through which he would play that role—that is, of course, the press article itself.[5] On the one hand, one finds in these articles a long and sometimes tortuous discussion concerning the role of the public intellectual and, above all, how it should differ from that of the politician. In the article "Servilismo y liberalismo" ("Servility and Liberalism"), published in *El Mercantil Valenciano* on 15 April 1921, for example, he implies that his job is to act as a "contrapeso a la autoridad" 'counterweight to authority' (*Political Writings* 2: 84), while in "De actualidad perdurable" ("On Lasting Actuality"), published in *El Liberal* (Madrid) on 30 April 1920, he adds that "Nuestro empeño es vitalizar, exaltar, entender, exasperar, acaso a unos y a otros, a blancos y negros, a los de la derecha y a los de la izquierda" 'Our duty is to vitalize, exalt, understand, exasperate those on all sides, perhaps, those in white and those in black, those on the right and those on the left' (1: 272). On the other hand, an analysis of all these writings can help to reveal what could be called the poetics of Unamuno's press articles: that is, the textual strategies that he develops in order to talk about current events, to express his indignation, to stir the conscience of his reader, and, ultimately, to forge a new intellectual community that might just become the blueprint for a freer and more just Spain in the future.[6]

Finally, there is the question of the relationship or even crossover between Unamuno's press articles and his writings that belong to other genres. It is interesting to note, by way of example, that Unamuno started preparing the definitive version of his major exile work *Cómo se hace una novela* ("How a Novel Is Made") at the same time (April or May 1927) that he started collaborating from Hendaye on the clandestine broadsheet *Hojas Libres*. The style of Unamuno's aggressively polemical articles, most of which were reproduced in Eduardo Comín Colomer's *Unamuno, libelista* ("Unamuno the Libeler"), can be seen invading *Cómo se hace una novela* at certain key moments, such as when Unamuno attacks what he sees as the profound stupidity of Primo de Rivera or the cowardice of those Spanish intellectuals who have refused to stand up to the dictator (Unamuno, *Manual* 190, 207). This incorporation of the style and texture of the (in this case clandestine) press article alongside and in the midst of the mini-essays, poems, and fragments of a short story that make up *Cómo se hace una novela* helps to reinforce the multigeneric or cross-generic status of what is probably Unamuno's most innovative and even avant-garde work. And this is just one example: the theme of the relationship between Unamuno's press articles and his novels, poems, essays, and dramas is a potentially very rich one that has hardly yet been explored.

NOTES

[1] For an analysis of García Blanco's position and of the politics of publishing Unamuno's "Complete Works," see S. Roberts, "Obras incompletas."

[2] All translations in this essay are my own.

[3] For an excellent analysis of Unamuno's response to these two events, and indeed of his developing political views and activity, see Urrutia León, *Evolución*.

[4] For an analysis of Unamuno's views on socialism at this time, see S. Roberts, "Miguel de Unamuno."

[5] Between them, these compilations reveal the sheer volume of Unamuno's journalistic output in the years between 1914 and 1924, when he seems to have been publishing a new article every two or three days, with some of them being syndicated in the regional press or republished abroad, above all in Latin America. It must be pointed out that there is some overlap between the compilations mentioned here: the articles that Unamuno wrote for *El Mercantil Valenciano*, for example, appear both in Robertson's volumes and in Robles Carcedo and Urrutia León's *Artículos desconocidos en "El Mercantil Valenciano"*; those he wrote for *El Socialista* at this time can be found both in Robertson's volumes and in Núñez and Ribas's *Unamuno y el socialismo*.

[6] On the dynamics and poetics of Unamuno's press articles, see S. Roberts, *Miguel de Unamuno* 170–85.

The Pathos of the Hero in Unamuno

Francisco LaRubia-Prado

One approach to teaching the rich and multifaceted figure of the hero in the works of Miguel de Unamuno involves four stages. First is the insertion of the hero in the intellectual and ethical framework that makes such a figure possible in Western philosophy, namely, individualism. Once this genealogy has been established, the instructor can begin to explore the protean figure of the hero in Unamuno's work. Second, the instructor must carefully select the works that illustrate Unamuno's understanding of heroism. Ideally, this selection will cover a wide spectrum of texts showing Unamuno's range and depth in the treatment of the subject. This treatment must simultaneously recognize the affinity of the hero with nature as well as a powerful movement within him- or herself toward internalization of the heroic spirit. Third, once the historical and critical framework has been established, the instructor can proceed to the analysis of the chosen texts. Finally, a contrast should be established between the previously discussed heroic figures, which can also include the antihero. This essay will analyze two charismatic figures within Unamuno's pantheon of heroes. Covering the four steps will ensure not only that students acquire an understanding of the *content* but that they also attain the systematic grasp of a methodology that will allow them to repeat similar analysis (*performance*) and thus the necessary *proficiency*.

Underlying Unamuno's treatment of the unique personality is the author's acutely felt sense of individualism, a characteristic Western cultural development. Distinctive individualism is a key component of the two works analyzed in this essay: Unamuno's first play, *La esfinge* (1898; "The Sphinx"), and his last novel, *San Manuel Bueno, mártir* (1931; "San Manuel Bueno, Martyr"). There are two reasons to choose these texts. First, they cover the entire temporal spectrum of Unamuno's literary production, showing that the figure of the exceptional individual was always important in his work. Second, both of these texts are closely connected by their central characters' pathos, by their feelings of despair, albeit channeled in diametrically opposed ways. The position of the central characters' self vis-à-vis the nonself—that is, the world—allows them to illustrate the cultural and ethical figures of the saint, the hero, and the antihero.

In the West, the assertion of individualism can be traced back to Greek hedonism—the pursuit of individual pleasure—and eudaemonism—the search for individual well-being. It was not until the Renaissance, however, when the individual became the source of all value. This recognition culminated with the granting of the hermeneutic power for individuals to interpret the Bible during the Reformation. After René Descartes, the Enlightenment enabled the birth of modern individualism. In *What Is Enlightenment?*, Immanuel Kant's words truly seal the new understanding of individual freedom and the rejection of ethical and intellectual authority over the individual: "Enlightenment is man's emergence from his self-imposed nonage. Nonage is the inability to use one's own understanding without another's guidance. *Dare to know!* (*Sapere aude.*) 'Have the courage to use your own understanding' is therefore the motto of the enlightenment." Other philosophers that decisively contributed to the development of Western individualism—and also questioned it—are John Stuart Mill, Friedrich Hegel, Karl Marx, Sigmund Freud, Søren Kierkegaard, and Friedrich Nietzsche.

Kierkegaard and Nietzsche were important in Unamuno's understanding of the greatest expression of individualism: heroism and sainthood. Victor Ouimette discusses at length Unamuno's concept of heroism and, in addition to Kierkegaard and Nietzsche, he cites Kant, Hegel, Benedict de Spinoza, Arthur Schopenhauer, Herbert Spencer, Ángel Ganivet, Étienne Pivert de Senancour, and Thomas Carlyle as major influences on his thinking about the subject. What Ouimette makes clear in his analysis is how behind Unamuno's understanding of heroism there is the conviction that the hero is "the best of any individual," displaying "the plenitude of a personality . . . , individual man's zenith" (12, 15). In Unamuno's *Vida de Don Quijote y Sancho* ("Life of Don Quixote and Sancho"), he sees Don Quixote "as the ultimate ego, the exemplary hero" (Ouimette 33). Luis Álvarez-Castro has treated Unamuno's literary heroism ("El héroe"). A poetic expression of heroic individuality in Unamuno is the genius who turns into the concrete expression of the people's spirit and decisively contributes to a people's self-awareness. This is possible, within Unamuno's metaphysics, thanks to the workings of the "creative imagination" and its symbolic power (LaRubia-Prado, *Alegorías* 88–93). In *Paz en la guerra* ("Peace in War"), the hero is not individualized but embodied by the people, the *intrahistóricos*, which include the inhabitants of Bilbao, the soldiers in the liberal and *carlista* armies, and the Basque farmers. It is the novel of what Unamuno called, in "Humilde heroísmo," "los héroes del heroísmo vulgar, cotidiano, difuso" 'the heroes of the everyday, daily, spread heroism' (1: 80). Aside from this novel, however, heroes in Unamuno's fiction are strong individualities.

In Unamuno's play *La esfinge*, Romantic individualism asserts itself as a powerful presence. Its main character, Ángel, displays features that do not entirely correspond to either the archetypal hero, the ethical hero, or the antihero, as exemplified in Fyodor Dostoyevsky's *Notes from Underground*. Ángel, the leader of a revolutionary party, suddenly decides to turn inward, abandons the cause that he had promoted, and focuses exclusively on himself in search of a more meaningful personal existence. He realizes that he lives the life of an actor: "No hago más que representar un papel" 'I only play a role' (5: 153).[1] Ultimately, he perceives his life is nothing but theater without foundation. This stems from the absence of what Kant calls, in his *Critique of Practical Reason*, a heteronomous conscience: a conscience that follows principles emanating outside itself, such as "divine commands" (60, 156). Instead, and despite his own wishes, he possesses an autonomous conscience—a self-determined one—which makes him feel divided, separated from an original and primordial innocence that he is desperate to recover. This situation causes Ángel acute anguish (5: 163) and self-pity (5: 169), prompting him to withdraw from the world in an attempt to become a child again (5: 189).

As a Romantic hero—a literary and cultural figure studied by Lilian Furst (55–67)—Ángel is at the center of the play. He takes over the scene with his long speeches about his own sentiments, relegating the other characters to mere spectators of his own psychodrama, not caring about anyone but himself: "Tengo que atender a mi salud. ¡Buscaos la vida!" 'I have to take care of my own health. You are on your own!' (5: 194). The only real freedom that matters to him is his own. Of the people's freedom, he declares, "¡Eso no es libertad!" 'That's not freedom!' (5: 190). Ángel rejects any possibility of finding existential meaning in action or a cause that transcends his own needs (5: 145–46). Consequently, he switches an ethos of service for an ethos where "the instincts and impulses of [his] heart" are supreme (Furst 56). Thus, he is neither the archetypal hero of Joseph Campbell's *The Hero with a Thousand Faces* nor a moral hero—one who performs beyond the call of duty, with great self-control, in situations in which others would not because of fear or concern for their self-preservation (Urmson 62). His "egocentric self-absorption" becomes what, in Furst's opinion about the Romantic hero, would make him represent the crucial turning point "from hero to anti-hero" (56).

Constantly facing nothingness—"esa nada, esa nada terrible que se me representa en cuanto cierro los ojos" 'That nothingness, that terrible nothingness that comes to me when I close my eyes' (5: 182)—Ángel finds his solution in inaction. He is also obsessed with sincerity, a typical trait of the Romantic hero (Furst 66–67): "Sinceridad, Eufemia, sinceridad!" 'Sincerity, Eufemia, sincerity!' (5: 151). His *Ichschmerz*, or dissatisfaction with the self, makes him become both a destructive force vis-à-vis his relationship with others as well as self-destructive. He ruins his relationship with all his friends, whom he sees as insincere, and he emotionally ill-treats his wife (5: 161) to the point that she feels compelled to abandon him, although her love for him makes her return when he is mortally wounded at the end of the play. Like many Romantic heroes, Ángel sees a return to nature and the love of a woman as part of his salvation, and he begs Eufemia to go to the country with him and embrace him as if he were her child (5: 195, 205, 218). The character's self-destructive drive and his desperate need to act, given his almost pathological indecisiveness, merge when he decides to immolate himself by provoking an angry crowd. When this happens, according to Furst, the hero of Romanticism is released "from the paralysis of his passivity" (63).

It is possible that the title of the play is ironic, as it presents a (self-)damaging androsphinx whose secret seems to be a mystery to both himself and those surrounding him, who all seem mystified as to the reasons for Ángel's behavior. However, and as is common in Romantic heroes, Ángel seems unable of any ironic distance regarding himself, although he is both self-conscious and self-reflective: "me paso la vida contemplándome, hecho teatro de mí mismo" 'I spend my life contemplating myself, performing a role' (5: 153). In the absence of self-irony, though, other characters let Ángel know what they think about him. Eufemia, for instance, accuses him of embracing "un egoísmo monstruoso" 'a dreadful selfishness' (5: 174). He also represents the "dissolution of values and forms" (Furst 67), as he rejects that life has an end in itself because "el universo no lo tiene" 'the universe does not have one' (5: 192).

Ángel's Romantic individualism—both heroic and antiheroic—has its antithesis in Don Manuel Bueno, the saint and hero in *San Manuel Bueno, mártir*. The two characters share features such as possessing an unhappy consciousness due to a fall into moral autonomy; both face a strong sense of nothingness; and both think about suicide. Their solution to their agonistic situation is, however, wholly divergent, as Don Manuel is determined to fully engage the world, the nonself, which the town of Valverde de Lucerna and its people embody. In *San Manuel,* Unamuno presents a powerful case for strong individualism, and the character is named both a saint and a hero. The novel includes the word *saint* thirty-three times (in a fifty-five-page novel), a sainthood that is also described as heroic (128).[2]

San Manuel portrays the case of a priest, Don Manuel Bueno, who devotes his life to helping his parishioners experience a joyful existence grounded on a heteronomous conscience, although he does not believe in immortality himself. Don Manuel's lack of faith causes constant agony in the priest, who continues ministering *as if* he still believed in God. From a moral philosophy perspective, a saint is the individual who "does actions beyond the limits of his duty, whether by control of contrary inclination and interest or without effort" (Urmson 62). First, Don Manuel's self-imposed behavior goes considerably beyond the code of duty of a priest, as he transcends what the *Código de derecho canónico* ("Code of Canon Law") establishes as the mission of a parish priest: to administer the sacraments and celebrate religious acts (358–82). Instead, Don Manuel believes that his main mission as Valverde de Lucerna's priest is to promote life and joy among his parishioners (127). In order to foster the joy of living, he promotes a "unitive" metaphysics of love (Abrams, *Natural* 431) that brings together parents and children and spouses, keeping his people as *one* (143). He also takes care of their material and emotional concerns (125–26). From an ethical perspective, though, Don Manuel's main supererogatory action, or moral action beyond the call of duty, is to carry alone the tormenting burden of what he believes is the human doom—a future of absolute nothingness after death—and its potentially devastating consequences on his people's lives. Indeed, it would be unwarranted to demand from a priest who does not believe in immortality to do what Don Manuel does while he remains a priest.

Second, Don Manuel's acts of supererogation are performed in situations where others would not do them "by control of contrary inclination and interest," including his rejection of a bright career within the Church to devote himself to his town (119). Lázaro, the person who knows the priest best, confirms Don Manuel's nonutilitarian goals (142). Of course, it is crucial to differentiate between a personal sense of finality and a utilitarian motivation, which is based on personal gain or the avoidance of unpleasantness. Don Manuel's motivations, I suggest, are not based on a utilitarian goal but on the fulfillment of his own being as prescribed by Aristotle (*Nicomachean Ethics*, bk. 1, ch. 1), Saint Thomas Aquinas (*Summa*, bk. 3, ch. 2), and Kant (*Critique of Judgment* 173) (LaRubia-Prado, "Sanctity" 221). Finally, Don Manuel shows an extraordinary amount of self-control, despite his agony, expressing that his life is "una especie de suicidio continuo, un combate contra el suicidio" 'a sort of continual suicide, a struggle against suicide' (147; 85). In order to promote joy and confidence, Don Manuel exercises great self-discipline, thus meeting moral philosophy's third condition in defining an individual as a saint.

But is he a hero as well? Pedro Cerezo Galán has described Don Manuel as a tragic hero. He sees a tragic conflict in the priest's lack of faith (*Las máscaras* 715). As a professor of classical Greek and a playwright, Unamuno makes Don Manuel's performance one that is deeply rooted in Greek classical culture. Indeed, the character accurately fits the characteristics of the most ancient Greek hero whose features have been methodically described and analyzed by Freud in *Totem and Taboo* (LaRubia-Prado, "Sanctity" 222–26). In the book, Freud discusses "the most ancient Greek tragedy," where there is "a company of individuals, named and dressed alike," who "surrounded a single figure, all hanging upon his words and deeds: they were the Chorus and the impersonator of the Hero. He was originally the only actor" (192–93).

In *San Manuel*, this actor is Don Manuel, and the chorus of figures "hanging upon his words and deeds" is his flock of parishioners, the *intrahistóricos*, the common people of Valverde de Lucerna. Over time, the ancient Greek tragedy adds a second actor to be the counterpart to the hero, a character that "split[s] off from him"—that is, from the hero's worldview (193). The second actor that figuratively separates from how Don Manuel sees existence is Lázaro Carballino, but, as Freud suggests, nothing between the hero and the chorus (Don Manuel and his people) changes when the second actor (Lázaro) appears on the scene (193). Lázaro is the traditional hero's friend to whom Fernando Savater refers in *La tarea del héroe* ("The Duty of the Hero"; 177). The hero, says Freud, "must suffer. To this day, that remains the essence of tragedy. He had to bear the burden of what was known as 'tragic guilt' [that] lay in rebellion against some divine or human authority" (193). Don Manuel's rebellion against a divine authority is the priest's lack of faith in the God that promises immortality.

In Greek mythology—among other mythologies—when a mortal sees the face of a god, the mortal dies. This is what happened, for instance, to Semele, when, at her request, Zeus showed himself to her in all his splendor. In Don Manuel's case, it is the exact opposite: when he sees the face of God, God dies for the priest. That is why Don Manuel does not want his people to see God's face: "que no le vea, pues, la cara a Dios este nuestro pueblo mientras viva, que después de muerto ya no hay cuidado, pues no verá nada" 'So don't let these people of ours see the face of God, as long as they live, but once they are dead don't worry, since then they won't see anything' (157; 95).

In *Totem and Taboo*, Freud describes a myth he created in which the primeval father, who had kept all the women for himself, is killed by his sons so that they can have access to the women. After this murder, the sons' shared guilt makes them create a law to prevent similar murderous acts from happening again. According to Freud, the brothers' guilt and the law that results from it form the pillars of civil society (176–79). Mutatis mutandis, Don Manuel executes the same kind of performance in Valverde de Lucerna. After he kills God, he fills that emptiness with foundational acts of his own in order to keep the cohesion of the community. Thus, he establishes the maternal institution of "La Santa Madre Iglesia de Valverde de Lucerna" 'Holy Mother Church of Valverde de Lucerna' (156; 93). In that church, Don Manuel is invested with different archetypal projections: that of the mother—"aquel varón matriarcal" 'that matriarchal man' (115; 95)—reminiscent of the Virgin Mary, as well as that of the earthly Christ, "nuestros dos Cristos, el de esta Tierra y el de esta aldea" 'our two Christs, that of this world and that of this village' (153; 91). Don Manuel is presented in *San Manuel* as the suffering figure discussed by Freud:

> But why had the Hero of tragedy to suffer? And what was the meaning of his "tragic guilt"? I will cut the discussion short and give a quick reply. He had to suffer because he was the primal father, the Hero of the great primeval tragedy which was being re-enacted with a tendentious twist; and the tragic guilt he had to take upon himself in order to relieve the Chorus from theirs. (193)

Don Manuel's suffering results, then, from throwing upon himself the tragic guilt of all humans—"la cruz del nacimiento" 'the cross of having been born' (130; 65)—so his people's lives can continue to be meaningful. His suffering is the sign of the demiurge, of Christ himself. Freud continues: "The crime which was thrown onto his shoulders, presumptuousness and rebelliousness against a great authority, was precisely the crime for which the members of the Chorus, the company of brothers, were responsible. Thus the tragic hero became . . . the redeemer of the Chorus" (193–94). If the tragic hero is "responsible for his own suffering" in the primeval Greek tragedy (Freud 194), Don Manuel throws upon himself the guilt of all of his people, redeeming the chorus from any guilt and the sin of birth, since "el delito mayor del hombre es haber nacido" 'our greatest sin is that of having been born' (154; 93). Don Manuel's sacrifice both frees his people from the crime committed at birth and prevents them from committing the crime that he himself has committed—that is, seeing the face of God with the eyes of their own intellect, which would certainly kill God, according to Don Manuel. Consequently, the priest's mission is to hide a crime already committed and to prevent a future crime from occurring. When the tragic hero dies, writes Freud, the chorus exhausts itself "with sympathy" (194), which is what happens before Don Manuel dies, when he "dio la bendición al pueblo, llorando las mujeres y los niños y no pocos hombres" 'gave his blessing to the village, while the women and children and not a few of the men wept' (158; 97).

Ángel's universe in *La esfinge* is that of an isolated individual centered on his own private obsessions. He represents a very real conflict for Unamuno—that of the human desire for coincidence and immortality—and yet he is shown in the text as a part disconnected from the whole (i.e., the community). Ángel displays the signs that make him the culturally hybrid figure of the Romantic hero—midway between the hero and the antihero. Within Unamuno's organic metaphysics, he is a mechanical figure whose solution to his crisis is ultimately false, as his only way to act to fill the vacuum of the nothingness he feels is the nothingness of death. According to Ouimette, Unamuno sees heroism as "the exceptional effort made by the individual to leave his mark upon society" (24). Using this notion, then, Ángel is certainly no hero, while Don Manuel turns out to be not just a hero but also a saint.

Don Manuel is in fact a true example of Unamunian heroic individuality, as he finds a communal, organic solution to his agonic pathos. The difference between Ángel and Don Manuel is clearly shown when they express their belief that existence has no purpose. Ángel, on the one hand, denies that life or the universe has an end in itself (5: 192), which leads him to a disengagement of self and nonself. Don Manuel, on the other hand, opts for a painful personal engagement with and protection of the nonself: "que [las personas] se consuelen de haber nacido, que vivan lo más contentos que puedan en la ilusión de que todo esto tiene una finalidad" 'let them console themselves for having been born, let them live as happy as they can in the illusion that all of this has a purpose' (151–52; 88–89). In the language of Savater, Don Manuel would be a hero because "el héroe es quien *quiere* y *puede*" 'the hero is he who *wants* [to accomplish something] and *can* [achieve it]' (168).

Ultimately, Ángel and Don Manuel are two ways in which protean Western individualism manifests itself in Unamuno's work. If Ángel becomes a halfway figure between the hero and the antihero, Don Manuel displays features attributable to the hero and the saint. Similarly, Ángel always remains bogged down by the conflict between his desire for the impossible dream to become a child again and his inability to be effective in any way. Don Manuel represents the powerful, agonistic individuality that projects itself effectively toward the outer world, even if his decision to conceal his truth to his people will always be questioned, since it is the result of his—to use Nietzsche's formulation—human, *all too human*, condition.

NOTES

[1] The text of *La esfinge* used in this essay is Manuel García Blanco's edition, included in *Obras completas*, published by Escelicer. All translations are mine.

[2] The text of *San Manuel Bueno, mártir* used in this essay is Mario J. Valdés's edition, published by Cátedra. All translations are by Paul Burns and Salvador Ortiz-Carboneres.

Of Love and Power: Teaching Unamuno's *Amor y pedagogía* to Undergraduates outside the Literary Major

Mark J. Mascia

A question that may arise for many college faculty teaching Miguel de Unamuno is whether his works, and in particular *Amor y pedagogía* ("Love and Pedagogy"), can be taught to undergraduates who are not involved in a strictly literary major. My answer is an emphatic yes. I chose this particular novel because it fit within a theme-based course of my own design, Love and Power in Spanish Literature. The learning environment at my institution is quite different from what one encounters in elite liberal arts colleges and universities or in doctoral programs. However, I have learned that it is just as possible to have a meaningful experience teaching Unamuno—and this less taught novel—to these students as it would be to anyone. In order to do so, instructors need to adjust their expectations and methods accordingly. This essay will show how I did just that in this course.

There are several observations I must make regarding our program and teaching environment. First, the Spanish major is the only foreign language major in our small department. The major involves thirty regular credits and a one-credit online senior portfolio project for assessment. In the major, only one class on literature is required. The rest of the credits are made up of culture and civilization classes, electives, and the foundational composition and grammar sequence. As a result, the major is not designed for the preparation of future doctoral candidates. Most of our students go on to careers in elementary or secondary education or are involved in other career paths with Spanish as a minor. Additionally, many of our students do not have prior experience reading complex literature in Spanish (or even in English); for some, this may be their first advanced course in Spanish after developing language skills. Many have not written analytical papers in Spanish before taking this course. Moreover, a large percentage of our students are first-generation college students and oftentimes do not have the cultural background of many PhD students or privileged undergraduates; instead, many resemble the undergraduates attending some state schools (including R1 universities such as flagship state schools) and other similar institutions. For some of them, this may even be the longest work they have ever read in any language. In some ways, reading Unamuno in the original Spanish is akin to the experience of many undergraduates reading Shakespeare in an English literature survey course. Without considering these factors—factors that characterize many of the nation's undergraduate programs—the instructor would be in error before teaching this work.

I should also note that many students do not choose to continue the study of literature after completion of this course or, for majors, upon graduating. A critical mass of my students is less interested in the texts per se than in completing the course and obtaining credit. In spite of all these factors, I have learned that it is still possible to teach this novel in the original Spanish to an audience like mine. In order to do so, the instructor must be empathetic and respectful of the students' backgrounds while maintaining a balance between achieving learning outcomes and helping students approach this text.

One of the first things the instructor must discuss is the social and cultural setting of Unamuno's Spain. Though the novel actually has two versions (the first one appeared in 1902 and the second one in 1934), Spain's place in the world and the author's place in his own environment need attention. I could not expect all of my students to know what the Spanish-American War and the Generation of 1898 were or about the rise of the urban middle class in Europe and the Americas during the 1800s. Bringing the students up to speed about the life and times of Unamuno and his characters is nearly as important as engaging in a close reading of the text itself, as is the fact that Unamuno wrote this novel within the context of nineteenth-century positivism. Once my expectations as a professor gave way to an understanding of what the students could be expected to know beforehand, I was able to undertake our journey.

To provide students with this background knowledge and to help them get ready to read this novel, there were several useful things that I did. One was to discuss the influence of positivism, a movement of which Unamuno was critical, and its legacy today. The obsession with raising a brilliant child (a theme central to an analysis of the novel) is nothing new, yet its roots are not always known prior to the students' engagement with the text. The novel is, after all, about an intellectual father's fixation with raising a genius son. The social stratification presented in the novel needs attention as well. Even simple phrases charged with discriminatory overtones merit explanation. See, for example, the beginning of chapter 12, when Clara harangues Apolodoro to attend Mass and show more outward religiosity in spite of his secularity. Here, she repeats, "Es que no te quiero judío" 'I don't want to see you Jewish' (133).[1] Students almost invariably do not know who Unamuno was or that he was actually a philosopher and the rector of the University of Salamanca. In explaining Unamuno's intimate knowledge of the world of intellectuals, the instructor will help students appreciate the novel. Plus, students do not immediately know that the section "Apuntes para un tratado de cocotología" ("Notes for a Treatise on Origami") at the end of the book was written to achieve a page count demanded by Unamuno's publisher (I do not require students to read this arcane addendum).

The next step is to begin a close reading of *Amor y pedagogía*. Though the quality of the language is not quite as challenging as, for example, baroque Spanish might be, at times the instructor might find it necessary to clarify at least some words or phrases. For many students, the experience could be doubly daunting if they are coming from a high school environment in which their teachers spoke mostly English. I chose to use the Alianza Editorial edition, edited by Julia Barella, because it has a helpful introduction and some explanatory notes, without there being too many notes to the point of distraction. The instructor can assign the relatively brief and manageable introduction if he or she so chooses. I also did not use any translations into English. Students were required to prepare themselves before each class by answering questions using the online program *Blackboard*, as the class had a discussion board for each week; they did this for a grade.

The course methodology merits some attention too. Love and Power in Spanish Literature was Peninsular but not confined to one time period. We began with the play *El médico de su honra* ("The Doctor of His Honor"), by Pedro Calderón de la Barca, in which the reader sees the relationship between love and the power of brutal social conventions leading to uxoricide. From the baroque, we moved to Romanticism and *Los amantes de Teruel* ("The Lovers from Teruel"), by Juan Eugenio Hartzenbusch. The topic there was the power of romantic love and its clash with the institution of marriage. Unamuno's novel was the third in line, as it deals with the power of love (both familial and romantic) conflicting with the power of, and obsession with, reason and the intellect. Then Federico García Lorca's play *Bodas de sangre* ("Blood Wedding") followed, focusing on the power of love and passion as its own theme, as well as some of his poetry (including "Llanto por Ignacio Sánchez Mejías" ["Lament for Ignacio Sánchez Mejías"; *Antología poética* 285–94], which treats the love of a close friend). Finally, we read the contemporary novelist Adelaida García Morales, whose novellas *El Sur* ("The South") and *Bene* treat women's perspectives on love and the power of the family, of the subconscious, and of bigotry and intolerance (against the Roma, as seen in *Bene*). My guiding principle behind developing the course was to show diverse works that treat multiple manifestations of love as well as those of power. This methodology can help attract and retain students in small programs who might want to choose a course that sounds interesting to them. I did not assign secondary sources, as I felt that they were unnecessary and would either overload the students or distract them from the work at hand.

The instructor must draw parallels between these texts and the students' own world, which I did in two ways. One was on a personal level, in which I helped students relate to individual characters. Another was on a more general level, in which the students drew parallels between their society and that of the characters. Although the Spain of 1902 (and of 1934) is not identical to the early twenty-first century, students could still find ideas to which they could relate. For example, one very easily observable theme is the obsession with educational success—more specifically, the obsessive focus on the intellect that Don Avito has for his son, Apolodoro (alternately called Luis by his mother, a name more familiar to students). Additionally, the ways in which affluent parents sometimes raise their children are not so far removed from the fictive world of Unamuno's novel; the concept of trophy children comes to mind. The ways in which some parents make decisions for and control their children, for the sake of what they believe to be their well-being, are as present in *Amor y pedagogía* as they are with today's helicopter parents. By making this often ignored text in undergraduate curricula appealing, the instructor is already well on the way to success.

I spent three weeks on this novel, and each third of the novel contains a plethora of subject matter to discuss. In the first reading (comprising the prologue through chapter 4), I encouraged the students to focus on Avito and his ideas. I solicited the students' reactions to this character and to how he approaches parental responsibility. Then I asked how the ideas of his time take hold in his self-reflective view as a father and whether these traits are visible in contemporary society. I also focused on relations between men and women, especially as it regards gender-based roles of parenting. Unamuno portrays Marina, the wife and mother, as not fully respected with equal status, but rather as a subordinate. My students must come to class ready to compare and contrast these ideas with today's ideas regarding parenthood and gender, as an analysis of the novel allows students to see how Unamuno judges restrictive gender roles. Though Avito's ideas are a product of bourgeois society and positivism in the nineteenth century, their legacy is still alive and well today. Unamuno willfully creates the somewhat pedantic Fulgencio as a tutor and mentor, and I asked the students whether Avito's plan to use him constitutes a proper way to raise a child. From this first reading, love and power are visible in the clout held by ideas and the fascination with the mind, along with the conflicting need to nurture a child's emotional development. Upon close reading, we see that Unamuno favors a balance involving the latter.

The second reading includes chapters 5 through 11, which contain many of the same ideas. I asked students to compare Avito's wishes for his son with some of today's parents' obsession with the goal of getting good grades, scoring high on standardized tests, and earning admittance to a selective college. The consumerist mentality of a student's paying tuition dollars for high grades and of parents' wanting a return on investment is a parallel worth discussing. This helps make the novel relevant to the students' own world. Apolodoro's emotional development as he matures and eventually falls in love with Clarita is a very relatable topic; instructors should connect an understanding of the text to the affective experiences of their students. Throughout this reading, Unamuno clearly shows how the neglect of a child's emotional development can damage him or her later in life. Additionally, it is always useful for instructors to draw on the other intellectual strengths of their students. For example, a student who is a double major in psychology and Spanish can use theories of personality or other knowledge acquired in the psychology program to discuss the characters.

The final reading comprises chapter 12 through the epilogue, excluding the "Notes for a Treatise on Origami" and the appendix. Students were asked to discuss whether Apolodoro really is a failure in balancing emotions and intellect, beyond trying to woo Clarita. Unamuno might instead place much of the blame on his father, Avito, as the author makes a statement regarding how intellectuals are in some way responsible for creating this environment. The sad and untimely deaths of both of Avito's children—the younger Rosa, by natural causes, and Apolodoro, by suicide—though never pleasant, should be discussed. The instructor might ask students whether they can see contemporary examples of parents pushing their children excessively. Unamuno shows that Avito has not learned from his mistakes, and I asked students whether the author is alternately presenting us with a cautionary tale, a parody of intellectuals, or something else entirely. After reading the text, the first two would be the logical conclusions. Perhaps the most open-ended and enigmatic phrase worthy of attention is "El amor había vencido" 'Love had won' (163), appearing as the last line before the epilogue. All of my students must bring ideas to the final class for paper writing.

I must make one final set of observations, regarding the use of online learning platforms. I require one posting of substance per week in a discussion group in *Blackboard*. I have learned that it makes students stay on task with their reading and arrive prepared to analyze the novel. For this novel, each of the three readings featured approximately a dozen separate questions and ideas for students to react to in *Blackboard* and to use as in-class discussion material; they could respond to one of them or come up with a subtopic of their own. Given the technological skills of today's students, the instructor should consider using programs like *Blackboard* or other tools such as blogs to help the students understand Unamuno. When one considers instructional technology like this, along with the need to establish connections between the novel and today's society, one will help the students learn and reduce anxiety in approaching Unamuno. In so doing, and in promoting any course like this, instructors would also allay the concerns of chairpersons or administrators who are more heavily focused on enrollments and course cancellations.

In sum, if the instructor uses methods such as the ones outlined in this essay, the experience of teaching *Amor y pedagogía* will be just as rewarding in a nonliterary undergraduate environment as it would be in any other. At the same time, it might help instructors to include it in a course that is more theme based and not a survey course. Other course ideas might include related themes or key words, such as "hearts and minds" or "the family in Spanish literature." Seeing how far students have come after reading this novel (to say nothing of the other texts in the course) and how they develop their skills in Spanish has been phenomenal; seeing how they can connect Unamuno's imagined world to their own is just as memorable. As long as the instructor factors empathy into his or her teaching, and as long as one realizes that literature was meant to be felt and not just analyzed, it is well worth teaching this novel and it is always an enjoyable experience.

NOTES

I would like to thank Kristen Ziemer for her inspiration, thoughtfulness, and insight in my writing of this essay.

[1] This essay uses Julia Barella's edition of *Amor y pedagogía*, published by Alianza. All the translations are mine.

Trains, Time, and Technology: Teaching "Mecanópolis" through Mobility and Science Fiction Studies

Benjamin Fraser

Given Miguel de Unamuno's well-deserved recognition as both a novelist and philosopher, canonical treatments seldom shine sufficient light on the short stories he wrote. It is much more common for such studies to highlight his novels and nonfiction. And yet the philosophical schisms expressed throughout the pages of the prolific writer's nonfiction essays and long-form narrative are present, nonetheless, even in his most concise literary products. The short story titled "Mecanópolis," in particular, has not received the attention it merits; moreover, it is of particular interest to engagements between Hispanic studies and contemporary interdisciplinary formations.

The story begins with a narrative-framing device—or said another way, an opening parenthesis—in which an unnamed narrator introduces the story related by a friend. What follows is a first-person account, related secondhand to readers by the narrator, of that friend's visit to "la ciudad de las máquinas" 'the city of the machines' (102).[1] This opening parenthesis is minimal; it seems designed to introduce, in distilled form, the figure of the narrator as a construction of the author, so often a prompt for addressing Unamuno's characteristic folds between truth and fiction, the individual and the multitude, intrahistory and national history. The embedded story that follows can be summarized in this way: its protagonist is lost in a desert—thirsty and close to collapse, not to mention death—when he sees an oasis. After much effort, he finally reaches the oasis, drinks from a spring, eats fruit from the trees, and promptly falls asleep. Upon waking, he sees a train station nearby and boards a car on the empty train, which is smoking and ready for departure. He is swiftly carried to a strange town where everything is automated.

This strange town is the titular Mecanópolis, which boasts not a single living thing. And yet its hotel kitchen serves food at the push of a button (103), empty trams and cars move through the streets of their own volition (103), instruments play themselves in a grand concert hall (104), and the print newspaper *El Eco de Mecanópolis* publishes and distributes itself, seemingly without the direction of a single human being. After days of this eerie solitude in a city of machines, the protagonist becomes overwhelmed and distraught, ultimately throwing himself in front of an electric streetcar (105). Immediately after this event, one whose consequences presumably would have been fatal, the traveler wakes up in that very oasis from which he had originally departed. He spends the night staring at the stars with a group of Bedouins, and, revitalized by human contact, he turns hateful of machines (105).

This essay explores "Mecanópolis" at once through two contemporary interdisciplinary formations. From the perspective of science fiction studies, the story presents elements that, functioning as references to the genre's evolution, fork in two directions. Whether we look backward to Washington Irving's "Rip Van Winkle" or forward to Alejandro Amenábar's internationally resonating film *Abre los ojos* ("Open Your Eyes"), the theme of fantasy versus reality that pervades Unamuno's short story provides a low barrier of entry for a generation of students highly conversant in the intertextual connections boasted by popular culture and film.[2] Moreover, the easy identification of this general theme with the early-seventeenth-century works of Miguel de Cervantes and Pedro Calderón de la Barca also allows instructors of Unamuno's short story to pique student interest in more canonical literature from the Iberian Peninsula.

Although instructors may be less familiar with the emerging interdisciplinary area of transportation and mobility studies, concerns central to that field are a driving force in "Mecanópolis."[3] Unamuno's story channels for readers fears about what the train represented symbolically, economically, and socially throughout the second half of the nineteenth century.[4] Simultaneously these fears are indicative of the nuanced links between technological advance and social progress that surface as a generalized theme in literature of the contemporary period. These links are, of course, essential preoccupations of the utopian and dystopian modes of the genre of science fiction. Neither aspect of these fears—neither their general resonance nor their concrete manifestation in a specific mode of transportation—can be disentangled from the other. Nevertheless, because the train appears prior to a full description of the automated town in the story, it is appropriate to begin with the transportation and mobility studies perspective and transition to the science fiction studies perspective.

Transportation and Mobility Studies

Although the appearance of the train in "Mecanópolis" is brief, it is nevertheless significant, central to the narrative, and echoed in the automation pervasive to the fictional city Unamuno has created. Noted transportation scholar Wolfgang Schivelbusch, in his canonical and philosophical book *The Railway Journey: The Industrialization of Time and Space in the Nineteenth Century*, drew attention to what he called the "Machine Ensemble" of the railroad: "The machine character of the railroad was dual: first, the steam engine (locomotive) generated uniform mechanical motion; secondly, that motion was transformed into movement through space by the combined machinery of wheel and rail" (20). This layered mechanization recapitulated the "detachment from nature initiated by the discovery of steam power," severing passengers from the natural landscape through which the train passed. It is important to note that the railroad's machine ensemble not only "interjected itself between the traveler and the landscape" (24) but also foregrounded the process of alienation experienced by travelers through telegraph poles and wires, which served as visible anchors of "the loss of a communicative relationship between man and nature" (11).

But train passengers were not only alienated from the landscape; they were also alienated from each other owing to the way in which experiences of social class figured into even the earliest train car designs (71–72). Moreover, in their passivity they became what Schivelbusch called "the object of an industrial process" (73)—human beings subjected to the same industrial forces as commodities and simultaneously carried along by those industrial forces. Alan Trachtenberg explains, in the foreword to Schivelbusch's text, "Personal travel by railroad inevitably (if unconsciously) assimilated the personal traveller into a physical system for moving goods. . . . It was a decisive mode of integration of people into their new status within the system of commodity production" (xiv). The speed of train travel was itself experienced by passengers as vertiginous and disorienting, a sign of the dehumanizing and industrial forces inducing a great transformation of nineteenth-century social life as well as the related upheavals characteristic of urban modernity (Berman).

The train in "Mecanópolis" functions as both a literal vehicle and a literary vehicle—ultimately it is a narrative device that delivers the story to an oneiric mode.[5] Having apparently awoken from a slumber at the oasis he has found in the desert, the protagonist spies a train and climbs on board (103). He experiences a horrible vertigo during travel. While the sense of awe experienced by the traveler upon exiting the train and entering the station might be seen in terms of traditional and overemphasized claims that Spain experienced an insufficient Enlightenment, a transportation and mobility approach suggests a different perspective.

Schivelbusch's account makes clear that train stations were located in oft-denigrated industrial areas of the city and served as gateways designed to connect city space and the railroad. Leaving town, the traveler gradually "experienced a process of expansion of space" and the station "prepared him for the industrial space of the railroad"; arriving at a destination, the "traveler experienced a process of spatial reduction" (174). Moving from the railroad through the liminal space of the station and into the city, however, Unamuno's arriving passenger does not experience any sort of perceptual spatial reduction. Instead, the sense of simultaneous estrangement and wonder he has endured over the "limitless space through which the train wheels have been carrying him for miles and miles" (Lucae, qtd. in Schivelbusch 175) is transposed first onto the station's grandeur and second onto the city's urban environment. As the unnamed traveler wanders through this urban sensorium, he experiences the sights and sounds of the new city with the same vertiginous wonder, awe, and even fear that characterized his experience of the railroad (103). The repetition of words expressing these feelings carries through the prose in its descriptions of a building, a control panel, and a park (103). In the Museo de Pintura, for example, each work of art is accompanied by "una doctísima explicación de su valor histórico y estético, hecha con la más exquisita sobriedad" 'a most learned explanation of its historical and aesthetic value, constructed with the most exquisite moderation' (104).

The transposition of this sense of awe from the train to the city is not that surprising once contemporary readers are reminded of the material, historical links between the two. The urban historian Lewis Mumford explores what he calls the paleotechnic city of the nineteenth century in *The City in History*, noting how the "generating agents of the new city were the mine, the factory and the railroad" (446) and the "main elements in the new urban complex were the factory, the railroad and the slum" (458). In "Mecanópolis," the saturation of the urban phenomenon by mechanization is necessarily a comment on the increased presence of industrial activity in and surrounding cities. Yet the city's automation has another meaning as well. Given that, as Mumford explains, "The factory became the nucleus of the new urban organism" (458), the city's mechanization also becomes a metaphor for the less tangible and more broadly social shifts in a nineteenth-century urban form that was now produced in the image of organized industrial production. That these wider social shifts owe their genesis to the railroad should not come as a surprise for the story's readers. But more important, there is a specifically spatial dimension to these social shifts. As Schivelbusch notes, train travel gave birth to a new paradigm in which "[m]otion was no longer dependent on the conditions of natural space, but on a mechanical power that created its own new spatiality" (10). A fully automated city, Mecanópolis carries the mechanical force inherent in the railroad to its logical conclusion by producing an entirely novel spatial environment.

In short, the significance of train travel in Unamuno's short story goes beyond what the brevity of its appearance would suggest. A transportation and mobility approach has the value of recovering the basic cultural associations that train travel would have had for early-twentieth-century readers of "Mecanópolis," reflecting the train as a multivalent signifier of progress and its price, as well as the traveler's experience of the shock, awe, anxiety, and wonder that accompanied the travel experience. But it also pushes contemporary readers to begin to think through the foundational links between the mechanized logic of the railroad and the spatial revolutions of urban modernity (Berman; Lefebvre).

Science Fiction Studies

As evident in the previous section, there is a certain form of literary realism reflected in the mechanized city of Mecanópolis. That is, in an immediate way the story documents the extent to which nineteenth-century society was affected by the railroad, understood as a technology. In one sense, the train was an agent of material change, bringing with it a new set of social, cultural, and economic relationships. In another sense, the train was itself a product of that same set of changing relationships, which was characterized by the production of a new spatial environment around organized mechanization. In this context, Fredric Jameson's assertion that science fiction is a spatial genre—that is, that "the distinctiveness of SF [science fiction] as a genre has less to do with time (history, past, future) than with space" (58)—provides a bridge with the transportation and mobility perspective. But at the same time that Unamuno's story reflects the cultural and spatial textures of an era of increased industrialization, it also moves into the terrain of utopian-dystopian science fiction and thus, ultimately, into consideration of the philosophical schisms that structure his other works. Despite the emphasis on the technological aspects of Mecanópolis, the philosophical and necessarily social emphasis of this story confirms Santoro Domingo's view that "[i]n the Spanish sf field, the scientific dimension of the genre is not widespread and, in any case, sf's potential for social extrapolation is more likely to be valued than its strictly scientific or technical potential" (327). In the end, "Mecanópolis" employs the dualistic nature of technological progress as a prompt to consider the more philosophical contradictions at the center of the human condition.

The philosophical core of Unamuno's story is tied to a terrifying science fiction–style insight that is revealed after the reader has moved through the social and technological descriptions of the city of Mecanópolis. While the more spectacular climax of the story may be the moment in which the traveler throws himself in front of an electric streetcar in the penultimate paragraph (105), there is a subtle but decisive turning point that occurs somewhat earlier. As the traveler explores the magnificent and automated city, there comes a key moment when his sense of awe and wonder turns to terror. Reading a posted sign, he realizes that the Museo de Pintura is considered to be part of the Museo Paleontológico (104). From this point on, the narration considers places in the city in succession—a music hall, libraries, and the Gran Teatro—without any of the amazement conveyed in previous passages. The traveler's recognition that human beings are now extinct, supplanted by machines, induces in him an enduring state of estrangement and horror, one whose meaning is only heightened by the banality of the city's everyday operations. As if driving this point home, when he reads of his own arrival to the city in its fully automated paper, *El Eco de Mecanópolis*, the harrowing thought that he has been under constant surveillance is juxtaposed with his sight of a minor misspelling ("nuestra ciuded" 'our citi') that effectively attributes to machines the disturbing possibility of committing a simple human error (104).

From this point on, the traveler becomes heavily depressed, suspecting he is sick or insane, and he comes to believe that "todas aquellas máquinas, aquellos edificios, aquellas fábricas, aquellos artefactos, eran regidos por almas invisibles, intangibles y silenciosas" 'all those machines, those buildings, those factories, those artifacts, were controlled by invisible, intangible and silent souls' (104). One day he wakes up terrified and once again reads about himself in the city's seemingly all-knowing automated newspaper (105). The thought that shakes him to the core and ultimately drives him to commit suicide by throwing himself in front of a streetcar is revealed in this singular instant of terror: the acknowledgment that "las máquinas tuvieran su alma, un alma mecánica" 'the machines possessed a soul, a mechanical soul' (105). Instead of dying, however, he suddenly wakes up in the same oasis where he had been before. What comes next is a life-affirming encounter with Bedouins that constitutes the story's brief dénouement, which is confined to the penultimate paragraph.

Crying, the protagonist hugs one of the Bedouins and experiences a form of understanding that transcends language. Most significant, during a single night of food, prayer, and lavish celebration—of human contact and emotion that were absent from the automated city—the unnamed traveler notes the absence of machines (105). This dénouement serves as a minimalistic but clear contrast with the exposition of Mecanópolis, and the traveler's final reunion with human beings expresses the core philosophical insights of Unamuno's work more broadly. This return to humanity can be seen in a simple sense as a figurative return to the material reality of the "hombre de carne y hueso" 'man of flesh and bone' (*Obras completas* [García Blanco] 7: 109; my trans.) and thus to the foundational role played by immediate experience in Unamuno's practical (and Bergsonian) philosophy.[6] The story's operative dichotomy between flesh and machine recapitulates the complex dualities of faith and reason, life and knowledge, and ultimately body and soul that run throughout Unamuno's philosophical texts such as *Del sentimiento trágico de la vida* ("On the Tragic Sense of Life") and philosophical novels such as *Amor y pedagogía* ("Love and Pedagogy").

Yet while the concluding words of "Mecanópolis" underscore the protagonist's newly developed hatred of progress, they also ring somewhat hollow in the context of Unamuno's overall work. Progress here has both a narrow and a broad meaning; it is easily equated both with technology and machines in the simple sense, but also suggests the rise of the industrial city and even, at a more conceptual level, the "machine ensemble" that characterized new forms of nineteenth-century urban spatiality. But the protagonist's concomitant rejection of culture and his facile idealization of a land untouched by progress mark him as a familiar Unamunian tragic figure, unable to hold the dualisms implicated in the story in balance.[7]

This notion of imbalance is reflected too in the story's tilted structural composition. Not without significance, the narrative parenthesis opened in the story's initial paragraphs is never closed—that is, the prose never returns from the traveler's embedded story to the framing voice of the unnamed narrator who introduced it. As a consequence, Unamuno's readers remain immersed in this contradictory philosophical terrain, feeling the pull between narrative and truth, faith and reason, the body and the soul. In "Mecanópolis," narrative is introduced as a creation, its creator is rendered invisible and set at a distance, and readers are left in limbo without a clear view of the narrator who set things in motion. This situation prompts readers to confront all the philosophical and existential contradictions we hail as uniquely Unamunian.

NOTES

[1] The text of "Mecanópolis" used in this essay is Eleanor Krane Paucker's edition, included in *Relatos de Unamuno*. English translations are mine.

[2] Both of these examples boast connections between anglophone fiction and the Hispanic world. Consider the story "Rip-Rip el aparecido," by the practitioner of *modernismo* Manuel Gutiérrez Nájera, or, for that matter, the remake of Amenábar's film as *Vanilla Sky* in 2001.

[3] For a concise introduction to mobility studies, see Hannam et al.; Cresswell; and Urry. On the intersections between train transportation and traditionally literary fields, see Misemer; Spalding and Fraser; and Fraser, "Urban Railways." Latham and McCormick's article convincingly ties together mobility studies and urban studies.

[4] Another story that might be taught in tandem with "Mecanópolis" is Pío Baroja's "Lo desconocido" ("The Unknown"), which also involves the train as a setting conveying a sense of alienation.

[5] The train as a vehicle of the oneiric mode appears as well in a canonical example of Spanish cinema, Víctor Erice's *El espíritu de la colmena* ("The Spirit of the Beehive").

[6] See Fiddian; Fraser, *Encounters* and "Unamuno."

[7] Consider here Ferrater Mora's discussion where he explores Unamuno's nuanced approach to the concept of humanity (28–29). Other areas for study include insights into the author's complex views on science (Eoff 187; Unamuno, "Cientificismo") and truth (Unamuno, "Verdad y vida").

Unamuno's Metafiction: *Niebla* as a Deviation from Convention

Craig N. Bergeson

Reading Miguel de Unamuno's fiction can be a daunting task, in part because much of it "dispenses almost entirely with the norms of the nineteenth-century realistic novel" (Ziolkowski x). As a result, readers may not know how to frame their reading, because they do not know what to expect. One of Unamuno's most famous works of fiction, *Niebla* ("Mist"), deviates from particular fictional conventions, reflecting some of its dominant themes, such as the ambivalent nature of human existence and the nebulous relation between reality and fiction; the work's deviation from convention can influence readers' reception of its themes. Consequently, a fruitful approach to teaching *Niebla* is to help students discover some of its deviations from fictional conventions and then determine how those deviations might affect the reader and how they relate to its most important themes.

I use this approach in my Modern Spanish Literature course, taught in Spanish, in which we begin with Leandro Fernández de Moratín's *El sí de las niñas* ("The Maidens' Consent") and continue with Benito Pérez Galdós's *Doña Perfecta* ("Mrs. Perfect"). We then move to selections from Gustavo Adolfo Bécquer's poetry and short stories and to Antonio Machado's poetry, which elicits a study of Hispanic modernity and is therefore a good segue into the study of Unamuno's *Niebla*, because it is in part Unamuno's participation in modernity that leads him to break with literary tradition and convention. I present Hispanic modernity as a reaction to a crisis of faith (Onís, "Sobre el concepto" 42), and after I show various examples of modernity—such as poetry by Machado, paintings by Joaquín Sorolla, and architecture by Antoni Gaudí—students are able to see Unamuno's disregard for conventions of nineteenth-century realism as a reaction to this modern crisis.

One way Unamuno disregards these conventions in *Niebla* is by violating supposed boundaries between author, text, and reader. For instance, a character from the novel writes the prologue, and therein he disputes Unamuno's version of the story's ending; that same character describes a new genre he is creating, which he calls a *nivola* and which is strikingly similar to the novel we are reading. Unamuno then invades the fictional text to comment about his own characters, and, in the most famous violation of fictional boundaries in *Niebla*, the protagonist, Augusto Pérez, has a face-to-face conversation with Unamuno. As we study these boundary violations in detail, we see that they each constitute a break with nineteenth-century realism, in which boundaries between author, text, and reader are generally respected.

Before students begin reading *Niebla*, I help them establish a framework for their reading. I begin this process by introducing them to Unamuno's life and works, especially mentioning his very personal crisis of faith (Rabaté and Rabaté, *Miguel de Unamuno* 159–80), related to his quest for immortality. I then ask students to look for evidence of that quest in *Niebla*, which helps students continue to build a framework for their reading. I also assign reading questions that they answer online before coming to class. The first few questions involve *Niebla*'s title. What might it mean? What images does it evoke? In their answers, and later during our class discussions, students often point out that a *niebla* distorts our vision to the point where nothing is clear or well-defined and that this fog or mist may cause us to think we see what is not really there and to not see what *is* there. I then ask students what this title might mean for our reading of this novel, and they usually reply that the title probably implies that the meaning of the novel will be blurry, or unclear, and that we should therefore read very carefully and be slow to make assumptions.

Keeping in mind the implications of the title, we begin to discuss the prologue and post-prologue. Many students struggle with the prologue because in it the prologist, Víctor Goti, wanders from one literary or philosophical concept to the next, making it difficult to extract what might be his main idea. The reading questions should help students overcome this difficulty by providing more framework and, therefore, more focus for their reading. For example, students will have been asked to consider the possible effect of the prologue and the post-prologue on the reader, specifically, the effect of a prologue written by one of the characters in the novel, who questions the truthfulness of the ending of the story as written by the author, and a post-prologue written by the author, who responds to the prologue and thereby engages in a dialogue with the fictional character. The questions offer the students hints, such as letting them know that Víctor Goti is a fictional character in *Niebla*.

After briefly discussing their answers to the questions, I introduce the students to the concept of metafiction, particularly as explained by Robert Spires in *Beyond the Metafictional Mode*, in which he suggests that narrative fiction, or the fictional mode, consists of three separate and distinct spheres of existence—those of the author, the text, and the reader—and explains that the metafictional mode results when an element from one of these spheres invades one of the other spheres, thereby blurring the boundaries between author, text, and reader (15–16). For Spires, a particular literary mode can be found in works of distinct sociohistorical and geographical contexts because, unlike a genre, a mode is not diachronic but rather synchronic (4). The metafictional mode is thus different from what Spires calls the metafictional movement, largely of the 1960s and 1970s (16), which incorporates the mode within a particular context. In most of my courses, and in this essay, the term *metafiction* refers to this metafictional mode and not to a particular movement that incorporates the metafictional mode.

In order to show students examples of the metafictional mode, I use clips from two films: *The Purple Rose of Cairo*, directed by Woody Allen, and *Stranger Than Fiction*, by Marc Forster. In the clip from *The Purple Rose of Cairo*, Jeff

Daniels's character steps out of the movie that Mia Farrow's character is watching and joins her in the "real" world; in the clips from *Stranger Than Fiction*, Will Ferrell's character discovers that he is the protagonist of a novel currently being written and that he will probably die at the end of the novel, which is why, in a scene similar to Augusto's interview with Unamuno, he meets with the author and asks her to spare his life. Students will recognize that conventional boundaries are breached in both films: in one, a character from the realm of fiction invades the realm of the spectator, and in the other, a character from the realm of fiction invades the realm of the author. When I ask students about the possible effect of these breaches of conventional boundaries, they point out that in both cases everything has become fiction, that the supposed boundaries between fiction and reality have disappeared, an idea we will return to later in our discussion of *Niebla*.

After being introduced to metafiction and seeing examples of it in film, students are asked to identify elements of metafiction in the prologue and post-prologue. They soon point out that when a character in the novel writes the prologue and then questions the novel's conclusion, as written by the author, the fictional character, from the sphere of the text, has invaded the sphere of the author, and that when, in the post-prologue, the author in turn questions the authority of the fictional character to question him, the author has invaded the sphere of the text. In other words, it appears that the character has become part of the author's "real" world and the author has become part of the character's "fictional" world. After students point out these metafictional boundary violations, I help them discover the effects of these violations by introducing them to Patricia Waugh's account of metafiction:

> *Metafiction* is a term given to fictional writing which self-consciously and systematically draws attention to its status as artefact in order to pose questions about the relationship between fiction and reality. In providing a critique of their own methods of construction, such writings not only examine the fundamental structures of narrative fiction, they also explore the possible fictionality of the world outside the literary fictional text. (60)

I then ask students to apply this definition to the prologue and post-prologue of *Niebla*, and, with a little prodding, they respond by pointing out that the elements of metafiction in the prologues show us that in *Niebla* Unamuno is questioning the supposed differences between his world and that of his characters, thereby questioning reality—Víctor's, his, and ours. When I then ask how this existential ambivalence might affect our reading of *Niebla*, students usually suggest that it may cause us to question the apparent reality or fiction of what we are reading, the man who wrote it, and those who read it, such as ourselves. Students then look for examples of Augusto or of someone else questioning his existence as they read the novel. They notice that Augusto implies that he doesn't really exist until he falls in love with Eugenia—that is, the image of

Eugenia he creates in his mind. In other words, he doesn't exist until he creates something or someone. His act of becoming the author of another's existence makes him feel alive. Yet, many times throughout the novel he continues to question his existence—that is, his reality.

As the students and I discuss *Niebla* over the next few weeks, they notice more examples of metafiction. For example, at one point in the novel, Víctor Goti tells Augusto about a novel he is writing, which he eventually calls a *nivola*. Once again, students come to class having answered reading questions. This time they are asked what Víctor's *nivola* has to do with the novel they are reading and how the discussion of the *nivola* in the novel might be considered metafiction. The students usually point out that when Víctor explains that the *nivola* is light on action and heavy on dialogue and that it is plotless, or that the plot and the characters create themselves (175–77), we should realize that the novel we are reading fits this description almost perfectly; therefore, Víctor is describing the book we are reading. In this case Víctor has not crossed from one sphere of reality to another; nevertheless, he has shown again, like he did indirectly in the prologue, that *Niebla* is literature about literature—in other words, metafiction. The effect of this instance of metafiction is that of a house of mirrors, in that one reflection (or fiction) reflects another, which reflects another, ad infinitum, making it almost impossible to determine whose story (Augusto's, Víctor's, Unamuno's, etc.), if any, is real; hence, it is as if we as readers are wandering aimlessly in a *niebla*, as is suggested in the title.

Another obvious example of metafiction occurs at the end of chapter 25, when Unamuno inserts the following comment: "Mientras Augusto y Víctor sostenían esta conversación *nivolesca*, yo, el autor de esta *nivola*, que tienes, lector, en la mano, y estás leyendo, me sonreía enigmáticamente al ver que mis *nivolescos* personajes estaban abogando por mí y justificando mis procedimientos" 'While Augusto and Victor were carrying on this "nivolistic" conversation, I, the author of this *nivola*, which you, my dear reader, are holding in your hand and reading—I was smiling enigmatically at the sight of my "nivolistic" characters advocating my case and justifying my methods of procedure' (228; 252).[1] Therefore, once again, the author has violated conventional boundaries of fiction. This time he appears to have entered both the world of his fictional characters as well as that of his readers; however, by addressing the readers within the fictional text, he has fictionalized them. That is, we as readers have become part of Augusto's fictional world and therefore cannot be certain of what has happened or will happen.

Of course, the most famous element of metafiction in *Niebla* is the interview between Augusto Pérez and Miguel de Unamuno. By the time we get to this point in the novel, students have seen several examples of fictional boundary violations, and I have warned them about this interview, so they are somewhat ready for the fantastic dialogue between an author and his character, which means that in class I don't have to explain what happens in this chapter. Instead, we can spend time discussing what this apparently absurd conversation may mean for the reader. During the discussion, students often focus on what Augusto says to

Unamuno after being told that he does not exist because he is just a figment of Unamuno's imagination:

> Mire usted bien, don Miguel . . . , no sea que esté usted equivocado y que ocurra precisamente todo lo contrario de lo que usted se cree y me dice. [. . .] [Q]ue sea usted y no yo el ente de ficción, el que no existe en realidad, ni vivo ni muerto . . . No sea que usted no pase de ser un pretexto para que mi historia llegue al mundo . . . (255)

> Listen to me, Don Miguel—it can't be that you are mistaken, and that what is happening is precisely the contrary of what you think and of what you have told me? . . . [T]hat it is you and not I who are the fictitious entity, the one that does not really exist, who is neither living nor dead? May it not be that you are nothing but a pretext for bringing my history into the world? (294–95)

Students mention that we see clearly in this episode that Unamuno and Augusto pertain to the same sphere; they are both fictions, one no more real than the other. They also mention that, according to Augusto, we as readers are also fictitious, in that we exist in the same plane of (fictitious) reality as Augusto and Unamuno (261). In other words, just as the metafictional nature of this novel has led Unamuno to question his existence, it may have led his readers to question their existence as well.

Later, as we discuss the conclusion of *Niebla*, I ask the students to share their opinions regarding Augusto's death: whether he died because Unamuno, as the author, wrote his death into the end of the story or whether Augusto committed suicide and Unamuno merely recorded the event. I then tell them that, according to one critic, if they say that Unamuno caused Augusto's death, they are admitting that *Niebla* has failed as an organic novel, or *nivola*, in which the characters create themselves through their own actions, which the author merely records on the paper. If, on the other hand, they say that Augusto did indeed commit suicide, they are saying that Unamuno was successful—that the plot and the characters created themselves (LaRubia-Prado, "Deconstrucción" 120). Most students feel that Augusto did indeed commit suicide, perhaps because the framing of their reading of a book that abandons fictional conventions through metafictional violations of those conventions helps them see new possibilities for the relationship between fiction and reality and between creation and creator.

By the time we finish our discussion of *Niebla*, the students have learned to read more judiciously. Reading *Niebla* as a work of metafiction has caused them to question almost every affirmation made by the author and his characters, which in turn may lead them to question their role as readers. For example, whereas they approached the realist novel *Doña Perfecta* from outside the text, the metafiction in *Niebla* has placed them inside the text, which strongly influences their interpretation of it because they are now on the same ontological plane as

Augusto and Unamuno, and as both Augusto and Unamuno question the nature of their existence, the students may now do the same. Therefore, framing *Niebla* as a work that deviates from fictional convention through metafiction helps students experience doubt and confusion in much the same way Augusto and Unamuno experience them, thereby allowing students to better sympathize with the protagonist and the author and thus enjoy an enriched reading experience. My hope is that they feel the existential angst of both Augusto and Unamuno, which in turn may allow them to begin to understand that angst in a way that may not have been possible had Unamuno attempted to write *Niebla* as a conventional nineteenth-century realist novel.

NOTE

[1] The text of *Niebla* used in this essay is Mario J. Valdés's edition, published by Cátedra. English translations are by Warner Fite (U of Illinois P edition).

Teaching Unamuno's Novels: Confrontation and Existence

Juan Herrero-Senés

Miguel de Unamuno is undoubtedly one of the key authors of Spanish modernism, but his work is not easily addressed. This is due to the quantity and variety of his production, which spans more than forty years in all genres, and especially to the difficulty of condensing Unamuno's thought into any type of system or sustained formulation. From that standpoint, Unamuno should be treated pedagogically as an author who escapes classification and who, throughout his career, understood both his life and his writing (deeply intertwined) as a quest, in the sense of both an investigation and a search.

This essay proposes an approach to teaching Unamuno from this idea of quest and through two vectors of interpretation: confrontation and existence. The two notions are equivalent in some sense, because for Unamuno existence is a constant struggle against the prejudices, misunderstandings, ignorance, and evil we encounter. Throughout life, we face multiple contradictions or tensions: between what we want and what we need, what we believe and what we do, what is right and what is wrong, and so on. These are not to be put aside (through laziness or ingenuity) but lived and experienced, as they cannot be solved, and they ultimately make what we are. In addition, confrontation and existence are for Unamuno essentially performative; that is, life is built and acquires meaning through actions. There is no prior meaning to be found. Meaning is produced, performed, in the quest—that is, in everyday existence and the reflection on it. The opposite of action is not thinking but domestication and conventionalism. This interpretation implies that Unamuno's texts seek primarily to compel readers to confront the construction of their own existence: think about how you live, what you believe in, and the purpose of your actions.

I will focus on two of Unamuno's most acclaimed narratives, written more than twenty years apart, where these themes are interwoven and fictionally dramatized: *Niebla* ("Mist"), Unamuno's most ambitious novel related to the topic of existence, and *San Manuel Bueno, mártir* ("Saint Manuel Bueno, Martyr"), probably his most popular text and considered today as a summary of his lifelong struggle with the role of religion and faith in life.[1] Confrontation and existence are present in both novels, not just as topics but as central to their compositional structure. I am aware the philosophical approach proposed here subordinates questions of literary history and literary (i.e., formal-rhetorical) analysis. It is also reductionist, as it leaves out many other possibilities of reading (in terms of gender, psychoanalysis, cultural history, or close reading, to name a few), and it leaves aside multiple themes proposed by the novels that confirm their status as classical texts.

The controversial nature of the topics addressed invites the teacher to assume primarily the role of facilitator for discussion. Sessions are therefore based on continuous dialogue and reflection from the students' perspective, because all of them can relate to the topic of existence. Comprehension, interpretation, and opinion are mixed, and consequently, assessment needs to be carefully crafted. I devote little time to lecturing apart from a brief introduction to Unamuno in the first class.

Niebla

Niebla recounts the story of Augusto Pérez's quest to find meaning in his life and take control of it, having progressively become aware of living a lonely life without purpose. As his attempts to find happiness through several sentimental relationships fail, Augusto feels increasingly deceived and frustrated, becoming unstable and uncontrollable in his decision-making until eventually the possibility of suicide is raised. When he decides to seek advice from the famous writer Miguel de Unamuno, it is revealed that Augusto is a fictional character with no actual existence and whose trajectory is at the mercy of his creator. Augusto rebels against his fictional destiny and finally dies. *Niebla* narrates the painful struggle of Augusto to be in charge of his own life only to find that Unamuno finally decides to dispose of him and finish the novel right away. The story presents students with a variety of possible meanings for the verb *exist* and claims that there are several levels of existence.

At one time or another, we have all probably felt that many people go through life without thinking about their actions or decisions. The character of Augusto represents, by exaggeration, the opposite attitude once he becomes aware of his purposeless life: that of someone who never ceases to consider how and why he acts. From the beginning, the novel is placed on a transcendental plane in which existential questions are continuously being raised through dialogues, monologues, and written statements. The plot seems to be an afterthought. Unamuno minimizes contextualization and characterization and replaces the narrative tension of adventure with existential conflict. Moreover, the multiple metanarrative strategies displayed reinforce the constructed, artificial status of the novel. Unamuno also removes much of the protagonist's individuality to allow a greater degree of identification between Augusto and the reader. However, from another perspective—and in my experience some complaints from students tend to go in this direction—the novel loses some appeal because Augusto is not a believable character; he is too existentially worried and his everyday life is practically nonexistent: no monetary or family issues, no commitments, and no job. In short, he does nothing (a trait shared with the typical protagonist of the Spanish avant-garde novel). That is not very realistic, which works against the intention of identification with the character, although some students may end up seeing it as the mere embodiment of a philosophical conflict.

As we entertain a broad interpretation of *Niebla*, the feedback from students generally fits into one of three possible readings: First, Augusto has indeed discovered that life has no meaning and is incapable of assimilating that perspective; his quest has failed, and he dies out of pity. Second, the novel is a macabre joke about people who think too much and do too little, neglecting to enjoy what life offers. Third, Augusto is merely a vehicle for Unamuno's metanarrative exercise, and in that sense, the novel functions as a fictionalized reflection on the process of fiction writing. Some points may expand the grounds for debate: in *Niebla* there is no room for religion or any other transcendental ideology to reassure the reader by offering a sense of individual or collective purpose in life, unless Unamuno himself is interpreted as God's counterpoint, a creator who judges his creature and reminds him of his fallen status. In any case, the lack of explicit thematization of a religious possibility places the novel on the opposite side of *San Manuel Bueno, mártir*, in which the presence of faith is pervasive. Another overall reading opens up if one accepts the perspective advocated by the character Víctor Goti—another instance of the novelist-creator—in chapter 30. He advises Augusto to adopt a comic vision of life and to laugh at conflicts—that is, to assume the vitally advisable position of reducing the feeling of tragedy by using humor to observe reality from other perspectives.[2]

The title also allows stimulating readings. Why *Niebla*? What does this mean? In addition to the phonetic similarity of *novela, nivola*, and *niebla*, the word *mist* communicates feelings of confusion, of being lost, of mental dullness, and of estrangement; it also functions as a metaphor for the portal of entry and exit of the novel and life itself. There is no definitive knowledge (or faith, as we will see later) in life that can dissolve the mist of the mystery of birth and death.

I have repeatedly noticed in class that students feel a special tenderness for Orfeo the dog; in fact, sometimes he is the only character in the novel that incites such feelings. Furthermore, his death next to his owner's bed and the fact that the novel concludes with an epilogue in which he is given the ability to speak and reason (logos) are signs of his overall importance (Collins). Any discussion on *Niebla* should make explicit mention of the value of Orfeo, the being who feels the death of Augusto most deeply—indeed, Orfeo dies of sorrow—and who offers a note of affection in the face of the mockery and cruelty exhibited by the other characters. This begs the question: what value do the animals and objects that surround us have in our lives? But, even more, by listening to Orfeo in the epilogue we can adopt a nonhuman point of view that allows us to reflect from the outside on the radical nakedness of human existence, more specifically on how we humans live, suffer, and die surrounded by innumerable discourses that try to comfort us from our own condition. Humans can be arrogant and self-sufficient. Other modernist novels, such as Mikhail Bulgakov's *Heart of a Dog* and Virginia Woolf's *Flush*, also use a canine point of view to interrogate the human condition.

At the end of the novel, we can identify several characters that call into question the idea that existence is possible only for real people. Unamuno argues for the existence of people who have already died (like himself, the writer of the novel we just read), for fictional people (Augusto), and for nonhuman beings (Orfeo). The first implication of this position is that, in a certain sense, death does not mean the end of existence but rather the entry into another mode or level of existence. The second implication is that any entity, and not only those of flesh and bone, exists to the extent that it is meaningful to someone: things and people that have disappeared survive as (and through) memories, as parts of the biographical trajectory of someone (i.e., an individual or a community). We are not only ourselves but the impact and the trace left by our existence in others and in the world. In this sense, loved ones survive in the existential mode of memory and affection, as well as through their progeny (a topic Unamuno addressed several times in his writing). Fictional characters live every time someone opens the book and starts reading.[3] And authors like Unamuno somehow exist every time we read and discuss their works in class. In this counterintuitive and hopeful sense, existence is not the opposite of immortality. But the existence of all the entities named above, like our own lives, must be claimed and built every day. They do not come by default. To exist is to continually perform the vindication of one's own life before, in front of, and with others, as existentialism will argue decades later.

The variety and depth of readings and existential suggestions, on the one hand, strengthens among students the sense of richness of the novel and highlights the idea of literary texts as open works. On the other hand, it reinforces the perception that Unamuno uses texts primarily as vehicles to push readers to think about and question themselves, endowing literature with a special mission as a spur to the spirit. While reading is a vehicle, a distraction, and an enjoyment, it also becomes a means for learning, an experience and a space where vital questions are asked. An unexamined life, Unamuno concludes, is not worthy. *Niebla* demands from the students a reflection on what is truly important in life.[4]

San Manuel Bueno, mártir

Published in 1931 (but rereleased in its definitive form in 1933), *San Manuel Bueno, mártir* is generally considered Unamuno's spiritual testament, as many of his deep lifelong concerns are condensed in a work strongly imbued with symbolism. It recounts the last few years in the life of Don Manuel Bueno, the Catholic priest of a small mountain village (Georges Bernanos's *Diary of a Country Priest*, published in 1936, uses a similar plot). He is beloved by the people as a friend and a guide, but with the arrival of the atheist Lázaro and his friendship with the priest, we discover that Don Manuel hides a terrible secret: he does not believe in what he preaches, specifically, in the afterlife. I propose to approach the text through six central, interconnected themes, all of which tackle the question of the meaning of life from different angles.

Progress versus a Simple Life

Lázaro's character symbolizes the values of progress and of economic and social enhancements. His involvement in social change clashes with the perspective of Don Manuel, for whom material concerns are secondary in people's lives as long as they have spiritual tranquility, behave kindly, and have faith that their (hard) life has a purpose. This contrast between Lázaro and Don Manuel can be treated in class as an interrogation of our basic priorities—that is, what we consider important in our existence. It can also be interpreted as a warning about how our engagement with political, social, and technological advances can turn us away from the perspective of a simple life. To what extent does progress confuse us or distract us from pursuing our aims and building our own path, simultaneously individualizing and dehumanizing us by articulating the measure of our achievements in material terms? What is the place of our belongings, economic or social status, or the accumulation of new and exciting experiences in our life?

The Impact on Others and the Ethical Life

If *Niebla* posited existence in individualistic terms, *San Manuel Bueno, mártir* links the value of existence to performing an ethical life in which helping others and fostering a sense of community become crucial. The priest demands goodness and advocates that our existence is judged according to the positive or negative impact we have on other people. Here again, Unamuno forces readers to question and analyze themselves and demands an ethical commitment to lives besides one's own.

The Role of Religion

The novel places at its center a crisis of religious belief and the implications this entails for the protagonist. In addition, religion is present throughout the story as the most powerful example of a totalizing discourse that endows individual and collective life with meaning. This allows us to raise questions about the role and weight of religion in the past and present, the importance of collective beliefs as creators of community, and, more generally, the function of transcendental beliefs (i.e., whether you believe in something) in the design and development of our lives, a topic central to all modernism since Friedrich Nietzsche's rebuttal of grand narratives.

Life as Agony and Construction

Don Manuel's intimate suffering stems from three different sources: his disbelief in immortality, the betrayal of his role as a guide of the people by his not believing what he preaches, and the possibility of someone uncovering his secret. Faced with this threat, Don Manuel decides to suffer in silence (with the exception of his revelation to Lázaro) and devote himself to his flawless parishioners. Sometimes students interpret this as a betrayal and argue that Don Manuel is a liar. This can lead to a fresh reassessment of Don Manuel as a complex and ambivalent character toward whom we as readers tend to feel empathy and even admiration but who is far from perfect (here the readings by Bilbao-Terreros and especially Mancing can be useful, as they offer a negative take on him). From there, discussions can be more general, touching upon such topics as the lies or secrets we all hide and the spread of hypocrisy in society; the intricate relation between our beliefs, our words, and our actions; the value of truth versus the impact of our actions on others (for example, the use of white lies); and the notion of personal integrity.

Afterlife, Again

A step further in a comprehensive reading would be to argue that the text as a literary and symbolic artifact contradicts the suspicion of the inexistence of immortality held by its protagonist. In *Niebla*, existence beyond death is mainly established through memory and evocation; that is, the deceased remain in memories as well as in the objects or texts they have produced. *San Manuel Bueno, mártir* collects and textually integrates both of these afterlife options: thus, Don Manuel survives in the manuscript of Ángela and in the devotion of his parishioners. But the novel also offers a more elusive possibility: to live in acts, which is to persist in the effect our actions have on the lives of others, again reinforcing the performative aspect of existence. Don Manuel's life makes sense as someone almost exclusively dedicated to helping others, although one of the motives of his anxious behavior was to silence the existential anguish in his heart.

Framing the Story

As with *Niebla*, *San Manuel Bueno, mártir* displays a powerful metanarrative frame: we know of Don Manuel's life from the manuscript of his assistant, Ángela, supposedly transcribed by Unamuno himself (Cela's *La familia de Pascual Duarte* ["The Family of Pascual Duarte"], published in 1942, uses a similar interplay of transcriptions). I emphasize in class that this carefully framed structure is not accidental, nor does it have purely aesthetic or formal value, but rather it is directly related to the philosophical theme of the novel. It allows readers to adopt different degrees of detachment from the main character, whose life we can contemplate as a whole, and to access several other characters' interpretations of that life, contrasting their opinions with our own. Thus, our judgment about Don Manuel is mediated by two interpretative framings: that of Ángela, for whom Don Manuel and Lázaro were not unbelievers but only they *believed* they were unbelievers, and that of Unamuno himself, who confronts Ángela's concern for belief and seems to reaffirm the evangelical idea that works are enough to judge the life of a person.[5]

The classroom discussions proposed here about *San Manuel Bueno, mártir* (which do not deplete the hermeneutic or the didactic aspects of the text) start with the basic question "What do we need for living?" and end with another: "How can we judge a life?" In the space between these two questions the novel seems to offer the following alternative: once material things (money, success, power) have been discarded as unimportant, an ethical life rests either on a transcendental belief that guides our actions (represented here by religious faith) or on helpful engagement with our fellow human beings.

Niebla and *San Manuel Bueno, mártir* share significant thematic and formal elements. I see the classes devoted to interpretation and discussion of both texts, either individually or in conjunction, as culminating by restating the invitation to students to use Unamuno's ideas as stimuli to reflect on and share their views about how they deal with their own lives and how they confront difficulties, conflicts, and decisions. An additional benefit of presenting the reading of Unamuno's novels as a personal and collective ethical quest into the meanings and values of living is to highlight how literature can be used (both inside and outside the classroom) as a powerful tool to examine existence.

NOTES

[1] See Lewis for a discussion of the place of religious experience in modernist fiction.

[2] See S. Roberts for a discussion of the role of humor in *Niebla*, which fits perfectly with the idea of producing a counter-reading of Augusto's conflicts: "To disturb their audience's reading and therefore their thinking patterns, to make them unsure as to whether they should laugh or cry, and to make them think, question, and wonder" ("Clowning" 60).

[3] In return, the same reader who makes Augusto alive in the first pages of the novel is bound to kill him in the last ones. I take this idea from Álvarez-Castro (*Los espejos* 76).

[4] On the type of reader demanded by Unamuno, see Marcos.

[5] Discussions about Ángela's feelings for Don Manuel can use Garrido Ardila's ("Amor") and Longhurst's ("Problem") interpretations that argue she is in love with the priest.

Abel Sánchez; or, The Reader's Personality as Textual Assemblage

Thomas R. Franz

Miguel de Unamuno wrote *Abel Sánchez* (1917) slightly more than halfway through his novelistic career. It was, as Julián Marías says, his coming of age as a writer of fiction ([Espasa] 156–57). It was in this novel—and not in the more innovative *Nuevo mundo* ("New World"), *Amor y pedagogía* ("Love and Pedagogy"), *Niebla* ("Mist"), and *Cómo se hace una novela* ("How to Make a Novel")—that the author first demonstrated thorough character delineation and, especially, control of his story. This new degree of control was achieved by sacrificing some of the spontaneity, chaotic structure, and self-creation on the part of his characters that we witness in some of his other novels. Some early critics tended to exaggerate the degree of this change based on the apparent simplicity of the novel and its clear allusions to well-known cases of biblical envy—Cain and Abel, Esau and Jacob, Lucifer and God—and their adaptation by subsequent literary works mentioned in Unamuno's novel (Round, *Unamuno* 47–61). It is true that the work's chapters are very brief, its vocabulary minimal, its sentences short, and its potential subplots mere allusions, but these characteristics disguise a technical complexity that is wanting in all of Unamuno's longer fiction outside *Niebla*, the underexamined and underrated *Cómo se hace una novela*, and *La novela de Don Sandalio, jugador de ajedrez* ("The Novel of Don Sandalio, Chess Player").

The organic nature of the metafictional structures in *Ábel Sánchez* has perhaps made it a less obvious influence than *Amor y pedagogía*, *Niebla*, and *Cómo se hace una novela* on postmodern Spanish American narrative.[1] Nevertheless, its displacement of traditional novelistic characters and narrators by the creative but unstable power of their character-readers has doubtless contributed to the progressive "subversion of [textual] authority" in Spanish American authors like Augusto Roa Bastos, Carlos Fuentes, and Julio Cortázar (Valdés, "Invention" 455). Jorge Luis Borges's frequent depiction of writers reading and incorporating other writers—even writers who never lived outside the pages of his fiction—doubtless reflects the Argentine's own reading of Unamuno works like *Abel Sánchez*. Borges corresponded with Unamuno, and recently Unamuno's biographer Jon Juaristi has called Borges "el más provechoso de sus discípulos trasatlánticos" 'the most purposeful of his transatlantic disciples' (*Miguel de Unamuno* 237).

The novel begins with the brief note of an unidentified narrator allegedly explaining how he or she came into possession of the manuscript and pointing out that it contains a second document, a confession that the alleged writer, Joaquín Monegro, bequeathed to his daughter (1: 677).[2] It is not stated whether it was Joaquín, the daughter, or the prologist who inserted the confession nor who is the author of the majority, non-confession part of the novel. The subtitle of *Abel Sánchez, Una historia de pasión* ("A Story of Passion"), is placed under the title in a gesture of equivalency, but we do not know who titled it, nor if someone has altered its text to any degree. The confession is styled in the first person, but the majority of the text is in the third person. Both narrators are diegetic (extradiegetic and homodiegetic), meaning that they and the story in which they appear (or which they create) are acts of invention, probably both involving the thoughts of the fictitious Joaquín (Sinclair 189). Despite this particular narratological grounding, the word *historia* (story, history) in the subtitle has an ambiguous ring, as if to suggest that an intensely invented story of a *pasión* (passion) can be real to its writer(s) and reader(s).

The painter Abel creates a portrait of Joaquín's love object, his cousin Helena, thus starting her transformation into Abel's mistress and, soon, wife and a symbol of immortal beauty, another Mona Lisa. Much later, he will paint her as the Virgin Mary, and her image will be so effective that the smitten Joaquín will end up praying to her. Chapter 2 begins the introduction of an endless series of allusions to Dante's *Inferno*, particularly to its fire and ice imagery, suggesting that Helena and Abel's temperamental coolness conceals a burning envy of Joaquín, a doctor, that only a literary account can reveal or, better yet, create in the mind of Joaquín (Clavería 116–17; R. Gullón, *Autobiografías* 125–39). Of note is the chapter's concluding allusion to the *Inferno*'s tale of Paolo and Francesca (canto 5, lines 127–38), whose sinful love finds provocation in a fictionalized tale of Lancelot and Guinevere. Chapter 8 sees Joaquín visiting a moribund patient and noting the presence of a portrait of her by Abel that restores all her lost youth, thus immortalizing her as Abel had done for Helena and Dante had succeeded in doing for Paolo and Francesca.

Abel subsequently announces his desire to paint a modern portrait of Cain in despair over the fratricide of his brother. In order to gain insight into the feelings of Cain, he reads Lord Byron's *Cain*, which sympathizes with the envious older brother. Learning of this injustice, Joaquín reads Byron's poem and questions why God would favor both the ritual sacrifice of the biblical Abel and the professional and amorous exploits of the painter. The reading of Byron's poem raises Joaquín's envy to the archetypal level of his biblical counterpart. He presides over a banquet he has organized to render homage to Abel's depiction of Joaquín as the despairing Cain and presents an imitation eulogy that outperforms the allegedly hypocritical sympathy for Cain/Joaquín represented in the painting. In the speech, Joaquín falsely compares Abel's love of the sufferer with John Milton's love for the victimized Satan of *Paradise Lost*. God seems to have created both Joaquín and Satan for his pleasure in scorning them. The banquet scene itself conforms to the many paintings of other artists' or writers' banquets that were popular in nineteenth- and early-twentieth-century Spain (Franz, "Painting" 65–76).

Much later Joaquín considers the fame and vengeance he might achieve from the future publication of his confession, originally intended only for the private illumination of his daughter. In case the confession is a failure, he decides to write a novel to be titled *Memorias de un médico viejo* ("Memoirs of an Old Doctor") that might recast him in a favorable light in comparison to the immoralities of his patients. Meanwhile, he encourages his new son-in-law to assemble a book detailing Joaquín's unpublished medical experiments. The reader never knows the extent to which the fame-seeking doctor and his admiring compiler will be truthful.

If metafiction is narrative that "openly comments on its own fictional status" and the "nature of fiction" itself (Baldick 133), and is not merely an impressive series of intertexts, we need to relate *Abel Sánchez*'s multiple literary allusions and comments on its own fictionality to those dynamic processes undergirding its composition. Here it is necessary to mention an existentialist detail that our emphasis on fiction and poetry has left out: the importance of the other in all of Unamuno's writing. Joaquín needs conflict with his adversary Abel in order to *exist* (Longhurst, Introduction 30; Olson, *Great Chiasmus* 113, 116). Likewise, *Abel Sánchez* needs the oppositional force of the Bible, *Inferno*, *Paradise Lost*, and Byron's *Cain* in order to proclaim its modern, practically Nietzschean treatment of the envy theme, one in which the envier and the envied change places when our perspectives of them become different. Brief allusions to the Pygmalion story make it clear that Abel is not really docile and that Joaquín is hoping that his rival will declare his hostility openly so as to justify his own aggression. This never quite happens, and thus the allusion to the Pygmalion fable is temporarily overturned, Abel remaining a mere potentiality until his son reveals his father's envious treatment of the son's artistic talent. The novel's continual reference to the transformative power of artistic allusions and images demonstrates its own power first to demonize Joaquín and second to reveal his status as a simultaneous victim.

The creative and transformative powers of literature come to the fore as the novel, in a Cervantine manner, begins to insert many small anecdotes that Joaquín's acquaintances relate to him. The first two of these appear in chapter 19, where two men, Ramírez and Carvajal, are unable to treat their children equally, much like the God who has too many children in *Paradise Lost* (Franz, *Parallel* 13–49). The tale of the self-centered politician Don Leovigildo intensifies these two stories. Chapters 22 and 23 present the similar cases of Federico Cuadrado and an Aragonese father who suffer and dispense inequality, illustrating the causes and effects of envy. The stories draw attention to themselves as literature by suddenly appearing out of nowhere, unlike Joaquín's early anecdotes about his patients. However, the earlier anecdotes become recast as art the minute Joaquín announces that he will not only assemble them but also—most pointedly—transform them into a novel. Being patently Cervantine in nature, the latter tales of the two fathers, the politician, Federico Cuadrado, and the Aragonese man simultaneously recall the novelized patient anecdotes and duplicate their fictional unity by appearing as an entire section of *Abel Sánchez*. By doing so they repeat the novel's suggestion that fictional processes underline all configurations of existence. Joaquín himself is a configuration of such processes. The fact that he is assembling anecdotes that reconfigure his own envy shows that *Abel Sánchez* never abandons the vision of self-creating characters like those of *Amor y pedagogía* and *Niebla*.

Although *Abel Sánchez* is embedded in the complexities of creating and nurturing the self, it is a very easy book for students to read and is extremely relevant to every reader's quest for authenticity and stability. If we no longer dedicate as much time as formerly to paintings and literary classics, we are bombarded every second with the images of life that advertisements, television, comics, and the Internet want to give us. All of these tend to either confirm or alter our personality. Meanwhile, the Bible and other sacred books purport to represent eternal values, but individuals tend to read them selectively and to interpret them in personal ways. Joaquín's reading of Genesis (Cain and Abel, Esau and Jacob, and their modern re-creations) reinforces his suspicion that life has favored Abel over himself. Unamuno does not label Joaquín's conviction as pathological—as Helena and Abel do and most of today's students probably would—because he sees it as tragically human. Classes might well discuss Unamuno's vision in light of contentions that sacred texts embody not only the divine but also older worldviews that demand an updating in our era of technology and science, necessarily recalling that Joaquín is a scientist and yet cannot—even with the help of his wife, his daughter, and a priest—disabuse himself of the idea that life made him inferior at the moment of his birth. Students and teachers alike have experienced envy and might discuss how far they have been willing to go in order to cure themselves of it or punish the persons they regarded as unfairly privileged.

Does Abel needlessly provoke Joaquín's envy, as both Unamuno's late prologue and Joaquín himself maintain, or are both Unamuno and Joaquín guilty of skewing the evidence to fit their circumstance? (Unamuno was in political exile and bitter toward his contemporaries who decided to support a dictatorship. Likewise, Dante was exiled when he wrote the extensive passages on envy that are spread through *Inferno*.) Does Unamuno pile up too many repetitive examples of envy, or is the weight of these examples necessary to reproduce the suffocation that Joaquín feels inside? What are some current examples of self-centeredness or envy that we see in today's politics or academic life? Would a reader feel Joaquín's envy to the same degree if Unamuno provided more details about the setting, about Helena, or about Joaquín's wife, Antonia, and their children? Do we remodel our lives or appearances according to some media-inspired vision in order to convince ourselves that we are normal? Can we ever novelize ourselves or others to our own satisfaction? Joaquín brings about Abel's death after literature's seeming confirmation that Abel is unfairly privileged. Are today's media responsible for similar violence? What are the emotions and who are the people that we need in order to feel like the same person every day or the person we want to be? Does Antonia initially fictionalize her rude and ungrateful husband in terms of his needful appearance? What role does the death of her mother play in her attempt to see Joaquín as an understanding person?

In the "Comentario" ("Commentary") forming part of *Cómo se hace una novela*, Unamuno states, "¿Qué me importa que no leas, lector, lo que yo quise poner en ella [mi obra] si es que lees lo que te enciende en vida?" 'What difference does it make to me reader if you don't read what I tried to put into the book, so long as you read something there that sets you ablaze in your life?' (7: 562; 6: 399). The dedication to *Amor y pedagogía* offers the same message. The reader, then, is the novel's final and definitive author, just as its characters have the illusion of freedom to reinterpret and interact with the individuals or literary texts that they encounter. Because Unamuno concedes to anyone this particular freedom, and because *Abel Sánchez* presents such an extreme story of human passions, it is tempting for us to hazard statements about the historical author Unamuno, who felt called upon to write it. Since there are countless studies on the historical Unamuno and his relationship to *Abel Sánchez*, and since our provisional re-creations of Unamuno will probably conflict with those of others, how can we resolve the discrepancies between our opinions and those of the experts? Should we take seriously the creative freedom Unamuno grants us, or is he exaggerating in the same way that he did in offering the outsized envy of Joaquín Monegro?

NOTES

[1] For more on this metafictional approach, see Álvarez-Castro, *Los espejos* 77–87.

[2] The texts of *Abel Sánchez* and *Cómo se hace una novela* used in this essay are those included in *Obras completas*, edited by Ricardo Senabre and published by Turner. Translations are by Anthony Kerrigan from *Selected Works of Miguel de Unamuno*.

Teaching *Cómo se hace una novela* and Its Legacy in Contemporary Spanish Autofictions

Cristina Carrasco

Miguel de Unamuno's most popular texts in undergraduate Spanish courses are *Niebla* ("Mist") and *San Manuel Bueno, mártir* ("Saint Manuel Bueno, Martyr"). Other works, such as *Abel Sánchez* or *Cómo se hace una novela* ("How to Make a Novel"), are not usually taught at the undergraduate level. In the case of *Cómo se hace una novela*, this pedagogical omission has a lot to do with the fact that, before Bénédicte Vauthier's recent critical edition,[1] we did not have a reliable version of this work (Álvarez Castro, *Los espejos* 88). Yet, teaching this work at the undergraduate level allows students to understand Unamuno's recurring themes and philosophical thoughts as well as current theoretical approaches on the novel (Zubizarreta 320). Given its hybrid nature, in many ways Unamuno's *Cómo se hace una novela* redefines the autobiographical novel as a literary genre, as it problematizes the representation of reality and the human subject, a concept that is fundamental to contemporary Spanish writers. This explains why many critics consider it a precursor of contemporary autofictions and why reformulations of the Basque writer's philosophical thoughts are found in the literature of the twenty-first century.

In this essay, I offer a few pointers on teaching *Cómo se hace una novela* in an advanced undergraduate course on Spanish autofictions of the twentieth and twenty-first centuries. Gonzalo Navajas considers Unamuno a postmodern writer, while others would classify him as an avant-garde thinker (*Unamuno*). Regardless of these labels that try to situate him in the literary spectrum of the twentieth century, Unamuno revolutionized several literary genres and influenced the European avant-garde movement, as can be seen in Luigi Pirandello's *Six Characters in Search of an Author* or in Ramón Gómez de la Serna's *Automoribundia*. Thus, I use Unamuno's masterpiece to discuss current polemics in regard to autobiography as a genre or theme and how it is problematized in contemporary works such as Rosa Montero's *La loca de la casa* ("The Madwoman in the House") and Enrique Vila-Matas's *París no se acaba nunca* ("Paris Never Ends"), among several others.[2]

In order to understand the relevance of studying Unamuno in a course on recent autofictions, at the beginning of the semester my students read Thomas Franz's "Envidia y existencia en Millás y Unamuno." This article allows us to discuss how Unamuno has influenced many contemporary Spanish authors who have, like Juan José Millás, become important literary figures thanks to their autofictions. This reading on the legacy of Unamuno's thought sets the tone for the entire semester. I also devote an introductory class to Unamuno's role as a precursor of the Spanish avant-garde, to show that his writings were revolutionary for the time. We continue our discussion on autofictions as a literary genre by reading Philippe Lejeune's "The Autobiographical Pact"; a selection from the book *El pacto ambiguo: De la novela autobiográfica a la autoficción* ("The Ambiguous Pact: From the Autobiographical Novel to Autofiction"), by Manuel Alberca; and a fragment of Ana Casas's compilation *La autoficción* ("Autofiction"). We also discuss Javier Marías's "Autobiografía o ficción" ("Autobiography or Fiction") and newspaper articles such as Winston Manrique Sabogal's "El yo asalta la literatura" ("The Self Assaults Literature"), which give students a good sample of most recent Spanish autofictions. When discussing these essays, we reflect on the limits of both fiction and autobiography and also on the polemics of the entire content of the course: fictions about the self.

First, in order to understand how Unamuno was a literary magician, in the sense that he experimented with several genres at once, we read his famous essay "A lo que salga" ("Whatever It Turns Out"; *Obras completas* [Senabre] 8: 694–96). In this essay, Unamuno explains the difference between two types of writers, the "vivíparo" 'viviparous,' and the "ovíparo" 'oviparous' (694). According to him, a viviparous writer is one who lets his characters surprise him. Through these texts, students grasp the idea that Unamuno was, indeed, a viviparous writer and that his texts conjugate life and fiction. After our discussion of this reading, I assign students an automatic writing exercise that gives them the opportunity to imitate Unamuno's writing style. In the process of internalizing Unamuno's writing, students learn how advanced he was for his time and how he was, indeed, a precursor of avant-garde narrative and contemporary autofictions.

What follows is an in-depth discussion, usually divided over two classes, of the sociohistorical context in which Unamuno wrote *Cómo se hace una novela*. One way of making Unamuno interesting to undergraduates is to tell them about the heated controversies that always surrounded him; his exile in Fuerteventura (Canary Islands), Paris, and Hendaye; and his opposition to the Spanish monarchy. In order to activate students' schemata, I ask them to compare Unamuno with other activists of the twenty-first century who are very critical of our current political situation in the United States. As a follow-up, I also show them a documentary called *Unamuno, apasionado*, which makes them more curious about the Basque writer, his legacy, and his enduring relevance.

By the time we begin reading *Cómo se hace una novela*, students are better prepared to understand the complexity and singularity of a hybrid text that depicts, through different layers of thought, the blurry lines that separate reality from fiction. I begin my lesson asking students to discuss in small groups why they think this work is called *Cómo se hace una novela.* Based on the title and their background knowledge on some of Unamuno's essays and novels, they have to formulate a hypothesis on what they may expect to read this time. In order to relate this work to the contemporary texts that we will discuss throughout the semester, I point out that most of the autobiographical texts penned by Montero, Millás, and Vila-Matas refer to novels, which emphasizes the idea that autofictions are autobiographies whose main challenge is to place reality and fiction at the same level.

Unamuno expresses the textualization of reality by creating a hybrid text composed of different layers. Working in pairs, my students have to write down a list of the different layers involved in the composition of *Cómo se hace una novela*, such as the main story; the novel of Unamuno's alter ego, Jugo de La Raza; and several Unamunian texts that appear as intertexts. Subsequently, we consider different paratexts and the chronological composition of the text, in the midst of Unamuno's exile. Because we have previously read "A lo que salga," we spend some time reflecting on this text as a "vivíparo" artifact that was composed over a two-year period, between 1925 and 1927. Students better understand the text's hybridity after a thorough discussion of the prologue to the Spanish edition, written by the author after its original publication in French. We also take the time to analyze not only the written portrait of Unamuno by Jean Cassou, who prepared the French edition,[3] but also Unamuno's commentary on this portrait, as well as the autofiction that narrates his years of exile.

After reading these paratexts together, students have a better idea of how Unamuno creates a hybrid text of multiple *cajas chinas* with political and intertextual comments about his exile, life, and works. Since students will have to write their own autofiction as a creative project for the class, they begin working on it early on, in order to avoid rushed and incoherent final products. Concurrent with our initial discussions on Unamuno's literary experiments, then, during the first two weeks of the semester, students have to begin writing a text about their life, relating it to fiction. This creative, hands-on assignment, which is completed gradually throughout the semester, helps students understand the topic. As we move forward to more contemporary readings, they have the opportunity to add layers to their original writing. And when they reflect on their own writing from an autofictional perspective, several weeks later, inevitably they return to Unamuno: to his in-depth literary reflections, his philosophical quests on the nature of the novel, and his aesthetic conjugation of life and fiction. Erasing the border between reality and fiction is closely related to the contemporary insistence on eliminating generic borders, as evidenced in the works of Cristina Fernández Cubas, Javier Marías, and Manuel Vicent, among many others.

As a way of further emphasizing the hybridity of *Cómo se hace una novela* and its contemporary significance, we discuss how Unamuno textualizes not only reality but also the human being, particularly when he becomes a character or a reader within his own text. The main difference between Unamuno's hybrid text and contemporary works that challenge literary genres, borders, and fluidity is that more recent writers explicitly transgress against several literary genres, playfully, writing against the grain, creating innovative metaphors, and challenging the idea that genres have parameters, rules, and regulations. Unamuno's text, students realize after our discussions, is the composite product of his years of exile and agony. In order to convey Unamuno's complexity, I allow students to read the English translation, as a way of explaining that this text is complex not only because of the language that Unamuno is using but also because it is crafted with the philosophical perspective of a higher work of art. In regards to the form of the novel, students are asked to discuss, for instance, the different types of genres that are gathered in a single text, the novelistic scenario, and the challenges of reading a first and second version of the same work.

After we go over the textualization of reality, specifically discussing the text's hybridity, we also discuss how Unamuno skillfully becomes a character and immortalizes his literary persona. When I introduce this idea to the students, I point out that, unlike Montero or Vila-Matas, Unamuno is obsessed with searching for God, and the overt textualization of himself on the written page reflects his hopes for immortality. What I try to illustrate to students is that Unamuno could not deny his authority as the creator (a godly figure) of his own creatures or characters, and he struggled with his own godly figure throughout his tormented life. We perceive this obsession in *Cómo se hace una novela* precisely because he does not want to stop being the author, the creator, and he is constantly critiquing the works of others, playing devil's advocate and behaving like a literary critic. Unlike him, the other authors whom we study throughout the course intentionally play with the textualization of themselves, distancing their contemporary works from the Basque writer's profound reflections on literary creation and authorship. This point becomes more evident as we read, for instance, Montero's *La loca de la casa*, where the narrator tells us the same story about her childhood in three different ways and becomes three different characters without any explicit reflections on the validity of one over the other or the legitimacy of a particular authorial voice.

When I discuss in class the different mechanisms that Unamuno sets in motion in order to textualize reality, I ask students to think about the role not only of the author but also of the reader. In *Cómo se hace una novela* we find different types of metatextual readers who invite us to see reality and fiction at the same level. As an implicit author, for example, Unamuno reads his own text through Cassou's written portrait. In the same vein, Jugo de la Raza represents the novel of his own existence, and he decides not to finish reading his novel as a way of escaping death. I tell students that, through these different active readers, Unamuno reminds us that fiction can be more real than reality. Unamuno wants to show that as long as we continue reading, the text will be alive, and that literary existence concurrently justifies our own presence as readers, yes, but also as human beings. If we stop reading, the author suggests, we will die. Finally, I remind students that although Unamuno recognizes the reader as one of the creators of the novel, he does not want to lose control of his creation, and he wants to remain an authoritative figure. In Vila-Matas's *París no se acaba nunca*, however, the narrator accepts a priori that the reader is the author of the autofiction.

The study of *Cómo se hace una novela* alongside contemporary autofictions facilitates a fruitful discussion on the topic of intertextuality. As students read works by Unamuno, Vila-Matas, Montero, Millás, Fernández Cubas, or Esther Tusquets, they are asked to identify implicit and explicit connections with other texts and to think about how a particular intertext rearticulates a previous work of art in an effort to create new knowledge. Thus, when reading *Cómo se hace una novela*, we discuss Unamuno's *Vida de Don Quijote y Sancho* ("The Life of Don Quixote and Sancho"), *Niebla*, and *La agonía del cristianismo* ("The Agony of Christianity"), among other titles. The inferential walk that we take thanks to the insertion of these intertexts allows us to discuss issues related to the role of the author and the reader, what constitutes originality in a work of art, and, perhaps more important, how major works of art are in fact ingenious reformulations of previous works.

By the time students read recent autofictions such as Montero's *La loca de la casa*, they know that such texts are crafted with a variety of intertexts, ranging from Saint Teresa's *Libro de la vida* ("Book on Life") to various topics covered by a number of nineteenth-century Russian writers. Because of their preparation with Unamuno's *Cómo se hace una novela*, when discussing these autofictions students are ready to tackle a double intertextuality present in many contemporary texts where the authors discuss other writers' works but also their own. Inspired by Unamuno's work, for instance, the main character in Vila-Matas's first novel, *La asesina ilustrada* ("The Illustrated Murderess"), will also die when she finishes reading her own novel. I usually let students work in small groups in order to identify these intertextual connections that take us back to Unamuno, and this group work also prepares them for their individual oral interviews, where they have the opportunity to discuss a theoretical article about autofictions. The oral presentations on a critical article are about ten minutes long, and students write an outline that includes the article's thesis, four key points for discussion, and two examples of how these critical or theoretical claims can be applied to the text that we are reading. Students find this assignment helpful because they can use this critical article for their final research essay on one of the contemporary autofictions.

When I teach my course on contemporary autofictions, I use *Cómo se hace una novela* as a critical text in order to analyze more recent texts. At the same time, canonical authors such as Unamuno give students an understanding of their importance in the development of the European avant-garde and postmodernism. Although we pay a great deal of attention to the narrative structures and the philosophical questions that these writers reflect on through their hybrid texts, we also analyze how they use their autofictions to articulate such topics as childhood, exile, and their role as writers. Studying these themes allows students to understand more deeply the sociohistorical and political situation in contemporary Spain. In sum, teaching Unamuno's masterpiece *Cómo se hace una novela* in the context of an undergraduate course on contemporary Spanish fiction shows once again his modernity and recovers a text that has not been paid the attention it deserves because of its formal complexity.

NOTES

[1] Published by Ediciones Universidad de Salamanca as the collection *Manual de Quijotismo, Cómo se hace una novela, Epistolario Miguel de Unamuno / Jean Cassou.*

[2] Other contemporary Spanish autofictions that can be incorporated into a comparative study of *Cómo se hace una novela* include *Habíamos ganado la guerra* ("We Had Won the War"), by Esther Tusquets; *Muchas veces me pediste que contara esos años* ("The Times You Told Me to Tell You About Those Years"), by Juan Cruz Ruiz; *Naturaleza infiel* ("Unfaithful Nature"), by Cristina Grande; *Cultivos* ("Crops"), by Julián Rodríguez; and *Lección de anatomía* ("Anatomy Lesson"), by Marta Sanz.

[3] Cassou's portrait is reprinted by Vauthier in his edition.

San Manuel Bueno, mártir as Literary Artifact

Brian Cope

> Y esta intolerancia popular lo mismo se ejerce en un sentido que en otro; tan intolerante es en España el librepensador como el católico.
> (And this common intolerance is exercised the same in one way or another; in Spain the freethinker is just as intolerant as the Catholic.)
>
> —Miguel de Unamuno, "Materialismo popular"

In 1900 Miguel de Unamuno delivered the convocation address at the University of Salamanca. In it, he challenged students to cultivate a mind-set conducive to independent learning and personal growth, which, he claimed, would protect them from the sectarianism and dogmatism that plagued civil society. He indirectly posited *skepsis*—the practice of disinterested inquiry and the modus operandi of Plato's Academy—as the manner of learning that yields the highest intellectual gratification, saying, "Lo que más hizo maestro de civilización al pueblo griego fue su siempre despierta curiosidad, curiosidad de niño, casi sin ulterior propósito, su espíritu platónico, su amor por la caza intelectual más que por la pieza que en ella pudiera cobrarse" 'What made the ancient Greeks masters of civilization was their always heightened curiosity, their childlike curiosity, almost without ulterior motives, their platonic spirit, their love for the intellectual hunt more than for the profitable catch' ("Discurso leído" 65; my trans.). Unamuno's emphasis on the pursuit rather than the attainment of knowledge situates him in the progressive camp of higher education, which drew much of its inspiration from ancient Greece and whose pioneers in Spain were Julián Sanz del Río and Francisco Giner de los Ríos, the latter of whom founded the Institución Libre de Enseñanza (Free Institution of Teaching).

I teach *San Manuel Bueno, mártir* ("San Manuel Bueno, Martyr") in a gateway course that targets close reading, argumentative writing, and critical thinking. I include *San Manuel Bueno* because of its poetic ambiguity and interpretive slipperiness and also because it derives from a tumultuous historical period that continues to hold much salience. My first step in teaching the novel is to introduce its author and share information about him as a public intellectual and champion of liberal principles. Keeping in mind that *San Manuel Bueno* is about the preservation of Catholicism through the presumably well-meaning suppression of freedom of conscience, and knowing that Don Manuel's purpose stands in antithetical relation to Unamuno's unwaveringly liberal worldview, I end my introductory lecture by sharing with the students a handout that contains selected passages from Unamuno's convocation address along with the following oft-quoted passage from "Mi religión" ("My Religion"):

> [L]os preguntones, si leen esto, volverán a preguntarme: "Bueno; pero ¿qué soluciones traes?" Y yo, para concluir, les diré que si quieren soluciones, acudan a la tienda de enfrente, porque en la mía no se vende semejante artículo. Mi empeño ha sido, es y será que los que me lean piensen y mediten en las cosas fundamentales, y no ha sido nunca el de darles pensamientos hechos. Yo he buscado siempre agitar, y, a lo sumo, sugerir, más que instruir. Si yo vendo pan, no es pan, sino levadura o fermento. (13)

> [T]he persistent questioners, if they read this, will turn right around and ask me: "So then, what solutions are you offering?" And I, to conclude, will tell them that if they want solutions, they'd better go to a different store, because in mine no such item is being sold. My endeavor has been, is and always will be, that those who read me think and meditate on the fundamental issues, and it has never been to give concrete answers. I have always tried to stir things up and, more than anything, to suggest rather than to instruct. If I sell bread, it is not bread, but yeast or ferment. (4)[1]

In the several sessions that I devote in my course to reading *San Manuel Bueno*, I strategically reiterate that Unamuno means not to instruct but rather to provoke thoughtful reflection. Because every text I assign constitutes an object of inquiry that allows my students to practice and hone their analytical, argumentative, and critical thinking skills, I refer to *San Manuel Bueno* as a literary artifact, which implies that the text contains unique attributes that can contribute to our emerging understanding of the historical milieu from which it derives, with the burden falling on us as readers to situate and interpret it.

In the immense archive of scholarly work on *San Manuel Bueno*, two studies prove valuable, if not indispensable, in establishing a framework for studying the text as a literary artifact. One is John Butt's landmark study of *San Manuel Bueno*, which locates the text in its historical context, discusses the circumstances of its creation, and reviews its critical reception. Butt stresses "the text's essentially poetic, mythical nature" (44); alleges that it contains an "allegorical message" (45); and insists that "by its very structure and language, the novel is designed *not* to reflect or be connected with contemporary history or social conditions" (32). The second is Howard Mancing's "The Lessons of *San Manuel Bueno, mártir*," which builds on several of Butt's positions and offers an incisive reading of Ángela as the character most imbibed with Unamuno's critical spirit. Both studies emphasize *San Manuel Bueno*'s interpretive elasticity and open-endedness. According to Butt, "It is really not possible to simplify or talk away the ambiguities and inconsistencies in his [Unamuno's] work" (9); similarly, Mancing affirms that "the text *affords*—allows us to construct—a number of possible understandings" (354).

My goal in teaching *San Manuel Bueno* as a literary artifact is to encourage my students to freely explore its *legitimate* range of signification, and unbeknownst to them, by doing so, they test the prevalent assumption in the criticism that the novel possesses little or no tangible relation to its historical milieu. Artifacts invite examination, and by labeling *San Manuel Bueno* a literary artifact I encourage students to draw from the knowledge and insight gained from previous assignments as they explore the complexity and signifying potential of the text. Prior to reading *San Manuel Bueno*, students complete at least one related historical reading; examine pictorial representations of *la niña bonita* (the pretty girl), the Spanish Republic's version of France's Marianne and the United States's Statue of Liberty; view the documentary *Misiones pedagógicas* ("The Pedagogical Missions") and the film *La lengua de las mariposas* ("Butterfly"); and read excerpts of the Constitución de la República Española (Constitution of the Spanish Republic) on the rights and responsibilities of citizens. Each of these assignments brings into focus Spain's liberal zeitgeist prior to or during the period of the Second Republic.

In an insightful article on teaching literature in the foreign language classroom, Sylvie Debevec Henning asks, "Are we encouraging students to do the work of establishing links with a text's multiple contexts? Are we helping them relate a text's themes and issues to pertinent concerns in their own world, either because these themes and issues are similar or because they are different?" (29). The mission of many liberal arts institutions, including my own, is to promote and facilitate inquiry that affords unique perspectives on the contemporary world. To this end, the gateway course that I teach is designed to allow for the possibility of synchronic *and* diachronic inquiry. I invite my students to draw connections to the world they inhabit, because the themes of factionalism, dogmatism, truth, division, and freedom of conscience hold such obvious relevance in the twenty-first century that to discourage exploring these connections is anathema to the cause of critical thinking, the liberal arts, and Unamuno's aim to prompt his readers to think about *fundamental* things. But more than this, I encourage my students to explore continuities between *San Manuel Bueno* and the content of previous assignments in order to put the novel in dialogue with its cultural milieu, understanding that while the text may be designed, as Butt affirms, to resist association to its historical context, it truly does have something to tell us about the time period from which it hails. Perhaps most important, however, exercising both close reading *and* relational inquiry fosters critical thinking.

According to bell hooks, in teaching critical thinking we teach discernment, and thinking critically "is a way of approaching ideas that aims to understand core, underlying truths, not simply that superficial truth that may be most obviously visible" (9). *San Manuel Bueno* is well suited for courses that emphasize critical thinking because of its ambiguity, its aesthetic richness, and the range of interpretation that it allows. To read *San Manuel Bueno* as a literary artifact is to challenge students to negotiate ambiguity, nuance, and contradiction and to practice the art of close reading. As Jonathan Culler affirms, "the work of close reading is not primarily to resolve difficulties but above all to describe them, to elucidate their source and implications" (10). Using *San Manuel Bueno* as a vehicle to practice close reading allows the students to independently cultivate their capacity to understand, argue, analyze, and reason objectively as they explore the implications of the text's ambiguity, nuance, and contradiction. In so doing, students continue to experience tangible growth in their linguistic competence as they gain the capacity for abstract thought and complex reasoning.

In the pedagogical enterprise described, the role of the teacher is paramount. Accordingly, I cast myself in the same role that Unamuno ascribes to himself: I suggest, provoke, and give yeast. In this sense, I subscribe to the view held by hooks that "[c]ritical thinking is an interactive process, one that demands participation on the part of teacher and students alike" (9). It is important to use pedagogical strategies that interrupt the students' comfortable routine and that encourage participation, but more important, the teacher must also welcome the students' point of view and cultivate a mind-set of acceptance. "Keeping an open mind," writes hooks, "is an essential requirement of critical thinking. I often talk about radical openness because it became clear to me, after years in academic settings, that it was far too easy to become attached to and protective of one's viewpoint, and to rule out other perspectives" (10). The success of the enterprise hinges, in my experience, on the radical openness that hooks describes. In the end, my conviction about what the story means is irrelevant. My role is to nurture the students' intrigue and hold them to reasonable standards of evidence as they construct their understanding of the text in relation to its multiple contexts.

Don Manuel occupies much of the students' attention as they discuss *San Manuel Bueno*, because he is the subject of Ángela's testimonial. Unamuno claims at the end of the novel that he did not write the text but rather discovered it. Its status as a found object therefore invites our examination of it as a literary artifact. According to Mancing, Ángela "is the closest thing to an Unamuno-figure in the story" and "is, like her creator, the character who respects others . . . and wants to give them yeast so that they can bake their own bread" (363). I like this interpretation because it gives me ample justification to emphasize to my students that Ángela is a character who models free inquiry. However, it is problematic in its implied celebration of Ángela's intellectual honesty. Not unlike the narrator of *Lazarillo de Tormes*—whose embellished narrative lays out a case to its esteemed reader—Ángela too presents the reader with a convenient version of events whose veracity in the end remains questionable. That she questions and exhibits intellectual curiosity should not imply that she does not also frame the facts to suit her purposes, as does the narrator of *Lazarillo*. Butt alludes to this when he writes, "The crucial point—nearly always glossed over by the critics—is that Ángela's version of events is almost certainly unreliable" (37). Yet despite recognizing that "Ángela's narrative undercuts the reliability of the story she relates" (355), Mancing still defends it as "her best version of the truth" and insists that "the mere fact of writing what she does . . . is an act of courageous defiance of everything don Manuel stood for: manipulation and deceit" (363). Any reader sympathetic to Ángela will naturally want to see the validity of this claim and look for evidence in the text to support it. In my view, however, it is unclear whether Ángela's testimony is not also manipulative and deceitful. Certainly Ángela's sincerity, frankness, and authenticity are easy to detect, but much less so are her subterfuge, duplicity, and innocent guile. Within the fictional labyrinth of the novel, her story could be completely fabricated or it could be the closest thing that exists to the truth. It cannot, however, be an objective and reliable account of the life of Don Manuel. Even Ángela notes that her testimonial is merely a confessional account of her "experiencia de la santidad ajena" 'contact with sainthood' (165; 19).[2]

The unit I teach on *San Manuel Bueno* begins and ends with Ángela. On the first day, my students and I carefully examine the first three pages of the text and discuss how Ángela draws the reader in with the force of her candor, eloquence, and sincerity. On the final day, I ask my students to consider what might be inferred from Unamuno's claim that he simply found the text (167), and I also assign for review select pages where Ángela shifts the focus to herself and her encounters with Don Manuel (130–34, 138, 145–46). These pages correspond to the sequences analyzed by Mancing (361–63) and describe Ángela's attempt to bring her doctrinal questions and spiritual doubts to the attention of Don Manuel. Remarkably, he treats her condescendingly and dismissively as he becomes agitated listening to her challenge the normative understanding of Catholic doctrine. Mancing's analysis of these sequences sheds light on the psychological abuse that Ángela endures from her trusted spiritual adviser. One important detail that Mancing ignores is that Don Manuel alleges that Ángela suffers from demonic possession as a result of her defiance of his expectation that she remain an embodiment of innocence and purity of faith: "Y esas preguntas, ¿sabes quién te las insinúa, quién te las dirige? Pues . . . ¡el Demonio!" 'And these doubts, do you know who gives them to you, who controls them? Well, . . . the Devil!' (133; 7). This passage exposes Don Manuel's penchant for acting in a mean-spirited and dogmatic way toward Ángela and should raise questions about both his goodness and the nobility of his enterprise. Does the text allow the reader to rightfully infer that he acts this way toward everyone with whom he perceives it will be effective—presumably women—or just with Ángela? Could Ángela's avowed "contact with sainthood" be insincere? These are just two questions that I pose to my students and for which I do not possess definitive answers.

Exploring the figure of Ángela and examining what her testimony of her "contact with sainthood" exposes unquestionably leads to the discovery that at the core of Don Manuel's benevolent enterprise is an agenda of unapologetic indoctrination, conformity, and despotism that Mancing describes in the following way: "For me, Don Manuel is like those individuals (some parents, politicians, professors: Inquisitors all) and those institutions (some governments, churches, universities: Inquisitions all) that paternalistically want to tell you what is good for you rather than have you decide for yourself" (359). Ángela's narrative documents the uncharacteristic aggression and misplaced contempt that Don Manuel directs toward her for exhibiting the spirit of *skepsis* but also attests to the process through which she becomes able to empathize with and accept him. Notwithstanding her apparent sympathy for Don Manuel, it is disingenuous to accept her account as an unqualified endorsement of his canonization, and thus much fruitful discussion can come from examining her written testimony as the "act of courageous defiance" that Mancing alleges (363). Certainly, the magnitude of Don Manuel's mistreatment of Ángela is sufficient to destabilize the reader's positive reception of her account and prompt a second look at the details she includes to render him in a positive light.

In spite of Ángela's evident empathy for Don Manuel there are details in her testimonial that reflect very poorly on him, and the reader is not unjustified in suspecting that her inclusion of them is by design. For example, she writes of Don Manuel, "Su acción sobre las gentes era tal que nadie se atrevía a mentir ante él, y todos, sin tener que ir al confesonario, se confesaban" 'Don Manuel's influence was so powerful that no one dared to lie to him, and even when they didn't need to go to the confessional, people still went to confess with him' (122; 3). What Ángela portrays uncritically as two positive effects of Don Manuel's laudable personal example might register with the reader as an objectionable social condition resulting from psychological coercion and intimidation. Furthermore, when Ángela discovers that her brother's conversion was a farce, the reader—especially a Catholic reader—might question Don Manuel's ethics in carrying out Lázaro's baptism since he does it knowing the conversion to be insincere. In the same way that Don Manuel previously attempted to *invalidate* Ángela by accusing her of demonic possession, the baptism of Lázaro can also be seen as a deliberate step by Don Manuel to *validate* the beliefs of his parishioners and feed their self-gratification. Those critics who accept the superficial validity of Ángela's apology of Don Manuel often place her account in the tradition of the biblical *Evangelios* ("Gospels"); it should be noted, however, that Ángela's *evangelio* does as much to expose Don Manuel's shortcomings as it does to celebrate his goodness. In what might be interpreted as a moment of supreme irony, Ángela innocently notes that she is unsure of the impact that her account will have on Don Manuel's canonization if it lands in the hands of the bishop (166). Considering Don Manuel's disapproval of Ángela's inquisitive and freethinking spirit, might not the bishop conveniently dismiss her account on the basis of her gender or on the suspicion that Satan is speaking through her? Questions such as this, which have no concrete answers, can spawn lively discussion and meaningful exploration of patriarchal authority and misogyny.

Mancing closes his article by asserting that "it is the lesson of Ángela, rather than that of Don Manuel, that is life-affirming; in the end, it is Ángela's positive lesson that I take from *San Manuel Bueno*" (363). Mancing makes this statement ignoring the probability of Ángela's deceit and manipulation; and yet I find myself sharing his conviction. In the end, Ángela's true intentions are unknowable, and should it be the case that she is sincere in her unconventional defense of Don Manuel, then she can be admired for the charity she affords him and her intellectual honesty. Should the opposite be true, then the treachery of her testimony merits respect for its subversion. After all, unlike Don Manuel or Lázaro, Ángela is a victim: she puts her trust in Don Manuel, and in exchange she receives only intolerance, disdain, and the indulgence afforded a child. In bringing her case into focus in the classroom, I hope the lesson for the students is about the value of intellectual honesty *and* the value of questioning, resilience, compassion, and resistance. The indetermination surrounding the figure of Ángela also affords another valuable lesson—that of suspending judgment and accepting ambiguity—for to practice and respect critical thinking is to recognize and honor the boundaries of knowing.

The appeal of using *San Manuel Bueno* as a vehicle for teaching close reading and critical inquiry is that so much of what can be argued about the story is open for debate and lends itself to a pedagogy structured around hooks's concept of radical openness. However one chooses to frame the students' examination of *San Manuel Bueno* as a literary artifact, stimulating, nurturing, and sustaining the students' curiosity is paramount.[3] For hooks, critical thinking can work only if it is driven by the engine of honest curiosity, asserting that it "involves first discovering the who, what, when, where, and how of things—finding the answers to those eternal questions of the inquisitive child—and then utilizing the knowledge in a manner that enables you to determine what matters most" (9). This observation is apt because, in assigning *San Manuel Bueno* in a gateway course, we should expect to devote attention to the who, what, when, where, and how. In the process, however, opportunities inevitably arise to draw the students into a space of bafflement from which to challenge their initial understanding and then shift the optic to whatever aspect of the text matters most. Indeed, the themes that come to light through Ángela's story—authoritarianism, misogyny, oppression, subversion, and freethinking—hold more relevance for the times in which our students are living than the metaphysical and doctrinal questions that arise from a traditionally sympathetic reading of Don Manuel. Therefore, it seems prudent to structure the analysis of the text more around Ángela than Don Manuel.

In closing, one benefit of teaching *San Manuel Bueno* at any level of instruction is that it both invites and resists interpretation and, as is so often the case, prompts inward reflection. These attributes are especially needed in the context of a gateway course, in which students can potentially overcome their initial insecurities about studying literature by having a meaningful reading experience and by cultivating their role as objective interpreters. Mancing's defense of the interpretive authority of the reader lends credibility to any such student-centered approach: "Let me repeat," he writes, "*we* readers each *construct* the meaning of the work" (354). *San Manuel Bueno* invites thoughtful reflection on the constructed nature of truth and the mediating role of the inquirer. I trust the process of critical inquiry to lead my students to a meaningful understanding of *San Manuel Bueno* that attests to the contours and frontiers of their intellectual curiosity and that respects the inscribed hermeneutical boundaries of the text. The lesson that my students invariably take away from this exercise is that succeeding in courses centered on literature hinges on playing the role of the close reader, critical thinker, and objective mediator of understanding. Indeed, the use of the term *literary artifact* implies this important role of the student and invites his or her objective inquiry and exploration.

NOTES

[1] The text of "Mi religión" used in this essay is the one included in the Espasa-Calpe edition of *"Mi religión" y otros ensayos breves*. The translation is by Armand Baker.

[2] The text of *San Manuel Bueno, mártir* used in this essay is Mario Valdés's edition, published by Cátedra. Translations are by Armand Baker.

[3] *San Manuel Bueno* can be used profitably in courses on European modernism. For more on the modernist qualities of Unamuno's literary production, see especially Soufas; M. Gómez. For more on the literary context of *San Manuel Bueno*, see Nepaulsingh.

Teaching Miguel Picazo's *La tía Tula* to College Students in the United States

Diana Roxana Jorza

Traditionally hailed as a masterpiece of the New Spanish Cinema of the 1960s, Miguel Picazo's *La tía Tula* ("Aunt Tula") has been customarily seen as a politically oppositional take on the Francoist gender ideology that favored female sexual repression. If Miguel de Unamuno's 1921 novel focuses on a protagonist who resolutely denies biological maternity to paradoxically found a kind of spiritual matriarchy, Picazo's film radically undermines Tula's virginal motherhood as subservient to the overpowering yearning for spiritual perpetuation that underlies Unamuno's narrative and thought. The movie's confessed attempt to construct an emblematic figure of provincial Catholic womanhood (that was both repressed and repressive) is set in postwar Spain, which departs from Unamuno's rather abstract sociohistorical setting, while it recycles the nineteenth-century regenerationist critique of the Spanish province.

By interrogating the historical and ideological rationale behind this cinematic adaptation and by critically repositioning the female protagonist through feminist approaches, this essay seeks to overcome the entrenched cliché of sexual repression applied to the main character. Furthermore, this hermeneutic shift serves to understand why contemporary American college students, particularly women, tend to see the Tula of 1964 as an empowering female figure within the rigid constraints imposed on women during Franco's regime.

I have taught this film four times so far: twice for a course titled Love and Education in Modern Spanish Culture, an advanced undergraduate class on various romance and education models and how they are sociohistorically and culturally informed; once for *El extraño viaje* / The Strange Journey: Cinema and (Hi)story Writing in Postwar Spain, an undergraduate film survey of postwar Spain; and once for *Tú y yo somos tres* / You and I Are Three: Reading Cinema in Franco's Spain, a graduate class on the diverse interpretations of postwar Spanish cinema in a historical context of uneven movie censorship. My undergraduate seminars satisfied one of the five elective requirements for majors and supplementary majors, mostly seniors in business, economics, premedical, or preprofessional studies. In both undergraduate seminars, I taught Picazo's *La tía Tula* in the later part of the course, after we examined Juan Antonio Bardem's *Calle Mayor* ("Main Street"), set in a similar provincial setting of postwar Spain, at a time of conflicting gender roles. My students had not read the original novel because of scheduling constraints, but they relied on my abstract of Unamuno's plot before watching the movie. The undergraduates of Love and Education in Modern Spanish Culture had also analyzed Unamuno's short novel *Dos madres* ("Two Mothers") during the first part of the course, while the students in my film classes, both graduate and undergraduate, read my personal synthetic notes on

Unamuno's thought and narrative through a handout posted online in advance. To sum up, I did not have to introduce many cultural references (belonging to Unamuno's time or the 1960s) in class before the actual film analysis, relying on what the students had already read and studied. What I added to this prior structure were some fragments from two feminist texts: Sandra Lee Bartky's "Foucault, Femininity, and the Modernization of Patriarchal Power" and Janice A. Radway's introduction (on Nancy Chodorow) to *Reading the Romance: Women, Patriarchy, and Popular Literature*. My students read these excerpts after watching the movie and making notes about their first impressions, so that the readings could help them better frame and analyze their viewing experience before class. Our primary task was to explore why this initial exposure contradicted existing canonic interpretations of Picazo's movie and was unwittingly feminist in its strong, empathetic identification with the female protagonist and in its visceral condemnation of the stark misogynistic treatment of Tula.

While I found the few feminist studies of Unamuno's *La tía Tula* (Gabriele; Feal Deibe) or of his *Dos madres* (Arrington Bruner Smith) very useful for understanding Picazo's 1964 movie, I was surprised that the many reviews, articles, or book chapters about the film conspicuously lacked feminist interpretations, which partially explained the silenced emancipatory readings of Tula within her sociohistorical setting. Furthermore, a critique of the institutionalized historiography of Spanish film studies (in respect to the cinema produced during Franco's time) is essential in assessing the sociohistorical and cultural legacy that marked the production and the critical canonization of Picazo's work. Combined readings not only in feminist studies but also in more recent Spanish film and cultural studies are therefore vital for a more comprehensive evaluation of this film adaptation of Unamuno's novel. In this essay, I attempt to shed light on this diverse critical panorama vis-à-vis the specific analytic aspects I emphasized with my undergraduates.

Prior to our in-class examination of the movie, my undergraduate students already knew, after studying *Dos madres*, about the paradoxical, irresolvable quest for immortality in Unamuno's thought and about his assumption that maternal desire is a specifically female way of coping with that yearning. Not only were they already familiar with some cultural roots of that tormenting metaphysical malaise, but they were also equipped to discern in Unamuno's narrative a contradictory legacy of the nineteenth-century patriarchal cult of motherhood, as summed up in Arrington Bruner Smith's complex analysis: nurturing motherhood was idealized and advertised as the most powerful role for women at that time, yet there was also considerable male anxiety about the son's (i.e., future man's) potential infantilization by the mother, whose domestic influence on her son was often seen as an obstacle to his future autonomy in the public sphere through a separation from the mother. Furthermore, not only was the mother's loss a prerequisite for her son's successful individuation (359), but this enforced separation would parallel a complete sacrificial devotion to the son (and to all other children). Unconditional maternal love, allegedly morally and religiously redeeming for women, was the foremost reason for marriage, and it was also extended to spousal relations, which downplayed erotic love to a sanitized version of attachment that transformed the married woman into an instrumental civilizing figure, "un remedio" 'a remedy' (to use Unamuno's wording from *La tía Tula*), meant to domesticate and redeem an otherwise wayward husband. The extensive cultural dissemination of this asexual "angel of the house" image by the patriarchal bourgeois society of the nineteenth century and beyond often meant in practice that the spouses lived alienated, unable to make each other the object of erotic desire, which helps to better explain Raquel's fixation with maternity in *Dos madres*, in which she objectifies and emotionally castrates her lover, Juan. While this short novel redefines the Don Juan myth by defamiliarizing conventional gender roles (e.g., Raquel's secret financial power in the public sphere, a realm commonly dominated by men), it also appears as a continuation of such a myth and of the related patriarchal expectations of womanhood: while the "black widow" Raquel is the feared, all-powerful mother who generates male anxieties as she ironically reverses the existing gender power relations, she desires only to experience motherhood, the traditionally most important female role whose achievement allegedly condoned any sacrifice.

Similarly, when my students watch Tula's strong desire for motherhood in Picazo's adaptation, which she dissociates from erotic desire and from a marriage institution that views women as sex objects (i.e., "remedios" 'remedies') for a "naturally" lustier man, they do not condemn her as domineering and sexually repressed, but rather they indict Ramiro's "excess" (to use Sally Faulkner's term) and the priest's overbearing contribution to the perpetuation of unfair gender roles. Their take on the movie is already discernible from the beginning of the class, during the small-group icebreaking conversations about their gut reactions to the film, when most students, especially the women, voice their strong criticism of the expected gender roles in the movie. I try to build on those initial stances as we talk about the main differences between the film and the novel: unlike Unamuno's generic milieu, deprived of clear marks of time and space, the movie has a specific sociohistorical setting (a provincial town in 1960s Spain, very similar to that of *Calle Mayor*, set in the mid-1950s, with which the students were already familiar); there is no cinematic focus on Ramiro's first marriage with Rosa, Tula's sister, nor with his last marriage with Manuela, thus concentrating on the twisted relationship between him and Tula after Rosa's death (roughly chapters 7 to 14 in the twenty-five-chapter novel); the 1964 Tula has more agency, as Ramiro and his kids come to live in her house (unlike what happens in the novel, where she goes to live in Ramiro's house after Rosa's death), and she owns and actively administrates the rural family property; the film includes Ramiro's attempted rape of Tula and his completed rape of her niece, the teenager Juanita; Tula is left alone in her house as Ramiro and his kids relocate after his rushed marriage to the pregnant Juanita (shortly before that, there is a grotesquely naive bachelorette party in which Tula participates and which is meant to showcase similarly sexually repressed single women whose educations have been shaped by a prude and authoritarian Catholic Church).

We begin our actual film analysis by examining the ambience of the provincial town and its dating rituals, as we watch Tula, in the street, silently followed by one of her suitors, Emilio, who is undeterred by her dismissive attitude, which she had expressed in writing before and expresses now through her obvious determination to run away from him and to protect herself from being accosted by flanking both her sides with a female friend. The undergraduates watching Tula trying to flee Emilio understandably identify his persistence as harassment and a lack of respect for her consent, so they cannot approve of his repeated marriage proposals, especially as they see him later in the movie as a voyeur at the outskirts of the town, where Madrid dwellers go out with apparent prostitutes. From the ongoing conversations between Tula and her female friends, students also realize that stories of domestic violence abound, which predisposes students to be very sympathetic toward Tula's rejection of Emilio and of other previous suitors because she would never let a man abuse her. She takes up this intractable position again later, when Ramiro tries to intercede for Emilio and Tula curtly replies that she does not want to "aguantar" 'put up with' any man. Having read Lee Bartky's text on the social construction of women as "docile and compliant companions for men" (143), disciplined into restraining their emotions in public, using constricting gestures and postures, casting their eyes downward, and showing vulnerability in alleged need of male protection (134–42), the students who analyze this movie are more likely to appreciate the magnitude of Tula's defiance (of conventional gender roles and corresponding power structures) than her parallel submission to some aspects of her patriarchal Catholic education. They also remember, in this respect, Carmen Martín Gaite's *Usos amorosos de la postguerra española* ("Courtship Customs in Postwar Spain"), a diagnostic of postwar female discipline (which they read to better understand *Calle Mayor*) based on an institutionalized fostering of naïveté (38); of a childlike vulnerability in need of (male) shelter (51); of body restraint, submissiveness, and patience (72); and, finally, of the ultimate model of a selfless, brave, and self-sacrificial mother (152).

As we discuss Tula's strong control of emotions and erotic desire in various moments of the movie (e.g., during the credits, when she appears like a frozen tableau at her sister's funeral; when she wakes up during the night in the countryside and keeps on drinking water and complaining of the hot weather in Ramiro's presence), we focus on her alleged repressed and repressive behavior as the effects of her patriarchal Catholic education by paying attention to the social construction (of gender) by which female subjects (and their bodies) are disciplined and turned into "docile bodies," to use Michel Foucault's well-known term from *Discipline and Punish*, a term that was fruitfully used by Lee Bartky and other feminist readers of Foucault. In so doing, we go against the simplistic but canonic Freudian reading of female repression in Picazo's film, which has been pervasive in most movie analyses and reviews since the movie's official release (e.g., Gubern; Faulkner; Aranda; Egido; del Amo; Belio; Rupérez) and which was apparently present even at the level of directorial intentionality, judging by the interviews with Picazo in the documentary *De Salamanca a ninguna parte* ("From Salamanca to Nowhere"). What is particularly problematic is that the critics and scholars indicting Tula and her behavior choose a Freudian reading of repression while neither questioning the patriarchal roots of her education nor perceiving the emancipatory bravery of her refusal to get married to Ramiro (or other men) in such a gender-constrictive environment. This oblivious interpretation has been undoubtedly catalyzed by the sociopolitical context of New Spanish Cinema, to which Picazo's movie is canonically ascribed. This cinema drew together a group of young filmmakers who embodied a novel art—auteurist Spanish cinema—directed toward an elite intellectual audience that, like the filmmakers, was in an oppositional political stance to the regime. Despite their careful craftsmanship and aesthetic pretensions, movies like Picazo's *La tía Tula* were therefore made and judged primarily through the lenses of political protest and denunciation. As the director states in an interview showed in *De Salamanca a ninguna parte*, Tula's trumpeted repression was thus meant to have an indexical function for the general (political and social) repression hovering over the Spain of the time. To say that Tula is, to a great extent, the product of a patriarchal society that goes beyond Franco's Spain and that most likely shaped the director (and the film critics) as well would therefore seem indecorous, as it appears to cast less culpability on a political system that should (canonically) be first and foremost condemned. In my undergraduate classes, I chose to only briefly mention this underlying sociopolitical reason for the simplistic interpretation of Tula's character, as I believe that, for my students and their overall ability to deconstruct and challenge gender stereotyping, it is more productive to focus on a feminist reading of the film rather than dwell on issues that are more relevant for a broader historiographical understanding of Spanish film and cultural studies. However, in my graduate film seminar, where we studied Picazo's movie within this larger framework, I assigned an additional critique on the institutionalized reception of New Spanish Cinema since the 1960s (Santos Zunzunegui's article on its literary roots); these students were already familiar with such field questioning because we had previously discussed Jo Labanyi's "Cinema and the Mediation of Everyday Life in 1940s and 1950s Spain" as well as Luis Alonso García's historiographical revision of postwar Spanish cinema.

The same patriarchal education that shaped Tula's outlook on love, marriage, and maternity, inspiring her to prioritize motherhood as the ultimate fulfillment, at the expense of denying her body and its desires, also taught her that the realm of her greatest power is the home, where she can help model good Christians by molding Rosa's children into similar, gender-differentiated patterns of conduct. However, both the body and the house—two traditional icons of female entrapment in a patriarchal society—are reconceptualized into symbols of rebellion and autonomy, as John P. Gabriele shows in his skillful analysis of

Unamuno's novel (111), a transformation that is also discernible in the 1964 film, despite the ideological bias of its adaptation. The kids unsurprisingly bear the protagonists' diminutivized names (Tulita and Ramirín), thus showing they are their aunt's and father's younger versions, meant to perpetuate the same role models. As we watch several scenes shot inside the house to see how Tula and Ramiro behave toward the children, the students do not fail to notice that Tula also introduces a significant personal imprint on this authoritarian pedagogical inheritance, somewhat similar to the protagonist's attempt in Unamuno's novel. On the one hand, she treats Ramirín more sternly than his sister and tries to stifle his (naturalized) pubescent interest in objectifying the female body, lightly condoned by his father as normal for his age; the fact that Ramirín hides newspaper cutouts among his school notes seems to point to the school as an institutional venue where boys share a double-standard culture that both gives them asexual images of women (i.e., the "angel of the house" model) and allows them to privately enjoy voyeuristic images of female bodies that are displayed for male pleasure. On the other hand, she repeatedly defends Tulita from her brother's bullying and from her father's condescending, gender-segregated treatment, a protective attitude stemming from the stereotyped patriarchal image of women as delicate and sensitive, in need of more protection and understanding. In so doing, Tula rewrites the conventional damsel-in-distress appeal to male guardianship by suggesting a special connection of women to their female heritage through the strong ties between mother/aunt and daughter/niece, which Gabriele also lucidly identifies in Unamuno's novel (108).

Even if Picazo's movie elides an explicit reference to Unamuno's central metaphor of the working bees model of "sororidad" 'sorority' as opposed to the drones' sole focus on mating, it still paradoxically succeeds in hinting that men are incapable of providing women with truly nurturing care. According to Radway's application of Chodorow's feminist revision of Freud (13–14), this kind of nurturing lets women adopt the pleasurable stance of the pampered child in relation to a protective and caring parental figure; combining traditionally masculine traits (e.g., strength, energy, authority) with attributes of maternal, nurturing care, the perfect male protagonist thus embodies both the father and the mother, which, in Chodorow and Radway's view, is an implicit "protest against the fundamental inability of heterosexuality to satisfy the very desires with which it engendered women" (Radway 14). To insist that Tula should have given in to Ramiro's excessive desire and harassment because she had a clear, though repressed, attraction to him, as most film critics have exhorted, completely disregards a more complex view of Tula's dissatisfaction with Ramiro's masculinity, reducing it to a question of merely appeasing an instinctual drive. Throughout the entire movie, Ramiro is presented as an immature, sex-crazed man, incapable of providing a respectful, nurturing companionship or of fulfilling his parental role, as he invariably delegates all upbringing responsibilities to Tula, who actually becomes both the mother and the father in the house, as Carlos Feal Deibe judiciously observed about the novel ("Nada" 76). Furthermore, Ramiro seems neither able nor willing to take care of most household errands or to make long-term family plans (e.g., to go on a vacation, to buy a television set). He is portrayed as an infantilized child in need of maternal care, which is evident when he burps after a meal, when he wears a bib-looking napkin around his neck at Tula's advice, when he abandons his (sick) body to Tula's care, and so on. In addition to these numerous shortcomings, he attempts to rape her, an abuse that is deviously purged of almost all male culpability by Tula's confessor, whose insistence on the (social) necessity of marriage between them after the attempted rape, despite Tula's dignified but resolute rejection of being a mere "remedio" for Ramiro's uncontrollable lust, is perhaps my students' most denounced patriarchal intervention. They can better explain their admiration of Tula, and their critical distancing from the priest's matter-of-fact, empathetic understanding of Ramiro's abusive behavior and from his harsh condemnation of Tula's alleged sinful pride (as she insists that "me estimo en más" 'I value myself more'), when they use Lee Bartky's observation that, in a society where ecclesiastical and civil authorities are conjoined (as was the case in 1960s Spain), an individual who holds both powers (i.e., the priest) is actually one of the last resorts to correct recalcitrant women left unconstrained by the male figures of their family (148).

As we conclude our analysis of Tula's constant defiance of traditional gender roles that confine women to a position of social subordination and passivity, we end our discussion by speculating on the film's ending, different from that in Unamuno's novel: if there Tula is finally raised to the revered (and contradictory) status of a guardian female saint of the home that, like San Manuel's character, dies doubting the means and the results of her lifelong mission, Picazo's adaptation deprives Tula of what she most desires, to mother and educate Rosa's children, thus depriving her of any personal fulfillment or molding power. As she says goodbye to Ramiro and his children at the railway station, what struck my students was not, as the movie's critics have tirelessly reiterated, how this ending can be seen as a belated awareness of her unconfessed attraction to Ramiro, whom she irreversibly loses as he is forced to marry the pregnant Juanita and relocate. Coming after the final confrontation between Ramiro and Tula, as she finds out about Juanita's rape and about his necessarily hasty marriage, the railway farewell scene has the unmistakable flavor of a final narrative punishment of Tula's unrepentant defiance of conventional gender roles through her resilient power over her body and her house. It is thus meaningful that, while Ramiro considers Tula guilty of his raping of Juanita (because Tula refused to give in to his uncontrollable sex urge in the countryside), Tula rightfully accuses him of reducing romance to sex, which made her rigorously take control of her body rather than give in to her instinctual attraction to him. Furthermore, when he tries to silence her uncomfortable accusations, she defiantly reminds him that she can say and do whatever she wants because she is in her own house. To be left alone there, as Ramiro immediately points out spitefully (without Rosa's children and with no future male interest in her body), cannot therefore but appear as a contrived ending, ensuring that the woman who questioned and stood up to all symbols of patriarchal power is narratively penalized at the level of the plot if no intradiegetic male authority figure is capable of disciplining her. To be able to read this enforced finale as a narrative retaliation strengthens, however, the film audience's feminist interpretation, generating even more constructive protest against unjust, naturalized power relations—not an insignificant learning perk of studying this sample of Spanish culture as part of a broader liberal education.

COMPARATIVE LITERATURE, PHILOSOPHY, AND RELIGION CLASSROOMS

Belief and Modernity in *Del sentimiento trágico de la vida*

C. A. Longhurst

Of all Miguel de Unamuno's texts, *Del sentimiento trágico de la vida* ("The Tragic Sense of Life") is probably the most challenging for the teacher trying to make it relevant to the students of today. First, religious belief over the past one hundred years since the work's first appearance has become a much more personal matter seldom discussed in public. Second, today's students rarely have the grounding in philosophical and religious thought that facilitates access to Unamuno's reformulations of what he has read. Third, Unamuno's idiosyncratic style of discourse does not help: while his language is always comprehensible, his habit of making provocative statements with no explanation can be off-putting; likewise, his inveterate digressions can be irritating.

These various aspects, not to mention the vast range of allusions in Unamuno's text, create pedagogical problems not susceptible to simple solutions, and the teacher will have to consider how best to approach the text in order to make it as accessible as possible to the particular group of students. For example, he or she may consider that providing a brief summary of each of the twelve essays or chapters of *Del sentimiento trágico* may be a useful tool in helping students to discern the progression in Unamuno's thesis about the role and importance of transcendent belief in human life. While not as obvious as the plot of a novel, *Del sentimiento trágico* does have a kind of plot or thread nonetheless. The work was not improvised; it was written and rewritten over many years, and only the closing chapter on what Spain's role should be in the new spirituality smacks of extemporization.

Del sentimiento trágico is not a theological treatise, nor is it a purely philosophical one, being much too personal for that. Yet it can be fitted into a religious studies course in which the source and nature of belief play a prominent role. Equally, it can perfectly well be included in a philosophical course on European existentialism in a line that goes from the tormented believer Søren Kierkegaard to the uncompromising atheist Jean-Paul Sartre. It would even find a place in a course on the psychology of spiritualism along the lines developed by William James (an important influence on Unamuno) and later existentialist psychologists such as Karl Jaspers (who shares with Unamuno the idea of philosophy as a psychological phenomenon) and even R. D. Laing and his view of personality as a psychopathological state that operates on a sliding scale between the sane and the psychotic. These various possibilities perhaps presuppose studying the text as a whole, but extracting individual chapters for particular study need not be discarded as a teaching strategy. For example, chapter 4, "La esencia del catolicismo" ("The Essence of Catholicism"), could be used in a survey of different Christian religions, and chapter 5, "La disolución racional" ("The Collapse of Reason"), in a philosophical course on reason and its uses. Chapter 7, "Amor, dolor, compasión y personalidad" ("Love, Sorrow, Compassion and Personality"), is relevant to mystical thought; and chapter 8, "De Dios a Dios" ("From God to God"), discusses the concept of God.

The approach adopted here revolves around the underlying themes that inform Unamuno's text. It consists in explaining the background against which *Del sentimiento trágico* should be seen and then describing as plainly as possible the main ideas around which Unamuno builds his case for belief, a case he is putting forward as an alternative to the traditional one based on defined dogmas. The explanation of the main thrust of *Del sentimiento trágico* is followed by, in an appendix, a teaching tool in the form of a list of questions that a teacher could use selectively in classroom discussions to bring out the relevance of Unamuno's text to the present day. Students who develop an interest in finding out where Unamuno's ideas are derived from should go on to read Nelson Orringer's *Unamuno y los protestantes liberales* ("Unamuno and the Liberal Protestants"), in which flesh is put on the bare bones offered here. Also, Orringer's own edition of the text (published by Tecnos) contains a wealth of informative notes helpful to both student and teacher. Those students who want to venture beyond *Del sentimiento trágico* and come to grips with the rather unusual nature of Unamuno's religious faith now have a helpful guide in Jan E. Evans's *Miguel de Unamuno's Quest for Faith*. The massive, detailed study *El problema del sobrenatural en Miguel de Unamuno* ("The Problem of the Supernatural in Miguel de Unamuno"), by Alfonso García Nuño, is recommended for very advanced students. Students whose knowledge of Spanish is limited may turn to Anthony Kerrigan's translation of *Del sentimiento trágico*, which carries the added bonus of a valuable essay by Martin Nozick.

Context

The book version of *Del sentimiento trágico* appeared for sale in 1913 after serialization in 1911–12. What prompted Unamuno to write this work, an earlier version of which, provisionally titled "Tratado del amor de Dios" ("Treatise on God's Love"), he had discarded?[1] Essentially, what he was trying to do was to find an alternative basis for Christian belief, an alternative, that is, to the traditional scholastic theology of the Catholic Church going back to Saint Thomas Aquinas.

Traditional Christian beliefs had come under attack from two sources: first from the increasing dominance, after Isaac Newton, of mechanistic science (bolstered by Darwinism in the nineteenth century) and its insistence on materialistic explanations of the universe and of mankind based on observed evidence; and second from the work of nineteenth-century biblical scholars who gave a very different view of the Gospels from the one that had been held for centuries by the Christian churches and especially the Catholic Church. Unamuno was probably less concerned with the scientific issue; he respected science but felt that its approach fell well short of explaining the human situation and mankind's longing for transcendence (i.e., for a transphysical or divine dimension) and survival beyond physical death, a longing that had been there since human records began. The scientific view of man was seriously incomplete and left room for spiritual belief.

The view that had emerged from the so-called modernist theology of the nineteenth century, however, posed a different and in some ways more difficult problem for traditional Christian belief, since it questioned the historicity of the New Testament; that is to say, it rejected the view of the Christian Gospels as historical documents. Most modernist theologians did not question the existence of Jesus of Nazareth, but they placed the accounts of his life in a completely new light. In particular, those scholars who initiated what came to be known as form criticism argued that the four evangelists had written their accounts in such a way as to fit in with the prophecies of the Old Testament. Whereas previously the Old Testament was seen to contain prefigurations or anticipations of the New Testament according to a divine plan, now, in the view of biblical scholars, the New Testament writings were seen as simply reproducing the expectations that the Gospel writers had picked up from the Old Testament. The Gospels were therefore mythopoetic rather than historical. By the time the mythical or figurative material was removed, there was not a great deal of biographical or historical information left, and what little remained appeared to refer to an ordinary human being with charismatic powers, not to a divine being. Instead of the supreme being predicated by the traditional doctrine of the Trinity, Jesus came to be seen not as a supernatural figure who emphasized abstract beliefs in a remote deity but as a social reformer whose teachings were impelled by concern for the welfare of his fellow humans. Indeed, this view of Jesus encouraged and was encouraged by a variant of emergent political socialism called simply Christian socialism, concerned with social reform rather than with achieving political power through revolution.

The new view of Jesus and of his teachings, and the concomitant attempt to modernize Christianity, provoked a severe backlash from the Catholic Church, which saw its authority threatened. Already, in 1879, Pope Leo XIII had issued an encyclical, "Aeterni Patris" ("Of the Eternal Father"), in which he denounced modernist theology and called for a return to the theological tradition known as scholasticism initiated by the thirteenth-century theologian Thomas Aquinas, which was regarded as the best way of countering the new Christianity, seen as an aberration by traditionalists. There then ensued a strong reactionary movement in Catholic Christianity, urged by Leo XIII's successor, Pope Pius X. This pope issued multiple decrees against the modernist movement in the Church, including, in 1907, the decree "Lamentabili sane exitu" ("With Truly Lamentable Results"), identifying no less than sixty-five errors in modernist theology, and the encyclical "Pascendi dominici gregis" ("Feeding the Lord's Flock"), condemning modernism as containing all possible heresies. The encyclical was followed by many other decrees and injunctions requesting obedience among Catholics, advising vigilance, and encouraging delation among the priesthood. This implacable attack on the reformers not only had a deleterious effect on Catholic biblical scholarship but also provoked dissidence and defections.

Brought up as a devout Catholic, Unamuno reassessed his faith when he read the modernist theologians, especially those from France and Germany,[2] concluding that his childhood beliefs were untenable and that Catholic Christianity needed to be reformulated if it was to endure and not become an irrelevance in a modern world governed by scientific thinking. This would require the abandonment of many traditional dogmas and of the Church's authoritarian attitude toward religious belief, since these dogmas had little or no foundation in the Bible or in rational thought. Unamuno was to a degree affected by Pope Pius X's attack on the modernists. His position in *Del sentimiento trágico* vis-à-vis Catholicism is more moderate and circumspect than it had been only a few years earlier. The encyclical of 1907 made him reconsider his views on faith as personal desire and faith as dictated by dogmatic truths. Now, for example, he admits the need for doctrinal content of some kind. He steers clear of criticizing Rome for its denunciations of modernism, even though in some respects Unamuno's position is perfectly modernist. He still believes that if Christianity is to exercise an impact on the population at large, a new basis for faith has to be found.[3] This became for Unamuno both a communitarian and a personal matter, for he felt very keenly the void left by his earlier unquestioning belief. Science had nothing to say on the important question of the human being's ultimate destiny, and this was for Unamuno the overriding question. If human beings are but momentary scintillations in the vastness of time and space, mere accidents in a purely contingent universe with no role or purpose, then neither morality, nor culture, nor altruism, nor personal striving makes much sense. It was therefore important to have a purpose, to give existence its "para qué" 'what for,' as he liked to put it (*Del sentimiento* 131). Aware of the gradual disappearance of transcendent or divine values from modern consciousness, he sought to point to a new way of retaining such values. That is what *Del sentimiento trágico* addresses. What follows are the main themes and succinct explanations of their content.

Major Themes

Thinking

Unamuno's starting point is what he sees as the major source of anxiety in human beings: survival. *Del sentimiento trágico* takes the form of a quasi-philosophical meditation on the human quest for perdurance. Humans are not just the knowing beings of traditional philosophy but beings who feel, who want, who imagine, who experience many different emotions. Real philosophy is not thought but thinking, a personal striving rooted deep inside ourselves and driven by disquiet and dissatisfaction, as well as by commitment to a personal quest rather than any abstract system. It is our feelings or sentiments that dictate what we think, but it is our thinking that subsequently enables us to formulate strategies for coping. To philosophize about the human situation requires more than the rational approach of the empirical sciences. Modern empirical science and the kind of philosophy that poses as scientific do not address the question of the high degree of self-consciousness in human beings and our concomitant desire for knowledge about ourselves and our universe. We are governed by our self-identity or consciousness of ourselves to such an extent that we search for a role and a purpose; we have somehow to come to terms with the fact of our existence by countering reason's intimation that we are nothing because we emerged from nothingness and will soon return to nothingness.

The search for a role or identity occupies a central place in *Del sentimiento trágico*, since it is an integral part of the basic theme of the work, namely, the impulse toward survival in this life and beyond, illogical as this yearning may seem in the light of reason and despite the conflicting tendencies and anxieties it can generate. What Unamuno wants to preserve above all is his personal identity, his self-consciousness, but who can guarantee the fulfillment of such a desire? In the face of this question, our thoughts turn to God as the only possible assurance. But what happens if our rational minds tell us that God is a human invention as much as were the gods of ancient pagan civilizations? And even if he is not an illusion, how can we know him? This, according to Unamuno, is the source of an unavoidable existential conflict. We long for the preservation of our self, of our individual being, but we have no very convincing reason to think that this longing is realistic. Our thinking about ourselves as both enduring and transient is the "tragic sense" of our existence.

Living

The whole thrust of *Del sentimiento trágico* is that each one of us tries to save his or her subjective consciousness; but in order to do this we need to keep alive the world around us, or, as Unamuno calls it, to personalize the world. The world exists for us whether we think of its existence in our consciousness or outside of it. Although still holding on to the idea of a subjective consciousness, Unamuno has no problem with the reality of the world and of other minds, as Cartesians might. It is not an epistemological question at all; it is not *saber* (knowing) but *sentir* (feeling), not a question of thinking existence but of experiencing it. We feel ourselves to exist, and this gives us some sense of the feelings of others. The world of others is revealed to each one of us not so much by cognitive acts as by intuition or insight. We imagine others to be capable of our feelings.

From recognizing in others the consciousness that we recognize in ourselves, Unamuno can posit his idea of a shared world without abandoning his precious principle of self-affirmation. This recognition that the others are like him because they are a reflection of his consciousness and he in turn is a reflection of theirs does not diminish Unamuno's own self-identity; but it underscores his need for the existence of others in order to affirm his own. This identity based on the distinction yet interdependence of different consciousnesses leads to a recognition of and a compassion for others (i.e., fellow feeling), others being the necessary condition for one's own individuality. We recognize, without needing to prove it, that others are not just bodily objects but are consciousnesses. This is implicit in wanting to be with others and, just as significantly, in wanting to be different from others, or, as Unamuno calls it, "singularizarse" 'to stand out' (164). What makes us human is the fact that we feel ourselves to be different from one another, and it is this quality of uniqueness that makes human relationships richly creative. Thus Unamuno holds that our lives should be a striving toward revealing our uniqueness to others (what he calls "hacerse insustituible" 'making oneself irreplaceable' [448]) while others reveal themselves to each one of us, a mutual sharing of our authentic singularity. This gives our lives a purpose. This purpose or sense of finality is necessary to counter the ever-present suspicion that we are nothing because what is not eternal lacks solidity. We try to combat this unreality, or purposelessness, by creating a purposive universe, and in Unamuno this takes the form of a substitute for the more traditional religious belief in eternal life based on divine revelation and Church dogma. Our mission or purpose is to become essential to others, irreplaceable, thereby countering our nothingness. To leave an imprint on others is to achieve a kind of immortality. This has both social and religious implications, and, indeed, at one point *Del sentimiento trágico* becomes a sociopolitical tract in which Unamuno advocates fidelity to one's calling in society and excoriates those who are less than enthusiastic about their occupation or the collective well-being. Renunciation of or withdrawal from normal life is an error since the next life can be envisaged only as a continuation of this one. We must be of and in the world and seek to influence others through a sense of solidarity with them. Unable to find a solution in either rationalism or dogmatic religion, Unamuno turns to his fellow humans for consolation and advocates a policy not of self-effacement but of mutual impression.

Loving

For humans, *being* is very much a *being with*. Our consciousness of ourselves and of the feelings we experience leads to consciousness of others. We imagine them capable of the same feelings. Sexual love—sharing an intimate experience with another being—gives rise to spiritual love, whose clearest manifestation is compassion—that is, shared suffering. Love and suffering go together because it is suffering above all that makes us self-aware and aware of other suffering beings. Compassion starts as a feeling of regret at one's finitude and from there spreads to other beings. The greater the similarity between other living entities and ourselves, the greater our feelings for them.

It is pain above all that tells us we are alive; what is dead or nonexistent does not suffer. Suffering is therefore an integral part of our being; it is our common bond, what unites us most, and what gives us our sense of solidarity. Suffering then begets compassion, which in turn begets love. Without suffering there would be no love; without love, no God. Suffering becomes a divine or universal attribute, as in the Christ story. This tells us that the love that emanates from our common suffering is more than mere sympathy or pity. It has deeper roots, serving to combat the sense of transience that we feel. The greatest love is for our children because they are most like ourselves and represent a sense of survival beyond our allotted time. Our social existence encourages us to survive through others, spreading our spirit to others, acting through society to fulfill its aims and to further its aspirations.

Love is therefore purposeful, not merely contingent, as science tells us that the universe is. Love is a projection into the future, an expectation of fulfillment. It is not time-bound, since we continue to love those whom we have lost; hence its intimation of lastingness. Our love for others reflects our intimate hope, and it is this hope that makes us turn to God—that is, to an eternal being. Love without hope, without commitment, is meaningless; it is reduced to mere expedience. Love impels us to believe in what we hope; it is therefore spiritual, not material, and it implies the existence of a transphysical realm. The *congoja*, or anguish, that we feel is an essential aspect of our intrinsic capacity for love. We feel anguish or anxiety (the existential angst) because we find it hard to accept our limitations in time and space. We aspire to overcome those limitations but cannot do so. It is this anguish that makes us turn to God, so God is the result of human suffering and incompleteness. Just as physical pain draws our attention to the material side of our existence, so anguish points to the spiritual dimension of our being. Our sense of nonfulfillment gives us God; and love for others (compassion) becomes love for God—that is, the fulfillment of our aspirations to perdurance. Our being is a *being with others*, and if we disregard the dead whom we have loved we annihilate part of our being. If we are committed to a person and our love is real, then that love must transcend temporality. Love thus becomes transcendent, godlike.

Believing

There are no rational proofs of the existence of God. If we believe, it is because we feel a need to believe, not because reason compels us. According to Unamuno, what is wrong with Catholicism is not its system of beliefs but its insistence that it offers a cast-iron guarantee of personal survival if you accept its dogmas. It has always insisted on the verifiability of dogma (e.g., the proofs of God's existence, the Trinity, the virgin birth; the historical reality of Christ's resurrection) in order to remove uncertainty from the human situation, since uncertainty threatens the social fabric. But in attempting to sustain faith through reason, the scholastic theology adopted by the Church has made unsustainable claims. Reason too has its limits. It may be able to establish partial truths, and it is an indispensable tool in our daily living, but it is unable to provide answers to fundamental questions about origins and purpose. Since our reason is conditioned by the world and by our social milieu, it cannot even establish that it itself is true—we have to believe that it is true—and therefore if taken to its ultimate conclusion leads to skepticism, robbing life of purpose. Scholastic theology has misused reason in support of its claims. The real question lies not in finding reasons for the existence of God but in explaining why we wish to believe and on what basis we believe. What does God represent in our lives?

The human creation of gods predates the reasoned explanation of God. The monotheistic religions refined earlier religions, but vestiges of these can still be observed in the Christian idea of the Trinity and the Mother of God. The God of theology is a mythical entity; his existence is part of our human civilization, not outside of it. God is thus a human necessity, a projection of our own self-consciousness onto the world, not something whose existence outside the human mind can be established. God is based on our existence, not on his. Does this then mean that belief in God is foolish or redundant? Unamuno certainly does not think so.

To decide to believe in God is to go outside the narrow bounds of reason, but that does not make belief nonsensical, although it does originate a conflict between our discursive intellect and our longing for purpose. But since the notion of God as a timeless presence is inherent in the human psyche, to abandon it is to put aside a part of our being. Belief in God is a natural desire, not an imposition from any constituted authority. It fulfills a double purpose. First, it satisfies, in part at least, the quest for transcendence, for going beyond our immediate world in search of answers to questions that human beings have always asked. Second, a shared God—an individual God makes little sense since we do not want to survive alone—provides us with a sense of belonging, a collective sense; it creates a community within which we find purpose, reassurance, and consolation. Belief in God gives a particular value to human life, defying the idea of a meaningless universe. Authentic Christian living in the modern world demands active involvement in society, not isolation. To be a Christian is to be so in civil life, not in a monastic cell. It is by working among others, by leaving an imprint on them and receiving their imprint on us, that we impose our will to live constructively and defy annihilation.

Dying

At the heart of *Del sentimiento trágico* lies human finitude and our reluctance to accept it. The "tragic sense" stems from the inherent contradiction between the rational and nonrational sides of the human brain. This contradiction is seen at its starkest in the uncertainty over the question of survival after death, which can be a source of considerable disquietude. For on the one hand, religion does not satisfy our brain's developed tendency to work things out by reasoning, yet on the other, rational discourse appears powerless to explain our fear of death, let alone our hankering for survival. This tension between our limited reason and our boundless aspiration is what underlies the religious philosophy of *Del sentimiento trágico*, and the recognition of such a state of affairs is what characterizes the authentic mode of existence advocated by Unamuno.

Awareness of our finitude is an essential characteristic of our being. Not to die would be more incomprehensible than to die, yet we still carry with us a deep, nonrational desire to not return to the nothingness from which we sprang, perhaps because nothingness is inapprehensible. This anxiety provoked by the greatest unknown factor in our lives is reflected in our wish to be remembered after death and is expressed, for example, through artistic creativity. This thirst for continued existence is very ancient and forms the real basis of religion. It nevertheless contains a paradox, because eternity seen from our vantage point is as incomprehensible as nothingness. For it is impossible to envisage how we can exist eternally except as a return to the godhead. But such a return denies the survival of individual consciousness, of self-identity, the longing for which creates the godhead in the first place.

The choice, then, appears to be between living on in God (or a universal consciousness), but not as ourselves (since we have lost our individual consciousness), and not living on at all; either way it means annihilation of the self. Despite wanting it, we cannot rationally explain a world of perpetual happiness or eternal existence. For as soon as we try to give some intelligible shape to our desire to live on as ourselves we create absurdities and contradictions. There is therefore no easy solution to the anxiety caused by having to live with the prospect of death. What Unamuno proposes is that we should accept this irreconcilability of opposites as an authentic part of our life struggle, that dying is indeed an integral part of living and not something to be put out of our minds as an unpleasant prospect. Dying represents the greatest uncertainty in the human situation, but its significance should lie in the acknowledgment that we cannot know, that our impending death is part of our innermost humanity and unites us in our common pursuit.

In conclusion, the pedagogical challenge posed by *Del sentimiento trágico* lies in getting students to appraise it in the light of Unamuno's objectives and judge the case it presents—whether on ethical, religious, or psychological grounds—sympathetically but firmly. *Del sentimiento trágico* offers a rather different view of Christianity and religion from the one Unamuno would have received as a child and even from the prevailing ones today. Has Unamuno succeeded in making a case for religious belief that offers an alternative to both theological dogmatism and uncompromising atheism?

NOTES

[1] He nevertheless kept the manuscript. The coincidences and discrepancies between the two works are studied by Orringer in his 2005 edition of both. References to *Del sentimiento trágico* are to this edition.

[2] The best known of these theologians were Friedrich Schleiermacher, David Friedrich Strauss, Albrecht Ritschl, Auguste Sabatier, Adolf von Harnack, Alfred Loisy, and George Tyrrell. For the influence of Protestant modernist theology on Unamuno and his modifications of it, see Orringer's book *Unamuno y los protestantes liberales* and his essay on the subject included in this volume.

[3] Unamuno would insist on his reinterpretation of Christianity some twelve years later in *La agonía del cristianismo* (1931, but first published in French in 1925; "The Agony of Christianity").

APPENDIX
Questions for the Classroom

The rather personal, even colorful, nature of the writing in *Del sentimiento trágico* gives rise to statements and arguments that seem at best dubious and at worst flawed. We find statements not always reconcilable with one another. This may perhaps serve to illustrate Unamuno's contention that our thoughts follow our feelings and not vice versa, but all the same these statements should not go unchallenged. The following list includes some of the many issues that call for further scrutiny.

Unamuno says that philosophers give a theoretical reason for their inquiries but seldom a practical or real one. What does he think motivates philosophers to make their inquiries?

Unamuno reverses René Descartes's "cogito, ergo sum" ("I am thinking, therefore I exist") and says that the truth is rather "homo sum, ergo cogito" ("I am human, therefore I am thinking"; *Del sentimiento* 141 [Tecnos]). Is this a sound and sensible criticism of Descartes's reasoning? If not, where has Unamuno gone wrong?

Unamuno says that everything that is vital (life-sustaining) is irrational and everything rational is antivital. How can we defend reason from the charge of being antivital?

Unamuno distinguishes two dimensions in human existence: the world of the sensible (what we access through our senses) and the world of the spirit (our sentiments and imagination). Is he falling into the Cartesian dualism that he criticizes?

Unamuno sees *pensar* (thinking) and *sentir* (feeling) as irreconcilable rivals. Does this have to be so?

Unamuno insists that a natural longing for personal survival, even survival after death, is what lies at the center of religious belief. Is he right? Are there no other explanations for the rise of religion in human affairs?

Unamuno holds that life becomes meaningless if we accept that death brings annihilation. Can a purely temporary and finite existence not be meaningful?

Unamuno regards a predominantly cerebral faith (one without passions or emotions) as not being real faith. Is this view of imperturbable or unemotional faith justified?

Why does Unamuno give priority to the teleological "para qué" 'what for' over the causal "por qué" 'why'? Is purpose independent of origins?

Unamuno states that God is a social and collective concept. How is this to be reconciled with his view of religion as a longing for personal survival?

Unamuno rejected the "argument from design" for the existence of God. Are his arguments persuasive?

Unamuno's questions about a possible next life all end in aporias. Why is this?

A critic has said that "Unamuno needs God to give meaning to his life and to guarantee his survival after death, but he dodges the question of whether that God exists outside of his need for him" (Evans, *Miguel de Unamuno's Quest* 60). Is this a valid criticism?

Unamuno places a great deal of importance on the role of suffering in our lives; it is what makes us human. But is suffering really as necessary as Unamuno makes out? Do you know anything of Unamuno's own circumstances that might help explain his raising of suffering to a transcendental level?

How does Unamuno treat the problem of evil, which historically has been one of the great challenges facing theologians?

Unamuno distinguishes between Protestantism and Catholicism by saying that in Protestantism religion is derived from ethics whereas in Catholicism ethics is derived from religion. Is this really so?

Unamuno seems to have an ambivalent attitude toward the idea of survival through fame. Why does he both emphasize and criticize the striving for fame?

Should we be persuaded by Unamuno's argument that the religious sentiment of Spaniards is essentially tragic?

In the final chapter of *Del sentimiento trágico* Unamuno does not synthesize but chooses instead to argue polemically against Spanish Europeanizers (such as José Ortega y Gasset) and in favor of Spain as leader of a spiritual world that northern Europe is losing. How can this be reconciled with his attempt to adapt Christian belief to modern times?

We could describe *Del sentimiento trágico* as a treatise on religious belief and ways of believing. But does it contain any practical advice on how to lead our lives?

Mist in a Comparative Literature Classroom: Unamuno, Dostoyevsky, and Dialogue

Tom Dolack

Miguel de Unamuno was a great paradoxalist. Contradiction runs unapologetically through much of his thought: peace in war, an atheist priest, authors who become their own characters. This is no less true of his relationship to world literature. On the one hand, Unamuno practically begs to be read in a comparative context. A professor of classics, he read over a dozen languages and championed the literature of supposedly minor languages such as Basque and Portuguese; references and quotes from all over the world litter his writings. Even his name seems to hint at "one world." He wrote as if he were a new Adam, putting pen to paper for the first time; as if there were no past or future, but at the same time trying to produce his past and future. Yet, despite his cosmopolitanism, he was also explicitly a Spanish author, repeatedly emphasizing his ties to Castilian culture and language despite being born in the Basque Country. A resolution to this contradiction is about as possible as to any of the other contradictions in his work, but the inherent tension can be used as a segue to a discussion of Unamuno and his broader context.

As with any rich text, there are many ways of approaching *Niebla* ("Mist"), and adding a comparative element only multiplies these. Sifting through the Spanish connections alone is a major task, from the Cervantesque metafictional aspects to Unamuno's play with the realist tradition of writers like Benito Pérez Galdós, which may be alluded to in the character Augusto Pérez's name. But opening the door to the many authors that Unamuno knew well—from Plato to Søren Kierkegaard—makes for a dizzying abyss of possibilities. Time spent on any of the traditions that inform the novel in order to place them in a larger context can be helpful. One could focus on Unamuno's beloved classics. In that case, instructors could do a lot with the Socratic dialogues—after all, dialogue is the central element of the *nivola*. There is another parallel in that Socrates's dialogues are really Plato's monologues. "Mis monólogos son diálogos" 'My soliloquies are dialogues,' Don Miguel de Unamuno, for his part, tells Augusto (2: 667; 220).[1] Further comparisons can be made in terms of genre and Unamuno's play with tragedy and epic, or "trigedia" 'trigidy' and "opopeya" 'opic' (2: 551; 18). A Greek tragedy can be virtually chosen at random and compared with *Mist* in terms of the role of fate, of free will, and of the gods or authors. Indeed, such a comparison can be useful in helping to make the depth of Unamuno's argument clearer. There is a tendency among students to either enjoy or dislike the novel based on the final conceit of the interview between Don Miguel and Augusto, but either way it can be easy to get distracted by the nivolistic fireworks and lose sight of the larger point. A comparison with heroes such as Oedipus or Orestes can shed light on the distinct roles of the different characters, with Don Miguel as a god enforcing fate or his will (see, for instance, the character Víctor Goti's prologue) and Augusto as a tragic (or even Romantic) figure trying to fight against destiny or a tyrannical god. Even some of the secondary characters can take on new importance with this approach, as the servants Domingo and Liduvina act like the chorus, commenting on the absurdity of Augusto's actions.

As a love story, *Mist* can also be viewed in the context of the European love lyric. It contains many of the tropes of Spanish and European love tales, including a Celestina figure (or two), the use of blazon, a love triangle, and a jilted lover. Comparing Unamuno's use of the love theme with students' preconceived ideas of love narratives, particularly Spanish ones, can lead to a productive discussion. It can be argued that either Unamuno flips the standard tale on its head (with the men being passive and the women being active) or that Augusto's failings as a lover stem from his taking the tropes of the lyric tradition to their most extreme and logical conclusion. There has always been something self-centered and self-serving about the love lyric dating back at least to Petrarch. The poet may spend his—or, to a lesser extent, her—time singing the praises of the beloved, but love lyrics seem to have a way of actually focusing on the poem that is elevating the beloved and the poet writing that poem. The actual achievement of the poet's goal can be detrimental to the poetic project in that it destroys the impetus for poetry. Augusto heads off this danger by starting off with an imaginary version of his love: "¡Oh, Eugenia, mi Eugenia, has de ser mía! ¡Por lo menos, mi Eugenia, ésta que me he forjado . . . !" 'O Eugenia! My Eugenia! You shall be mine! At least the Eugenia I created, my Eugenia . . . !' (2: 563; 38). This fits with the thought that starts the novel: "La función más noble de los objetos es la de ser contemplados" 'The noblest role of any object is that of being contemplated' (2: 557; 27). But how, students should ask, does this square with the idea of dialogue that is so central to the novel?

A starting point to this question can be a discussion of Augusto's progression over the novel. He moves from a solipsistic obsession with a single woman to two and eventually three women who speak to his head, heart, and stomach (2: 643; 179), before winding up with none. It is his relationships with these women that lead him through his successive realizations. It is being the other in relation to Eugenia that begins the breakdown of his solipsism; it is in seeing his own reflection in Rosario's eyes that he begins to establish a dialogic relationship with the outside world (2: 645–46; 183), which in turn sets up his dialogues with Víctor Goti and Don Miguel himself. The love story and its relationship with earlier tradition are inextricable from the philosophical message of the novel and can serve as a user-friendly means of delving into it.

In class, the most relevant plot elements and thematic points can be used to transition into the deeper philosophical issues of the novel, especially the issue of dialogue. I have taught *Mist* in a ten-week comparative literature course that focuses on the literature of existentialism (albeit a rather generous interpretation of that movement) in translation that begins with Fyodor Dostoyevsky's

Notes from Underground as well as "The Grand Inquisitor" and "The Russian Monk" sections of *The Brothers Karamazov* (these two should be done together; "The Grand Inquisitor" without the tale of Zosima is like *Inferno* without *Paradiso*). Then I teach Rainer Maria Rilke's *The Notebooks of Malte Laurids Brigge* (where class discussion of masks fits quite well with *Mist*) before getting to Unamuno. The second half of the course features works by the usual suspects: André Malraux (*Man's Fate*), Jean-Paul Sartre (*Nausea*), Albert Camus (*The Stranger*), and Samuel Beckett (*Waiting for Godot* and some of the short plays).

Beginning with Dostoyevsky, especially *Notes*, is particularly useful for Unamuno, even if (or perhaps specifically because) Dostoyevsky's worldview is so different from that of every other thinker in the course. Indeed, at first blush the two works would seem to be polar opposites. *Notes* is an extended monologue describing, in painful detail, the psychologic torture wrought on and by the "Underground Man" as a result of his isolation and the brutal conditions of St. Petersburg. But Dostoyevsky's works are very much based on the idea of dialogue. There too, "soliloquies are dialogues." Nowhere is this more evident than in *Notes*.

I begin my teaching of *Notes* by going through the opening paragraph in a detailed way that relies very heavily on Mikhail Bakhtin's reading of the passage (*Problems* 127–30, 227–30). My class is aimed at students new to comparative literature and literary theory, so I do not assign Bakhtin's text but instead give a digested version of the material and point the interested to the original text. Passages of Bakhtin could be assigned to more advanced students.

The first lines of the novel are: "Я человек больной . . . Я злой человек. Непривлекательный я человек. Я думаю, что у меня болит печень. Впрочем, я ни шиша не смыслю в моей болезни и не знаю наверно, что у меня болит. Я не лечусь и никогда не лечился, хотя медицину и докторов уважаю" 'I am a sick man . . . I am a spiteful man. I am a most unpleasant man. I think my liver is diseased. Then again, I don't know a thing about my illness; I'm not even sure what hurts. I'm not being treated and never have been, though I respect both medicine and doctors' (5: 99; 3).[2] A reliable way of getting class discussion moving is to trust students' gut reactions. I start by asking their initial reaction to the words "I am a sick man." This is generally something along the lines of sympathy. But the reaction to the second sentence, "I am a spiteful man," is far more negative (what kind of man calls himself "spiteful"?). Moving on, "unpleasant" isn't nearly as negative. Then: the diseased liver brings on more sympathy, only to be replaced by confusion or consternation at the avowals of ignorance and his willful passivity toward his disease, despite his respect for medicine. And so on for the rest of the paragraph and, indeed, the novel. Once students have a visceral feel for what's happening rhetorically, I move on to what's going on beneath the surface, and the key to this is the ellipsis after the first sentence. What is going on in the head of the Underground Man during that marked pause? According to Bakhtin, he is hearing his own words as if he were someone else, which forces him to try to correct or change the impression that he has made on his interlocutor. This begins a “дурная бесконечность” ‘vicious circle’ (129; 229) whereby he must constantly respond to the perceived reaction his own words make. He is in dialogue with himself but also must have the last word, and so he can never stop. This Sisyphean task imposed by his self-consciousness is a form of oppression, even horror, for Dostoyevsky, one that can only be overcome through Christian love.

To add levels to this, but levels that can serve as a useful bridge to Unamuno, time should also be spent going over the footnote at the very start of the work. Even before the strange opening lines comes a brief commentary from the author placed seemingly innocuously at the bottom of the page: “И автор записок и самые «Записки», разумеется, вымышлены. Тем не менее такие лица, как сочинитель таких записок, не только могут, но даже должны существовать в нашем обществе. . . . / *Фёдор Достоевский*” ‘Both the author of these notes and the *Notes* themselves are fictitious, of course. Nevertheless, people like the author of these notes not only may, but actually must exist in our society. . . . / *Fyodor Dostoyevsky*’ (5: 99; 3; trans. altered to include author’s name). Dostoyevsky was far from the first author to break the fourth wall, but the footnote, especially with its authorial signature, sets up expectations not only about the work itself (what is the purpose of the entire work, then, if he reveals its fictionality from the get-go?) but also about the relationship between author and reader. Dostoyevsky is trying to change his reader, to control him or make him see the reality around him in a new way. And he does so through this form of dialogue, through the conversation (or half conversation) the fictional Underground Man has with his perceived reader and the conversation the real Dostoyevsky starts with his actual reader. This line of thought continues throughout the novel, culminating in the Underground Man’s failure to accept the love offered to him by the prostitute Liza, a failure caused in part by his inability to exercise free will precisely because of the constant dialogue in his head: “Мне не дают . . . Я не могу быть . . . добрым!” ‘They won’t let me . . . I can’t be . . . good!’ (5: 175; 84). This “they” is a stone around his neck, dragging him down. Dialogue, which should open him up to the possibilities of other people (Liza certainly tries; Dostoyevsky points us in the right direction), instead traps him in his own mind and locks him in a never-ending cycle of self-consciousness.

In short, Dostoyevsky’s work can set up a lot of the important questions for *Mist*. For starters, there is the relationship between author and reader or author and character. Dostoyevsky’s footnote makes clear that the author holds special knowledge about society and its problems and, presumably, how to fix them. The fiction is no more than a means of getting that knowledge to the public. It is, of course, important that the means Dostoyevsky chooses is a novel, and a novel so steeped in dialogue. Clearly Dostoyevsky thinks that his message will have a greater effect if he makes his readers work through the problems of the Underground Man in a dialogic way, to live his life and think his thoughts. But in the end there is a lesson to be learned. That conclusion lies in the Christian meekness of Liza and her renunciation of the self and, to a lesser extent, in the Underground Man’s servant Apollon. Compare this with the appearance of Don

Miguel in *Mist*. Unamuno first intrudes himself into the narration (not including two of the three prologues) at the end of chapter 25, after a discussion between Augusto and Víctor about doubt: "¿Dudas?, luego piensas; ¿piensas?, luego eres" 'You doubt, therefore you think. You think, therefore you are' (2: 649; 189). Doubt, then, becomes just as much a defining characteristic of the *nivola* as dialogue. In fact, it is what necessitates the need for dialogue. It is just this point that can allow for a glimpse of the depth of what Unamuno is trying to achieve (and therefore a good point to mull over in class discussion), for it is at this point that Don Miguel introduces the conflation of author and god, a conflation that began in the prologue and will reach its height a few chapters later. The key to this first intrusion is to apply Víctor's logic to Don Miguel himself. Unamuno as narrator attempts to speak in the same manner as Dostoyevsky's footnote: the voice of a narrator/god imposing some truth on the narrative. Students should be able, like Augusto, to use the knife of doubt to cut deeper than the narrator himself has. If, indeed, Don Miguel is the god of Víctor and Augusto's universe, who is the god of Don Miguel's universe? And the god of that god's universe? (This also sets up an interesting class discussion of whether Unamuno was an atheist, a large difference between him and the Sartre and Camus they read later in the course.)

All of this, of course, builds up to the events of chapter 31, where Augusto, debating suicide, goes to visit Don Miguel, author of some relevant articles as well as of the *nivola* Augusto himself inhabits. The scene plays out almost like the conclusion of a dystopian novel, where the hero is interviewed by the leader of the state and learns why the authoritarian regime is necessary, only to have his logic thrown back in his face: "Pues bien, mi señor creador don Miguel, también usted se morirá. . . . Porque usted, mi creador, mi don Miguel, no es usted más que otro ente *nivolesco*" 'Very well, my lord creator, Don Miguel de Unamuno, you will die too! . . . Because you, my creator, my dear Don Miguel, are nothing more than just another "*nivolistic*" creature' (2: 670; 226). Augusto departs with a newfound desire to survive that will prove to be fleeting. Don Miguel holds true to his despotic word to kill his character off—and kills him with the means of life: food. Or does he? Don Miguel later proves incapable of resuscitating his supposed creation and is visited by the ghost of Augusto, who appears to have superseded his creator before disappearing into the mist.

This leaves some good questions for discussion in class. For instance, given the final lines of the book (excluding the epilogue), it could be argued that Don Miguel is the real hero of the novel, as it is his life—perhaps only second to that of Orfeo—that is most substantially changed by the events of the work. Are there similarities in Augusto's and Orfeo's deaths or in their result? Why is the dog named Orfeo—he undergoes a similar grief as Orpheus, but is there a similar descent and return? What, after all, is the mist? In this last connection it can be useful in class to have students go through all instances of the word *niebla* and related words (*nebuloso*, *tiniebla*) in the novel (a copy of the Spanish text, if not the English, is available on *Project Gutenberg*), where they will notice certain patterns linking mist with everyday life, the spirit, and confusion and doubt.

This discussion should provide a means of coming full circle. The grand theme of Unamuno (among so many) is the fate of human consciousness after death (Julián Marías 11 [Harvard UP]). At the end of the novel we see both Augusto's and Orfeo's consciousnesses emerge from the mist in order to speak to Don Miguel and the reader, respectively. This is an important clue, because it is, as Robert Richmond Ellis phrases it, "only through contact with the Other [that] this nothingness take[s] on form" (60). Dialogue, then, becomes the means of forming a coherent consciousness out of the inchoate mist (can students find specific examples of this in the text?).

While teaching Unamuno, it seems a shame to me to avoid some discussion of his biography, particularly in connection with Dostoyevsky, because the final moments of Unamuno's public life appear taken from a Dostoyevsky novel, specifically the dueling speeches General José Millán-Astray and Unamuno, then rector of the University of Salamanca, gave as Francisco Franco and the Falangists came into power. The clash recalls, at least for me, the Grand Inquisitor chapter from *The Brothers Karamazov*. The shouts of "¡Viva, viva la Muerte!" 'Long live Death!' could have been uttered by the Inquisitor himself with his hatred of freedom; the shout of "¡Muera la Inteligencia!" 'Death to the Intelligentsia!' (Rudd 298, 301) is a snug fit for the Inquisitor's comment "Да ты и права не имеешь ничего прибавлять к тому, что уже сказано тобой прежде" 'Thou hast no right to add anything to what Thou hadst said of old' (14: 228; 217).[3] However, Unamuno was, it goes without saying, no Jesus. First of all, Dostoyevsky's Jesus makes no reply but merely kisses the Inquisitor before leaving his cell, while Unamuno begins by saying, "A veces, quedarse callado puede interpretarse como aquiescencia" 'At times to remain silent can be interpreted as approval' (Juaristi, *Miguel de Unamuno* 438). But Unamuno resigns himself to the inevitable with the infamous phrase "Venceréis . . . Pero no convenceréis" 'You will conquer . . . But not convince' (440). Unamuno would spend his remaining months under house arrest, a testament to the power of his convictions and an example that the real Unamuno should not be confused with either Augusto, who is afraid of ruining the nobility of his umbrella by opening it, or the fictive Don Miguel, who is a petty tyrant over his creations.

NOTES

[1] The text of *Niebla* used in this essay is Manuel García Blanco's edition, included in *Obras completas*, published by Escelicer. All the English translations are by Anthony Kerrigan.

[2] The text of *Notes from Underground* used in this essay is from volume 5, pages 99–179 of Полное собрание сочинений (*Polnoe sobranie sochinenii*; *Complete Works*), published by Nauka. All the English translations are from Michael R. Katz's edition.

[3] I cite *Brothers Karamazov* in volume 14 of Полное собрание сочинений (*Polnoe sobranie sochinenii*; *Complete Works*), published by Nauka.

"My Imitators Are Better Than I Am": Clarice Lispector, Unamuno, and the Agony of Creation

Adam Morris

As the modernist scholar Lisa Ruddick persuasively argues in her 2015 essay "When Nothing Is Cool," a careerist market logic willingly internalized by humanities scholars strangles the study of literature in the United States. This hyperprofessionalism in the academy has not only stalled critical thought but also discourages any curiosity that might expose the deficiencies of orthodox methods and beliefs in contemporary literary criticism. It facilitates the casualization of academic labor and the correlated cheapening of the humanities as an area of study by creating a fearful, self-policing, and compliant workforce devoid of the creativity, humor, and independence that are inconvenient to the corporate university yet so vital to art and the humanities.

What does all this have to do with Miguel de Unamuno or Clarice Lispector? First, this sort of accommodating and reactionary attitude in the academy was one against which Unamuno rebelled for many years. The intellectual climate during the time of the Primo de Rivera dictatorship was bureaucratic and complacent and did not, in Unamuno's view, offer much evidence of backbone when it came to social and political critique. In fact, the insipid and gutless intellectual culture in post-Restoration Spain was almost as much the bane of Unamuno's existence as the dictatorship itself: its moral failings were those of what Jean-Paul Sartre would later call bad faith.

The Incurious Scholar: Unamuno's Academic Satire

Unamuno was a student of faith and its agonies and dilemmas. His novel *San Manuel Bueno, mártir* ("Saint Manuel Bueno, Martyr") is a dramatization of his writings on the quandary of faith in the modern rationalist era, when the enlightened man of reason is prevailed upon to surrender faith as a vestige of medieval thinking. Unamuno stated that this novel was a creative exposition of the ideas he later set forth in *La agonía del cristianismo* ("The Agony of Christianity"). Similarly, *Niebla* ("Mist") offers a novelistic, or, more precisely, a *nivolistic*, exposition of the ideas Unamuno developed in *Del sentimiento trágico de la vida* ("The Tragic Sense of Life"). For Unamuno, the "tragic sense of life" was the result of having lost Pascal's wager: Unamuno *wanted* to believe in God and in the certainties offered by religion. But the religion he describes in "Mi religión" ("My Religion") is not one of dogma and accepted truths. Rather, it is a faith riddled with constant and inevitable doubt. This doubt is the mist or fog (*niebla*) of uncertainty at the heart of human existence. As Unamuno wrote in

"Mi religión," he could neither affirm nor deny the existence of God because he had not seen adequate proof for either conclusion. The "tragic sense of life" is that humankind must navigate life without certain answers to these fundamental questions.

In Unamuno's view, doubts, not certainties, lead to human self-knowledge. He wasted few opportunities to declare his opposition to the positivist philosophies that prevailed in the early twentieth century, particularly their application to social and humanistic questions. He expressed this opposition continually in his work, including the 1902 novelistic satire *Amor y pedagogía* ("Love and Pedagogy"), which is the comedy of a man's eugenic attempt to produce a genius offspring; the 1907 essay "Cientificismo" ("Scientism"), which deals with his opposition to scientificism directly; and even *Niebla*, in which the character Antolín S. Paparrigópulos, a theorist of women's psychology, functions both as a plot device and the butt of an academic joke.

Paparrigópulos is a foil for Unamuno: from the solitary confines of his study, Paparrigópulos believes he can study and theorize women's psychology. One of *Niebla*'s protagonists, Augusto, goes to consult Paparrigópulos after deciding to write a two-volume book on feminine psychology called *Eugenia and Rosario*. This book is titled after the two women who tantalize Augusto; their names are also a nod to the Marquis de Sade, who perhaps represents the opposite method of contemplating feminine psychology to Paparrigópulos's dry and cloistered methodology. Paparrigópulos was not, the narrator explains, one of those curious youths who throw themselves into diverse projects with equal enthusiasm, nor the kind of intellectual capable of any great insights. This is because—and Unamuno is explicit about this—the young man, although at the beginning of his career, has already made up his mind about what kind of study must be done, what sort of books need to be written, and what conclusions they should reach. The likelihood that Paparrigópulos will make any insightful discoveries is quite low given his focus on his own fixed ideas.

Unamuno's satirical critique is of the sort of scholar who never allows himself to stray from the path of his intentions. His results are always the ones he seeks, an activity that Unamuno considered a foolish act of self-reinforcement, typical of the anti-intellectualism that sandbagged Restoration Spanish society: Paparrigópulos values academic success more than sound ideas.

Enter Lispector

Scholars of transatlantic modernism might recall that a similar critique was made decades after Unamuno published *Niebla*, by a writer who became one of Unamuno's sincerest flatterers—albeit without ever naming him conspicuously. This writer is Clarice Lispector. In her final work of fiction, *Um sopro de vida: Pulsações* ("A Breath of Life: Pulsations"), published posthumously in 1978, Lispector's protagonist, known simply as Author, tells the reader,

> Se este livro vier jamais a sair, que dele se afastem os profanos. Pois escrever é coisa sagrada onde os infiéis não têm entrada. Estar fazendo de propósito um livro ben ruim para afastar os profanos que querem "gostar." Mas um pequeno grupo verá que esse "gostar" é superficial e entrarão adentro do que verdadeiramente escrevo, e que não é "ruim" nem é "bom." (20)
>
> If this book ever comes out, may the profane recoil from it. Since writing is something sacred where no infidel can enter. I am making a really bad book on purpose in order to drive off the profane who want to "like." But a small group will see that this "liking" is superficial and will enter inside what I am truly writing, which is neither "bad" nor "good." (12)

In this passage, the Author of *Um sopro* rejects the importance of superficial readings and of any criticism that does not take his work on its own gnostic terms. In so doing, he articulates one of Lispector's own frustrations with her life's work: that no one had really understood her, despite her popularity. Writing, for Lispector and for several of her narrators, was an attempt to communicate the personal and nontransferable energy and timbre of that which exists beyond language and even beyond thought. For this reason, it was always both a success and a never-ending failure.

With this introduction by the Author, Lispector responded to critics who had begun to characterize her as a Satrean existentialist. These critics, including Benedito Nunes, identified parallels between European existentialist philosophy and the ideas Lispector expressed in her fiction. However, they paid little attention to another thinker who, departing from an independent reading of Søren Kierkegaard, Benedict de Spinoza, Blaise Pascal, and William James, produced his own outsider existentialist philosophy, known to us in title and in summary as *Del sentimiento trágico de la vida*. Lispector read Unamuno and used her late fiction to address some of the paradoxes Unamuno explored in his work, particularly those set forth in *Del sentimiento trágico de la vida*. She did this through works of fiction that dramatize the inscrutability and occasional absurdity of the human condition and that meditate on the role of the creative process as a method for exploring and coping with the contradictions of faith and belief, much as Unamuno did.

Um sopro reads as an homage to *Niebla*: in it, the Author struggles with a character he created and named Ângela Pralini. The Author writes that he created Ângela because he needed the company of her dialogue, even if invented; he consoles her by reminding her that he too must suffer the knowledge that he was created for the same reasons. The Author, who claims to have authored books with the same titles as Lispector's early novels, is a cipher for Lispector. Ângela shares her initials with Augusto Pérez, the protagonist of *Niebla*, and shares her first name with Ángela Carballino in Unamuno's *San Manuel Bueno, mártir*, a character who elicits her confessor's crisis of faith. San Manuel resolves the problem of a parishioner's suicide by asserting that people who commit suicide repent of their actions at the last instant. This fractional instant in which salvation is achieved is something that Lispector, through her narrators, had been seeking and theorizing since at least the publication of *Agua viva* ("Living Water"), which is essentially a book-long meditation on that subject.

The theme of suicide likewise unites the two novels. In *Niebla*, Augusto is not permitted to commit suicide, but his death nevertheless resembles one, and it leaves open the question of whether he dies of his own free will or whether he successfully manipulates his author, Don Miguel, into killing him. This scenario is repeated in *Um sopro*, a book that—similar to *Niebla*—likens the creative process to an act of suicide. Lispector's Author creates an equivalence between inventing Ângela and killing himself, establishing an analogy between creation and self-destruction.

Elsewhere, the Author writes that if Ângela weren't so paralyzed by contemplating her own existence, she would also be able to see into herself from without, and she "descobriria que era uma pessoa voraz: come com um desregramento que beira a completa sofreguidão como se lhe tirassem o pão da boca" 'would discover that she was a voracious person: she eats with such abandon that it borders on the complete suffering of having bread ripped out of her mouth' (26; 35–36). This is, of course, exactly the way Augusto kills himself—or is killed by Don Miguel—in *Niebla*: he gorges himself on rich foods and dies shortly after he learns, during his interview with Don Miguel, that because he has dared to suggest killing either Don Miguel or himself, the author of the novel has reasserted his authority by condemning his character to die another way.

Lispector's Author realizes that a similar situation confronts him with regard to Ângela. He writes, "Se Ângela é uma suicida em potencial, como terminei por entender, faço-a suicidar-se? Não. Não tenho coragem: sua vida me é muito preciosa. Só que ela tem gosto pelo risco e eu também" 'If Ângela is a potential suicide, as I ended up realizing, do I make her commit suicide? No. I don't have the courage: her life is very precious to me. It's just that she has a taste for danger and so do I' (54; 47). Here he echoes, in modified form, the thought voiced by Don Miguel in *Niebla*, who abhors the idea of dying by the hand of one of his own fictional creations. But whereas Don Miguel reacts this way out of indignant resentment, the Author of *Um sopro* ponders the question of Ângela's suicide with trepidation. In a manner that recalls *Niebla*, the Author slowly loses control over his creation as his dialogue with her progresses, to the point where he says to himself, "Pergunto-me às vezes se ela quer que eu a mate para me levar ao cúmulo do ódio" 'I sometimes wonder if she wants me to kill her to bring me to the summit of my hatred' (133; 133).

The similarities and coded references to *Niebla* are too numerous to mention. Lispector might even coyly acknowledge this when she has the Author of *Um sopro* state, "Noto que os meus imitadores são melhores que eu. A imitação é mais requintada que a autenticidade em estado bruto" 'I recognize that my imitators are better than I am. Imitation is more refined than raw authenticity' (30; 23). The concern, for me, is not whether these two works are related. This appears obvious. The more interesting question is why they have not been studied together, particularly considering that both writers were strongly influenced by Friedrich Nietzsche, if not also Kierkegaard, and both wrote metafictional novels in which characters threaten the reality or existence of their authors.

The first answer is that American literary critics, beginning with Lispector's translator Gregory Rabassa, were determined to compare her with canonical European modernist writers like Virginia Woolf, James Joyce, and Franz Kafka. A second answer is more germane to this volume and brings us back to academic fashions. Unamuno is not fashionable in twenty-first-century Latin American literary studies, despite his tremendous influence over Latin American intellectual culture. Nor was he widely read and understood in the 1960s and 1970s by Lispector's critics, who were determined to demonstrate Lispector's inheritance from Sartre and Simone de Beauvoir, or in the 1980s and 1990s by poststructuralist critics, who leaned heavily on Hélène Cixous's writings on *écriture féminine*. Much American and Brazilian literary criticism on Lispector's work remains indebted to Derridean deconstruction, another fashion that eclipsed comparative study of Lispector and Unamuno.

Too many critical Paparrigópuloses, especially in Brazilian literary criticism, have preferred to read Lispector along with French philosophers like Jacques Derrida, Gilles Deleuze, and Cixous rather than alongside a writer whom she almost certainly studied and emulated. Additionally, it remains unfashionable in literary studies to bring two writers with disparate historical and cultural contexts into conversation on the unproven, undocumented grounds that one of them read and was influenced by the other. This is the old Harold Bloom style of literary criticism that looks for what Bloom calls in *The Anxiety of Influence* the "strong misreadings" that one writer makes of a predecessor's text—a game of literary agon that Bloom believes to be at the heart of the development of Western literature. This mode of criticism flies in the face of everything we were supposed to have learned about the death of the author and other poststructuralist commonplaces that have become critical blinders in the field. But students, lacking the blind spots of trained humanists, realize that literary genealogies do in fact exist and are tremendously useful for understanding the ideas an author wishes to discuss or transmit.

Teaching Lispector with Unamuno

Thus my proposition: why not teach Lispector and Unamuno together? For those teaching Latin American women's literature or the Brazilian novel, it may seem counterintuitive to add Unamuno to the syllabus when so many other texts are clamoring for inclusion. However, Lispector's unique contribution to the Latin American literary-philosophical tradition is best understood when the context of her agon with Unamuno is acknowledged. It is insufficient to offer impressionistic comparisons to Europeans like Sartre, de Beauvoir, Woolf, and Katherine Mansfield. When students understand that Lispector is playfully reappropriating

Unamuno's novel, which itself is deeply indebted to *Don Quijote*, they may begin to make sense of the scattershot readings of the canon that make up most departmental offerings.

Likewise, a course on Unamuno could easily be organized in this dialogic way, around the Latin American writers who responded directly to his work, including Jorge Luis Borges, who sent Unamuno all his early works, and Lispector, who ceased naming her philosophical interlocutors explicitly after her first novel but who nevertheless kept up the dialogue and agon throughout her career, up to and including her final unpublished novel.

Questions of particular relevance to a discussion of Lispector and Unamuno can focus on their common interests: why do these authors link the ideas of artistic creation and suicide? What textual passages could be offered as evidence? What emotional affects do the texts solicit? For example, are they sad? Humorous? Why or why not? Because suicide is such a freighted topic, it is best not to begin by dropping these questions on students in class. Instead, they might be posed as prereading response prompts that prepare students for the text or as postreading questions that follow up on textual themes. These reflective responses allow students the opportunity to write to read or to read to write in order to "compose" meaning, a technique "at the heart of reading" (Hirvela 107). I have used a course wiki to tailor response-journal questions as a bridge between one course discussion and the next; they can easily be written in ten minutes after class, when memories of course discussion—of what we covered and what we didn't get to—are still fresh.

In courses taught in the target language, it is important to design these questions according to the American Council on the Teaching of Foreign Languages recommendation of warming up students to tackle a more advanced goal of linguistic production. Courses that function as a bridge between language and literature should aim to create a "symbiotic relationship between language and literature" that can help students make strides in their language proficiency by combining prior knowledge with the sophisticated concepts under discussion in literary texts (Bernhardt, *Understanding* 85). Like Lispector and Borges, Unamuno offers a unique opportunity to coach Spanish students in the use of speculative language, such as the subjunctive clauses used in hypothetical situations and expressions of doubt.

If working on these language constructs were paired with the discussion of suicide and artistic creation, and if this is made clear to students by offering discrete models to follow, students who are less invested in literary studies but who take upper-division literature courses to improve their Spanish—and we must acknowledge there are many on our rosters—will buy into the assignments and enrich class discussions with perspectives from their own major fields of study, whether those be physics, psychology, biology, or philosophy. This requires that we commit to embracing the diversity of reasons students take second language literature courses and surrender the habits that have thinned course enrollments and created a generation of Paparrigópuloses from those who remained.

Unamuno in the Context of Jean-Paul Sartre and Modern Existentialist Literature

Robert Richmond Ellis

I feel as if I have lived with Miguel de Unamuno for much of my lifetime. I began reading his works in high school and college, and for my doctoral degree I wrote a dissertation in which I examined him as a precursor of Jean-Paul Sartre. For much of my career I have taught Unamuno at the undergraduate level in courses on modern Spanish narrative and theater as well as in seminars on literary theory and existentialist literature in translation. Some of my students come to my classes having already read Unamuno in high school, and they are almost always delighted to delve more deeply into his works. Those in my Spanish courses tend to find the language of his texts accessible, although they often require background preparation in order to grasp the literary and cultural references.

In my courses on existentialist literature I usually begin with texts by Unamuno, Franz Kafka, and Albert Camus, because I have discovered over the years that students are more receptive to those writers' thinking than to Sartre's. In fact, students sometimes find Sartre dogmatic, and they can be put off by both his uncompromising atheism and his insistence on radical freedom, as if the former were too pessimistic and the latter too idealistic. Overall, they appreciate the ambiguities in Unamuno's writing and his open-ended vision of life, which allow them to engage in philosophical speculation of their own.

One of the most intriguing philosophical problems that Unamuno and many existentialist writers explore is the ontological dynamic of the relationship between the self and the other. This essay examines this topic as represented in Unamuno's *Niebla* ("Mist"), Sartre's *La nausée* ("Nausea"), and, more briefly, Kafka's *Die Verwandlung* ("The Metamorphosis") and Camus's *L'étranger* ("The Stranger"). In so doing I hope to provide instructors with insights that will assist them in conducting guided readings of these texts. I also reflect on strategies and activities designed to make them accessible and meaningful to contemporary students.

Representations of the Self and the Other in Four Existentialist Narratives

Unamuno stands as one of the most significant figures of the existentialist tradition. As generations of scholars have observed, his worldview shares affinities with the most noted existentialist thinkers, including Søren Kierkegaard, the reputed founder of modern existentialism, and Sartre, the leading exponent of the philosophy. Unamuno expresses his existentialist vision throughout his numerous essays and literary works, and although he does not produce a philosophical treatise of the scope of Sartre's *L'être et le néant* ("Being and Nothingness") and *Critique de la raison dialectique* ("Critique of Dialectical Reason"), he articulates a profound existentialist ontology. In *Del sentimiento trágico de la vida* ("The Tragic Sense of Life") he asserts that on the deepest level humans are nothing (7: 191).[1] When they recognize their nothingness, they experience an all-consuming anguish as well as an overpowering hunger for being. In *Niebla* the life of the protagonist, Augusto Pérez, is compared to a mist or fog. Eugenia, the woman he loves, goes so far as to describe him as "hueco" 'hollow' (159); and according to the character Víctor Goti, both he and Augusto are empty: "Nosotros no tenemos dentro" 'We have no inside' (250). Unamuno nevertheless believes that humans achieve a degree of concrete objectivity through their relationships with others. In *Aforismos y definiciones* ("Aphorisms and definitions") he argues that they exist for themselves only insofar as they exist for others. He thus affirms that "ser para sí es ser para los otros" 'being-for-itself is being-for-others' (7: 1518). In the absence of others, humans would have no discrete personality or identity and would be nothing more than an anguished desire for an ontological plenitude that is quelled only by death.

According to the ontological system elucidated by Sartre in *L'être et le néant*, being-for-itself (or consciousness) is not reducible to being-for-others, and personal identity arises through a continuous interplay of intentions over which being-for-itself, as long as it is alive, always has some control. For Sartre, the two primary modes of being are not being-for-itself and being-for-others but being-for-itself and being-in-itself, the being of inanimate matter. On the most fundamental level being-for-itself is a consciousness of being-in-itself. Through its acts of consciousness it posits being-in-itself as being. In so doing it negates itself as not being the being-in-itself of which it is conscious. It is a nothingness insofar as it is pure action, devoid of substance or essence. In fact, its only essence would be the freedom that nothingness implies. As a freedom, moreover, being-for-itself must always choose, and for this reason it bears responsibility for the world in which it lives. Sartre dramatizes the ontology of *L'être et le néant* in *La nausée* as well as his other early novels and plays. In *La nausée* the protagonist, Antoine Roquentin, is acutely aware of the things in his midst, which he experiences in all their brute and absurd materiality. He thus differs from Augusto, who focuses his attention almost exclusively on himself and other human beings.

Through what Sartre calls the revealing intuitions of being (anguish, boredom, and nausea), Roquentin discovers that both he and the world that he inhabits have no transcendental meaning. Augusto also experiences anguish and boredom as well as a kind of reverse nausea through his overwhelming desire at the end of the narrative to fill himself through eating. But he is ostensibly less free and more passive than Roquentin. Whereas for Sartre passivity is a mode of action through which consciousness chooses to deny its freedom and responsibility (thereby engaging in what he calls bad faith), for Unamuno passivity results from the inability of consciousness to assert itself over the other. Nonetheless, the greatest point of convergence in their respective ontologies lies precisely in their depictions of the relationship between the self and the other. For both authors this relationship is one of conflict. Sartre categorically denies the possibility of an ontological bond between the self and the other, or what Martin Heidegger calls the *Mitsein* 'being with' (qtd. in Sartre, *L'être* 502). Augusto perhaps experiences a kind of *Mitsein* with his mother and his dog, Orfeo. But his relationships with his adult peers are all conflictive.

According to Unamuno and Sartre, consciousness seeks objectivity through the other. But to the extent that the other objectifies consciousness, consciousness experiences alienation, since it is unable to control completely the meaning of its objectivity. Under the look of the other it senses that its freedom is threatened. In fact, consciousness desires the objectivity made possible by the other, but it simultaneously wants to remain free. In *Niebla*, Augusto continually pursues fulfillment through the other, while also attempting to reject the negative essences that the other imposes on him. Yet he is ultimately unable to preserve his autonomy. In *La nausée*, Roquentin is better able to maintain control of his objective identity. He seems stronger than Augusto and for this reason more like the traditional hero of realist literature.

Sartre argues in *L'être et le néant* that consciousness experiences in shame its objectivity under the look of the other. At the outset of *Niebla*, Augusto naively imagines that the love of the other would function like a "lluvia bienhechora en que se deshace y concreta la niebla de la existencia" 'beneficent rain in which the mist of existence dissolves and becomes concrete' (117). But his interactions with people are more often than not traumatic. On one occasion, Augusto wields the power of the look when he regards the character Rosario: "Nunca te he visto ponerte así colorada. Y además me pareces otra" 'I have never seen you become so red. And moreover, you seem like another person' (141). In this scene Rosario not only feels shame, as demonstrated when she turns red, but through Augusto's look she seemingly undergoes an ontological transformation. On another occasion Augusto attempts to grasp his image in Rosario's eyes (222). But like the characters Cosme and Damián in Unamuno's play *El otro* ("The Other") and Estelle in Sartre's play *Huis-clos* ("No Exit"), he is unable to do this because her intentions ultimately elude him, and he thus declares that he must defend himself against her (223). In the presence of Eugenia the shame and concomitant objectivity that he experiences nearly cause him to lose consciousness, as if in her presence he were reduced to the status of a thing: "Los ojos de Eugenia se le borraron de la vista y no vio ya nada sino una niebla, una niebla roja. Un momento creyó perder el sentido" 'Eugenia's eyes disappeared from his sight and he now saw nothing but a mist, a red mist. For a moment, he thought he was losing consciousness' (136). In his encounter with the character Don Miguel de Unamuno, Augusto attempts to turn the tables and direct the look against the ultimate incarnation of the other, the author who created him, gazing into his eyes and threatening to kill him (258–59). Yet as he concedes in the letter that he leaves before dying, Don Miguel has his way with him and kills him when he writes Augusto's death into the narrative. In contrast to Augusto, Roquentin is never really threatened by the look of the other, including even the look of Medusa that his former lover Annie displays (202), and in *La nausée* the shame of being-for-others is largely the experience of other characters.

Being-for-others, as elucidated in the theoretical and literary works of Unamuno and Sartre, is constituted not only by the look of the other but also by language. In describing the narrative that he is writing (in a sense a *mise en abyme* of *Niebla* itself), Víctor explains that the characters will realize themselves primarily through words. Yet according to Augusto, the words that humans speak are always false. Through language they don masks and assume roles in society, but their masks do not express their authentic selves. Yet ironically, all that they conceal is the anguished desire of humans to affirm a distinct, individual identity and to persist in their being beyond death. Here, then, is one of the greatest conundrums of Unamuno's existentialist ontology: with others we are not who we are, but alone we are nothing.

In *L'être et le néant* Sartre defines language as the basic constituent of being-for-others. Whereas in this treatise he limits his discussion of being-for-others and by extension language to the personal sphere of human interactions, in *Critique* (a text in which he attempts to meld existentialism and Marxism) he situates human relationships in a larger social context. In so doing he formulates a theory of what he calls the *pratico-inerte* 'practico-inert' in order to account for those aspects of materiality that have been imbued with human praxis and seemingly turn back on humans and reify them. Language as a constituted system of communication can function as a *pratico-inerte* insofar as it defines humans in exteriority and alienates them from their freedom. Although in *Niebla* Unamuno expresses an existentialist vision more evocative of the philosophy of *L'être et le néant*, his reflections on language as an alienating social structure share commonalities with the theory of language propounded by Sartre in *Critique*. Augusto rarely senses that he is a unique individual: "sólo a solas podía decirse a sí mismo, tal vez para convencerse: '¡Yo soy yo!'" 'only alone could he tell himself, perhaps in order to convince himself: "I am I!"' (188). In society he ostensibly loses control over language, and as a result he is unable to recognize himself and feels as if he were nothing.

Both *Niebla* and *La nausée* have metatextual dimensions, but these are more significant in *Niebla*. At the outset of *La nausée* Roquentin is writing a historical biography, which he eventually abandons because he realizes that he is unable to capture the lived experience of his subject. As he sees it, a narrative, whether historical or fictional, endows life with a teleological dimension that it does not have in the lived moment, when consciousness must freely choose its future in the light of its past actions. The belief that life unfolds like a story, where each moment necessarily leads to the next and ultimately to some sort of conclusion, is what Sartre calls the retrospective illusion (*Les mots* 212). Roquentin attempts to reject the retrospective illusion and write a diary in which he records his conscious moments as he lives them. He nonetheless maintains the hope that this work, when finished, will give his life meaning and relieve him of the anguish of existence.

In *Niebla*, in contrast, the characters, including not only Augusto but also Víctor and even to a certain extent Don Miguel, are more deeply self-reflexive than Roquentin insofar as they are compelled to recognize that they are fictional. In the culminating scene, when Augusto visits Don Miguel in his studio in Salamanca and Don Miguel informs him that he is a product of his authorial imagination, Augusto vehemently insists that he is real and that he will survive long after Don Miguel and the readers of the text are dead. This scene can be interpreted as a dramatization of Unamuno's ontology, for although the self, according to Unamuno, is a nothingness, it nevertheless expresses an overwhelmingly real desire for being. Yet in *Niebla* the recognition of this desire is ultimately the experience of the readers, who through Augusto's words are drawn into the discourse of the text. Whereas a more conventional literary or philosophical discourse might lead readers to reflect on the existential condition from a position of exteriority, the metatextuality of *Niebla* makes possible their own existential awakening, since it explicitly identifies them as existential subjects of the narrative.

If the encounter between Augusto and Don Miguel is the climax of *Niebla*, the pivotal scene of *La nausée* occurs when Roquentin enters a public garden and perceives the world as if it has been stripped of all its conventional meanings. What he discovers in this moment is universal contingency—the notion that humans and things are not necessary beings but meaningless and absurd. He remarks that over the ages some individuals have attempted to overcome contingency by inventing a causal being, but he concludes that contingency is absolute and inescapable. His recognition of the absence of the divine might seem more radical than Unamuno's depiction of religion in his literary and philosophical texts. Yet as Sartre reveals in his reflections on his own early idealism, Roquentin in fact harbors a kind of belief insofar as he imagines that he has a mission to make others aware of the contingency of existence (*Les mots* 211).

Throughout his career, Unamuno was preoccupied with religion and the desire of humans for immortality. Yet the ethos of *Niebla* is in some ways more atheistic than that of *La nausée*. Even if Augusto's meeting with Don Miguel is read as an encounter with God, the God figure represented by Don Miguel is altogether human in his egoism, anger, and lack of compassion for others, despite the furtive tear that he sheds when Augusto departs. Indeed, he is no different from the alienating figures that threaten Augusto throughout the narrative. In contrast to Roquentin, who turns to artistic creation as an escape from anguish, Augusto is granted no release from his suffering short of death—and death and annihilation, regardless of his original intention to kill himself, are what he most desperately hopes to avoid. *Niebla* is hence deeply existentialist in its representation of the tragedy of the human condition.

The existential intuitions that Unamuno and Sartre express in *Niebla* and *La nausée*, respectively, and in particular their depictions of the dynamics of the relationship between the self and the other, are present in numerous existentialist texts, including Kafka's *Die Verwandlung* and Camus's *L'étranger*. In *Die*

Verwandlung the character Gregor Samsa is even more overdetermined by being-for-others than Augusto. When Gregor awakens one morning to discover that he has been transformed into a cockroach, his reaction is surprisingly nonchalant, and he seems solely concerned about maneuvering his cumbersome body out of bed and appeasing his superiors for not arriving at work on time. He realizes the horror of his condition only when others look at him. His reaction is one of shame. Moreover, although he is capable of speaking, the sounds that he utters are unintelligible to others. He is thus defined by language but unable to use it to counter the identity that others confer on him. In his case, being-for-others ultimately triumphs over being-for-itself. As Sartre argues in *L'être et le néant*, this triumph can only occur when being-for-itself dies and the other assumes absolute control of the meaning of its existence. From the Sartrean perspective, therefore, either the living Gregor is in bad faith or Kafka has created a character who is not ontologically free. As an example of bad faith, Gregor continually subordinates his desires to those of his family and accepts the identity that they place on him. Yet he does demonstrate agency and freedom when he periodically emerges from his room. By the end, however, he has internalized the look of the other and in a sense gives up and dies. Augusto, in contrast, never ceases to assert himself in opposition to those who would deny his ontological integrity as an independent subject; and even if he dies at the hands of Don Miguel, as his final letter suggests, he remains valiant in his struggle against his fate.

Camus's *L'étranger* also highlights the ontological structures of being-for-itself and being-for-others. In this text the protagonist, Meursault, commits a murder and is found guilty and condemned to death. The motive for his action is never established, and even if it were, the text suggests that it would not alter his ontological status in the present, as if the human subject were impervious to whatever essence its actions might imply. Yet in the eyes of society Meursault is guilty. What is more, he often expresses feelings of guilt—when the old people stare at him at his mother's wake; when his victim looks at him under the glaring sun and laughs; and when the jurors scrutinize him at his trial. Meursault's guilt is an internalization of his being-for-others, a negative essence akin to the identities conferred on Augusto and Gregor. Meursault nevertheless manages to embrace his guilt while rising above it and affirming his self-worth in opposition to society. In so doing he comes to incarnate the hero of the absurd, recognizing the absence of transcendental values in the world yet affirming himself in spite of his situation. He is thus similar to Augusto, who continually struggles to fulfill his ontological desire despite his ever-increasing realization of the impossibility of his endeavor. Unlike the characters in *Niebla*, *La nausée*, and *Die Verwandlung*, Meursault also finds solace in nature. Whereas the images of nature in existentialist literature are typically indicative of the despair and meaninglessness of the human condition (for instance, the mist and fog in the three aforementioned texts), in *L'étranger* the natural world can be a source of peace and contentment.

In the Existentialist Classroom

Unamuno, Sartre, Kafka, and Camus share numerous existentialist insights, not only in their depictions of being-for-others and being-for-itself but also in their reflections on epistemology, ethics, aesthetics, and religion. In my courses in existentialist literature, my students typically complete a long research paper on one of these themes or on another of their choosing. In preparation, they compile an annotated bibliography of primary and secondary sources that they share with their peers. They also give an extended presentation of their work in progress. Through the presentation they gain valuable feedback while providing the class with further topics for discussion. In addition to the research paper they write several short papers that often feed into their research project. Some topics that I have proposed for short papers related to *Niebla* are the look, the body, love, good faith and bad faith, metatextuality, and the relationship between literary praxis and existential self-knowledge.

For a more creative writing exercise I often have my students keep a journal throughout the semester, which I call their "journal of existentialism." I ask them to use their journals to reflect on the readings of the class and to formulate topics for discussion and papers. I also invite them to relate the readings to their personal lives and to describe some aspect of their own existential experience or what they might regard as significant moments of heightened existential awareness. I normally do not assign a grade for this exercise, although I award greater credit for more fully developed journals.

In several iterations of my courses in existentialist literature I have had my students write an autobiographical vignette. For this project I require them to formulate a paradigm explaining and justifying the structure of their narrative and to highlight experiences in their pasts that exemplify themes of existentialism represented in the readings. To guide them, I suggest that they identify a moment of fundamental choice and examine how it informed their subsequent life choices. I derived the idea for this format from Sartre's autobiography, *Les mots* ("The Words"), which unfolds in a spiral fashion, with the writing subject continually returning to an early life choice from different temporal vantage points. Unamuno's writing corpus provides a clear model of a life informed by a fundamental ontological choice insofar as he continually revisits the existential crisis of 1897, when one of his children died, and transforms it into the linchpin of his existentialist worldview.

From my perspective young students today seem far more pragmatic than their counterparts a generation ago, and at times they are impatient with texts whose basic message, as they see it, is simply that life has no meaning. Rather than appreciate the characters of these texts as rebels against oppressive values and traditions, they sometimes regard them as failures. Nevertheless, I find that this occurs much less often with the characters of Unamuno than with some more universally acclaimed existentialist heroes. I attribute this to the ability of Unamuno to generate tremendous empathy for his literary creations. Such empathy, I believe, is the greatest gift that we as instructors in the humanities can impart to our students. I further believe that the clearest way to teach empathy is by guiding students to draw our subject matter into their lives and make it their own. This is what Unamuno hoped to achieve with all his readers, when he challenged them to imagine a human bond grounded not in conflict but reciprocity.

NOTE

[1] The text of *Niebla* used in this essay is Mario J. Valdés's edition, published by Cátedra. Other works by Unamuno are quoted from volume 7 of *Obras completas*, edited by Manuel García Blanco and published by Escelicer. All translations are mine.

Teaching *Abel Sánchez* to Undergraduates

Jan E. Evans

In *Del sentimiento trágico de la vida* ("The Tragic Sense of Life") Miguel de Unamuno rails against philosophers who are not "de carne y hueso" 'of flesh and bone' (*Obras completas* [García Blanco] 7: 109–20). By that he means to emphasize that a true philosopher must engage all of life in his philosophy—the concerns of the head and of the heart—in facing the truth of existence that our destiny is to die. Theory that does not take into account the demands of both the intellect and the heart does not address the tragic sense of life. At the end of the first chapter of Unamuno's defining philosophical treatise, he names a small number of philosophers whom he considers to be philosophers "de carne y hueso." Among those philosophers is the Danish thinker Søren Kierkegaard.

That Unamuno read Kierkegaard at the beginning of the twentieth century when his *Samlede Værker* ("Collected Works") was published is surprising but indisputable. Mario Valdés asserts that Unamuno bought each of the fourteen volumes as they were published in Copenhagen from 1901 to 1906 (Valdés and Valdés, *Unamuno Source Book* xx [n7]). But did Unamuno read them? We know that Unamuno turned the pages of all but two volumes because there are words glossed in German and Spanish in the margins, and there are various types of underlining that Unamuno used to mark passages of interest. How much Kierkegaard influenced Unamuno has been much debated.[1] Did Unamuno learn from Kierkegaard, or did he just find in Kierkegaard a "hermano" 'brother' for his own well-developed philosophy (*Obras completas* [García Blanco] 7: 174)? The purpose of this essay is not to answer that question, though my sense of the debt Unamuno owes Kierkegaard will come through. Rather, I propose to show how an 1849 Kierkegaardian text, *The Sickness unto Death*, can enrich the reading of *Abel Sánchez*. In this approach students are introduced to an important nineteenth-century philosopher while grappling with one of Unamuno's most disturbing protagonists, Joaquín Monegro. By combining Kierkegaard's understanding of despair and the clear example of that despair in the character of Joaquín, students are helped in facing their own existence, which is what Unamuno would want.

The following are questions I want students to consider as they approach the reading of *Abel Sánchez*: what is the true nature of Joaquín's affliction? How does it start? How does it progress? Is there any possibility of change for Joaquín? Are there pivotal moments when he might have changed?

Joaquín is a person who is consumed with envy. From a Kierkegaardian perspective, the envy he feels and his inability to control it are a manifestation of his despair. It is worth noting a long quote from *The Sickness unto Death* that Unamuno underlined for emphasis, in which Kierkegaard explains offense as an intense form of despair:

> For what is offense? Offense is unhappy admiration. Thus it is related to envy, but it is an envy that turns against the person himself. . . . The

> uncharitableness of the natural man cannot allow him the extraordinary that God has intended for him; so he is offended.
>
> The degree of offense depends on how passionate a man's admiration is. The more prosaic people, lacking in imagination and passion and thus not particularly given to admiration, are also offended, but they limit themselves to saying: Such a thing I just can't understand; I leave it alone. They are the skeptics. But the more passion and imagination a person has—consequently, the closer he is in a certain sense (in possibility) to being able to believe, N.B., to humbling himself in adoration under the extraordinary—the more passionate is his offense, which finally cannot be satisfied with anything less than getting this rooted out, annihilated, trampled into the dirt. (86)

Joaquín is one of the most passionate and unsettling of Unamuno's protagonists, and yet he is the closest to faith, as this quote indicates. This story is full of darkness without much light. However, it is not Kierkegaard's purpose to portray authentic existence without hope, nor is it Unamuno's. The ultimate value for students reading *Abel Sánchez* is to recognize Unamuno's hints as to how Joaquín's offense might have been "rooted out." Finally, students must ask themselves if such a solution does, in fact, make sense in their world.

If *Abel Sánchez* were taught in a philosophy class, perhaps one focused on existentialism, I would assign the first eighty-seven pages of *The Sickness unto Death* before reading the novel as the groundwork for understanding the protagonist. If the novel were part of a twentieth-century Peninsular literature class, I would have students begin the novel first and introduce Kierkegaard at a crucial moment in Joaquín's downward spiral. It happens at the end of chapter 21, when the tortured Joaquín demands of God why he has made him to hate himself. The biblical command is to love one's neighbor as oneself, but Joaquín has the self-revelation that the reason he cannot love is that he hates himself, and he thinks that God is responsible for that hate. He is in tears when his young daughter, Joaquina, comes to the door and asks to be let in. Joaquín asks his daughter to pray for him, and Joaquina, clearly upset, asks him if he is sick. Joaquín responds, "Sí, estoy enfermo" 'Yes, I am sick' (2: 728; 102).[2] At this point I introduce *The Sickness unto Death* as a way to understand Joaquín's illness in Kierkegaardian terms.

Ideally, students should read *The Sickness unto Death* themselves. Kierkegaard's meaning is not easily transparent, but they should not give up before getting through the eighty-seven pages. Questions they should be able to answer from the reading are: what is a self? How does one become a self? How does despair come about? What are the stages of despair? Why is despair essential in the process of becoming a self? What is the opposite of despair? Since the teaching situation is rarely ideal, I will sketch the important Kierkegaardian concepts that apply to the reading of the novel.

Despair is defined as a failure to become a self. But what is a self? The text is dense, but most students can see that Kierkegaard is talking about the self as a synthesis of the "infinite and the finite, of the eternal and the temporal, of freedom and necessity" (13). However, the self for Kierkegaard is more than just a healthy balance. What is crucial is that we are aware of the disparate parts of our lives, and that awareness Kierkegaard calls consciousness. Being aware of the qualities that need to be in balance implies an ability to step back and choose oneself. The ideal synthesis can be realized only when consciousness is in proper relation to "the third," the power that created it (13–14). What is that proper relation? To rest "transparently in the power that established it [the self]" (14) and to will to be the self that one was created to be.

For Kierkegaard, personhood, becoming a self, is a lifelong process. There is a part that is temporal and finite—a bodily being born in a particular situation—and there is a part that is infinite—the ability to imagine, on which feeling, knowing, and willing are dependent. When one aspect dominates the other and there is no synthesis, despair results. For example, the despair of infinitude or possibility is found in a person who constantly imagines possible careers for himself but never gets down to the basics of training for any meaningful work. The despair of finitude is found in a person who is never able to break out of his given circumstances for fear of what others will think (33). Kierkegaard believes that to rightly relate these two aspects, there must be an awareness and dependence on God: "The self is the conscious synthesis of infinitude and finitude that relates itself to itself, whose task is to become itself, which can be done only through the relationship to God" (30). So becoming a self is becoming the self the person was created to be by God.

There are stages of increasing intensity in despair depending on the extent to which a person is conscious of despair. It is entirely possible to be in despair without being aware of it. Kierkegaard says that most of the world is ignorant of its own despair. One can try to keep oneself in the dark with busyness, but life has a way of unfolding such that one cannot avoid facing the despair one feels at some point. When one becomes conscious of a lack of a self, one becomes conscious of despair and can react in one of two ways, in weakness not to will to be oneself or in defiance to will to be oneself.

A person in the despair of weakness despairs over earthly concerns, those circumstances of life that are dealt to a person by "fate" that cause unhappiness (51–52). Joaquín is in the despair of weakness as the story begins. He is very conscious of his unhappiness even in school, as his peers embrace Abel and reject him. When Joaquín learns of Abel's pursuing Helena and of her preference for his friend, Joaquín's unhappiness turns to hate, and he purposes to conceal it while feeding it and allowing it to overtake his life. Here we can see that Joaquín has entered into yet another stage of despair that Kierkegaard calls "inclosing reserve": "A person in this kind of despair will hurl himself into life, perhaps into the diversion of great enterprises; he will become a restless spirit whose life certainly leaves its mark" (65–66). Joaquín throws himself into his work, seeking to eclipse the fame of Abel, but he despairs over himself, which is a step toward despairing over what is really important, the eternal. Kierkegaard says that at this point it is possible for the pain to bring the self "to lose itself in order to win itself" and to come to the opposite of despair, which is faith (67). But if a self does not lose itself in the eternal, then the person is on the path to go on to the next level of despair, the despair of defiance.

As the two titles—despair of weakness and despair of defiance—indicate, the first is passive and the second is active. In the despair of weakness the person despairs over externals, allows himself to be buffeted by fate. In the despair of defiance, the person's despair is "conscious of itself as an act; it does not come from outside as a suffering under the pressure of externalities but comes directly from the self" (67). Joaquín moves quickly into the despair of defiance. He sees his envy and hate as the makeup of who and what he is. Joaquín goes on to write his *confesión* (confession) so that his daughter will know the depth of his passion and see him as a misunderstood "héroe de la angustia tenebrosa" 'darkly afflicted hero' (2: 746; 144). Kierkegaard describes Joaquín perfectly:

> The person who despairs in defiance embraces his weakness and glories in it. He has convinced himself that this thorn in the flesh gnaws so deeply that he cannot abstract himself from it (whether this is actually the case or his passion makes it so to him), and therefore he might as well accept it forever, so to speak. He is offended by it, or more correctly, he takes it as an occasion to be offended at all existence, . . . he wills to be himself with it, takes it along, almost flouting his agony. (70–71)

Joaquín embraces and flouts his hate, saying in his *confesión*, "Mi vida, hija mía, ha sido un arder continuo, pero no la habría cambiado por la de otro. He odiado como nadie, como ningún otro ha sabido odiar, pero es que he sentido más que otros la suprema injusticia de los cariños del mundo y de los favores de la fortuna" 'My life, my daughter, has been one long passion, and yet I would not have exchanged it for another. I have hated like no one else ever has, for I have felt more than anyone the supreme injustices of the world's favors' (2: 746; 144).

Kierkegaard predicts Joaquín's downward spiral as he describes the person in the despair of defiance:

> The more consciousness there is in such a sufferer who in despair wills to be himself, the more his despair intensifies and becomes demonic. . . . So now he makes precisely this torment the object of all of his passion, and it finally becomes a demonic rage. . . . Once he would gladly have given everything to be rid of this agony, but he was kept waiting; now it is too late, now he would rather rage against everything and be the wronged victim of the world and all of life. (71–72)

Joaquín's behavior becomes more outrageous. He dismisses a maid whom he sees as threatening him with her goodness and is afraid that she will tell the world that he is mad. The crescendo of hate and envy rises to the point of an attempt to kill Abel.

The fact that the despair of defiance is wholly embraced underscores that it is chosen, a matter of the will. A person's ability to freely choose, *el libre albedrío* 'free will,' is at the center of Unamuno's concerns throughout his corpus, and nowhere is it more important than with Joaquín. Is he capable of change, of choosing a different course?[3] What are the moments of possible transformation? One of the most dramatic is Joaquín's decision to host the banquet to celebrate Abel and his award-winning painting of Cain and Abel.[4] Joaquín's motives are mixed; he believes that by his rhetoric he can eclipse the importance of the work, but on some level he wants to expiate the demon that controls his life. However, even though Joaquín's speech is a tremendous success, his demon tempts him to kill Abel in their embrace after the speech. The next day Joaquín wishes he had criticized the painting as he had wanted to.

The failure of the banquet to cure Joaquín sets up the crucial next scene where Antonia sends him to talk with the priest. It is in the confessional that Joaquín gives voice to the reigning paradigm for intellectuals, the deterministic philosophy of positivism on which nineteenth-century science was based and in which Unamuno was schooled as a university student. When the priest tells Joaquín that he must make an effort to change his hate and envy into something noble, as God made him free to do, Joaquín responds, "Soy médico. . . . No, no creo en la libertad humana, y el que no cree en la libertad no es libre" 'I am a doctor. . . . No, I do not believe in human liberty, and whoever cannot believe in liberty is not free' (2: 719; 79). To change, Joaquín would have to abandon his scientific worldview that says that everything is determined. To change, one must believe that one can be changed. Without that possibility, change is impossible.

Interestingly, Kierkegaard emphasizes that the freedom to choose is itself a gift from the eternal even though it can be misused. The consciousness of the choice brings the person closer to faith, as already noted in the passage above where Kierkegaard connects despair to offense. Joaquín reveals himself as being close to faith in a scene with Abel in chapter 16. Abel is outraged that Joaquín has been seen going to Mass and accuses him of having become a reactionary. Abel has no religion other than his art and asks Joaquín point-blank if he actually believes. Joaquín replies not that he believes but that he needs to believe. This helps make plausible the insights of the deathbed scene at the very end of the novel.

I ask my students if they can find any rays of hope in this very sad, climactic scene, in which the family of Joaquín gathers around him to hear his last words. The students point to Joaquín's asking forgiveness of his grandson and pleading with him not to forget his other grandfather as acts of contrition and reparation. Joaquín confesses in the presence of both Helena and Antonia that he did not love Antonia. He says if he had been able to love Antonia, he would have been cured. In this moment, there is the recognition that love could have overcome the hate and envy, and there is a willingness to love if only there were a chance to start over.[5]

This marks a change. Many times Joaquín had come close to being able to change, but in his despair there was always someone or something else to blame. As the overarching frame of the Cain and Abel story plays out, it is most pointedly God whom Joaquín accuses of making him the way he is, the victim, unable to do anything else. It is here that the matter of free will comes full circle. Did Joaquín have a real choice to love and use the power that would have cured him? Now Joaquín takes responsibility and concedes that there was a choice, and he could have chosen differently. "Pude quererte, debí quererte, que habría sido mi salvación, y no te quise" 'I could have loved you, I should have loved you, it would have been my salvation, but I did not' (2: 759; 176).

For Kierkegaard, the opposite of despair is faith. Does Joaquín come to faith? The text has prepared the reader for this possibility, since Joaquín goes from declaring the world to be determined to admitting that he needs to believe in God, though of course the text does not settle the matter. According to Kierkegaard, the person who is cognizant of his deep despair, the despair of defiance, is close to faith. Despair and faith are opposite passions, but one must believe that one has the power to choose to make a choice. At the end of his life, Joaquín perceives clearly that he had the option to love and he had rejected it. In this moment Joaquín has the first element of faith. He understands his despair and his ability to have done otherwise. Kierkegaard says, "The despair that is the thoroughfare to faith comes also through the aid of the eternal; through the aid of the eternal the self has the courage to lose itself in order to win itself" (67). In the last moments of his life, Joaquín loses his life in order to win it, and he can die in peace.

When students read *Abel Sánchez* through the eyes of Kierkegaard and *The Sickness unto Death*, they can more clearly understand Joaquín and his crippling envy. It is a way of helping them see some light in this dark tale, and it is a way of presenting them with existential choices of their own.

NOTES

[1] For further reading on the relationship of Kierkegaard and Unamuno, see the monographs by Collado; G. Roberts; and Evans (*Miguel de Unamuno's Quest* and *Unamuno*). Recent articles on this subject include Garrido Ardila's "Nueva lectura de *Niebla*" and "The Origin of Unamuno's *Mist*" and Evans's "*La enfermedad mortal* de Kierkegaard y *San Manuel Bueno, mártir* de Unamuno." For Unamuno's own story as to how he came to read Kierkegaard, see "Ibsen y Kierkegaard."

[2] The text of *Abel Sánchez* used in this essay is Manuel García Blanco's edition, included in *Obras completas*, published by Escelicer. English translations are by Anthony Kerrigan.

[3] Longhurst has an excellent, more thorough discussion of free will in *Abel Sánchez* in his *Unamuno's Theory of the Novel* (163–67). My reading concurs with his.

[4] For an illuminating, careful study of the banquet scene, see Franz, "Painting."

[5] Longhurst affirms that in this scene Joaquín expresses "the view that Unamuno had expressed in *Del sentimiento trágico de la vida*, the view that we are redeemed by our capacity to love" (*Unamuno's Theory* 166).

Unamuno and the "Protestant Left"

Nelson R. Orringer

Around 1897 Unamuno began seriously studying liberal Protestant theology, called by him the "izquierda protestante" 'Protestant left' (Unamuno and Zulueta 22–23) and spearheaded by the liberal Lutheran school of Albrecht Ritschl of Göttingen, Germany (Unamuno, "Epistolario" 11). To ease understanding of the depth and breadth of Unamuno's religious thinking, relevant to our age of crisis, it is a reliable method in the classroom to draw comparisons between his most typical writings and the specific theological ideas of members of the Ritschlian school read by Unamuno. A comparative examination of his main works can illustrate: his deepest essayistic effort, *Del sentimiento trágico de la vida* ("The Tragic Sense of Life"), debates with Ritschl; his best-studied novel, *Niebla* ("Mist"), dialogues with the younger Ritschlian Georg Wobbermin; and his most intense poem, *El Cristo de Velázquez* ("Velázquez's Christ"), reacts against the historian of dogma, Ritschl's student Adolf von Harnack. If we treat each of Unamuno's works as a living exchange of ideas with a different one of these three thinkers, we bring Unamuno's creations to life in the minds of our thinking students of philosophy, theology, or literature.

Around 1904 Unamuno invented his own religion, combining elements of liberal Protestantism and Catholicism (3: 9). He exercised his creative energies on his religious feeling while maintaining "creer es crear" 'to believe is to create' (*Del sentimiento* 539n100).[1] Unamuno wanted to be a Catholic, albeit a creative heterodox. Ritschlianism pointed the way, criticizing Catholicism for its uncertainty of salvation, while God guarantees forgiveness of sin and salvation afterward to Protestants. All believers' efforts, according to Ritschl, should concentrate on obtaining forgiveness (*Geschichte* 1: 28–29; *Die christliche Lehre* 2: 10–11, 3: 582). Now, the uncertainty of salvation seemed negative to the Ritschlians. However, Unamuno decided to make his doubt a positive force to forge a dynamic faith in God, struggling against every uncertainty to acquire new vigor. In volume 3 of his greatest theological work, *Die christliche Lehre von der Rechtfertigung und Versöhnung* ("The Christian Doctrine of Justification and Reconciliation"), Ritschl bases a philosophy of religion on God's guarantee of forgiveness of sin. Unamuno, however, reinvents Ritschl's philosophy by substituting uncertainty of salvation for forgiveness. Students can be stimulated to perceive how consistently Unamuno made this substitution to forge his chief work of religious philosophy, *Del sentimiento trágico de la vida*. He believed that he and the Spanish people in general felt uncertainty of salvation and that such uncertainty formed the authentic religion of Spain (9: 817, 3: 9).

Ritschl in The Tragic Sense of Life

From volume 3 of Ritschl's *Die christliche Lehre*, Unamuno derives the system of problems posed in his own book and most of the order of its ideas. Like Ritschl, Unamuno prefers the conservation of the personality to the entire world and to all knowledge. In Unamuno, personal preservation forms a principle regulating the theory of being, the theory of knowledge, religious dogma, individual and social ethics, everyday life, and aesthetics. This principle supposes the salvation of the complete man in body and soul.

Unamuno's religious philosophy, like Ritschl's theology, begins with a conception of the human being. Ritschl gives equal emphasis to morals and to forgiveness of individual sin (*Die christliche Lehre* 3: 9). Yet Unamuno, guided by Ritschl's conception of Catholicism, gives maximum importance to individual salvation. Ritschl and Unamuno both subordinate theoretical cognition to practical and religious knowledge. However, in Unamuno, all knowledge is reducible to life's only problem, human destiny after death. This problem originates the struggle between discursive reason and the desire for immortality. The head says no to immortality after death, while the heart says yes. The conflict between head and heart, reason and passion, defines what Unamuno calls the tragic sense of life (*Del sentimiento* 116).

With Ritschl, Unamuno rejects the ancient idea of God for its intellectualism: the mere idea of God does not equal God himself. Both Ritschl and Unamuno instead favor the view of God as a person. In Ritschl, the divine person forgives sins and guarantees salvation. In Unamuno, though, that person saves the human being through love. Both Ritschl and Unamuno, at the end of their philosophies of religion, synthesize all their doctrines in their ethics, their doctrine of right daily living. Yet in Ritschl the good human being lives in peace with himself, certain of salvation, while in Unamuno, he lives in a state of perpetual inner war, struggling to believe in salvation. Like the French author Étienne Pivert de Sénancour, Unamuno urges living every day to deserve salvation, and if the nothingness is awaiting us, "hagamos que sea una injusticia esto" 'let us make this an injustice' (*Del sentimiento* 433).

Wobbermin and the Divine World Plan in Unamuno's Mist

Wobbermin broaches the same philosophical issues as Unamuno in *Mist*, decisively affecting the novel. The I and causality, life after death, the personality of God, and moral freedom lie at the crux of *Mist*. For the sake of brevity and for greater clarity in the classroom, we may limit our focus to the question of freedom, central to the novel. Wobbermin asks: if God, our creator, preserver, and redeemer, must operate with the power to cause events, do we attain salvation through our own wills or seek divine intervention? Is God the only cause of salvation? For Wobbermin, God's omnipotence is limited by his ability to do everything to materialize his world plan; his omniscience is reduced to his knowledge of everything concerning that plan. Wobbermin does not believe, as the ancients did, that God foresees all human decisions and actions, or human will would be superfluous. Wobbermin conceives God as guaranteeing human freedom, but controlling its exercise only insofar as that freedom impedes the divine governance of the world. Likewise, Wobbermin disputes the view of God as foreseer of all free decisions of rational creatures. Otherwise, the world plan would function like a watch, set in motion for all time.

Instead, Wobbermin prefers William James's notion of a creator who predetermines beforehand all universal possibilities of his plan, leaving many details undetermined. Some come about by chance and are determined only at the moment of their realization. Others await their turn to be realized after the actualization of the possibilities reserved by God for causality. The rest of the world plan, including its final result, stays predetermined throughout history. Wobbermin summarizes using a clarifying example read in James: two unequal chess players sit at the board. The expert has a plan to defeat the novice but cannot foresee his moves. Yet the expert (i.e., God) knows all possible moves and the defenses to assure his victory. He infallibly wins by putting his opponent's king in checkmate (230n1).

The competitive relationship between divine player and human player passes from Wobbermin's treatise to Unamuno's novel. The chess game between Augusto and his prescient friend Víctor Goti proves the influence. The vision of Eugenia's eyes has endowed Augusto's life with meaning. When he moves his chessmen, he glimpses divine will behind his encounter with Eugenia. But the game, which leads to his defeat, offers a foreshadowing of the will of the author-god Don Miguel Unamuno to deprive Augusto of Eugenia and his life of significance. Augusto monologues: "Aquí sí que hay lógica, en esto del ajedrez, y, sin embargo, ¡qué nebuloso, qué fortuito después de todo! ¿No será la lógica también algo fortuito, algo azaroso? Y esa aparición de mi Eugenia, ¿no será algo lógico? ¿No obedecerá a un ajedrez divino?" 'There is surely logic in this business of chess playing, and yet how nebulous, how fortuitous after all! May not logic too be something fortuitous, something governed by chance? And that appearance of my Eugenia, may it not be logical? May it not obey a divine chess game?' (2: 564). James and Wobbermin recognize the role of chance in the world plan and compare life to a chess game in which the human being inexorably loses his king. When Augusto announces to Víctor his love of Eugenia, Víctor prophetically exclaims, "¡Jaque!" 'Checkmate!' (2: 565).

Yet the novelist Unamuno protests against this world plan in view of his tragic sense of life. If God's world plan deprives Unamuno's life of meaning by withholding from him the immortality he desires, his actions must demonstrate God's injustice. The gauntlet that Unamuno tosses to God appears in Sénancour's statement, already mentioned, that "si es la nada lo que nos está reservado, hagamos que sea una injusticia esto" 'if the nothingness is reserved for us, let us not make that fair' (*Del sentimiento* 433).

Mist hinges on a main issue: either I have free will, hence real existence and a just universe in which to live, or I form part of a superior being, execute his decisions, lack real existence, and must tolerate divine injustice. The German philosopher Arthur Drews expresses the dilemma by denying free will:

> If I do not exist as a real being (precisely because free will is not really at hand in my consciousness); if my I is rather only the subjective representation in which the actions of the Absolute are reflected, . . . it is thereby clear that it is only a deceitful illusion that any action comes from me. Therefore I am only the passive instrument or means by which the absolute Subject acts. Consequently, I have no freedom of action. (qtd. in Wobbermin 269)

The genial innovation of Unamuno as novelist consists of placing Drews's rationale in the mouth of an unjust author-god named Don Miguel, who says to his character Augusto Pérez, "No, no existes más que como ente de ficción; no eres, pobre Augusto, más que un producto de mi fantasía y de las de aquellos de mis lectores que lean el relato que de tus fingidas venturas y malandanzas he escrito yo" 'No, you do not exist except as a fictional being; you are only, poor Augusto, a product of my fantasy and of those of my readers that read the story that I have written of your feigned fortunes and misfortunes' (2: 666). Hence no action comes from Augusto. He cannot commit suicide, for instance, unless the absolute subject wishes: "como tú no existes más que en mi fantasía . . . y como no debes ni puedes hacer sino lo que a mí me dé la gana, y como no me da la real gana de que te suicides, no te suicidarás" 'Since you only exist in my fantasy . . . and since you shouldn't or can't do anything except what I damn well feel like having you do, and since I don't damn well feel like having you commit suicide, you will not commit suicide' (2: 667).

Confronted by the sarcastic joke of his own fictionality, Augusto nonetheless attempts to affirm his independence, even superiority, to his author-god. His arguments harmonize with Wobbermin. Miguel de Cervantes's narrator says of Don Quixote, "Para mí solo nació Don Quijote, y yo para él; él supo obrar, y yo escribir" 'For me alone was born Don Quixote, and I for him; he knew how to perform, and I to write' (qtd. in Unamuno 3: 254). Augusto brandishes the same argument against the author-god Don Miguel to assert the superiority of his own creatural reality to his creator's reality. With irony, Augusto cites to his author-god his own words: "¿no ha sido usted el que no una, sino varias veces, ha dicho que Don Quijote y Sancho son no ya tan reales, sino más reales que Cervantes?" 'wasn't it you who, not once, but several times, said that Don Quixote and Sancho are not only real, but more real than Cervantes?' (2: 667). Possibly at the base of this argument is a theological doctrine of Richard Rothe, paraphrased by Wobbermin (205–06): the endpoint of all creation is creatural spirit, which by definition has existence in and for itself. To emphasize the superiority of his own existence, Augusto offers the example of the dream as apparently more real than the inert dreamer. For Wobbermin, the active I is real. It argues in favor of Augusto's existence that he disputes his author-god. Likewise, Wobbermin quotes Wilhelm Dilthey's idea that we presume there is existence outside us from the resistance or contrast that our will encounters (286). Augusto also hints the reciprocity of resistance between creator and creature: if the author-god decrees a relationship of opposition with respect to him, he can oppose the author-god in accordance with his own inner law or logic. Wobbermin attributes to the I the right to free self-determination (206). Augusto reasons that he has the right to commit suicide. Given the unfair treatment he feels he has received from his creator, Augusto tells his author-god that suicide serves as a practicable substitute for deicide.

The author-god reacts with fury by decreeing the time and place of Augusto's death (2: 669). That god's conduct adheres to the limits of omnipotence set by Wobbermin and James: he does only what is strictly necessary to bring about his world plan. Since Augusto has spoken of assassinating him, he finds that notion "anarchic" (2: 669)—that is, contrary to the governance of the novelistic world. It is ironic that Augusto's deicidal attitude catches his author-god by surprise. Until this point he has known the most intimate sentiments of Augusto as well as Augusto himself (2: 665). If Wobbermin's theology functions within the universe of *Mist*, Augusto's sentimental evolution before his dialogue with the author-god has constituted the substance of the novel, which that deity would have to know to bring about his original plan. On the other hand, he would not have had to forecast Augusto's deicidal challenge, because, rebellious or not, Augusto, a weak character, could not have hindered the author-god's objective: the goal of producing in Augusto the experience of the tragic sense of life. Why, then, does harmless Augusto receive the death sentence? If the instructor poses this question to students, they may respond that the novelist is stressing the injustice of the author-god, who, since Augusto has served his novelistic purpose, affirms a theory that has tormented the essayist Unamuno: "No sé qué hacer ya de ti. Dios, cuando no sabe qué hacer de nosotros, nos mata" 'I don't know what to do with you. God, when he doesn't know what to do with us, kills us' (2: 670). In daily living, nobody knows the cause of death, although a pessimistic Unamuno feels that a malicious God makes determinism likely. *Mist* fulfills its mission when Augusto screams for life eternal, feeling the tragic sense of life, the conflict between the will to live and the awareness of mortality. Hence Wobbermin, countered by Sénancour, generates Unamuno's most debated novel.

Velázquez's Christ *and Harnack's Critique of Popular Catholicism*

Mist posits the possibility of a competitive God. However, Unamuno desires with Ritschl a God of personality, love, and will to save humankind. This vision predominates in *Velázquez's Christ*. In *The Tragic Sense of Life* appears Unamuno's explanation of how he came to envision Diego Velázquez's painting *Christ Crucified* as the expression par excellence of the faith of the Spanish people. Unamuno contrasts Johann Sebastian Bach with Velázquez: the composer gave to world art the maximum contribution of Protestantism, and the painter that of Catholicism. Unamuno identifies the Ritschlian Ernst Troeltsch as the source of the idea that Bach's music constitutes the loftiest expression of Protestantism (*Del sentimento* 191). Unamuno's own preference for painting—an opinion worthy of student debate—derives from a rationale found in two liberal Protestants: Harnack and the American Unitarian William Ellery Channing. Channing maintains that the plastic arts, especially painting and sculpture, show that matter exists in the universe to serve spirit (87). Hence Unamuno prefers painting for its tangibility, materiality, and permanence (*Del sentimiento* 191). This taste for painting has its roots in Harnack, who attributes religious materialism to popular Catholicism, always desiring to seek "signs of the love of God" (1: 151). Unamuno identifies with Spanish Catholics in the same sense: "como los judíos, queremos señales, algo que se pueda agarrar con todas las potencias del alma y con todos los sentidos del cuerpo" 'Like the Jews, we want signs, something that can be grasped with all the potencies of the soul and all the senses of the body' (*Del sentimiento* 196). Velázquez's *Christ Crucified* furnished Unamuno such a sign. Yet, he could not be certain of salvation, or he would have ceased being Catholic in the sense understood by him and Harnack of a Christian uncertain of being saved. He wrote to Teixeira de Pascoaes, "A mí me ha dado ahora por formular la fe de mi pueblo, su cristología realista, y . . . lo estoy haciendo en verso" 'Now I have taken it upon myself to formulate the faith of my people, its realist Christology, and . . . I am doing it in verse' (6: 24). Here Unamuno translates the materialistic *Realismus* that Harnack deplored in the Christology of popular Catholicism (Harnack 1: 426, 444). What Harnack censures in popular Catholic religion, Unamuno approves as his own and as essentially Spanish. Hence he accepts the conception of popular Catholicism read by him in Harnack, while substituting a favorable value judgment for Harnack's negativity. Intellectually, Unamuno is Ritschlian; affectively, he feels Catholic, though in a heterodox sense defined by Harnack. This disparity between sentiment and thought appears both in *The Tragic Sense of Life* and *Velázquez's Christ*.

Unamuno debates Harnack about the materialism of Catholic piety. Favoring intelligence and spirit over matter, Harnack rejects the sacrament of the Eucharist for its obscurantism and materialism. However, Unamuno, agreeing with the materialism ascribed to this sacrament by Harnack, defends it by relating it to the traditional Spanish desire for the resurrection of the flesh. *Velázquez's Christ* abounds in allusions to the Eucharist derived from Harnack, though positive in the poet and negative in the theologian. Here, let us summarize Harnack's idea of popular Catholic piety; show that the seven historical stages attributed to it by Harnack are to be found in the faith praised in *Velázquez's Christ*; and point out that Harnack's negative attitude toward that faith is reversed by Unamuno in his poem.

Harnack opposes natural theology, the metaphysical doctrine of God, based on ancient cosmology. Therefore Harnack disputes the metaphysical Christology of the ancient and medieval church. He finds that faith rests on the historical work of Jesus, not on mere value judgments about his nature (Meijering 23–56). Harnack deplores the religion of amulets, fetishes, and magic toward which, in his opinion, Christianity declined six centuries after its founding. The Greek church, he thinks, made too many concessions to the masses. It ceased to give a spiritual treatment to knowledge of divine realities, reducing it to a body of doctrines half comprehensible, half secret, supposedly derived straight from God and communicated through sacred festivals. Although the magic and mysticism seemed to indicate that God overcomes reason, Christianity, Harnack explains, tended toward paganism. Doctrine became mystagogy, combining spirituality and sensualism. Ritual, fixed ceremony, predominated. Mystagogical theology reduced persons, epochs, and objects to mysterious symbols and vehicles of meaning. Hence such theology submitted to mass preference for the annihilation of spirit and the sanctification of matter.

Since the end of the second century, when Christianity started preaching a public doctrine, there has existed what Harnack calls a religion of second order, popular, underground, and polytheistic. Catholicism, he thinks, legitimized it and joined it with public doctrine. Harnack distinguishes seven evolutive stages of this legitimization, visible in *Velázquez's Christ*: (1) Christian doctrine received a structure affected by Greco-Latin culture and philosophy, interwoven with mythology and superstition. (2) Christianity's public doctrine sanctioned the Old Testament, utilizing it to legitimate sacred ceremonies. (3) Sacred activities like baptism and the Eucharist introduced popular religion into official Christianity. Into it entered new mysteries, magic, liturgical miracles, and fetishes. (4) Although angels and demons had already figured in primitive Christianity, public doctrine could not control popular representations of those spirits. Monks fantasized a world of them, giving Christian labels to ancient mythological figures. The church welcomed the Neoplatonic doctrine of spirits. (5) The belief arose that an epoch of heroism had arrived, led by the Old Testament patriarchs and prophets, martyrs, ascetics, and saints. All these figures could intercede with God and maintain a special relationship with Christ. The Virgin took center stage, giving feminine form to divinity. (6) Since antiquity, Christians had valued death as sacred. Pagan fetishism, therefore, easily passed to the cult of the relics of saints. (7) The veneration of saints and the service demanded by the relics led to honoring images and icons.

Let us now consider how Unamuno transforms Harnack's historiography of popular Christianity. It does not disturb Unamuno that the Eucharist and baptism paved the way for popular religion in official Christianity. In *The Tragic Sense of Life*, he sees the sacrament of the Eucharist as the "eje de la piedad popular católica" 'crux of popular Catholic piety.' In it "se administra el cuerpo de Cristo, que es pan de inmortalidad" 'is administered the body of Christ, that is the bread of immortality' (184–85). The sacrament may well defy reason, yet for Unamuno it preserves its value. Miracles, magic, and mysteries form the substance of *Velázquez's Christ*; the painter's art seems magical, his theme miraculous, and spectators feel the love emanating from the mystery of salvation:

> Vara mágica
> nos fue el pincel de don Diego Rodríguez
> de Silva Velázquez. Por ella en carne
> te vemos hoy. Eres el hombre eterno
> que nos hace hombres nuevos. (6: 417)
>
> Magic wand
> for us was the brush of Don Diego
> Rodríguez de Silva Velázquez. Hence in the flesh
> We see you today. You [Christ] are the eternal man
> That makes us new men.

Into this poetry, dazzled by human magic and divine grandeur, enter angels and demons. In the segment "Miguel," the archangel frightens away "infernal" vultures, comparable to demons, trying to feed on Christ's body. Satan shudders with envy and wrath while Christ triumphs (6: 456). Unamuno's poem conveys an atmosphere of heroism. A victorious Christ joins patriarchs, prophets, ascetics, and saints. Among the patriarchs, Jacob (6: 428, 440, 446) and Moses (6: 430, 477) stand out. Beside them militate ascetics and saints. Christ the Nazarene compares to Samson (6: 466–67). Among saints, Unamuno prefers Athanasius, intensely hoping for immortality. For him, "No, pues . . . siendo hombre se hizo después Dios, sino que, siendo Dios, se hizo después hombre para que mejor nos deificara" 'not, therefore, for being a man did [Christ] afterward become God, but being God, he afterward became a man to deify us' (qtd. in *Del sentimiento* 181). Athanasius's quotation passes to the verses of Unamuno's poem (6: 456).

Harnack disapproves Mariolatry, with roots in pagan worship of "mothers of God" like Demeter, Venus, Juno, and others, all united into a single great mother (1: 442). Unamuno, as always, agrees with Harnack as historian, yet approves the pagan heritage as specifically Catholic. Attributing multiple personalities to God appears to Unamuno to be one of many ways for human beings to save the personality of God, so that he in turn may save them (*Del sentimiento* 327). In *Velázquez's Christ*, according to Calvin Cannon (28–39), Unamuno associates the Virgin with Mother Earth, Christ with the moon, and God the father with the sun (6: 433).

The ideas of three liberal Protestants dialogue with three major works by Unamuno: Ritschl with *The Tragic Sense of Life*, Wobbermin with *Mist*, and Harnack with *Velázquez's Christ*. All illustrate that believing (*creer*) is creating (*crear*). Aside from the aesthetic enjoyment Unamuno's works provide, they form creations through discrepancies with the intertexts. We could easily have extended our comparisons to many of his writings. Suffice it to say that the creativity of Unamuno's faith relies on the creative theology of liberal Protestantism. It makes sense to bring Unamuno's dialogue with Ritschlianism to the attention of students eager to witness how his main works came into being.

NOTE

[1] The text of *Del sentimiento trágico de la vida* used in this essay is my own edition, published by Tecnos. Unless noted otherwise, other works by Unamuno are quoted from *Obras completas*, edited by Manuel García Blanco and published by Escelicer. All English translations are mine.

SAN MANUEL BUENO, MÁRTIR IN AN INTEGRATED SPANISH MAJOR

Unamuno's *San Manuel Bueno, mártir*: An Integrated Performance Assessment Approach

Dawn Smith-Sherwood

A staple of introductory Hispanic literature courses throughout the United States, Miguel de Unamuno's *San Manuel Bueno, mártir* ("San Manuel Bueno, Martyr") often presents undergraduate minors and majors in Spanish their first true second-language reading challenge. While celebrated among Unamuno scholars, its dense thematic concerns regarding tradition and progress, faith and disbelief, combined with a complex narrative structure and rich discursive features, are unfamiliar and potentially off-putting to second-language learners at the intermediate level. In the face of these challenges, professors may resort to explanation and lecture, acceding to a coverage rather than competence pedagogical model. As a result, while students may become skilled at memorizing and repeating what their professors communicate to them about a literary text, they may also stagnate in their development of linguistic proficiency across all modes, never reaching the advanced levels necessary for future academic and professional success.

This essay encourages second-language literature professors to consider how they might alter their course planning and classroom practices to ensure that they are meeting students where they actually are linguistically and show them the way forward, so that students not only know about challenging works of the literary canon but also learn how to engage with texts in meaningful ways that will additionally serve to develop their linguistic proficiency. This essay details the transformation of my own pedagogical approach from coverage to competence in the context of Unamuno's *San Manuel Bueno, mártir* in an Introduction to Hispanic Literature setting. Specifically, it proposes the adoption of the Integrated Performance Assessment (IPA) as a way to better serve students and perhaps save the teaching of literature in the postsecondary second-language setting.

A course that is common to many Spanish program curricula, Introduction to Hispanic Literature traditionally serves as a bridge between the language, conversation, and composition courses characteristic of the first two years of college-level study and the linguistics, culture, and literature courses of the third and fourth years. I have taught Introduction to Hispanic Literature, a course required of all Spanish majors and minors at my institution, more than a dozen times since the fall of 2003. A review of my syllabi reveals a drastic reduction in the number of primary texts covered as well as a complete elimination of the *panorama histórico* 'historical introduction' that accompanies each genre—narrative, poetry, drama, and essay—treated in the oft-used textbook for such a course, *Aproximaciones al estudio de la literatura hispánica* ("Approaches to the Teaching of Hispanic Literature"), now in its seventh edition.

Following a university-wide assessment initiative, course objectives were changed dramatically to reflect student learning outcomes, or what we call student performance objectives: what students would be able to do rather than what and how much they would be expected to know. In this context, Elizabeth Bernhardt's "Teaching Literature or Teaching Students?" also urges that we consider our own motivations. In this brief, powerful piece, Bernhardt asks, "[A]re we in our classrooms for the benefit of students as individuals, or are we there to ensure that certain bodies of work remain in the consciousness of literary scholarship?" (6). Additional incentive to guide the course from coverage to competence stems from Richard Donato and Frank Brooks's seminal 2004 piece that demonstrated, albeit somewhat painfully, that even the discussion in which well-intentioned literature professors thought they were engaging their students was mired in the traditional initiation-response-evaluation sequence, in which a professor initiates an interaction, a student responds, and the professor, in effect, closes down the potential for further conversation with an evaluative comment.

Subsequent replication studies, such as those by Mark Darhower, have yielded similar results but few suggestions or solutions. Fortunately, scholars like Chantal Thompson, in her *ADFL Bulletin* piece "Preparing Students for Writing and Talking About Literature," have begun to provide practical advice to literature professors. For example, Thompson's continuum model, focusing on form in support of function—from full control of intermediate tasks, to partial control of advanced tasks, to emerging control of superior tasks—is most useful in planning in-class activities that spiral up in a manner similar to the ACTFL Oral Proficiency Interview (OPI) and ACTFL Writing Proficiency Test.

My own teaching responds to Bernhardt's 2002 assertion that "[t]he point of departure must be what the student understands is in the text, not what the teacher tells him or her it is about. The task . . . is to look for and to diagnose misunderstandings arising from cultural misconstructions, linguistic deficiencies, or both" ("Research" 202). Most recently, I have been experimenting with the use of the IPA, developed initially for L2 instruction in the K–12 context, in order to explore its applicability within a literature course at the postsecondary level.

Informed by the ACTFL Proficiency Guidelines and National Standards for Learning Languages and grounded in second language acquisition theory and research, the IPA provides a useful protocol to help shift the focus away from content to competence, from a literature professor's recourse to lecturing when confronted with blank stares to the needs of the second-language learners who occupy their classrooms. The IPA and its associated interpretive, interpersonal, and presentational tasks engage and assist students in the further development of linguistic proficiency and cultural competence as they participate in the cycle of modeling, practice, performance, and feedback that results from the related concept of backward design (Adair-Hauck et al. 3).

The tasks associated with the IPA's initial interpretive communication phase deploy "the use of both top-down and bottom-up processing in concert" (Adair-Hauck et al. 15) and guide students from an initial exploration of the authentic text—through searches for key words, phrases, and supporting details (literal comprehension)—to a more complex second look, informed by organizational features, context, inference, and cultural perspective (interpretive comprehension). As the focus is on receptive rather than productive skills, interpretive tasks are not second-language exclusive; that is, there is no insistence on use of the second language to complete them. The activities associated with the interpretive task draw on what students do know and encourage them to take risks and make educated guesses about what remains less familiar to them.

Next, in the interpersonal communication phase, students are provided a related situational conversation prompt to respond to orally with the aim of encouraging them to produce the thematic, lexical, and grammatical features discovered through previous completion of interpretive tasks. Emphasis here is on problem solving and negotiation of meaning, features that resonate with the ACTFL OPI.

In the culminating presentational communication phase, students create a product, in written or spoken form, for a real audience with a real purpose. In both the interpersonal and presentational communication phases, there is increased insistence upon accurate use of the second language, as the focus shifts from receptive to productive linguistic skills. Assessed in terms of four criteria—language function, text type, comprehensibility, and language control—the presentational product is additionally evaluated for its impact—that is, "The degree to which a written or oral message maintains the attention of the reader or listener" (Adair-Hauck et al. 115).

San Manuel Bueno, mártir is a literary tour de force. Ángela, the work's first-person narrator, brilliantly underscores for students that a first-person narrator is not necessarily the author. The work also suggests the existence of an implied narratee, the Bishop of the Diocese of Renada, who may one day read Ángela's testimony. The abrupt and unanticipated interruption of a second first-person narrator near the work's conclusion, whose commentary disrupts the veracity of all that has come before, exemplifies the concept of the unreliable narrator. *San Manuel Bueno, mártir* employs foreshadowing, intertextuality, and leitmotif and offers abundant dialogue as well as robust description replete with multiple examples of figurative language. Unamuno's signature hypotactic syntax and playful use of word families combine to create rich paradoxical truths. Consequently, a class could spend an entire semester exploring this one text.

These many and varied formal aspects contribute to the underlying texture of complex thematic concerns regarding such matters as faith, reason, tradition, progress, personal struggle, and loss. While one must encourage students to be wary of easy biographical answers to complex questions, Unamuno's own losses—personal (death of a child), professional (removal from university positions), and political (exile and house arrest)—in the context of a Spain that changed dramatically during his lifetime arguably impacted his work. Unamuno lived, both indirectly and directly, the fallout of the Spanish-American War, the dictatorship of Miguel Primo de Rivera, and the onset of the Spanish Civil War. *San Manuel Bueno, mártir* is a work that one hopes students return to multiple times over the course of their lives, for linguistic, intellectual, and even spiritual reasons.

Prior to approaching *San Manuel Bueno, mártir*, a culminating work for the course, students will have studied short stories, poetry, and drama, all within the broad theme of family, more specifically, the misunderstandings that result from generation gaps, who is considered family other than those to whom one is related, and how individuals form families of friends outside of their families of origin. Students will be familiar with the major features of narrative (types of narrator, narrative frames, dialogue, description, figurative language), poetry (rules of versification, rhyme, literary figures and tropes), and drama (written versus performed, dramatic devices).

In order to prepare students for completion of the summative assessment, I provide them with a global view as well as individual task summaries associated with each phase of the IPA (appendix 1). These tasks are pitched at the intermediate-high level, and the interpersonal and presentational tasks will be assessed using rubrics calibrated to this level. It should be noted, however, that the IPA is adjustable across all levels of linguistic proficiency, and the manual *Implementing Integrated Performance Assessment* provides interpersonal and presentational rubrics from novice through advanced. The interpretive task rubric can be used at all levels of linguistic proficiency.

Compared to the traditional questions, identifications, and theme activities that often accompany works in standard literary anthologies, the tasks of the IPA cannot be completed in "look back and lift off" manner. When combined with prompt and high-quality feedback—an essential component of the IPA's cyclical approach—"[t]he IPA is an assessment system that can promote a growth mindset in student language performance" (Adair-Hauck et al. 5).

As mentioned earlier, the IPA works in tandem with the major tenets of what has come to be known as backward design, in which the teacher determines, before even entering the classroom, how the desired results for and acceptable evidence produced by students will be accomplished through learning activities (Adair-Hauck et al. 115). As Adair-Hauck et al. assert, "The advantage of the IPA within a backward design approach is that the target for performance is always in focus, and consequently both learners and instructors understand what the goal is and how instruction and assessment work as one system to enable learners to reach that goal" (3). A list of sample learning activities associated with the first part of *San Manuel Bueno, mártir* for the three modes of communication prior to completion of the IPA as a summative assessment is provided in appendix 2.

In 2007 and 2009 the Modern Language Association (MLA) released reports that critiqued the traditional two-tiered model within undergraduate modern language programs, whereby language study and communicative proficiency are relegated to the beginning and intermediate levels, while third- and fourth-year courses focus primarily on literary and cultural analysis, what some have called an instructor-focused content curriculum. At the 2017 MLA Annual Convention, a series of five sessions, organized in recognition of the tenth anniversary of the 2007 report, considered what had been done, in effect, to mend the traditional language-literature split. From what Elizabeth Redden of *Inside Higher Ed* reported, the progress was somewhat discouraging. It seems that creating new structures had been met with considerable resistance. In 2002 Heidi Byrnes predicted as much, explaining, "While college FL [foreign language] faculty, the majority of whom are specialists in literary cultural studies, see themselves as committed teachers, they do not consider task as a viable construct for describing their intellectual work nor do they view assessment as contributing substantively to their professional self-identification and their role as teacher-scholars" (420).

College foreign language faculty, especially literature professors, urgently need to reconsider their long-held positions and get engaged. We need to respond and move proactively. If, as Redden reports, the last decade of curricular reforms "include diversifying their curriculum and study abroad offerings, *phasing out the emphasis on literature*, developing interdisciplinary initiatives, and engaging with the community" (emphasis added), Unamuno may soon disappear altogether from undergraduate programs. We do not need to phase out literature but rather to rethink the ways that we teach it in order to ensure that its study contributes to students' growth as second-language learners. The application of the IPA cycle of interpretive, interpersonal, and presentational tasks in the teaching of Unamuno's *San Manuel Bueno, mártir* has proven effective in shifting the focus from professor to student, from explanation to engagement, from content coverage to linguistic and cultural competence, in order to produce increasingly confident, capable readers of authentic Spanish literary texts.

APPENDIX 1

San Manuel Bueno, mártir: IPA Overview

You have been studying *San Manuel Bueno, mártir*, by Miguel de Unamuno. This reading has sparked your curiosity to learn more about Unamuno's worldview. First, you will read a poem by Unamuno. Based on what you discover, you and a classmate will explore the question of poetic voice. Finally, you will write a proposal to rename the Spanish language cluster at your university in honor of Unamuno for his continued relevance to today's students of Spanish-language letters.

Interpretive Task

Your professor will give you a second work by Unamuno, a poem, to read. Your job is to comprehend as much as you can of this poem so that you may deepen your understanding of Unamuno's worldview. Take up to twenty minutes to read and complete the comprehension guide.

Interpersonal Task

You and your classmate must decide which character from *San Manuel Bueno, mártir* gave poetic voice to the poem "Oración del ateo" ("Prayer of the Atheist"): Ángela, Lazarus, their mother (la Simona), Don Manuel, or Little Blaise. Propose at least one possibility individually and consider the merits of an additional possibility collectively (for a total of three different possibilities) and give reasons for the likelihood or unlikelihood of each choice. Finally, choose one of the characters and give solid, concluding reasons for the choice.

Presentational Task

Based on learning activities, readings, and your discussion with your classmate, write a proposal of approximately two hundred words (three well-developed paragraphs) about why the Spanish language cluster at your university should be renamed to honor Miguel de Unamuno. Take up to forty minutes to prepare your proposal.

APPENDIX 2

Sample Learning Activities to Prepare for the IPA: *San Manuel Bueno, mártir* (Part 1)

For the purposes of my course, I divide the novel into three parts. Part 1, which marks the narrative time prior to Ángela's return to the town following her formal education, ends with "Yo no podría llevar solo la cruz del nacimiento" 'I could not bear alone the burden of being born' (Friedman et al., lines 257–58; my trans.).

Interpretive Task Related

Key words: Valverde de Lucerna, Renada, matriarcal
Main ideas: What is the main idea of the first part of the work?
Supporting details: Ángela's age when she returns home from school, Don Manuel's saint's day
Organizational features: chronological, parabolic
Guessing meaning from context: "The important thing is that Ángela *be finished* and that she not remain among those *uncivilized* townswomen."
Inferences: "he would fall silent," "six planks, that he kept at the foot of his bed"
(Author's) narrator's perspective: personal, factual, religious
Comparing cultural perspectives: celebration of saint's day, use of refrains

Interpersonal Task Related (completed in pairs or as a whole class)

Draw Ángela's family tree, Ángela's father's library, or Ángela's town.
Conduct interviews (Bishop interviewing townspeople: Ángela, Lazarus, la Simona, Don Manuel).

Presentational Task Related

Write a letter from Don Manuel to another character.
Write a parable about someone you admire.

Supplemental Learning Activities

View excerpts from Fernando Trueba's film *Belle Epoque* (1992).
View or listen to excerpts from Unamuno documentaries from Televisión / Radio Nacional Española (TVE / RNE).
Read article from *El País* regarding the popularity of Pope Francis, compare and contrast personal characteristics of Don Manuel and Pope Francis.

Discovery Learning and Unamuno's *San Manuel Bueno, mártir*

Emily Joy Clark

Inquiry-based learning places college students at the helm in constructing meaning from passages through literary analysis, pushes them to develop critical thinking skills, and allows them to reconsider their own preconceptions when approaching a text. Miguel de Unamuno's novels, which negotiate existential questions of reality, religion, and tradition, provide an ideal medium for opening a dialogue surrounding existential topics in the text and in students' belief systems. By selecting specific codified quotations to start students on an exploratory path to find the religious symbolism hidden in Unamuno's *San Manuel Bueno, mártir* ("Saint Manuel Bueno, Martyr"), I have successfully pushed them to develop and test hypotheses about the novel's metaphorical subtext. This process allows learners to discover for themselves the double reading of certain characters as biblical figures (e.g., Jesus, Mary, Lazarus, and the disciples) and to uncover the symbolism behind repeated images (e.g., the lake and the mountain). Individual groups working on a specific character or image can test the concepts they are developing as we continue to read by recording relevant quotations and ideas to share with the class about their topic. As the groups fit their information with that of other groups and reformat their interpretations through class discussion, the novel's metaphorical messages come into focus by the conclusion, with learners taking an active approach in unearthing existential ideas. Using this method provokes exciting dialogue, partly because Unamuno invites this type of questioning from his readers. By offering students aid in uncovering the text's hidden messages in an inquiry or discovery learning process, professors can facilitate students' collective detection of the novel's religious ideas, augment intrinsic motivation, and make literature relevant in students' lives.

Discovery and inquiry-based learning techniques stem from learning and development research such as Jean Piaget's constructivist theories that learners construe meaning from direct experience, interaction, and even reformulation of ideas, rather than from passive absorption of concepts. Many education theorists who design inquiry-based teaching techniques thus organize their models around students' active learning by constructing questions, searching for evidence, and considering conflicting viewpoints. Although this approach was initially applied to the sciences, where hypothesis testing fits perfectly with an inquiry model, it is effective in a variety of fields (Audet 2). Gordon Wells makes a strong case for introducing more inquiry-based techniques when approaching books, which have, unfortunately, traditionally been treated like "repositories" of information learned through "reading and memorizing." A better approach to synthesize the content that books present, Wells argues, would be for "novices

[to] actively participate in the activities in which the knowledge is used, [and] construct their own understanding of it" (178). In Unamuno's works, philosophical questions are not simply understood by lecture but by inquiry, a search for textual evidence, and dialogue. While classical discovery learning activities were largely student directed, later permutations of these techniques allow teachers to better guide learners in their search for meaning (Wells 177). In my experience, guided inquiry works well for literature promoting theoretical concepts, as it can allow students to formulate questions and hypotheses, reevaluate original impressions, and engage in critical thinking.

Such learning techniques can provide a richer engagement with Unamuno's works, especially since Unamuno was likely a follower of scientific inquiry, classical skeptic philosophy, and the scientific method, as Brian Cope has argued (183). In *San Manuel*, the title character's life and doubts directly parallel those of Christ, allowing readers to question Jesus's beliefs and, subsequently, Catholicism, an argument that critics such as Pelayo H. Fernández (*El problema*), Francisco LaRubia-Prado ("Sanctity"), and Eduardo Godoy Gallardo have made. Just as Don Manuel shares much in common with Jesus (and Moses), other characters also mirror biblical figures (for example, Ángela and the writers of the Gospels, Mary, and Mary Magdalene; Lázaro and his biblical namesakes as well as Jesus's disciples), as Douglas Carey and Phillip Williams, Carlos Longhurst (*Unamuno's Theory*), and others explore. When students read the novel and make queries about specific characters, they examine links between the novel and the story of Jesus, which elucidates doubt at the story's core. Since Don Manuel, a Christ-like martyr, questions Catholicism, *San Manuel* suggests that Jesus could have doubted the existence of God and his own divinity, a concept that intrigues students. Ultimately, students realize that the type of Christianity being promoted by Don Manuel and Lázaro is not one rooted in faith but rather in the illusion of faith, to tranquilize the populace facing existential questions that are symbolically reflected in the lake, the mountain, and the town of Valverde de Lucerna. These parallels are evident to critical readers and are ones that other theorists have pointed out; however, many students do not immediately see such connections when reading, and pushing them to create questions, find evidence, and craft hypotheses facilitates their discovery of the text's deeper meanings.

With guided inquiry methods in mind, I start by assigning students to work groups for weeks 1–2, in which I cover the novel to provide structure while allowing students to uncover the text's symbolism. After letting the groups select their character or image from a list, I offer them a few quotations about their topic that provide a starting point for brainstorming. Later, students add further textual support to their ideas at home and in class during in-group discussion. After applying this technique in several classes, I believe the best characters and images for group topics are Don Manuel, Lázaro, Ángela, the lake, the mountain, and Valverde de Lucerna. Blasillo also works well for critiquing the text's presentation of disability and incorporating theory from disability studies into discussion.

Each day, after summarizing the section read for homework, students work with quotations from that day's reading about their groups' topics. At the end of the session, they share their impressions, hypotheses, and possible symbolic interpretations with the rest of the class. During group time, I give individual groups one or two printed quotations related to their theme, and they should bring a quotation they found while reading that is relevant to their questions and postulations about their topic. By having the groups first work separately on quotations related to their character or image, they can format possible symbolic and, eventually, allegorical interpretations of the text as it progresses. During this process, I circulate around the classroom to guide the interpretation of the quotations if groups seem lost. Toward the end of each session, once all the groups have analyzed their quotations, I bring everyone back together to discuss the quotations. Progressing in order by page numbers, each student group reads its assigned quotations aloud and discusses possible interpretations. With guidance, we add the interpretations and evidence together as each group contributes quotations to better the understanding of the topic. Each group's viewpoints are further shaped by evidence and ideas about other central characters and images that the remaining groups contribute.

To motivate students to discover possible biblical allegories in the text, I tell them that there are other possible ways to read the novel, which encourages them to try to figure out what they are and spurs hypotheses. At the end of each class session, I ask them to take a few minutes to write down questions and thoughts that they have about their topic or about the novel's themes and symbols in general. Queries could include "what does Lázaro believe after his conversion?" or "why are the lake and the mountain mentioned together?" If they have difficulty understanding the significance of a quotation, I emphasize certain words for them. Alternatively, teachers can make open-ended comments about certain aspects of a quotation if students seem lost, such as "I wonder why Unamuno uses that word," or "I wonder if that quotation relates to the one that the group studying Ángela mentioned." Sometimes students produce random comments in this process, but the free exploration of ideas also permits more creative insights. Finally, by our last day studying the novel, I ask the entire class to piece together other possible interpretations of the story. Relying on one another and their hypotheses, students are able to decipher allegorical readings of the text by this point. Their discovery of these ideas is more valuable for critical thinking skills than a lecture would have been.

Unamuno's short novel is a treasure trove of worthwhile passages, but some are particularly salient for linking the protagonists to Jesus and New Testament figures, thus sowing doubt into the interpretation of biblical stories. These quotations guide students to see this symbolism and have been highlighted by other critics such as Godoy Gallardo. Early in the novel, for instance, readers see that Don Manuel has Christ as his patron saint (121).[1] Later, his mother is compared with the Virgin in an iconic scene in church (122), and he is referred to as one of "nuestros dos cristos" 'our two Christs' as the text progresses (153). Multiple sections of the novel also point to Don Manuel's Christlike actions. Crucially, some of these are also in unorthodox scenes where Don Manuel defies Catholic doctrine, such as his forgiveness of victims of suicide (126) and his statements leading Ángela to question if he believes in hell (133). Upon his death, which may represent a martyrdom for the painful cause of convincing others to believe his prophesy, Unamuno describes Don Manuel's hands, invoking the image of Christ on the cross: "Tenía entre sus manos un crucifijo" 'He had a crucifix in his hands' (125). Like Christ, Don Manuel doubts the existence of God while leading others in religious worship, a paradox echoed in the words of Christ on the cross, which reappear throughout the novel: "Díos mío, Díos mío, ¿por qué me has abandonado?" 'My God, my God, why have you forsaken me?' (121). Such passages where Don Manuel confesses doubt effectively guide the group studying him.

Of course this link between Don Manuel's doubt and Christ's doubt is further strengthened by Lázaro's retelling of conversations he has with Don Manuel, which are effective for both groups working on these characters. For instance, Lázaro explains how Don Manuel "acabó confesándome que creía que más de uno de los más grandes santos, acaso el mayor, había muerto sin creer en la otra vida" 'ended up confessing to me that he believed that more than one of the great saints, perhaps the greatest, had died without believing in life after death' (162). Since Lázaro and Ángela function as disciples of sorts, students may detect these biblical parallels. Sections regarding Lázaro's conversion not to Christianity but to Don Manuel's religion of self-sacrifice and feigned belief establish him as a follower of this alternate faith (see Carey and Williams 298). Lázaro and Ángela later receive guidance from the dying saint regarding caring for his flock: "Oíd: cuidad de estas pobres ovejas que se consuelen de vivir, que crean lo que yo no he podido creer. Y tú Lázaro, cuando hayas de morir, muere como yo" 'Listen: care for these poor sheep so that they are consoled in living, so that they believe what I have been unable to believe. And you, Lázaro, when you have to die, die like me' (156). As Manuel Blanco posits, here death is cast as a ritual for Don Manuel's disciples in order to occlude doubt and establish "faith" (154). Lázaro follows these instructions on his own deathbed, and the town prays to Don Manuel (not Jesus), showing the creation of a new religious following (163). Lázaro's death also can open a discussion of what sainthood and martyrdom mean in the novel. His depiction as a new saint helps cement the faith created by Don Manuel (again in parallel to the Jesus story).

With Ángela, students can be guided to a discussion of the writing process and the New Testament. Longhurst has connected Ángela to Mary Magdalene, and this fits with an interpretation of the novel's narrator as a female disciple (*Unamuno's Theory* 43). Students may find evidence of love between Don Manuel and Ángela, in line with J. A. Garrido Ardila's reading of the text as a romance ("Amor" 99). As Longhurst explains, regarding Ángela's authorship, Don Manuel is "consistently depicted by Ángela as a Christ-figure in her 'gospel'" (*Unamuno's Theory* 43). Of course, the faith that Don Manuel espouses is based in Catholicism, like Jesus's teachings were based in Judaism, but Ángela reveals the church of Don Manuel to be that of a false prophet who sacrificed himself for the faith of his followers. Quotations guiding students should focus on Ángela's reasons for writing, the writing process, intertextual references, her interactions with Don Manuel, and the idea of doubt. References to Ángela as sacrilegious or possessed (133–34) are also relevant because they undermine her narrative or "gospel." In several sections, Ángela also mentions her "afecto maternal" 'maternal feelings,' linking her to Mary and opening a discussion of Unamuno's portrayal of women (134, 146). Ángela's role as writer will also lead students to see Unamuno's undermining of the Gospels' truths, versus their historical value (Longhurst, *Unamuno's Theory* 45).

Finally, Unamuno's questioning of the text's source and accuracy in the conclusion underscores a larger query related to the truth of the written word. After showing many parallels between the doubts of Jesus and Don Manuel, Unamuno enters the text and questions the novel and its source, which, as it parallels the Bible, also allows readers to question the Gospels. Since some books of the Gospels are mysterious in origin and were debated for inclusion in the New Testament, the inception of the Scriptures is thus debated here. When analyzing the conclusion, fixations on the writing process can also incite dialogue about intertextuality and metaliterature relating to Unamuno's other compositions, as critics such as Álvarez-Castro (*Los espejos*) have described.

While some student groups are employed with the parallels between the characters in the novel and Jesus and his disciples, others work on the symbolism related to organized religion, tradition, and doubt in quotations about the lake, the mountain, and Valverde de Lucerna. As Fernández has argued, the mountain may represent faith and religion (126) and the lake doubt, or, as Godoy Gallardo claims, those places could refer to the Old and New Testaments (33). Students can explore these ideas and the juxtaposition of tradition and progress in location motifs. One useful quotation exploring these ideas, which Julia Biggane has highlighted ("Introjection" 336), describes Don Manuel's leadership of prayer: "Y no era un coro, sino una sola voz . . . como una montaña, cuya cumbre . . . era Don Manuel. Y al llegar a lo de 'creo en la resurrección de la carne y la vida perdurable,' la voz de Don Manuel se zambullía, como en un lago . . . y era que él se callaba" 'And it wasn't a chorus, but a single voice . . . like a mountain, whose peak . . . was Don Manuel. And when arriving at "I believe in the resurrection of the flesh and eternal life," Don Manuel's voice wavered, like in a lake . . . because he became silent' (123). Another interesting description joins Valverde with the lake, and the protagonist tells the myth of the lost town below the water's surface, which is likened to the secret buried in Don Manuel's soul (117). Learners can use these place depictions and others, such as those contrasting America and Valverde, to examine tradition and doubt.

Ultimately, by writing questions and hypotheses for inquiry-based learning related to different topics in groups, students encounter the existentialist questions Unamuno proposes by the novel's conclusion. The beautiful thing about a discovery approach is that students arrive there themselves through examination, guided reading of quotations on themes about which they become experts, and dialogue. The emergence of the idea of doubt, which Unamuno sows into the narrative, is something students uncover, which is more rewarding than having their teacher tell them. Many students say that studying Unamuno is their favorite part of the semester, and I believe it is because they are pushed to think for themselves. By allowing students to associate Don Manuel's story and doubts with those of Jesus through inquiry, they are able to unravel the novel's biblical references and questions about faith's ultimate role.

NOTE

[1] The text of *San Manuel Bueno, mártir* used in this essay is Mario J. Valdés's edition, published by Cátedra. Translations from the text are mine.

NOTES ON CONTRIBUTORS

Luis Álvarez-Castro is professor in the Department of Spanish and Portuguese Studies at the University of Florida, where he serves as associate chair and director of graduate studies. His research centers on nineteenth- through twenty-first-century Spanish literature and culture. In addition to several annotated editions of nineteenth-century works, he is the author of *Los espejos del yo: Existencialismo y metaficción en la narrativa de Unamuno* (2015), *La palabra y el ser en la teoría literaria de Unamuno* (2005), and *El universo femenino de Ángel Ganivet* (1996). He is coeditor of the journal *Decimonónica* and associate editor of the journals *Siglo diecinueve* and *Hispania*.

Tracie Amend has held teaching positions at several universities. A lifelong singer and actor, she specializes in the theater of Spain with an emphasis on nineteenth-century drama. She is the author of *The Adulteress on the Spanish Stage: Gender and Modernity in Nineteenth-Century Romantic Drama* (2015) and of several articles published in peer-reviewed journals.

Craig N. Bergeson is professor of Spanish and chair of the Department of Foreign Languages at Weber State University. He has published articles about Unamuno's narrative fiction and about narrative fiction of Spain's postwar period. His research interests also include the role and function of time in literature and methods of teaching language, literature, and culture.

Cristina Carrasco is teaching associate professor of Spanish at the University of North Carolina, Chapel Hill. Her research focuses mainly on contemporary Peninsular and transatlantic studies. Building on her doctoral work on the autobiographical metafictions of Unamuno, Rosa Montero, Enrique Vila-Matas, and Juan José Millás, she examines the ways in which contemporary hybrid genres continue to reconfigure Spanish and Latin American literature in an age of globalization and new cultural *mestizajes*. Other interests include transatlantic cinema and literature, particularly texts that address recent immigration to Spain, exotic representations of women and other marginalized groups, and transnational identities in the Iberian Peninsula.

Emily Joy Clark is assistant professor of Spanish at Sonoma State University, specializing in nineteenth-century Hispanic literature. Her research interests include Romanticism, modernism, women's writing, existentialism, and monetary and economic questions emerging in Latin American nation-building narratives. She has published scholarly articles in journals such as *Revista de estudios hispánicos*, *Decimonónica*, and *Letras femeninas*.

Brian Cope is associate professor of Spanish at the College of Wooster. His research interests include philosophy and literature, the twentieth-century Spanish novel, and contemporary Spanish film. His articles have appeared in *Hispanic Review*, *Revista de estudios hispánicos,* and *Anales de la literatura española contemporánea.* His current book project examines philosophical skepticism in Unamuno's works.

Tom Dolack is visiting assistant professor of Russian at Wheaton College. His research interests include translation studies, theories of imitation, the twentieth-century novel, and Russian literature. He is currently working on a book on imitation and the work of the Russian poet Osip Mandelstam.

Robert Richmond Ellis is Norman Bridge Distinguished Professor of Spanish at Occidental College. He is the author of *They Need Nothing: Hispanic-Asian Encounters of the Colonial Period* (2012); *They Dream not of Angels but of Men: Homoeroticism, Gender, and Race in Latin American Autobiography* (2002); *The Hispanic Homograph: Gay Self-Representation in Contemporary Spanish Autobiography* (1997); *San Juan de la Cruz: Mysticism and Sartrean Existentialism* (1992); and *The Tragic Pursuit of Being: Unamuno and Sartre* (1988).

Jan E. Evans is professor and graduate program director at Baylor University, where she has taught since 2002. She is the author of *Unamuno and Kierkegaard: Paths to Selfhood in Fiction* (2005) and *Miguel de Unamuno's Quest for Faith: A Kierkegaardian Understanding of Unamuno's Struggle to Believe* (2013) and of articles in journals such as *Symposium*, *Philosophy and Literature*, and *Hispania*.

Thomas R. Franz is professor emeritus of Spanish at Ohio University. He is the author of books on Juan Valera, Benito Pérez Galdós, Unamuno, and Antonio Machado as well as of many articles on Spanish authors of the last century and a half. In addition to being a founding editor of *Decimonónica*, he is on the editorial board of *Hispanic Studies Review* and a member of the *comité científico* of *Cuadernos de la Cátedra Miguel de Unamuno*.

Benjamin Fraser is professor and head of Spanish and Portuguese at the University of Arizona. He has published eighty essays and sixteen books. His single-authored monographs include *The Art of Pere Joan: Space, Landscape, and Comics Form* (2019); *Cognitive Disability Aesthetics* (2018); *Toward an Urban Cultural Studies* (2015); *Digital Cities* (2015); *Antonio López García's Everyday Urban Worlds* (2014); *Disability Studies and Spanish Culture* (2013); *Understanding Juan Benet* (2013); *Henri Lefebvre and the Spanish Urban Experience* (2011); and *Encounters with Bergson(ism) in Spain* (2010). Fraser is executive editor of the *Journal of Urban Cultural Studies*, a senior editor of the *Arizona Journal of Hispanic Cultural Studies*, editor-in-chief of *Hispania*, and coeditor of the Hispanic Urban Studies book series.

Edward H. Friedman is Gertrude Conaway Vanderbilt Professor of Spanish and professor of comparative literature at Vanderbilt University. His major field of research is early modern Spanish literature, with special emphasis on Miguel de Cervantes, picaresque narrative, and theater. He has published plays based on classic Spanish authors as well as a collection of poetry, *Quixotic Haiku*. He has served as president of the Cervantes Society of America, editor of *Bulletin of the Comediantes*, and director of the Robert Penn Warren Center for the Humanities at Vanderbilt.

Leslie J. Harkema is associate professor of Spanish at Yale University. Her research and teaching focus on the literature and culture of nineteenth- and twentieth-century Spain, with particular interests in literary modernism, science and literature, and the history of translation in the Iberian Peninsula. She is the author of *Spanish Modernism and the Poetics of Youth: From Miguel de Unamuno to "La Joven Literatura"* (2017), in which she argues for the prominent role played by Unamuno as a poet, essayist, and public figure in Spanish writers' conceptualization of youth during the first third of the twentieth century.

Juan Herrero-Senés is associate professor of Spanish at the University of Colorado, Boulder. His main areas of research are Spanish avant-garde literature, science fiction, and modernist intellectual history. His latest book is *Mensajeros de un tiempo nuevo: Modernidad y nihilismo en la literatura de vanguardia, 1918–1936*. He has published critical editions and articles on Benjamín Jarnés and Miguel de Unamuno, among others.

Diana Roxana Jorza is assistant professor of Spanish at Saint Mary's College, Notre Dame. She specializes in modern and contemporary Spanish culture, focusing especially on Spanish intellectual history and on cinema in its relation to the public spheres. Her book manuscript on the Spanish postwar comedy examines a largely unknown cinematic corpus that has greatly contributed to the visibility of new, alternative role models during Franco's long dictatorship.

Francisco LaRubia-Prado is professor in the Department of Spanish and Portuguese at Georgetown University. He has also taught at Princeton University and Johns Hopkins University. He has published and edited books on Unamuno, José Ortega y Gasset, the Enlightenment, the Romantic period, Miguel de Cervantes, and intellectual history. He has published many essays on Spanish and comparative literature. His latest books are *Imperialism and the Wider Atlantic*, coedited with Tania Gentic (2017), and *The Horse in Literature and Film* (2017).

C. A. Longhurst is professor emeritus at the University of Leeds and formerly professor of Spanish at the University of Exeter. He was visiting professor at several institutions, including, in 2000, the Cátedra Extraordinaria Miguel de Unamuno at Universidad de Salamanca. He has published ten books and editions and some eighty articles in specialized journals, mostly on modern Spanish literature, including various editions of Unamuno's works and *Unamuno's Theory of the Novel* (2014). He was joint general editor of the *Bulletin of Spanish Studies* for eleven years.

Mark J. Mascia is associate professor of Spanish at Sacred Heart University. His publications include articles on Golden Age Spanish literature, twentieth-century Latin American poetry, and the twentieth-century Spanish novel. He is secretary-treasurer of the Society for Renaissance and Baroque Hispanic Poetry.

Juan Francisco Maura is professor of Spanish in the Department of Romance Languages at the University of Vermont. He has published books, editions, and articles on the explorer Cabeza de Vaca, on the presence of Spanish women in the conquest of the Americas, as well as on the Black Legend, the Spanish presence in Asia and the Pacific, and Unamuno. Currently he is working on Spanish and Portuguese exploration in Canada before the arrival of Jacques Cartier.

Adam Morris is a writer and translator. He is coeditor, with Bruno Carvalho, of *Essays on Hilda Hilst: Between Brazil and World Literature* (2017). He is the recipient of the 2012 Susan Sontag Foundation Prize for Literary Translation and a 2017 PEN/Heim translation grant. He is the author of *American Messiahs: False Prophets of a Damned Nation* (2019).

Gonzalo Navajas is distinguished professor of Spanish at the University of California, Irvine. He is the author of books and more than two hundred essays on modern Spanish and European literature, intellectual history, film, critical theory, and contemporary culture. His latest books include *El intelectual público y las ideologías modernas: De* *los años 30 a la posmodernidad*; *Literatura y nación en el siglo XXI*; *El paradigma de la enfermedad y la literatura en el siglo XX*; *La utopía en las narrativas contemporáneas: Novela, cine, arquitectura*; *La modernidad como crisis: Los clásicos modernos ante el siglo XXI*; and *La narrativa española en la era global: Imagen, Comunicación, Ficción*. He serves on the editorial board of many national and international journals, and he lectures and teaches regularly in various universities and cultural institutions in the United States and Europe.

Salvador Oropesa is professor of Spanish and chair of the Department of Languages at Clemson University. His teaching and research areas of specialization are Peninsular and Mexican literature. He is the author of *Literatura y comercio en España: Las tiendas, 1868–1952* and coeditor, with Maureen Ihrie, of *World Literature in Spanish: An Encyclopedia*.

Nelson R. Orringer is professor emeritus at the University of Connecticut, Storrs. He has written seventeen books and over 150 articles, including a monograph on Unamuno, the first critical edition of his essay *El sentimiento trágico de la vida*, and Spanish and English editions of his *Tratado del amor de Dios* ("Treatise on Love of God"). Orringer won the 2011 Menéndez y Pelayo Prize for Humanistic Research for his 2009 coauthored encyclopedia, *Legado filosófico español e hispanoamericano del siglo XX*. In memory of his mother, a concert pianist, he published *Lorca in Tune with Falla*, a music-literature comparative study.

Stephen G. H. Roberts is associate professor and reader in modern Spanish literature and intellectual history at the University of Nottingham. He has published numerous articles and book chapters on the literature, politics, and philosophy of Unamuno and is editor of *Miguel de Unamuno: Political Speeches and Journalism, 1923–1929* and author of *Miguel de Unamuno o la creación del intelectual español moderno*. He has also published on the intellectual relationship between Spain and Latin America, on late-nineteenth- and early-twentieth-century poetry and prose fiction, and on Spanish cinema, with articles and book chapters on Benito Pérez Galdós, José Enrique Rodó, José Ortega y Gasset, Juan Ramón Jiménez, Federico García Lorca, Pablo Neruda, Juan Antonio Bardem, and Víctor Erice. He is finishing a literary biography of García Lorca and a monograph on Unamuno's period in exile (1924–30).

Dawn Smith-Sherwood is associate professor of Spanish at Indiana University of Pennsylvania. She has published several essays on the works of Spanish women writers of the post-Franco era. Her recent scholarship focuses on the teaching of literature and culture in foreign language classrooms and bridging the disciplinary divide between faculty members who teach second language acquisition and those who teach literature and culture.

Stephen J. Summerhill is professor emeritus in modern Spanish literature at Ohio State University. He has published articles on the modern sublime and the allegorical in Unamuno and on the instability of lyric voice in contemporary poetry. He is also coauthor of *Sinking Columbus: Contested History, Cultural Politics, and Mythmaking During the Quincentenary* (2000).

Ana Urrutia-Jordana is professor in the Department of Modern and Classical Languages at the University of San Francisco, where she has taught since 1996. She is currently director of the Spanish studies program, and her academic area of expertise focuses on the literature and culture of Spain. Her publications examine Unamuno's poetry of exile, in particular *De Fuerteventura a París* and *Romancero del destierro*.

SURVEY PARTICIPANTS

Tracie Amend, *Independent Scholar*
Laura J. Beard, *University of Alberta*
Catherine Bellver, *University of Nevada, Las Vegas*
Craig N. Bergeson, *Weber State University*
Julia Biggane, *University of Aberdeen*
Christine Blackshaw Naberhaus, *Mount Saint Mary's University*
María José Bordera-Amérigo, *Randolph-Macon College*
Cristina Carrasco, *University of North Carolina, Chapel Hill*
Emily Joy Clark, *Sonoma State University*
Brian Cope, *College of Wooster*
Diego del Río Arrillaga, *Yale University*
Tom Dolack, *Wheaton College*
Robert Richmond Ellis, *Occidental College*
Jan E. Evans, *Baylor University*
Matthew I. Feinberg, *Case Western Reserve University*
Thomas R. Franz, *Ohio University*
Benjamin Fraser, *University of Arizona*
Edward H. Friedman, *Vanderbilt University*
J. A. Garrido Ardila, *University of Malta*
Leslie J. Harkema, *Yale University*
Juan Herrero-Senés, *University of Colorado, Boulder*
Keith Johnson, *Georgia Regents University*
Diana Roxana Jorza, *Saint Mary's College, Notre Dame*
Francisco LaRubia-Prado, *Georgetown University*
C. A. Longhurst, *University of Leeds*
Patricia W. Manning, *University of Kansas*
John Marchese, *University of Notre Dame*
Mark J. Mascia, *Sacred Heart University*
Juan Francisco Maura, *University of Vermont*
Carlos Miguel-Pueyo, *Valparaiso University*
Gonzalo Navajas, *University of California, Irvine*
Debra J. Ochoa, *Trinity University*
Salvador Oropesa, *Clemson University*
Nelson R. Orringer, *University of Connecticut, Storrs*
Dale Joseph Pratt, *Brigham Young University*
Itziar Rodríguez de Rivera, *Cornell University*
Robert Simon, *Kennesaw State University*
Dawn Smith-Sherwood, *Indiana University of Pennsylvania*
Carol Snell-Feikema, *Eastern Mennonite University*
Stephen J. Summerhill, *Ohio State University*
Ana Urrutia-Jordana, *University of San Francisco*
Elizabeth Willingham, *Baylor University*
David Wood, *Millsaps College*

WORKS CITED

Abella Maeso, María José. *Dios y la inmortalidad: El mundo religioso de Unamuno*. Verbo Divino, 1997.

Abellán, José Luis. "El '¡que inventen ellos!' de Unamuno." Fundación March, 10 May 1994. *Fundación Juan March*, www.march.es/conferencias/anteriores/voz.aspx?p1=22216&l=1.

Abrams, M. H. *Natural Supernaturalism: Tradition and Revolution in Romantic Literature*. W. W. Norton, 1971.

———. "Structure and Style in the Greater Romantic Lyric." *The Correspondent Breeze: Essays on English Romanticism*. Foreword by Jack Stillinger, W. W. Norton, 1984, pp. 76–108.

Adair-Hauck, Bonnie, et al. *Implementing Integrated Performance Assessment*. ACTFL, 2015.

Alas, Leopoldo (Clarín). *His Only Son*. Translated by Margaret Jull Costa, New York Review Books, 2016.

———. *Su único hijo*. Edited by Francisco Caudet, Castalia, 2012.

Alberca, Manuel. *El pacto ambiguo: De la novela autobiográfica a la autoficción*. Biblioteca Nueva, 2007.

Alonso García, Luis. "Anomalías históricas y perversiones historiográficas: De *La malquerida* a *La niña de tus ojos*." *La herida de las sombras: El cine español en los años cuarenta*, edited by Luis Fernández Colorado and Pilar Couto Cantero, Academia de las Artes y las Ciencias Cinematográficas de España / Asociación Española de Historiadores de Cine, 2001, pp. 575–604.

Álvarez-Castro, Luis. "De la metaficción al metacine: Cuatro adaptaciones de *Niebla*, de Unamuno." *Hispania*, vol. 93, no. 1, 2010, pp. 11–22.

———. *Los espejos del yo: Existencialismo y metaficción en la narrativa de Unamuno*. Ediciones Universidad de Salamanca, 2015.

———. "El héroe, el profeta y la crisis del individualismo en Unamuno." *Perfiles del heroísmo en la literatura hispánica de entresiglos (XIX–XX)*. Edited by Luis Álvarez Castro and Denise DuPont, Universitas Castellae, 2013, pp. 191–200.

———. "La novela modernista de Miguel de Unamuno: Entre el ser de la ficción y la ficción del ser." *Teoría(s) de la novela moderna en España: Revisión historiográfica*, edited by Bénédicte Vauthier, Genueve Ediciones, 2019, pp. 85–106.

———. *La palabra y el ser en la teoría literaria de Unamuno*. Ediciones Universidad de Salamanca, 2005.

———. "¿Quién mató a Augusto Pérez? Control hermenéutico y chantaje existencial en *Niebla*, de Unamuno." *Revista de estudios hispánicos*, vol. 46, no. 1, 2012, pp. 25–47.

———. "'Yo, individuo, poeta, profeta y mito': Los sujetos líricos de *Romancero del destierro*." Garrido Ardila, *El Unamuno eterno*, pp. 258–91.

Álvarez Gómez, Mariano. *Unamuno y Ortega: La búsqueda azarosa de la verdad*. Biblioteca Nueva, 2003.

Anderson, Benedict. *Imagined Communities: Reflections on the Origin and Spread of Nationalism*. Verso, 1991.

Ángeles Cerón, Francisco de Jesús, editor. *Unamuno: El poeta del pensamiento*. Anthropos, 2018.

Aquinas, Thomas. *Summa contra Gentiles: Basic Writings of Saint Thomas Aquinas*. Translated by Anton C. Pegis, Random House, 1945, pp. 3–224.

Aramburu, Fernando. *Patria*. Tusquets, 2016.

Aranda, J. F. "*La tía Tula* (Revelación del Festival de San Sebastian)." *Ínsula*, no. 214, 1964, p. 14.

Aristotle. *Nicomachean Ethics*. Translated by R. W. Browne, Henry G. Bohn, 1850.

Arrington Bruner Smith, Elizabeth. "(S)Mothering in Miguel de Unamuno's *Dos madres*: The Fatal Repercussions of the Nineteenth-Century Idealization of the Mother." *Hispanic Journal*, vol. 20, no. 2, 1999, pp. 351–62.

Ascunce Arrieta, José Ángel, editor. *La poesía de Miguel de Unamuno*. Universidad de Deusto, 1987.

Asier eta Biok. Directed by Amaia Merino and Aitor Merino, Doxa Producciones, 2015.

Audet, Richard H. "Part I: Teaching and Learning through Inquiry in the Content Areas." *Integrating Inquiry across the Curriculum*, edited by Richard H. Audet and Kinda K. Jordan, Corwin Press, 2005.

Auster, Paul. *City of Glass*. Penguin, 1987.

"La aventura del pensamiento: Part 13: Miguel de Unamuno." Hosted by Fernando Savater, produced by Canal Encuentro. *YouTube*, uploaded 14 Oct. 2013, www.youtube.com/watch?v=pE0Yi3U9xic.

Baker, Armand F., translator. *Miguel de Unamuno*. 2011–17, www.armandfbaker.com/unamuno.html.

Bakewell, Sarah. *At the Existentialist Café: Freedom, Being, and Apricot Cocktails*. Other Press, 2016.

Bakhtin, Mikhail. *Problems of Dostoevsky's Poetics*. Edited and translated by Caryl Emerson, U of Minnesota P, 1984.

———. Собрание сочинений. 2, Проблемы творчества Достоевского; Статьи о Л. Толстом [*Sobranie sochinenii. 2: Problemy tvorchestva Dostoevskskogo*; *Stat'i o L. Tolstom*; *Zapisi kursa lektsii po istorii russkoi literatury*; *Collected Works 2: Problems of Dostoevsky's Poetics*; *Essays on L. Tolstoy*; *Notes for Lectures on the History of Russian Literature*]. Russkie Slovari, 2000.

Baldick, Chris. *The Concise Oxford Dictionary of Literary Terms*. Oxford UP, 1990.

Barbieri, Marie E. "La 'tragedia desnuda' en *Fedra* y *Yerma*." *Explicación de textos literarios*, vol. 19, no. 1, 1990–91, pp. 38–47.

Baroja, Pío. "Lo desconocido." 1900. *Vidas sombrías*, by Baroja, Biblioteca Nueva, 1998, pp. 135–38.

Basdekis, Demetrios. *Unamuno and the Novel*. U of North Carolina P, 1974.

Batchelor, Roland E. "Form and Content in Unamuno's *Niebla*." *Forum for Modern Language Studies*, vol. 8, no. 3, 1972, pp. 197–214.

———. *Unamuno, Novelist: A European Perspective*. The Dolphin Book Company, 1972.

Bécquer, Gustavo Adolfo. *Rimas y leyendas.* Espasa-Calpe, 1944.

Belio, M. A. "*La tía Tula* de M. Picazo." *Cuadernos para el diálogo*, no. 12, 1964, p. 13.

Benavente, Jacinto. *La malquerida*. 1913. Edited by José Montero Padilla, Castalia, 1996.

Berman, Marshall. *All That Is Solid Melts into Air: The Experience of Modernity*. Penguin, 1988.

Bernhardt, Elizabeth. "Research into the Teaching of Literature in a Second Language: What It Says and How to Communicate It to Graduate Students." *SLA and the Literature Classroom: Fostering Dialogues*, edited by Virginia Scott and Holly Tucker, Heinle, 2002, pp. 195–210.

———. "Teaching Literature or Teaching Students?" *ADFL Bulletin*, vol. 26, no. 2, 1995, pp. 5–6.

———. *Understanding Advanced Second-Language Reading.* Routledge, 2011.

Bhabha, Homi K. *The Location of Culture.* Routledge, 1994.

Biggane, Julia. "Introjection, Loss, and the Politics of Possession in Unamuno's *San Manuel Bueno, mártir*." *Hispanic Review*, vol. 73, no. 3, 2005, pp. 329–50.

———. "Yet Another 'Other': Unamuno's *El otro* and the Anxiety for Influence." *Bulletin of Hispanic Studies*, vol. 77, no. 5, Dec. 2000, pp. 479–91.

Biggane, Julia, and John Macklin, editors. *A Companion to Miguel de Unamuno*. Tamesis, 2016.

Bilbao-Terreros, Gorka. "Ética y liminaridad en *San Manuel Bueno, mártir*: Una lectura kierkegaardiana." *Hispanic Review*, vol. 80, no. 2, 2012, pp. 243–65.

Blanco, Manuel. *La voluntad de vivir y sobrevivir en Miguel de Unamuno*. AB Editor, 1994.

Blanco Aguinaga, Carlos. "De nuevo: El socialismo de Unamuno." *Cuadernos de la Cátedra Miguel de Unamuno*, vol. 18, 1968, pp. 5–48.

———. "El socialismo de Unamuno: 1894–1897." *Revista de occidente*, vol. 41, Aug. 1966, pp. 166–84.

———. "Unamuno's *Niebla*: Existence and the Game of Fiction." *MLN*, vol. 79, no. 2, 1964, pp. 188–205.

———. *Unamuno, teórico del lenguaje*. El Colegio de México, 1954.

Blanco Prieto, Francisco. *Unamuno en las Cortes Republicanas.* EDIFSA, 2017.

———. *Unamuno, profesor y rector en la Universidad de Salamanca*. Hergar Ediciones Antema, 2011.

Blasco, Javier, et al. *Miguel de Unamuno, poeta*. Universidad de Valladolid, 2003.

Bloom, Harold. *The Anxiety of Influence: A Theory of Poetry*. Oxford UP, 1973.

Borges, Jorge Luis. *El Aleph*. Alianza Editorial, 1971.

———. The Aleph *and Other Stories*. Translated by Andrew Hurley, Penguin, 2004.

Boulé, Jean-Pierre. *Hervé Guibert: Voices of the Self.* Translated by J. Fletcher, Liverpool UP, 1999.

Bradbury, Malcolm, and James Walter McFarlane, editors. *Modernism: A Guide to European Literature, 1890–1930*. Penguin Books, 1991.

Britt-Arredondo, Christopher. *Quixotism: The Imaginative Denial of Spain's Loss of Empire*. State U of New York P, 2005.

Brooks, Peter. Review of *Flaubert*, by Michel Winock, translated by Nicholas Elliott. *New York Review of Books*, 9 Mar. 2017, pp. 24, 26.

Butt, John. *Miguel de Unamuno:* San Manuel Bueno, mártir. Grant and Cutler, 1981.

Byrnes, Heidi. "The Role of Task and Task-Based Assessment in a Content-Oriented Collegiate Foreign Language Curriculum." *Language Testing*, vol. 19, 2002, pp. 419–37.

Calderón de la Barca, Pedro. *El médico de su honra*. Edited by D. W. Cruikshank, Castalia, 1989.

Calle Mayor. Directed by Juan Antonio Bardem, produced by Cesáreo González and Manuel J. Goyanes, 1956.

Calvino, Italo. *If on a Winter's Night a Traveler*. Translated by William Weaver, Harcourt Brace Jovanovich, 1982.

Calvo Carilla, José Luis. *La cara oculta del 98*. Cátedra, 1998.

Camus, Albert. *L'étranger*. Gallimard, 1942.

Cannon, Calvin. "The Mystic Cosmology of Unamuno's *El Cristo de Velázquez*." *Hispanic Review*, vol. 28, 1960, pp. 28–39.

Carey, Douglas M., and Phillip G. Williams. "Religious Confession as Perspective and Mediation in Unamuno's *San Manuel Bueno, mártir*." *MLN*, vol. 91, no. 2, 1976, pp. 292–310.

Carlson, Marvin. *The Haunted Stage: Theater as Memory Machine*. U of Michigan P, 2003.

La casa de mi padre. Directed by Gorka Merchán, Media Films, 2008.

Casas, Ana, editor. *La autoficción: Reflexiones teóricas*. Arco/Libros, 2012.

Caudet, Francisco. Introduction. *Paz en la guerra*, by Miguel de Unamuno, Cátedra, 1999, pp. 10–112.

———. *Romancero de la Guerra Civil*. Ediciones de la Torre, 1978.

Caudillo. Directed by Basilio Martín Patiño, Retasa, 1977.

Cela, Camilo José. *La familia de Pascual Duarte*. Destino, 1993.

———. *The Family of Pascual Duarte*. Translated by Anthony Kerrigan, Dalkey Archive, 2004.

Cercas, Javier. *Soldados de Salamina*. Tusquets, 2001.

———. *Soldiers of Salamis*. Translated by Anne McLean, Bloomsbury, 2003.

Cerezo Galán, Pedro. *El mal del siglo: El conflicto entre Ilustración y Romanticismo en la crisis finisecular del siglo XIX*. Biblioteca Nueva, 2003.

———. *Las máscaras de lo trágico: Filosofía y tragedia en Miguel de Unamuno*. Trotta, 1996.

———. *Miguel de Unamuno: Ecce homo: La existencia y la palabra*. Ediciones Universidad de Salamanca, 2016.

Cervantes, Miguel de. *Don Quijote*. Edited by Tom Lathrop, Juan de la Cuesta, 2012.

———. *Don Quixote*. Translated by Edith Grossman, Ecco, 2003.

———. *Exemplary Novels*. Translated by Edith Grossman, edited by Roberto González Echevarría, Yale UP, 2016.

———. *Novelas ejemplares*. Edited by Harry Sieber, Cátedra, 1988. 2 vols.

Chaguaceda Toledano, Ana, editor. *Miguel de Unamuno: Estudios sobre su obra*. Ediciones Universidad de Salamanca, 2003–09. 4 vols.

Chandler, Richard E., and Kessel Schwartz. *A New History of Spanish Literature*. Louisiana State UP, 1991.

Channing, William Ellery. *The Complete Works of William Ellery Channing*. Christian Life, 1884.

Charlebois, Lucile C. "El teatro desnudo de Unamuno: Un teatro de palabras." *Hispanic Journal*, vol. 8, no. 1, Fall 1986, pp. 19–29.

Ciplijauskaité, Biruté. "Perspectiva irónica y ambigüedad en *Paz en la guerra*". *Homenaje a Antonio Sánchez Barbudo: Ensayos de literatura española moderna*, edited by Benito Brancaforte et al., U of Wisconsin P, 1981, pp. 139–55.

Clavería, Carlos. *Temas de Unamuno*. 2nd ed., Gredos, 1970.

Código de derecho canónico. 5th ed., Ediciones de la Universidad de Navarra, 1992.

Collado, Jesús Antonio. *Kierkegaard y Unamuno: La existencia religiosa*. Gredos, 1962.

Collins, M. S. "Orfeo and the Cratyline Conspiracy in Unamuno's *Niebla*." *Bulletin of Spanish Studies*, vol. 79, nos. 2–3, 2002, pp. 285–306. *Taylor and Francis Online*, www.tandfonline.com/doi/abs/10.1080/147538202317345032.

Comín Colomer, Eduardo. *Unamuno, libelista: Sus campañas contra Alfonso XIII y la Dictadura*. Colección Siglo Ilustrado, 1968.

Cope, Brian. "Unamuno's *San Manuel Bueno, mártir*: Philosophical Skepticism in a Time of Political Upheaval." *Revista de estudios hispánicos*, vol. 45, no. 1, 2011, pp. 177–99.

Cresswell, Tim. *On the Move: Mobility in the Modern Western World*. Routledge, 2006.

Criado Miguel, Isabel. *Las novelas de Miguel de Unamuno*. Ediciones Universidad de Salamanca, 1986.

Cruz Ruiz, Juan. *Muchas veces me pediste que contara esos años*. Alfaguara, 2008.

Las cuatro novias de Augusto Pérez. Directed by José Jara, 1975. Filmax, 2008.

Culler, Jonathan. "The Closeness of Close Reading." *ADFL Bulletin*, vol. 41, no. 3, 2011, pp. 8–13.

Cunningham, Michael. *The Hours*. Picador, 2000.

Dante Alighieri. *La divina commedia*. Edited by Ettori Mazzali, vol. 3, Nuova Accademia, 1964.

Darhower, Mark. "Literary Discussions and Advanced-Superior Speaking Functions in the Undergraduate Language Program." *Hispania*, vol. 97, no. 3, Sept. 2014, pp. 396–412.

del Amo, A. "*La tía Tula* de M. Picazo." *Cuadernos para el diálogo*, no. 12, 1964, p. 13.

del Molino, Sergio. "Lo que Unamuno nunca le dijo a Millán Astray." *El País*, 9 May 2018, elpais.com/cultura/2018/05/07/actualidad/1525711624_377047.html.

De Salamanca a ninguna parte. Directed by Chema de la Peña, Artimaña Producciones, 2002.

Días contados. Directed by Imanol Uribe, Aiete Films, 2000.

Díaz, Elías. *El pensamiento político de Unamuno*. Tecnos, 1965.

———. *Revisión de Unamuno: Análisis crítico de su pensamiento político*. Tecnos, 1968.

Díaz-Peterson, Rosendo. *Estudios sobre Unamuno*. Verbum, 2012.

Díaz-Plaja, Guillermo. *Modernismo frente a noventa y ocho: Una introducción a la literatura española del siglo XX*. Espasa-Calpe, 1951.

Díez, Ricardo. *El desarrollo estético de la novela de Unamuno*. Playor, 1976.

Donato, Richard, and Frank B. Brooks. "Literary Discussions and Advanced Speaking Functions: Researching the (Dis)Connection." *Foreign Language Annals*, vol. 37, no. 2, 2004, pp. 183–99.

Dostoyevsky, Fyodor. The Brothers Karamazov*: A Revised Translation, Contexts, Criticism*. Edited by Susan McReynolds Oddo, W. W. Norton, 2011.

———. Notes from Underground*: A New Translation, Backgrounds and Sources, Responses, Criticism*. Translated by Michael R. Katz, W. W. Norton, 1989.

———. Полное собрание соцчинений: В тридцати томах [*Polnoe sobranie sochinenii: V tridtsati tomakh*; *Complete Works: In Thirty Volumes*]. V. G. Bazanov, general editor, Nauka, 1972–91.

Dotras, Ana M. *La novela española de metaficción*. Júcar, 1994.

Echegaray, José. *El gran Galeoto*. Edited by Jame Hoddie, Cátedra, 1989.

Egido, L. G. "La agonía de Unamuno: Adaptación cinematográfica de *La tía Tula*." *Ínsula*, nos. 216–17, 1964, p. 35.

Elizalde, Ignacio. "Unamuno y el mito griego: 'Electra.'" *Letras de Deusto*, vol. 20, no. 47, May 1990, pp. 117–25.

Ellis, Robert Richmond. *The Tragic Pursuit of Being: Unamuno and Sartre*. U of Alabama P, 1988.

Eoff, Sherman. *The Modern Spanish Novel*. New York UP, 1961.

Ereño Altuna, José Antonio. *Artículos inéditos de Unamuno en* La Lucha de Clases, *1894–1897*. Beta, 2002.

Estar o no estar. Directed by Marcelo González, Cinetzin Films, 2015.

Evans, Jan E. "*La enfermedad mortal* de Kierkegaard y *San Manuel Bueno, mártir* de Unamuno." *Revista de filosofía*, vol. 137, 2014, pp. 59–71.

———. *Miguel de Unamuno's Quest for Faith: A Kierkegaardian Understanding of Unamuno's Struggle to Believe*. Pickwick Publications, 2013.

———. *Unamuno and Kierkegaard: Paths to Selfhood in Fiction*. Lexington Books, 2005.

Faulkner, Sally. *A Cinema of Contradiction: Spanish Film in the 1960s*. Edinburgh UP, 2006.

Feal Deibe, Carlos. "Nada menos que toda una mujer: *La tía Tula* de Unamuno." *Estelas, laberintos, nuevas sendas: Unamuno, Valle-Inclán, García Lorca, la Guerra Civil*, edited by Ángel G. Loureiro, Anthropos, 1988, pp. 65–80.

Fernández, Pelayo H. *Bibliografía crítica de Miguel de Unamuno*. José Porrúa Turanzas, 1976.

———. *El problema de la personalidad en Unamuno y en San Manuel Bueno*. Mayfe, 1966.

Fernández Cifuentes, Luis. *Teoría y mercado de la novela en España: Del 98 a la República*. Gredos, 1982.

Fernández de Moratín, Leandro. *El sí de las niñas*. Duckworth Publishing, 1996.

Ferrater Mora, José. *Unamuno: A Philosophy of Tragedy*. Translated by P. Silver, U of California P, 1962.

Fiddian, R. W. "Unamuno-Bergson: A Reconsideration." *Modern Language Review*, vol. 69, no. 4, Oct. 1974, pp. 787–95.

Flórez Miguel, Cirilo, editor. *Tu mano es mi destino: Congreso internacional Miguel de Unamuno*. Ediciones Universidad de Salamanca, 2000.

Fontana, Josep. *La época del liberalismo*. Crítica / Marcial Pons, 2007.

Foster, David William. *Unamuno and the Novel as Expressionistic Conceit*. Inter American UP, 1973.

Foucault, Michel. *Discipline and Punish: The Birth of the Prison*. Random House, 1975.

Fox, E. Inman. "'La Generación de 1898' como concepto historiográfico." *Divergencias y unidad: Perspectivas sobre la Generación del '98 y Antonio Machado*, edited by John P. Gabriele, Orígenes, 1990, pp. 23–28.

Franco, Andrés. *El teatro de Unamuno*. Insula, 1971.

Franz, Thomas R. "Envidia y existencia en Millás y Unamuno." *Revista canadiense de estudios hispánicos*, vol. 21, no. 1, 1996, pp. 131–42.

———. Niebla *inexplorada: Midiendo intersticios en el maravilloso texto de Unamuno*. Juan de la Cuesta, 2003.

———. "The Painting of the Banquet Scene in *Abel Sánchez*." *Hispanic Review*, vol. 72, no. 1, 2004, pp. 65–76.

———. *Parallel but Unequal: The Contemporizing of* Paradise Lost *in Unamuno's* Abel Sánchez. Albatros/Hispanófila, 1990.

———. *The Word in the World: Unamuno's Tragic Sense of Language*. Strathmore Press, 1987.

Fraser, Benjamin. *Encounters with Bergson(ism) in Spain: Reconciling Philosophy, Literature, Film, and Urban Space*. U of North Carolina P, 2010.

———. "Unamuno and Bergson: Notes on a Shared Methodology." *Modern Language Review*, vol. 102, no. 3, 2007, pp. 753–67.

———. "Urban Railways in Buenos Aires: Spatial and Social Alienation in the Documentary Film *El tren blanco*." *Transfers: Interdisciplinary Journal of Mobility Studies*, vol. 5, no. 2, 2015, pp. 5–22.

Freud, Sigmund. *Totem and Taboo*. W. W. Norton, 1989.

Friedman, Edward H. *Cervantes in the Middle: Realism and Reality in the Spanish Novel from* Lazarillo de Tormes *to* Niebla. Juan de la Cuesta, 2006.

———. *Into the Mist*. Juan de la Cuesta, 2011.

Friedman, Edward H., et al., editors. *Aproximaciones al estudio de la literatura hispánica*. 7th ed., McGraw-Hill, 2008.

Furst, Lilian. "The Romantic Hero, or Is He the Antihero?" *Studies in the Literary Imagination*, vol. 9, no. 1, 1976, pp. 53–67.

Gabriele, John P. "From Sex to Gender: Toward Feminocentric Narrative in Unamuno's *La tía Tula* or 'cómo se hace una novela feminista.'" *Hispanic Journal*, vol. 20, no. 1, 1999, pp. 105–17.

Galbis, Ignacio. "De técnicas narrativas e influencias cervantinas en *Niebla* de Unamuno." *Cuadernos americanos*, vol. 221, no. 6, 1978, pp. 197–204.

García, Carlos Javier. *Metanovela: Luis Goytisolo, Azorín y Unamuno*. Júcar, 1994.

García Blanco, Manuel. *América y Unamuno*. Gredos, 1964.

———. Introduction. *Obras completas*, by Unamuno, edited by Manuel García Blanco, Vergara and Afrodisio Aguado, 1958–64, vol. 7, pp. 7–126.

García Lorca, Federico. *Antología poética*. Edited by Allen Josephs, Plaza y Janés, 1999.

———. *Bodas de sangre*. Edited by Allen Josephs and Juan Caballero, 15th ed., Cátedra, 2001.

García Morales, Adelaida. *El Sur* seguido de *Bene*. 15th ed., Anagrama, 1991.

García Morejón, Julio. *Unamuno y Portugal*. Gredos, 1971.

García Nuño, Alfonso. *El problema del sobrenatural en Miguel de Unamuno*. Ediciones Encuentro, 2011.

Garner, Stanton. *Bodied Spaces: Phenomenology and Performance in Contemporary Drama*. Cornell UP, 1994.

Garrido Ardila, J. A. "Amor y religión en *San Manuel Bueno, mártir* de Unamuno." *Romance Quarterly*, vol. 58, no. 2, 2011, pp. 94–113.

———. *La construcción modernista de* Niebla *de Unamuno*. Anthropos, 2015.

———. "La génesis de la novela unamuniana: La parodia de Galdós y de la novela realista." Garrido Ardila, *El Unamuno eterno*, pp. 67–91.

———. "Nueva lectura de *Niebla*: Kierkegaard y el amor." *Revista de literatura*, vol. 70, no. 139, 2008, pp. 85–118.

———. "The Origin of Unamuno's *Mist*: Unamuno's Copy of Kierkegaard's *Diary of the Seducer*." *Modern Philology*, vol. 109, no. 1, 2011, pp. 135–43.

———, editor. *El Unamuno eterno*. Anthropos, 2015.

———. "Unamuno y Cervantes: Narradores y narración en *Niebla*." *MLN*, vol. 125, no. 2, 2010, pp. 348–68.

George, David. "Unamuno on Naturalism, 1896." *Naturalism and Symbolism in European Theatre, 1850–1915*. Edited by Claude Schumacher, Cambridge UP, 1996, p. 484.

Gies, David T., editor. *The Cambridge History of Spanish Literature*. Cambridge UP, 2004.

Los girasoles ciegos. Directed by José Luis Cuerda, produced by Fernando Bovaira et al., 2008.

Godoy Gallardo, Eduardo. "El trasfondo bíblico en *San Manuel Bueno, mártir* de Miguel de Unamuno." *Revista chilena de literatura*, vol. 58, 2001, pp. 19–34.

Gómez, Michael A. "Unamuno and Schopenhauer: Art, Artistic Imagination, and the Relation to Modernism." *Confluencia*, vol. 23, no.1, 2007, pp. 43–61.

Gómez de la Serna, Ramón. *Automoribundia*. Sudamericana, 1948.

Gómez Molleda, Dolores, editor. *Actas del congreso internacional Cincuentenario de Unamuno*. Ediciones Universidad de Salamanca, 1989.

———, editor. *Volumen-Homenaje Miguel de Unamuno*. Ediciones Universidad de Salamanca, 1986.

González Martín, Vicente. *La cultura italiana en Miguel de Unamuno*. Ediciones Universidad de Salamanca, 1978.

Gossdenovich Feldman, Leticia. *Un primer intento de bibliografía crítica de Miguel de Unamuno*. Xlibris, 2005.

Grande, Cristina. *Naturaleza infiel*. RBA Libros, 2012.

Granjel, Luis. *Panorama de la Generación del 98*. Guadarrama, 1959.

———. *Psicobiografía de Unamuno: Un ensayo de interpretación*. Ministerio de Educación y Cultura, 1999.

Gubern, Román. "*La tía Tula* 1963 [1964]." *Antología crítica del cine español, 1906–1995: Flor en la sombra*, edited by Julio Pérez Perucha, Cátedra / Filmoteca Española, 1997, pp. 561–63.

Gullón, Germán. "*Paz en la guerra* y la interiorización de la novela española moderna." *Ojáncano*, vol. 2, 1989, pp. 41–57.

Gullón, Ricardo. *Autobiografías de Unamuno*. Gredos, 1964.

———. "La invención del 98." *"La invención del 98" y otros ensayos*. Gredos, 1969, pp. 7–19.

Haddon, Mark. *The Curious Incident of the Dog in the Night-time*. Vintage, 2004.

Hannam, Kevin, et al. "Editorial: Mobilities, Immobilities, and Moorings." *Mobilities*, vol. 1, no. 1, 2006, pp. 1–22.

Hansen, Keith W. *Tragic Lucidity: Discourse of Recuperation in Unamuno and Camus*. Peter Lang, 1993.

Harkema, Leslie J. *Spanish Modernism and the Poetics of Youth: From Miguel de Unamuno to "La Joven Literatura."* U of Toronto P, 2018.

Harnack, Carl Gustav Adolf von. *Lehrbuch der Dogmengeschichte*. Mohr, 1890–94. 3 vols.

Harrison, Joseph, and Alan Hoyle, editors. *Spain's 1898 Crisis: Regenerationism, Modernism, Post-colonialism*. Manchester UP, 2000.

Hartzenbusch, Juan Eugenio. *Los amantes de Teruel*. Edited by Carmen Iranzo, 10th ed., Cátedra, 2005.

Hay, Marion J. "Informal Glimpses of Don Miguel de Unamuno." *Hispania*, vol. 16, no. 1, 1933, pp. 66–68.

Henning, Sylvie Debevec. "Strategies for Promoting the Study of Literature." *ADFL Bulletin*, vol. 41, no. 3, 2011, pp. 26–32.

Hirvela, Alan. *Connecting Reading and Writing in Second Language Writing Instruction*. U of Michigan P, 2004.

hooks, bell. *Teaching Critical Thinking: Practical Wisdom*. Routledge, 2010.

Hwang, David Henry. *Yellow Face*. Theatre Communications Group, 2009.

Ilie, Paul. *Unamuno: An Existential View of Self and Society*. U of Wisconsin P, 1967.

Imízcoz Beunza, Teresa. *La teoría poética de Miguel de Unamuno*. EUNSA, 1996.

La isla del viento. Directed by Manuel Menchón, Mediagrama, 2015.

James, William. *"The Will to Believe" and Other Essays in Popular Philosophy*; *Human Immortality*. Dover, 1956.

Jameson, Fredric. "Science Fiction as a Spatial Genre: Generic Discontinuities and the Problem of Figuration in Vonda McIntyre's '*The Exile Waiting*.'" *Science Fiction Studies*, vol. 14, no. 1, 1987, pp. 44–59.

Jiménez Hernández, Adolfo. *Unamuno y la filosofía del lenguaje*. Editorial San Juan, 1973.

Johnson, Roberta. "Archetypes, Structures, and Myth in Unamuno's *El otro*." *The Analysis of Hispanic Texts: Current Trends in Methodology*, edited by Lisa Davis and Isabel Taran, Bilingual, 1976.

———. *Crossfire: Philosophy and the Novel in Spain, 1900–1934*. UP of Kentucky, 1993.

———. *Fuego cruzado: Filosofía y novela en España, 1900–1934*. Translated by Teresa Fernández, Libertarias/Prodhufi, 1997.

———. *Gender and Nation in Spanish Modernist Novel*. Vanderbilt UP, 2003.

Juaristi, Jon. *El chimbo expiatorio: La invención de la tradición bilbaína, 1876–1939*. Espasa, 1999.

———. *Miguel de Unamuno*. Taurus, 2012.

Jurkevich, Gayana. *The Elusive Self: Archetypal Approaches to the Novels of Miguel de Unamuno*. U of Missouri P, 1991.

Kafka, Franz. *Die Verwandlung*. K. Wolff, 1917.

Kagan, Richard L. "The Spanish Craze in the United States: Cultural Entitlement and the Appropriation of Spain's Cultural Patrimony, ca. 1890–ca. 1930." *Revista complutense de historia de América*, vol. 36, 2010, pp. 37–58.

Kant, Immanuel. *Critique of Judgment*. Translated by Werner S. Pluhar, Hackett, 1987.

———. *Critique of Practical Reason*. Translated by T. K. Abbott, Prometheus, 1996.

———. *What Is Enlightenment?* Columbia U, www.columbia.edu/acis/ets/CCREAD/etscc/kant.html. Accessed 15 Feb. 2017.

Kierkegaard, Søren. *The Sickness unto Death*. Translated by Howard V. Hong and Edna H. Hong, Princeton UP, 1980.

King, Willard. "Unamuno, Cervantes y *Niebla*." *Revista de occidente*, no. 47, 1967, pp. 219–31.

Krauel, Javier. *Imperial Emotions: Cultural Responses to Myths of Empire in Fin-de-Siècle Spain*. Liverpool UP, 2013.

Kuhn, Thomas S. *The Structure of Scientific Revolutions*. 2nd ed., U of Chicago P, 1970.

Labanyi, Jo. "Cinema and the Mediation of Everyday Life in 1940s and 1950s Spain." *Alternative Voices in European Cinemas*, edited by M. Topping and G. Armstrong, special issue of *New Readings*, no. 8, 2007, ojs.cf.ac.uk/index.php/newreadings/article/view/23/18.

———. *Gender and Modernization in the Spanish Realist Novel*. Oxford UP, 2000.

Laín Entralgo, Pedro. *El cuerpo humano: Teoría actual*. Espasa, 1989.

———, editor. *La edad de plata de la cultura española (1898–1936): Identidad, pensamiento y vida, hispanidad*. Espasa-Calpe, 1993. Vol. 39 of *Historia de España*.

LaRubia-Prado, Francisco. *Alegorías de la voluntad: Pensamiento orgánico, retórica y deconstrucción en la obra de Miguel de Unamuno*. Libertarias/Prodhufi, 1996.

———. "Deconstrucción: *Niebla* de Miguel de Unamuno: Ironía y deconstrucción." *El hispanismo en los Estados Unidos: Discursos críticos, prácticas textuales*, edited by José M. del Pino and Francisco LaRubia-Prado, Visor, 1999, pp. 111–32.

———. "Sanctity, Heroism, and Performance in Miguel de Unamuno's *San Manuel Bueno, mártir*." *Hispanófila*, vol. 171, 2014, pp. 217–36.

———. *Unamuno y la vida como ficción*. Gredos, 1999.

Lasagabaster, Jesús María, editor. *El teatro de Miguel de Unamuno*. Universidad de Deusto, 1987.

Latham, Alan, and Derek P. McCormack. "Moving Cities: Rethinking the Materialities of Urban Geographies." *Progress in Human Geography*, vol. 28, no. 6, 2004, pp. 701–24.

Lazarillo de Tormes. Edited by Francisco Rico, Cátedra, 1987.

Lazarillo de Tormes. Translated and edited by Ilan Stavans, W. W. Norton, 2015.

Lee Bartky, Sandra. "Foucault, Femininity, and the Modernization of Patriarchal Power." *Writing on the Body: Female Embodiment and Feminist Theory*, edited by Katie Conboy et al., Columbia UP, 1997, pp. 129–54.

Lefebvre, Henri. *Writings on Cities*. Edited and translated by E. Kofman and E. Lebas, Blackwell, 1996.

Lejeune, Philippe. "The Autobiographical Pact." *On Autobiography*, edited by Paul John Eakin, translated by Katherine Leary, U of Minnesota P, 1989, pp. 3–30.

La lengua de las mariposas. Directed by José Luis Cuerda, Twentieth Century Fox Home Entertainment, 2000.

Lennox, Charlotte. *The Female Quixote*. Oxford UP, 1994.

Lewis, Pericles. *Religious Experience and the Modernist Novel*. Cambridge UP, 2010.

Los libros: Niebla. Directed by Fernando Méndez-Leite, 1976. *RTVE*, www.rtve.es/alacarta/videos/los-libros-ficcion/libros-niebla/2760134/.

Lispector, Clarice. *A Breath of Life: Pulsations*. Translated by Johnny Lorenz, New Directions, 2012.

———. *The Hour of the Star*. Translated by Benjamin Moser, New Directions, 2011.

———. *Um sopro de vida. (Pulsações)*. Nova Fronteira, 1978.

Longhurst, Carlos A. Introduction. *Abel Sánchez*, by Miguel de Unamuno, Cátedra, 2000, pp. 9–71.

———. *Modernismo, noventayochismo y novela: España y Europa*. Peter Lang, 2014.

———. "The Problem of Truth in *San Manuel Bueno, mártir*." *Modern Language Review*, vol. 76, no. 3, 1981, pp. 581–97.

———. *Unamuno's Theory of the Novel*. Legenda, 2014.

———. "Unamuno, the Reader, and the Hermeneutical Gap." *Modern Language Review*, vol. 103, no. 3, 2008, pp. 741–52.

Luby, Barry J. *The Uncertainties in Twentieth- and Twenty-First-Century Analytic Thought: Miguel de Unamuno the Precursor*. Juan de la Cuesta, 2008.

Lucae, Richard. "Über die Macht des Raumes in der Baukunst." *Zeitschrift für Bauwesen*, vol. 19, 1869, pp. 293–306.

Machado, Antonio. "Por tierras de España." *Poesías completas*. Foreword by Manuel Alvar, 9th ed., Espasa-Calpe, 1983, pp. 139–40.

Maeterlinck, Maurice. *The Plays of Maurice Maeterlinc, Series I–II*. Translated by Richard Hovey, Kraus Reprint, 1972.

Mainer, José-Carlos. *La edad de plata, 1902–1939: Ensayo de interpretación de un proceso cultural*. 4th ed., Cátedra, 2016.

Mancing, Howard. "The Lessons of *San Manuel Bueno, mártir*." *MLN*, vol. 121, no. 2, 2006, pp. 343–66.

Manrique Sabogal, Winston. "El yo asalta la literatura." *El País*, 13 Sept. 2008, elpais.com/diario/2008/09/13/babelia/1221262752_850215.html.

Marcos, Luis Andrés. "El lector unamuniano como clave filosófica." Chaguaceda Toledano, vol. 3, pp. 89–97.

Marías, Javier. "Autobiografía o ficción." *Literatura y fantasma*, Siruela, 1993, pp. 62–69.

Marías, Julián. *Miguel de Unamuno*. 3rd ed., Espasa, 1997.

———. *Miguel de Unamuno*. Translated by Frances M. López Morillas, Harvard UP, 1966.

Marichal, Juan. *El designio de Unamuno*. Taurus, 2002.

Martín-Estudillo, Luis. *The Rise of Euroskepticism: Europe and Its Critics in Spanish Culture*. Vanderbilt UP, 2018.

Martínez-López, Ramón, editor. *Unamuno: Centennial Studies*. U of Texas, 1966.

Martínez-Nadal, Rafael, editor. *Miguel de Unamuno y José María Quiroga Pla: Un epistolario y diez* Hojas libres. Editorial Casariego, 2001.

Martín Gaite, Carmen. *The Back Room*. Translated by Helen R. Lane, Columbia UP, 1983.

———. *El cuarto de atrás*. Destino, 1980.

———. *Usos amorosos de la postguerra española*. Anagrama, 2002.

Martín Gijón, Mario. *Un segundo destierro: La sombra de Unamuno en el exilio español*. Iberoamericana / Vervuert, 2018.

Martín-Márquez, Susana. *Disorientations: Spanish Colonialism in Africa and the Performance of Identity*. Yale UP, 2008.

Meijering, E. P. *Theologische Urteile über die Dogmengeschichte: Ritschls Einfluss auf von Harnack*. E. J. Brill, 1978.

Méndez, Alberto. *Los girasoles ciegos*. Anagrama, 2004.

Meyer, François. *La ontología de Miguel de Unamuno*. Gredos, 1962.

Mientras dure la guerra. Directed by Alejandro Amenábar, Mod Producciones / Movistar+, 2019.

Miguel de Unamuno y la fotografía. Ediciones Universidad de Salamanca, 2012.

Misemer, Sarah M. *Moving Forward, Looking Back: Trains, Literature, and the Arts in the River Plate*. Bucknell UP, 2010.

Misiones pedagógicas. Directed by Gonzalo Tapia, Acacia Films, 2007. *YouTube*, Acacia Films, 7 May 2011, www.youtube.com/watch?v=tYmfcvXqUBM.

Modern Language Association. "Report to the Teagle Foundation on the Undergraduate Major in Language and Literature." 2009, apps.mla.org/pdf/2008_mla_whitepaper.pdf.

Modern Language Association Ad Hoc Committee on Foreign Languages. "Foreign Languages and Higher Education: New Structures for a Changed World." *Profession*, 2007, pp. 1–12.

Montero, Rosa. *La loca de la casa*. Alfaguara, 2003.

Morón Arroyo, Ciriaco. *Hacia el sistema de Unamuno: Estudios sobre su pensamiento y creación literaria*. Cálamo, 2003.

Morrison, Toni. *The Bluest Eye*. Vintage, 2007.

Mumford, Lewis. *The City in History: Its Origins, Its Transformations, and Its Prospects*. Harcourt, Brace and World, 1961.

Nada menos que todo un hombre. Directed by Rafael Gil, 1972. Filmax, 2008.

Navajas, Gonzalo. *El paradigma de la enfermedad y la literatura del siglo XX*. Publicaciones de la Universidad de Valencia, 2013.

———. *Unamuno desde la posmodernidad: Antinomia y síntesis ontológica*. 2nd ed., PPU, 1992.

Nepaulsingh, Colbert I. "In Search of a Tradition, Not a Source, for *San Manuel Bueno, mártir*." *Revista canadiense de estudios hispánicos*, vol. 11, no. 2, 1987, pp. 315–30.

Newcomb, Roger Patrick. *Iberianism and Crisis: Spain and Portugal at the Turn of the Twentieth Century*. U of Toronto P, 2018.

Nicholas, Robert L. *Unamuno narrador*. Castalia, 1987.

Niebla. Directed by Pedro Amalio López, 1965. *RTVE*, www.rtve.es/alacarta/videos/niebla/.

Nozick, Martin. *Miguel de Unamuno: The Agony of Belief*. Princeton UP, 1971.

Núñez, Diego, and Pedro Ribas, editors. *Unamuno y el socialismo: Artículos recuperados, 1886–1928*. Comares, 1997.

Olson, Paul R. *The Great Chiasmus: Word and Flesh in the Novels of Unamuno*. Purdue UP, 2003.

———. "Sobre el arte de *Paz en la guerra*." *Actas del IX Congreso de la Asociación Internacional de Hispanistas*, vol. 2, Vervuert, 1989, pp. 319–26.

———. *Unamuno*: Niebla*: Critical Guides to Spanish Texts*. Grant and Cutler, 1984.

———. "Unamuno's Break with the Nineteenth Century: Invention of the *Nivola* and the Linguistic Turn." *MLN*, vol. 102, no. 2, 1987, pp. 307–15.

Onís, Federico de. "Crónica literaria de España." *Hispania*, vol. 1, no. 1, 1918, pp. 46–48.

———. "Sobre el concepto del modernismo." *Estudios críticos sobre el modernismo*, edited by Homer Castillo, Gredos, 1974, pp. 35–42.

Orringer, Nelson R. "Philosophy and Tragedy in Two Newly Discovered *Fedras* by Unamuno." *Anales de la literatura española contemporánea*, vol. 22, 1997, pp. 549–64.

———. *Unamuno y los protestantes liberales: Sobre las fuentes de* Del sentimiento trágico de la vida. Gredos, 1985.

Ortega y Gasset, José. *La deshumanización del arte*. Revista de Occidente, 1925.

———. *Ensayos sobre la generación del 98*. Alianza Editorial, 1989.

Ouimette, Victor. *Reason Aflame: Unamuno and the Heroic Will*. Yale UP, 1974.

Pardo Bazán, Emilia. *The House of Ulloa*. Translated by Paul O'Prey and Lucia Graves, Penguin, 2013.

———. *Los pazos de Ulloa*. Edited by Marina Mayoral, Castalia, 1987.

París, Carlos. *Unamuno: Estructura de su mundo intelectual*. 2nd ed., Anthropos, 1989.

Parker, Alexander A. "On the Interpretation of *Niebla*." *Unamuno: Creator and Creation*, edited by José Rubia Barcia and M. A. Zeitlin, U of California P, 1967, pp. 116–38.

Pascual Mezquita, Eduardo. *La política del último Unamuno*. Globalia Ediciones Anthema, 2003.

Pedraza Jiménez, Felipe B., and Milagros Rodríguez Cáceres. *Generación de fin de siglo: Prosistas*. Cénlit, 1987. Vol. 9 of *Manual de literatura española*.

La pelota vasca: La piel contra la Piedra. Directed by Julio Medem, Alicia Produce, 2003.

Pereda, José María de. *Peñas arriba*. Edited by Antonio Ray, Cátedra, 1999.

Pérez, Janet. "Rhetorical Integration in Unamuno's *Niebla*." *Revista canadiense de estudios hispánicos*, vol. 8, no. 1, 1983, pp. 49–73.

Pérez de la Dehesa, Rafael. *Política y sociedad en el primer Unamuno*. Ciencia Nueva, 1966.

———. Prologue. *Obras completas* [García Blanco], by Unamuno, vol. 9, pp. 465–68.

Pérez Galdós, Benito. *La de Bringas*. Edited by Alda Blanco and Carlos Blanco Aguinaga, Cátedra, 2006.

———. *Doña perfecta*. Planeta, 2003.

———. *Episodios nacionales*. Edited by Yolanda Arencibia, Cabildo de Gran Canaria, 2010.

———. *Fortunata y Jacinta: Dos historias de casadas*. Edited by Francisco Caudet, Cátedra, 1983. 2 vols.

———. *That Bringas Woman*. Translated by Catherine Jagoe, Orion, 1996.

———. *Tristana*. Translated by Margaret Jull Costa, New York Review Books, 2014.

———. *Tristana*. Edited by Isabel Gonzálvez and Gabriel Sevilla, Cátedra, 2008.

Piaget, Jean. "Piaget's Theory." *Carmichael's Manual of Child Development*, edited by P. H. Mussen, Wiley, 1970, pp. 703–32.

Pirandello, Luigi. Six Characters in Search of an Author *and Other Plays*. Translated by Mark Musa, Penguin, 1996.

Portela, Edurne. *El eco de los disparos: Cultura y memoria de la violencia*. Galaxia Gutenberg, 2016.

———. *Mejor la ausencia*. Galaxia Gutenberg, 2017.

The Purple Rose of Cairo. Directed by Woody Allen, MGM, 1985.

Rabaté, Colette, and Jean-Claude Rabaté. *En el torbellino: Unamuno en la Guerra Civil*. Marcial Pons, 2018.

———. "Enfrentamiento en el paraninfo: Unamuno, 'fulminado.'" *El País*, 27 May 2018, elpais.com/cultura/2018/05/26/actualidad/1527331721_207393.html.

———. *Miguel de Unamuno: Biografía*. Taurus, 2009.

Rabaté, Jean-Claude. *Guerra de ideas en el joven Unamuno, 1880–1900*. Biblioteca Nueva, 2001.

Radway, Janice A. "Introduction: Writing *Reading the Romance*." *Reading the Romance: Women, Patriarchy, and Popular Literature*. U of North Carolina P, 1984, pp. 1–18.

Ramos Gascón, Antonio. "Spanish Literature as a Historiographic Invention: The Case of the Generation of 1898." *The Crisis of Institutionalized Literature in Spain*, edited by Wlad Godzich and Nicholas Spadaccini, Prisma Institute, 1998, pp. 167–93.

Ramsden, H. *The 1898 Movement in Spain: Towards a Reinterpretation*. Manchester UP, 1974.

Redden, Elizabeth. "Call to Action on Languages, 10 Years Later." *Inside Higher Ed*, 6 Jan. 2017, www.insidehighered.com/news/2017/01/06/survey-looks-foreign-language-programs-response-decade-old-call-transform-teaching.

Resina, Joan Ramon. "'For Their Own Good': The Spanish Identity and Its Great Inquisitor, Miguel de Unamuno." *The Battle over Spanish between 1800 and 2000*, edited by José del Valle and Luis Gabriel-Stheeman, Routledge, 2002, pp. 106–33.

Ribas, Pedro. *Para leer a Unamuno*. Alianza Editorial, 2002.

Ribbans, Geoffrey. *Niebla y soledad: Aspectos de Unamuno y Machado*. Gredos, 1971.

———. "The Structure of Unamuno's *Niebla*." *Spanish Thought and Letters in the Twentieth Century*, edited by Germán Bleiberg and E. Inman Fox, Vanderbilt UP, 1966, pp. 395–406.

Ritschl, Albrecht Benjamin. *Die christliche Lehre von der Rechtfertigung und Versöhnung*. Adolph Marcus, 1870–74. 3 vols.

———. *Geschichte des Pietismus in der reformirten Kirche*. Adolph Marcus, 1880–86. 3 vols.

Rivera de Ventosa, Enrique. *Unamuno y Dios*. Ediciones Encuentro, 1985.

Roberts, Gemma. *Unamuno: Afinidades y coincidencias kierkegaardianas*. Society of Spanish and Spanish American Studies, 1986.

Roberts, Stephen G. H. "Clowning and Tragic Clowning: Miguel de Unamuno as a Funny Writer." *Romance Quarterly*, vol. 63, no. 2, 2016, pp. 53–62.

———. *Miguel de Unamuno o la creación del intelectual español moderno*. Translated by María José Martínez Jurico, Ediciones Universidad de Salamanca, 2007.

———. "Miguel de Unamuno y su relación con el socialismo entre 1914 y 1924: Una primera aproximación." *Cuadernos de la Cátedra Miguel de Unamuno*, vol. 43, no. 1, 2007, pp. 89–98.

———. "Obras incompletas: La historia textual póstuma de la obra de Unamuno y sus efectos en la crítica." *Los textos del 98*, edited by Juan Carlos Ara and José-Carlos Mainer, Universidad de Valladolid, 2002, pp. 143–66.

———. "Unamuno contra Primo de Rivera: 10 artículos de 1923–24." *Sistema*, vol. 75, Nov. 1986, pp. 83–112.

Robles, Laureano, editor. *Azorín-Unamuno: Cartas y escritos complementarios*. Conselleria de Cultura, Educació i Ciencia de la Generalitat Valenciana, 1990.

———, editor. *Epistolario completo Ortega-Unamuno*. El Arquero, 1987.

Rodríguez, Julián. *Cultivos*. Literatura Random House, 2008.

Rojas, Carlos. *¡Muera la inteligencia! ¡Viva la muerte!: Salamanca, 1936, Unamuno y Millán Astray frente a frente*. Planeta, 1995.

Round, Nicholas G., editor. *Re-reading Unamuno*. U of Glasgow P, 1989.

———. *Unamuno:* Abel Sánchez. Grant and Cutler, 1974.

Rudd, Margaret T. *The Lone Heretic: A Biography of Miguel de Unamuno y Jugo*. Introduced by Federico de Onís, U of Texas P, 1963.

Ruddick, Lisa. "When Nothing Is Cool." *The Point*, 2015, thepointmag.com/2015/criticism/when-nothing-is-cool.

Ruiz-Manjón, Octavio, and Alicia Langa, editors. *Los significados del 98: La sociedad española en la génesis del siglo XX*. Biblioteca Nueva and Universidad Complutense de Madrid, 1999.

Rupérez, J. "*La tía Tula* de M. Picazo." *Cuadernos para el diálogo*, no. 12, 1964, pp. 13.

Said, Edward. *Orientalism*. Random House, 1979.

Salcedo, Miguel. *Vida de don Miguel: Unamuno en su tiempo, en su España, en su Salamanca: Un hombre en lucha con su leyenda*. 2nd ed., Anaya, 1998.

Salinas, Pedro. Pedro Salinas Papers, ca. 1912–75, Houghton Library, Harvard U, MS Span 100, series 9, folder 1133.

Sánchez Barbudo, Antonio, editor. *Miguel de Unamuno: El escritor y la crítica*. Taurus, 1974.

Sanmiguel, Manuel. "Presentación." *Obras completas* [Sanmiguel and García Blanco], by Unamuno, vol. 1, pp. 7–15.

Santa Teresa de Jesús. *Libro de la vida*. 1565. Edited by Fidel Sebastián Mediavilla, Real Academia Española, 2014, www.rae.es/sites/default/files/HOJEAR_Libro_de_la_vida_0.pdf.

Santoro Domingo, Pablo. "Science Fiction in Spain: A Sociological Perspective." *Science Fiction Studies*, vol. 33, no. 2, 2006, pp. 313–31.

Santos-Rivero, Virginia. *Unamuno y el sueño colonial*. Iberoamericana, 2005.

Sanz, Marta. *Lección de anatomía*. RBA Libros, 2008.

Sartre, Jean-Paul. *L'être et le néant: Essai d'ontologie phénoménologique*. Gallimard, 1943.

———. *Les mots*. Gallimard, 1964.

———. *La nausée*. Gallimard, 1938.

Savater, Fernando. *La tarea del héroe*. Destino, 1992.

Schivelbusch, Wolfgang. *The Railway Journey: The Industrialization of Time and Space in the Nineteenth Century*. U of California P, 1986.

Schmidt, Rachel. "The Poetics of Resuscitation: Unamuno's Anti-Novelistics." *Forms of Modernity:* Don Quijote *and Modern Theories of the Novel*. U of Toronto P, 2011, pp. 162–96.

Sedgwick, Eve Kosofsky. *Between Men*. Colombia UP, 1985.

Serrano Poncela, Segundo. *El pensamiento de Unamuno*. Fondo de Cultura Económica, 1964.

Shaw, Donald. *La Generación del 98*. Translated by Carmen Hierro, 5th ed., Cátedra, 1985.

———. *The Generation of 1898 in Spain*. Ernest Benn, 1975.

Silva, Lorenzo, et al. *Sangre, sudor y paz: La Guardia Civil contra ETA*. Ediciones Península, 2017.

Sinclair, Alison. *Uncovering the Mind: Unamuno, the Unknown, and the Vicissitudes of Self*. Manchester UP, 2001.

Sotelo Vázquez, Adolfo, editor. *Miguel de Unamuno: Artículos en "Las Noticias" de Barcelona, 1899–1902*. Lumen, 1993.

Soufas, C. Christopher. *The Subject in Question: Early Contemporary Spanish Literature and Modernism*. Catholic U of America P, 2007.

Souza, Francisco de. *Tratado das Ilhas Novas*. 1570. 2nd ed., Typografia do Archivo dos Açores, 1884.

Spalding, Steven, and Benjamin Fraser, editors. *Trains, Literature, and Culture: Reading and Writing the Rails*. Lexington Books / Rowman and Littlefield, 2012.

Spires, Robert. *Beyond the Metafictional Mode: Directions in the Modern Spanish Novel*. UP of Kentucky, 1984.

Sprinchorn, Evert. "Introduction to *A Dream Play*." *Selected Plays*, by August Strindberg, U of Minnesota P, 1986, pp. 641–43.

Stapfer, Paul. *Des réputations littéraires: Essais de morale et d'histoire*. Hachette, 1893.

Stoppard, Tom. *Rosencrantz and Guildenstern Are Dead*. Grove, 1994.

Stranger Than Fiction. By Zach Helm, directed by Marc Forster, Colombia Pictures, 2006.

"The Ten Best Books of 2016." *The New York Times*, 1 Dec. 2016, www.nytimes.com/interactive/2016/books/review/best-books.html.

Terzakis, Angelos. *Homage to the Tragic Muse*. Translated by Athan H. Anagnostolopoulos, Houghton Mifflin, 1978.

Thompson, Chantal. "Preparing Students for Writing and Talking About Literature." *ADFL Bulletin*, vol. 40, no. 1, 2008, pp. 20–23.

La tía Tula. Directed by Mario Picazo, produced by José López Moreno et al., 1964. Video Mercury Films, 2010.

El tiempo de Miguel de Unamuno y Salamanca. Ediciones Universidad de Salamanca, 1998.

Tollinchi, Esteban. *La ontología de Unamuno*. Universidad de Puerto Rico, 1978.

Torrealdai, Joan Mari. *La censura de Franco y los escritores vascos del 98*. Ttarttalo, 1998.

Trachtenberg, Alan. Foreword. Schivelbusch, pp. xiii–xvi.

Trapiello, Andrés. *Las armas y las letras: Literatura y Guerra Civil, 1936–1939*. Planeta, 1994.

Turner, David G. *Unamuno's Webs of Fatality*. Tamesis, 1974.

Tusquets, Esther. *Habíamos ganado la guerra*. Bruguera, 2007.

Unamuno, Miguel de. *Abel Sánchez*. Edited by José Luis Abellán, 3rd ed., Castalia, 1990.

———. *Abel Sánchez*. Edited by Ángel del Río and Amelia del Río, Dryden Press, 1947.

———. *Abel Sánchez*. Edited by Carlos A. Longhurst, Cátedra, 2004.

———. *Abel Sánchez*. Translated and introduced by John Macklin, Aris and Phillips, 2009.

———. *Abel Sánchez*. Edited by Susan G. Polansky, Cervantes and Company, 2008.

———. *Abel Sánchez*. *Obras completas* [García Blanco], vol. 2, pp. 683–759.

———. Abel Sánchez *and Other Stories*. 1956. Translated by Anthony Kerrigan, introduced by Mario J. Valdés, Regnery Publishing, 1996.

———. *Abel Sánchez; San Manuel Bueno, mártir; Cómo se hace una novela y otras prosas*. Edited by Domingo Ródenas de Moya, Crítica, 2006.

———. *La agonía del cristianismo*. Edited by Victor Ouimette, Espasa-Calpe, 1996.

———. *The Agony of Christianity*. Translated by Pierre Loving, Payson and Clarke, 1928.

———. *The Agony of Christianity*. Translated and introduced by Kurt F. Reinhardt, Frederick Ungar, 1960.

———. "A lo que salga." *Obras completas* [Senabre], vol. 8, pp. 691–705.

———. *Alrededor del estilo*. Edited by Laureano Robles, Ediciones Universidad de Salamanca, 1998.

———. *Amor y pedagogía*. Edited by Julia Barella, Alianza Editorial, 2000.

———. *Amor y pedagogía*. Edited by Bénédicte Vauthier, Biblioteca Nueva, 2002.

———. *Antología: Poesía, narrativa, ensayo*. Introduction by José Luis López Aranguren, afterword by Pedro Cerezo Galán, Fondo de Cultura Económica de España, 2007.

———. *Antología poética*. Edited by Roberto Panoli, Espasa-Calpe, 2000.

———. *Antología poética*. Edited by José María Valverde, Alianza Editorial, 2015.

———. *Artículos desconocidos en "El Mercantil Valenciano" (1917–1923)*. Edited by Laureano Robles Carcedo and Manuel M.ª Urrutia León, Generalitat Valenciana, 2003.

———. *Artículos en* La Nación *de Buenos Aires, 1919–1924*. Edited by Luis Urrutia Salaverría, Ediciones Universidad de Salamanca, 1994.

———. *Artículos olvidados sobre España y la Primera Guerra Mundial*. Edited by Christopher Cobb, Tamesis Books, 1976.

———. *Aunt Tula / La tía Tula*. Edited and translated by Stanley Appelbaum, Dover Publications, 2005.

———. *Aunt Tula / La tía Tula*. Translated and introduced by Julia Biggane, Aris and Phillips, 2013.

———. *Cancionero: Diario poético*. Losada, 1953.

———. *Cartas del destierro: Entre el odio y el amor, 1924–1930*. Edited by Colette Rabaté and Jean-Claude Rabaté, Ediciones Universidad de Salamanca, 2012.

———. *The Christ of Velazquez*. Translated by Eleanor L. Turnbull, Johns Hopkins UP, 1951.

———. *The Christ of Velázquez*. Translated by Jaime R. Vidal, Franciscan Press, 1999.

———. "Cientificismo." Unamuno, *"Mi religión" y otros ensayos breves*, pp. 132–39.

———. *Cómo se hace una novela*. Edited by Teresa Gómez Trueba, Cátedra, 2009.

———. *El Cristo de Velázquez*. Edited by Víctor García de la Concha, Espasa-Calpe, 1987.

———. *Cuentos*. Edited by Eleanor K. Paucker, Minotauro, 1961. 2 vols.

———. *Cuentos completos*. Edited by J. Óscar Carrascosa Tinoco, Páginas de Espuma, 2017.

———. *De Fuerteventura a París*. Prologue by Gregorio San Juan, El Sitio, 1981.

———. *Del sentimiento trágico de la vida*. Alianza Editorial, 1986.

———. *Del sentimiento trágico de la vida en los hombres y en los pueblos*. *Obras completas* [García Blanco], vol. 7, pp. 106–302.

———. *Del sentimiento trágico de la vida en los hombres y en los pueblos* y *Tratado del amor de Dios*. Edited by Nelson Orringer, Tecnos, 2005.

———. *Del sentimiento trágico de la vida; La agonía del cristianismo*. Edited by Antonio Sánchez Barbudo, Akal, 2017.

———. *De patriotismo espiritual: Artículos en* La Nación *de Buenos Aires, 1901–1914*. Edited by Victor Ouimette, Ediciones Universidad de Salamanca, 1997.

———. *Diario íntimo (1897)*. Edited by Etelvino González López, Ediciones Universidad de Salamanca, 2012.

———. "Discurso en la velada en honor de Gabriel y Galán." *Obras completas* [García Blanco], vol. 9, pp. 145–48.

———. "Discurso leído en la solemne apertura del curso académico de 1900 a 1901, en la Universidad de Salamanca." *Obras completas* [García Blanco], vol. 9, pp. 60–67.

———. *Dos novelas cortas*. Edited by James R. Stamm and Herbert E. Isar, Xerox College Publishing, 1961.

———. *Ensayos*. Prologue by Fernando G. Candamo, Aguilar, 1942. 2 vols.

———. *Ensueño de una patria: Periodismo republicano, 1931–1936*. Edited by Victor Ouimette, Pre-Textos, 1984.

———. *En torno al casticismo*. Edited by Jean-Claude Rabaté, Cátedra, 2005.

———. *Epistolario I, 1880–1899*. Edited by Colette and Jean-Claude Rabaté, Ediciones Universidad de Salamanca, 2017.

———. *Epistolario americano, 1890–1936*. Edited by Laureano Robles, Ediciones Universidad de Salamanca, 1996.

———. "Epistolario entre Unamuno y Giner de los Ríos." *Revista de occidente*, vol. 25, no. 73, Apr. 1969, pp. 1–18.

———. *Epistolario inédito*. Edited by Laureano Robles, Espasa-Calpe, 1991. 2 vols.

———. *Escritos socialistas: Artículos inéditos sobre el socialismo, 1894–1922*. Edited by Pedro Ribas, Ayuso, 1976.

———. *La esfinge*. *Obras completas* [García Blanco], vol. 5, pp. 141–220.

———. *La esfinge; La venda; Fedra*. Edited by Guadalupe Gómez Ferrer, Castalia, 1988.

———. *El espejo de la muerte*. Espasa-Calpe, 1967.

———. *Essays and Soliloques*. Translated by J. E. Crawford Flitch, A. A. Knopf, 1925.

———. *Fedra: Tragedia desnuda*. *Obras completas* [García Blanco], vol. 5, pp. 299–363.

———. *Filosofía lógica*. Edited by Ignacio García Peña and Pablo García Castillo, prologue by Cirilo Flórez Miguel, Tecnos, 2016.

———. *Fog: A Novel*. Translated by Elena Barcia, introduced by Alberto Manguel, Northwestern UP, 2017.

———. *El hermano Juan o el mundo es teatro*. *Obras completas* [García Blanco], vol. 5, pp. 713–826.

———. "Humilde heroísmo." *Obras completas* [García Blanco], vol. 1, pp. 80–82.

———. "Ibsen y Kierkegaard." 1907. *Obras completas* [García Blanco], vol. 3, pp. 289–93.

———. *Life of Don Quixote and Sancho according to Miguel de Cervantes Saavedra Expounded with Comment by Miguel de Unamuno*. Translated by Homer P. Earle, A. A. Knopf, 1927.

———. *Love and Pedagogy*. Translated by Michael Vande Berg, Peter Lang, 1996.

———. *Manual de Quijotismo, Cómo se hace una novela, Epistolario Miguel de Unamuno / Jean Cassou*. Edited by Bénédicte Vauthier, Ediciones Universidad de Salamanca, 2005.

———. "Materialismo popular." *Obras completas* [García Blanco], vol. 3, pp. 363–67.

———. "Mecanópolis." Unamuno, *Relatos*, pp. 102–05.

———. *Medea*. *Obras completas* [García Blanco], vol. 5, pp. 827–56.

———. *Miguel de Unamuno: An Anthology of His Poetry*. Edited and translated by C. A. Longhurst, Aris and Phillips, 2015.

———. "Mi religión." Unamuno, *"Mi religión" y otros ensayos breves*, pp. 7–14.

———. *"Mi religión" y otros ensayos breves*. 1907. Espasa-Calpe, 1978.

———. *Mist*. Unamuno, *Selected Works*, vol. 6, pp. 3–246.

———. *Mist. A Tragi-comic Novel*. Translated by Warner Fite, A. A. Knopf, 1928.

———. *Mist: A Tragicomic Novel*. Foreword by Theodore Ziolkowski, translated by Warner Fite, U of Illinois P, 2000.

———. *Mist / Niebla*. Translated and introduced by John Macklin, Aris and Phillips, 2014.

———. "My Religion." Translated by Armand Baker. 4 Feb. 2017, www.armandfbaker.com/translations/unamuno/my_religion.pdf.

———. *Niebla*. Edited by Juan Herrero Senés, Stock Cero, 2010.

———. *Niebla*. Edited by Mario J. Valdés, 26th ed., Cátedra, 2013.

———. *Niebla*. Edited by Armando F. Zubizarreta, Castalia, 2012.

———. *Novelas completas*. Edited by Juan Antonio Garrido Ardila, Cátedra, 2017.

———. *Nuevo mundo*. Edited by Laureano Robles, Trotta, 1994.

———. *Obras completas*. Edited by Manuel García Blanco, Escelicer, 1966–71. 9 vols.

———. *Obras completas*. Edited by Manuel Sanmiguel and Manuel García Blanco, Afrodisio Aguado, 1950–58. 16 vols.

———. *Obras completas*. Edited by Ricardo Senabre, Turner, 1995–2009. 10 vols.

———. *Obras selectas*. Foreword by Julián Marías, Espasa-Calpe, 1998.

———. *El otro*. Edited by Ricardo de la Fuente Ballesteros, Colegio de España, 2002.

———. *El otro*. *Obras completas* [García Blanco], vol. 5, pp. 651–710.

———. *El otro; El hermano Juan*. Edited by José Paulino, Espasa-Calpe, 1992.

———. *Paz en la guerra*. Edited by Francisco Caudet, Cátedra, 1999.

———. *Peace in War*. Translated by Allen Lacy and Martin Nozick with Anthony Kerrigan, Princeton UP, 1983.

———. *Perplexities and Paradoxes*. Translated by Stuart Gross, Philosophical Library, 1945.

———. "El poder de la palabra." *Biblioteca Digital Hispánica*, bdh.bne.es/bnesearch/biblioteca/El%20poder%20de%20la%20palabra%20:%20parte%20I%20[y]%20II%20/qls/Unamuno,%20Miguel%20de%20(1864%201936)/qls/.

———. *Poems*. Translated by Eleanor L. Turnbull, Johns Hopkins UP, 1951.

———. *Poesía completa*. Prologue by Ana Suárez de Miramón, Alianza Editorial, 1987. 4 vols.

———. *Poesías.* Edited by Manuel Alvar, Cátedra, 2009.

———. *Political Speeches and Journalism, 1923–1929.* Edited by Stephen G. H. Roberts, U of Exeter P, 1996.

———. *Political Writings, 1918–1924.* Edited by Graham David Robertson, Edwin Mellen Press, 1996. 3 vols.

———. *Por tierras de Portugal y de España.* Edited by Ángel Rivero, Alianza Editorial, 2014.

———. *Por tierras de Portugal y de España.* Aguilar, 1953.

———. *Raquel encadenada. Obras completas* [García Blanco], vol. 5, pp. 527–90.

———. *Relatos de Unamuno.* Edited by Eleanor Krane Paucker, Meredith Corporation, 1969.

———. *República española y España republicana.* Edited by Vicente González Martín, Ediciones Almar, 1979.

———. *Rimas de dentro.* Mondadori, 2000.

———. *Romancero del destierro.* Introduced by David Robertson and José María González Helguera, El Sitio, 1982.

———. *Saint Manuel Bueno, Martyr.* Translated by Armand Baker. 4 Feb. 2017, www.armandfbaker.com/translations/unamuno/san_manuel_bueno_martir.pdf.

———. *Saint Manuel Bueno, Martyr / San Manuel Bueno, mártir.* Translated by Paul Burns and Salvador Ortiz-Carboneres, introduced by Paul Burns, Aris and Phillips, 2009.

———. *San Manuel Bueno, mártir.* Edited by Paola Bianco and Antonio Sobejano-Morán, Focus Publishing, 2005.

———. *San Manuel Bueno, mártir.* Edited by Cirilo Flórez Miguel, Tecnos, 2012.

———. *San Manuel Bueno, mártir.* Edited by Joaquín Rubio Tovar, 3rd ed., Castalia, 2011.

———. *San Manuel Bueno, mártir.* Translated by Francisco de Segovia and Jean Pérez, G. G. Harrap, 1957.

———. *San Manuel Bueno, mártir.* Edited by Mario Valdés, 24th ed., Cátedra, 2003.

———. "San Manuel Bueno, mártir." *Aproximaciones al estudio de la literatura hispánica*, edited by Carmen Virgillo et al., 7th ed., McGraw-Hill, 2012, pp. 110–34.

———. *San Manuel Bueno, mártir.* Espasa-Calpe, 1985.

———. *Selected Works of Miguel de Unamuno.* Translated by Anthony Kerrigan, Princeton UP, 1967–1976. 7 vols.

———. "Soledad." *Obras completas* [García Blanco], vol. 1, pp. 1251–63.

———. *Sombras de sueño; Soledad.* Edited by José Paulino Ayuso, Biblioteca Nueva, 1998.

———. *Teatro completo.* Edited by Manuel García Blanco, Aguilar, 1956.

———. *Teresa.* Edited by M.ª Consuelo Belda Vázquez, Cátedra, 2018.

———. *Three Exemplary Novels.* Translated by Ángel Flores, introduced by Ángel del Río, A. and C. Boni, 1930.

———. *La tía Tula.* Edited by Carlos A. Longhurst, 3rd ed., Cátedra, 2005.

———. *La tía Tula.* Espasa-Calpe, 2007.

———. *The Tragic Sense of Life in Men and in Peoples*. Translated by J. E. Crawford Flitch, introduced by Salvador de Madariaga, Macmillan, 1921.

———. *The Tragic Sense of Life in Men and Nations*. Translated by Anthony Kerrigan, edited by Martin Nozick, Princeton UP, 1978.

———. *A Translation of* Niebla ("Fog") *by Miguel de Unamuno*. Translated by Juan Cruz, Forma Arts and Media Limited, 2005.

———. *Treatise on Love of God*. Translated and edited by Nelson R. Orringer, U of Illinois P, 2007.

———. *Tres novelas ejemplares y un prólogo*. Calpe, 1920. *Internet Archive*, archive .org/details/tresnovelasejemp00unam.

———. *The Velázquez Christ*. Translated by William Thomas Little, UP of America, 2002.

———. *La venda*. *Obras completas* [García Blanco], vol. 5, pp. 221–44.

———. "Verdad y vida." Unamuno, *"Mi religión" y otros ensayos breves*, pp. 16–22.

———. *Viajes y paisajes: Antología de crónicas de viaje*. Preface by Jaime-Axel Ruiz Baudrihaye, La línea del Horizonte, 2014.

———. *Vida de Don Quijote y Sancho*. Edited by Alberto Navarro, Cátedra, 2004.

———. *Vida de Don Quijote y Sancho*. Espasa-Calpe, 1981.

———. "Y va de cuento." *Cuentos completos*, edited by Óscar Carrascosa Tinoco, Páginas de Espuma, 2011, pp. 297–300.

Unamuno, Miguel de, and Joan Maragall. *Epistolario y escritos complementarios: Unamuno-Maragall*. Foreword by Pedro Laín Entralgo, afterword by Dionisio Ridruejo, Seminarios y Ediciones, 1971.

Unamuno, Miguel de, and Luis Zulueta. *Cartas, 1903–1933*. Aguilar, 1972.

Unamuno apasionado. Directed by Rafael Alcázar, performance by Luis Hostalot, Radio Spanish Television Documentaries, 2018, www.rtve.es/television/20180315/unamuno-apasionado/1019921.shtml.

Unamuno Pérez, María de la Concepción de. *Miguel de Unamuno y la cultura francesa*. Ediciones Universidad de Salamanca, 1991.

Urmson, J. O. "Saints and Heroes." *Moral Concepts*, edited by Joel Feinberg, Oxford UP, 1970, pp. 61–73.

Urrutia-Jordana, Ana. *La poetización de la política en el Unamuno exiliado:* De Fuerteventura a París *y* Romancero del destierro. Ediciones Universidad de Salamanca, 2003.

Urrutia León, Manuel M.ª. *Evolución del pensamiento político de Unamuno*. Universidad de Deusto, 1997.

———. "Miguel de Unamuno y *España con Honra* (1924–1925)." *Cuadernos de la Cátedra Miguel de Unamuno*, vol. 47, no. 1, 2009, pp. 193–234.

Urry, John. *Sociology beyond Society: Mobilities for the Twenty-First Century*. Routledge, 2000.

Valdés, Mario J. *Cultural Hermeneutics: Essays after Unamuno and Ricoeur*. U of Toronto P, 2016.

———. *Death in the Literature of Unamuno*. U of Illinois P, 1964.

———. "The Invention of Reality: Hispanic Postmodernism." *Revista canadiense de estudios hispánicos*, vol. 18, no. 3, Spring 1994, pp. 456–68.

Valdés, Mario J., and María Elena de Valdés. *An Unamuno Source Book: A Catalogue of Readings and Acquisitions with an Introductory Essay on Unamuno's Dialectical Enquiry*. Introduced by Mario J. Valdés, U of Toronto P, 1973.

Valera, Juan. *Pepita Jiménez*. Edited by Leonardo Romero, Cátedra, 1989.

Vargas Llosa, Mario. *Aunt Julia and the Scriptwriter*. Translated by Helen R. Lane, Picador, 2007.

———. *La tía Julia y el escribidor*. Seix Barral, 1977.

Vauthier, Bénédicte. *Arte de escribir e ironía en la obra narrativa de Miguel de Unamuno*. Ediciones Universidad de Salamanca, 2004.

Vila-Matas, Enrique. *La asesina ilustrada*. Lumen, 1977.

———. *París no se acaba nunca*. Anagrama, 2003.

Vilanova, Antonio. "La teoría nivolesca del *bufo trágico*." Gómez Molleda, *Actas*, pp. 189–216.

Waugh, Patricia. "What Is Metafiction and Why Are They Saying Such Awful Things about It?" *Metafiction*, edited by Mark Currie, Longman, 1995, pp. 39–54.

Weber, Frances W. "Unamuno's *Niebla*: From Novel to Dream." *PMLA*, vol. 88, no. 2, 1973, pp. 93–120.

Wells, Gordon. "The Case for Dialogic Inquiry." *Action, Talk, and Text: Learning and Teaching through Inquiry*, edited by Gordon Wells, Teacher's College P, 2001, pp. 171–94.

Witthaus, Jan-Henrik. "El tema de África en la obra ensayística de Miguel de Unamuno: Identidad cultural y ubicación intelectual." *Iberoamericana*, vol. 56, 2014, pp. 91–102.

Wobbermin, Georg. *Theologie und Metaphysik: Das Verhältnis der Theologie zur modernen Erkenntnistheorie und Psychologie*. Duncker, 1901.

Wright, Doug. *I Am My Own Wife*. Farrar, Straus and Giroux, 2004.

Wyers, Frances. *Miguel de Unamuno: The Contrary Self*. Tamesis Books, 1976.

Zambrano, María. *Unamuno*. Introduced by Mercedes Gómez Blesa, Debate, 2003.

Zavala, Iris M. "*Niebla*: La lógica del sueño." *La Torre*, vol. 1, no. 1, 1987, pp. 69–92.

———. *Unamuno y el pensamiento dialógico: M. de Unamuno y M. Bajtin*. Anthropos, 1991.

Ziolkowski, Theodore. Foreword. *Mist*. By Miguel de Unamuno, translated by Warner Fite, U of Illinois P, 2000, pp. v–xvii.

Zubizarreta, Armando F. *Unamuno en su nivola*. Taurus, 1960.

Zulaika, Joseba. *Polvo de ETA*. Alberdania, 2007.

Zunzunegui, Santos. "De cuerpo presente: En torno a las raíces literarias del 'Nuevo Cine Español.'" *La imprenta dinámica: Literatura española en el cine español*, edited by Carlos F. Heredero, Academia de las Artes y las Ciencias Cinematográficas, 2002, pp. 103–16.